Human Virtuality and Digital Life

This book is a psychoanalytic and philosophical exploration of how the digital is transforming our perception of the world and our understanding of ourselves.

Drawing on examples from everyday life, myth, and popular culture, this book argues that virtual reality is only the latest instantiation of the phenomenon of the virtual, which is intrinsic to human being. It illuminates what is at stake in our understanding of the relationship between the virtual and the real, showing how our present technologies both enhance and diminish our psychological lives. The authors claim that technology is a pharmakon – at the same time both a remedy and a poison – and in their writing exemplify a method that overcomes the polarization that compels us to regard it either as a liberating force or a dangerous threat in human life. The digital revolution challenges us to reckon with the implications of what is being called our posthuman condition, leaving behind our modern conception of the world as constituted by atemporal essences and reconceiving it instead as one of processes and change. The book's postscript considers the sudden plunge into the virtual effected by the 2020 global pandemic.

Accessible and wide-reaching, this book will appeal not only to psychotherapists, psychoanalysts, and philosophers, but anyone interested in the ways virtuality and the digital are transforming our contemporary lives.

Richard Frankel is a faculty member and supervisor at The Massachusetts Institute for Psychoanalysis. He is a teaching associate and supervisor in psychiatry at Harvard Medical School and has a private practice in Cambridge, MA. He is the author of *The Adolescent Psyche: Jungian and Winnicottian Perspectives.*

Victor J. Krebs is professor of philosophy at the Pontifical Catholic University of Peru and philosophical curator at VJK Curaduría Filosófica. He is author of *La imaginación pornográfica: contra el escepticismo en la cultura,* and editor (with William Day) of *Seeing Wittgenstein anew.*

Human Virtuality and Digital Life

Philosophical and
Psychoanalytic Investigations

Richard Frankel
Victor J. Krebs

Routledge
Taylor & Francis Group

LONDON AND NEW YORK

First published 2022
by Routledge
2 Park Square, Milton Park, Abingdon, Oxon OX14 4RN

and by Routledge
605 Third Avenue, New York, NY 10158

Routledge is an imprint of the Taylor & Francis Group, an informa business

British Library Cataloguing-in-Publication Data
A catalogue record for this book is available from the British Library

Library of Congress Cataloging-in-Publication Data
Names: Krebs, Victor J., 1957- author. | Frankel, Richard, 1961- author.
Title: Human virtuality and digital life : psychoanalytic and philosophical perspectives / Victor J. Krebs and Richard Frankel.
Description: New York : Routledge, 2021. | Includes bibliographical references and index. |
Identifiers: LCCN 2021009102 (print) | LCCN 2021009103 (ebook) | ISBN 9781138505148 (hardback) | ISBN 9781138505155 (paperback) | ISBN 9781315146423 (ebook)
Subjects: Internet--Psychological aspects. | Virtual reality--Psychological aspects. | Human-computer interaction--Psychological aspects.
Classification: LCC BF637.C45 K74 2021 (print) | LCC BF637.C45 (ebook) | DDC 153.60285--dc23
LC record available at https://lccn.loc.gov/2021009102
LC ebook record available at https://lccn.loc.gov/2021009103

ISBN: 978-1-138-50514-8 (hbk)
ISBN: 978-1-138-50515-5 (pbk)
ISBN: 978-1-315-14642-3 (ebk)

Typeset in Stone Serif
by MPS Limited, Dehradun

Highlighting the toxicity of the digital [...] may be salutary, but forgetting how it can be beneficial, and how it is pharmacological, is dangerous.

–Bernard Stiegler (2019)

Contents

x   Contents

xii *Contents*

Preface

The writing of this book has been an experiment in shared virtuality. Composing it between two countries – Peru and the United States – on Skype, with a Google Doc between us, we entered one common mindspace. The immediacy of the other's presence on the shared screen as we talked and wrote and thought together, generated a singular mode of intimacy that emerged from the virtual, which encouraged more spontaneity, risk-taking, and freedom. The vulnerabilities that are typically activated when sharing one's writing process – now intensified by the transparency of the virtual medium – could be lived out in the open, with less exposure.

Though the digital screen inevitably intensified our narcissism, it also enabled us to identify more quickly whenever its head slowly reared. Territorial and proprietary with our thoughts and words at the beginning, we began to feel less so with time. When we would divide up our tasks, elaborating on one's own idea or recomposing a paragraph we had worked on together, each of us would come back with an independently constructed text that often uncannily echoed the other's, provoking surges of unexpected synergy that resulted in a genuinely hybrid voice, with one invisible author. We started to notice that sentences almost seemed to write themselves. It felt, in fact, as if something beyond our individual minds started constellating.

Alive in the strange presence of our digital images on the screen, sometimes blurred and then again sharply clear, sometimes glitching or trailing behind our words, garbling sounds that echoed or muted themselves, our bodies were routinely reconstituted into virtual selves. Welded together in the virtual page, at the pace and rhythm of our tapping keys, our hands would blend our words together into a single flow. We have been unable to erase the traces that remain of each other's personal idiosyncracies, but that is only proof of the body's resilience and irreducibility to the digital. There is always some trace that will emerge, like a Barthesian "punktum," in the digital image.

When we had the opportunity to write in the same physical location (whether in Lima or Boston) dealing with the hard reality of our material lives, the contrast with working in our usual shared digital mindspace was poignant. On those occasions, even though present together – ironically enough – we felt more separate. The now-familiar intimacy ushered in by the virtual screen dissipated as we faced each other in our embodied difference, two separate minds working on a shared project experiencing together the drag of the real. The contrast between the virtual and the embodied modes of interaction – something we try to capture again and again throughout the book – was striking and elusive at the same time. We were no longer dancing on clouds but firmly tethered to the ground.

Initially we were each personally committed to different and sometimes contrary stances. One of us was inside technology, familiar with its inner workings, and naively optimistic about digital life; the other stood slightly askance, weary and pessimistic, assiduously resisting its pull. But as the result of composing in virtual space we discovered and experienced new thoughts and ideas spontaneously emerging; orientations shifted and – as two alternating helmsmen aboard a ship weathering an unpredictable tide – we found ourselves each oscillating between the various positions. In this liquid environment we began to feel safe enough to abandon our previous commitments, and follow the ideas without restriction. We no longer expected the other to remain faithful to earlier positions and even became critical of what was once previously defended. ("Consistency is the hobgoblin of little minds," Emerson kept reminding us.) We deliberately resisted the kind of defensive argumentation so common in discussions about technology which we have started to recognize as symptomatic of the poison that is part of the technological pharmakon. In our particular case, we lived that pharmacological tension both in our writing and digital lives, and in our growing capacity to surrender our individual convictions and see them from different and even opposing perspectives.

We wish that the readers of our text, regardless of their feelings or ideas about technology, will be able to let themselves also enter into this (pharmacologically) fluid space. All the different positions there interact, resonate, and expand each other, rather than oppose, forming a complex mosaic that gives image to the relationship with technology that we have attempted to forge in the writing of this book.

We have been talking about these issues continuously over 25 years, and it has taken us nearly a decade to birth the book. The digital revolution has had such profound and far-reaching effects on everyday life, it could have been a century. But it has also felt like a single blink, for the transformation to the new mode of life that we are exploring has already become a global fact and it is advancing at lightning speed with the onset of the pandemic.

Disclaimer

We should warn the reader that the words we use are, some of them, borrowed from others. Deleuze's, Freud's, Benjamin's, Flusser's, or Winnicott's words will appear under their original guise, but may very well acquire a life of their own. These borrowed terms repeat their original meanings, (and so they are duly attributed to their authors in their inception here) but, as with any repetition in a new setting, they may be called to perform quite different functions from those of the originals. This may cause confusion, and may seem, at some points, to do a disservice to the original authors, but it is in the nature of the rhizomatic field from which we hope to be writing, that chaos and cosmos (chaosmos), understanding and confusion together hold the tension.

No expectations should be placed on us or our words to adhere to their same original meanings, for that would only perpetuate the repetition of the same. Here, they may turn out to be quite different in the end. To put it in the language we use in this book, our writing "in-corporates," rather than simply "re-inscribes" the concepts, so variations may appear at any point and anywhere in the text.

Acknowledgements

Everything would have been very different were it not for our families who, in one way or another, nurtured us and put up with our constant preoccupation with the virtual. We want to thank Magali, Art, Antonio, Susan, Rachel, and Greti for their love and support; Lisa (undoubtedly our celestial muse), whose voice so often tempered and grounded us; Eve and Isaac, who, immersed in their digital lives, taught us more than they could have suspected.

Our work has also benefited from the keen intelligence of many friends and colleagues. Mario Montalbetti, whose careful reading and incisive comments on an early draft of the book confirmed to us that we were on a good track; Humphrey Morris, who, in spirited conversation, challenged and inspired us to push further and think deeper; Eduardo Villanueva, whose expertise in media studies helped clarify some issues in the first two chapters of the book; Marjorie and Doug Kinsey who, at one remove from the everyday digital, gave us a fresh perspective from which to see more clearly. We are both also indebted to Charles E. Scott, whom we met in the Philosophy department at Vanderbilt University in the eighties, and whose influence has been with us ever since.

We would also like to mention for supporting us in various ways: Richard Ying, Gordon Bearn, Jorge Villacorta, Greg Shaw, Stephen Pinals, Dan Monroe, Lorena Rojas Parma, Daniel Esparza and the Hampolindos, Adam Phillips, George Makari, José Medina, Juliet Floyd, Glen A. Mazis, Sherry Turkle, Patricia Llosa, Roque Carrión, Joshua Day, Rodrigo Luque, Robert Riethmiller, Ed Corrigan, Mark Steinberg, Jeff Meyerhoff, Francis Lang, Lucinda Ballantyne, Juan Pablo Bruno, Kristopher Spring, Carlos Schoof, Talia Wong, Alessandra Oshiro, Antonio Pomposini, and Vania Alarcón. Our editors Kate Hawes and Hannah Wright and, last but not least, Tori and Blue.

Parts of this book were written during a sabbatical leave from the Pontifical Catholic University of Peru, for which time we are both grateful.

Permissions

Introduction

Prelude

The astounding omnipresence of the virtual in contemporary consciousness is radically restructuring our psychology, changing our societies and culture, and having profound effects on who we are, how we behave with one another, and on the kind of world we are inhabiting. This is clearly evident in the indispensable and ubiquitous smartphone, the tiny home for quick and always accessible virtuality; in the screens that have become permanent fixtures in our houses, our offices, our social spaces, and, of course, our pockets; in our increasingly automated ways of life; and in our growing cohabitation with innumerable virtual presences and artificial intelligences.

Any adolescent, merely 30 years ago, had to go past the censoring mediation of a parent or authority figure in order to reach the person they were pursuing: "Let it be their sibling who answers the phone and not their parent!" was their common prayer. Back then, you could stay out all day. Nobody could reach you and you lived undisturbed and disconnected from anyone until you were back home.

Today, things are very different. Having a permanent line to the other is something we have come to take for granted. Thanks to our digital devices, we can chat with the person we want, reach them directly and immediately, unencumbered by any mediating presence. We can't even remember, much less imagine now, a life without a smartphone connecting us all to each other, like an umbilical cord that we are unable (and by now most likely unwilling) to shed.

Conversations, too, had a different dynamic. They flowed uninterrupted by virtual promptings, and whenever voids in memory or information cropped up, they were not replaced by the immediate consultation of the Google oracle; rather, they were endured together, opening spaces of interaction that could be personally enriching in ways that seem almost impossible nowadays. When the last pre-digital generation dies out, and their time becomes something for the history books, our children and their children will have only known a time in which mind and psyche were thoroughly permeated by a digital sensibility.

The speed and instantaneousness of digital communication radically unsettles both time and space. "Real time" and "virtual space" are new categories in our existence that introduce dramatic transformations in our form of life. The digital spreads through all our interactions and makes the virtual a space where we can now share experiences, with anyone, anywhere, something previously unimaginable. The difference between the public and the private that was so essential to modern life and culture is gradually disappearing. And in the compulsive desire it has ignited to expose our most intimate thoughts and feelings in the social media, we may be witnessing today the gradual disappearance of the boundaries that give shape and meaning to our collective lives.

As the god of communication, inventor of language, maker of borders, Hermes presides over the virtual. But he is also the trickster and thief, misdirecting us when he is supposed to guide, disabling us when he is supposed to enable. Hermetic undercurrents wind their way through our contemporary absorption in the digital. The virtual world provides a screen where we are tricked into believing that all our wishes and desires, our passions and aspirations can be fulfilled and hence made "real" without the work and labor required by actual life.

It is not surprising, therefore, that in such a short time, we have so unhesitatingly and uncritically surrendered to the power of digital technology. Our living in the "digital-now" – as we could call the immediacy of our digital lives – has transformed our relationship to temporality, scrambling the links between past, present, and future, making us often impervious to the passage of time and changing our experience and understanding of history.

McLuhan pointed out, already in the 1960s, that the media had become all-important. The ways the new technologies modulated the message began to re-define not just the mode, but the very nature of communication. *How* things were said started to take precedence over (and even make obsolete or irrelevant) *what* was said. "The medium," McLuhan prophetically proclaimed, "is the message," thus anticipating the situation – nowadays pervasive – where truth no longer matters, and where the way something is transmitted – whether it be through instant messaging, the TV news cycle, blogs, webpages, Twitter, or Instagram accounts, etc. – not only transforms what we communicate, but also reshapes it, beginning to determine how we think and what we believe.

In the vertiginous contingency of our digital lives, what really matters is less the message than that mediatic power that makes it ripple through the collective mind. Accuracy, objective representation, proof or argument are literally irrelevant when faced with a "trending topic."

The fake-news wars are predicated on the volatility of the social media that makes it easy to manipulate, or sway and convince the public. Democratic elections everywhere have become living proof of this power. Immediate impact displaces actual facts in this bewildering time of "post-truth."

Changing our very understanding of knowledge and ignorance, of subjectivity and objectivity, digital technology is reforging our needs and interests, affecting all areas of human experience. Our traditional habits and assumptions, our culture, our politics, our philosophy, and our morals are subverted by the multiple new forms of digital communication proliferating in our lives today. These profound transformations have been so rapid that we are only now beginning to notice and slowly assimilate their psychic effect. So much of it still remains unconscious, that it becomes important not only to attend to what seem to be the digital's very clear perils, but also to try to discern what may be its still unknown or unseen potential. Indeed, we might be witnessing an enhancement and extension of our existence beyond anything we are as yet able to imagine.

1 Human virtuality

In this book, we have made the concept of the virtual the fulcrum of our whole investigation. Although we all have learned to think of the virtual as a second "world," an artificially constructed environment or object that emulates, and sometimes amazingly mimics reality, it is important to see that it is not only that. Indeed, the concept of the virtual has a long history in philosophy, as well as crucial significations for psychoanalysis; it brings with it issues of time, embodiment, and mortality, shedding an important light on what it means to be human. The virtual, then, as a concept, as an idea and as a force in nature, packs a forceful multi-dimensional punch whose impact we will explore throughout the book. But we begin here, with its most familiar usage, which is derived from our contemporary digital world.

The "virtual" in the term "virtual reality" serves to qualify something as secondary, fake or unreal, even something illusory. Virtual objects in cyberspace are mere copies that only represent or replicate reality but are themselves not quite real. A virtual kiss, a virtual flower, a virtual friend, for example, are less than a real kiss, an actual flower, or a friend. Shooting at someone in a videogame is not the same as shooting a real person. We have naturally gauged the "reality" of the virtual in terms of how close it comes to the empirical real. The underlying assumption is, of course, that the virtual and the real will never be the same. But it is precisely that unquestioned belief in the radical separateness of real and virtual that needs to be contested.

Ironically enough, our digital lives are forcing us to seriously question it, and may in the end reveal as utterly mistaken our assumption that the virtual, like the pilot fish on the shark, is parasitic on the real.

In striking opposition to our contemporary notion of the virtual as denoting something false or illusory, the pre-digital understanding of the virtual has more to do with force. As Brian Massumi (2014) observes, "virtual" is derived from the Latin word for strength or potency, so that the primary definition of the virtual is not simulation, as we usually assume, but "potentiality," which, as Aristotle taught us, is that which may come to be, the latent potency of a thing. The virtual should be understood, not as an illusory, artificial reality, but as the *dimension of possibility* inherent to all reality. As Massumi puts it,

> [The virtual] concerns the potency in what is, by virtue of which it really comes to be. It connotes a force of existence: the press of the next, coming to pass. The virtual pertains to the power to be, pressing, passing, eventuating into ever new forms, in a cavalcade of emergence. (p. 55)

Technology has always contended with the emergent force of the virtual, its open possibilities, as something it must mold or modulate. But each new modulation confirms that the potential of the virtual in its "cavalcade of emergence" always surpasses the technological. Every technology draws from this prime matter that is the virtual and brings something out of it that was never there before.

In the shift that took place with the advent of writing, for example, when the oral tradition was superseded by the scribal, the new technological modulation of the virtual changed the topography of communication, for in writing it was no longer required to happen in a shared (physical) space, nor in real time. The scribal modulation dislocated time and vanished space. The book could be read by anyone, anywhere in the world. Leaving behind the intimacy of the oral and confining it to the solitude of each individual's mind, it paradoxically broadened the range of the exchange.

With the digital modulation, another topographical shift takes place. No matter where we are we can directly interact with the other in virtual space, restoring the immediate presence of the oral that was lost to scribality. In bringing forth its own unique modulation, each technological advance, in its particular configuration of time, space, and matter, displaces the modulation that has preceded it, laying the ground for innumerable new shifts and transformations, thus confirming the inexhaustibility of the virtual.

The history of the virtual is as long as that of language, as we will see in the brief history of the media in Part I of the book, so the meaning of the virtual does not follow from the advent of digital technology or the invention of the virtual world. Our ability to speak, to articulate experience in words, and so "lift," as it were, the empirical world into the abstract dimension of concepts and images, marks the emergence of the human virtual. It has always referred to the potentiality that subjectivity adds to sensible experience, and, as the realm of the mind, has been the concern of philosophy since the beginning.

We will distinguish the "human virtual," that mental space wherein we are able to think, imagine, fantasize, invent the world, from the "digital virtual" also a place for thought, fantasy and imagination, yet located in that virtual space behind our screens, that we call virtual reality. But let us not forget that both the human and the digital virtual emerge out of the very immanence of our lived existence as mortal, embodied beings in an actual world, in other words, the inexhaustible virtual itself. The virtual *tout court*, moreover, distinct from the human and the digital virtual, is the source of change and temporal movement that cuts through the world and underwrites the mind. It is precisely the fate of our relation to the virtual in the age of digital technology that is the central concern of the book.

a Virtuality and psychoanalysis

The digital virtual is another version – expressed in a different register and with a different set of terms – of what has also been an object of profound concern for psychoanalysis. Although psychoanalysis does not speak of virtual reality *per se*, it does speak of psychic reality, dream and play space, fantasy and reverie, and the central role of the imagination in constituting the real. Indeed, human virtuality could be seen, from this perspective, as nothing other than the always decentered play between the free and open realm of autonomous desire and fantasy (i.e., the unconscious psyche), and the conscious mind.

Our repeated turn toward the digital in the course of everyday life (searching, checking, updating, and posting) has significant parallels to the inwardly directed turn toward our own minds (thinking, fantasizing, and dreaming). Pre-digitally, in a less distracted era, we may remember (no doubt for some, tinged with a certain amount of nostalgia) that it was far easier than it is now to be attuned to an inwardly generated cognitive and emotional space where thoughts, fantasies and ideas could spontaneously play out in the mind's eye. This interior space of psychic life, which includes the figures that appear in dream and fantasy form, as well as reveries, thoughts and ideations, is what we will call the *virtual within*. It is from this well-spring of internally sourced virtuality that virtual reality technologies seem to draw their dynamism. The virtual-within, in contrast with the artifice of the digital media, springs from the vital spontaneity of the

imaginative mind. Whereas "virtual reality" arises from the collecti-
vized archive of human subjectivity as it is now assembled in the
Internet, the virtual within is sourced in the interior of the in-
dividualized, embodied self and depends on experience, memory, and
the creative workings of fantasy.

The difference this makes to our experience of the virtual is illustrated by the case of Frank, a psychotherapy client who once had one
of those crystal clear dreams, in which he found himself taking a walk
in the woods with his father and speaking to him as he was before his
mind and body were ravaged by Parkinson's. In the dream, he was
thinking to himself, "Yes, this is how my father used to walk, this is
how he was physically present, ambling through the natural world,
before he got the disease." Frank was very moved by this dream, as it
resonated with a sad and split-off part of himself that was not quite
ready to mourn what he was losing. Some time later, Frank spoke of
the experience he had had upon seeing old family videos of his father
before Parkinson's. Although he was affectively moved, Frank
observed that the images on the screen did not have the same emotional weight or valence for him. There was something missing. But
what exactly was the difference, what is the missing experience? Is
there something about the creative power of the dream, as an unbidden image that comes out of the depths of one's own being, that is
different from the technological registration of a past event? How do
we make sense of the difference between the way the psyche creates
virtual-reality worlds in the form of dream images, fantasies, reveries,
flights of fancy in one's mind, etc., and the digital realm of imaginative, affective, and emergent reality that is materialized in the virtual world? What is the vantage point from which we see the
superiority of the dream experience over its video counterpart?

Today, of course, the psyche is constituting the digital, both individually and collectively. The unconscious force of our psychic
lives structures the particular ways in which each of us invites the
digital into the most intimate aspects of our subjective being. But
the digital is also transforming our experience of psychic reality. The
imagination of an event on the screen weaves new associations and
meanings and so re-fashions the actuality of the event itself, closely
paralleling the re-fashioning of reality that takes place in our inner
lives. This paradox – the psyche simultaneously constituting reality
and being constituted by the digital modulation of experience – is
our point of access for probing what is happening to the virtual in
this new world.

In order to hold open a space in which to explore the difference
between the digital-virtual and the virtuality inherent to our psychic
lives (i.e., the virtual within), we will continually keep in mind their
resonances and dissonances. In other words, we will pinpoint where

they seem to draw together and where they seem to split apart. Nowhere is this poignant play between them better exemplified today than in the dissociation that happens when we use our digital devices. In opening up the laptop or peering at the phone, we seek contact with a virtual realm that is not immediately available in the present, just as we do, at any moment, when we inwardly shift our attention toward our own thoughts and feelings. In both cases – the turn toward our mind and the turn toward our devices – we dissociate in order to enter another kind of mindspace or even to flee the empirical present. But, in our digitally permeated split-screen lives, we are becoming evermore dissociative creatures, our attention constantly wavering, here one minute, gone the next. Yet all of this consciousness-fragmenting behavior that plagues us in our digital engagements, takes place against the inescapable backdrop of the human psyche's vulnerability to distraction, splitting and dissociation.[1] If, as Freud contends, unconscious life is intimately tied to psychic defenses, then we have to explore what it is that we are obliged to evade about ourselves, about others, and the world, in order to stay so immersed in the digital flow.

We will see how our fixation with our digital devices makes us blind to the impact they are having on our affective and erotic lives. In the vital interplay between the erotic possibilities of the virtual and the everyday exigencies of reality, the digital makes desire more familiar and accessible while at the same time dissociatively estranging us from its unconscious roots. At the most fundamental level of embodied existence, we will argue, eros and desire fuel our virtual attachments, not just in the ubiquity of Internet pornography, but also in virtual shopping, browsing, recording, chatting, and all social networking.

We will not systematically differentiate creative from pathological dissociation through sociological or empirical investigation. Rather, we aim to think more broadly about what is being split and what is being dissociated, as well as what is being reconfigured and reconnected when the digital so pervasively enters into the innermost dimensions of our acquisitive and erotic lives. This takes us into the depths of the problematic regarding the changing relationship between the virtual and the real in the digital era (the theme of Part II of the book) and will also help us understand how our use of digitality both serves us, on the one hand, to escape and, on the other, to potentiate our engagement with the virtual.

b *Virtuality and philosophy*

It is by now increasingly evident that traditional Western metaphysics is no longer adequate for our contemporary world. The digital age is drastically changing not just our psychology but also our ontology, the basic makeup of our world. We need only consider the previously unheard-of entities and relations that begin to people it: virtual space and "real time," digital screens and smartphones, telematic action and perception, cybersex and virtual objects, hard disks and holograms, live photographs, downloads and .gifs, algorithms and bitcoins, "ghosting" and "phubbing" and "blocking" and "sharing," and so on. In this alternative universe, our understanding of how things are ordered is rapidly and radically changing. David Weinberger (2007), for example, considers how the lay-out of an office supply store is changed in the digital era:

> Instead of atoms that take up room, [this space] is made of bits. Instead of making us walk long aisles, in the digital world everything is only a few clicks away ... [But] something much larger is at stake than how we lay out our stores. The physical limitations that silently guide the organization of an office supply store also guide how we organize our businesses, our government, our schools. They have guided – and limited – how we organize knowledge itself [....] Now, for the first time in history, we are able to arrange our concepts without the silent limitations of the physical. (pp. 6–7)

The result of this ontological expansion is a world that forces and stretches the categories by which we normally order and give meaning to experience, and slowly undermines our standards, shattering some of our most familiar presuppositions and criteria. But when our clothes no longer fit our bodies, as Galileo once said, we must look for others that do. So, we need to find a new paradigm through which to make sense of this changing order.

From the beginning of time, each technology has inevitably modified the ways we structure and find meaning in what we experience. Each new technological innovation either extends and so potentiates the previous one, as, for instance, the printing press did to writing, or film did to photography or else, a pre-existing technology is destabilized by what comes next, as different perceptions and experiences emerge that shatter old orders and force the establishment of new criteria and a reshuffling of perceived reality. We can see this, for example, in how the affective intensity of oral communication was disrupted by the new ways of ordering our thinking imposed by the linearity of the written text. Each new technological innovation introduces novel forms of modulation by which the virtual is now actualized, thus transforming our perception. The development of impressionistic painting, for instance, resulted in a perception of reality not in brushstrokes, as the previous styles had done, but in points or smudges of color that affected our reception and apprehension of the world. The virtual is actualized and new aspects are made visible by the powers of each new medium.

In the particular case of the latest technologies, as we will see, aspects of orality and scribablity are further potentiated, but also shattered by the new ontology introduced by the digital medium. Whereas, from the scribal perspective, the world was made up of permanent substances and qualities, the digital turns this worldview on its head. The metaphysics of permanence that underwrites the modern mindset is displaced by a world of processes in constant movement. Thus, change – which had been seen as an illusion of sensible experience unveiled by means of scientific knowledge – becomes the very essence of the world within the digital framework.

This current medium provides us with new modulations of reality – new ways in which the virtual is actualized – that broaden our perception and deepen our understanding of experience. We can now modulate the temporality of an event and either accelerate or decelerate it, thus revealing aspects of its makeup that were otherwise imperceptible. For example, the action of peeling an orange seen again through a slow motion video allows us to begin not only to notice things that remained unconscious before, but, precisely because of that, leads to weaving experience into ever more complicated brocades that enrich reality.

Unknowingly anticipating the novel modulations of the virtual that the digital media introduce us to, Wittgenstein, Benjamin, and Deleuze rebel against the fixed and sedimented concepts of substances and qualities inherent to the modern worldview. For this reason we will appeal and enter in dialogue with these three thinkers. Their experiments in language and methodologies unsettle our conceptions of identity and permanence, of space and time, and reality and illusion. They provide us with valuable tools that are more suitable for the mode of thinking that emerges with the digital and useful for finding our way through the thicket of problematics that begin to arise with it. Even without having any inkling of the hegemony of digital life that has occurred in our times, they were all intent, in different ways as we will see, on entering into the dance of the virtual and the actual, where – liberated by the temporal movement of the real – the virtual becomes a new creation itself.

As the temporality of the things in the world becomes central to the modulation of the digital, the issue of whether what we see is true or not, authentic or illusory, becomes secondary or even dispensable. As Massumi (2014) observes, "the question of perception is no longer one of truth or illusion, but of differing modes of reality, in the movement of emergence through which the forms of experience come to pass" (p. 56). The new modes of actualizing virtuality no longer depend on a fixed representational relationship with what already is, but rather constitute a wholly new production of experience. The actualized virtuality that constitutes the ontology of the virtual world makes it evident, that contrary to what the modern metaphysic of presence suggested, the virtual need not be always considered in the framework of original and copy. As Massumi (2014) asserts of the virtual, from a Deleuzian post-representational perspective, "[f]ar from [being] a replica of the real, [it] is the very motor of its continued becoming" (pp. 55–6).

And if we return to the notion of the virtual as potential, then the virtual is a potential that "never appears as such. What appears is that which it gives rise to – which is precisely not it, but its fulfillment" (p. 56). What we are dealing with in the book then is not primarily "virtual reality" (in the digital sense), but the reality of virtuality, that potential of which Massumi speaks, which is nothing other than the inscrutable and inexhaustible immanence of the virtual, where we are unable to discern anything prior to the new modulations, but which is the source of all emerging meanings. The virtual as potentiality is always behind what we perceive, underwriting it all with pure possibility; it is situated behind perception as its invisible double, out of which reality emerges. "Potential is [...] never actually present as such [...] It is as evasive of the present as it is effective in its formation" (p. 56).

That is why, in what follows, we continually return to the question of the negative or unsayable or – in psychoanalytic terms – the unrepresentable, as manifestations of this potential which never appears as such. The paradox of virtuality is found in the fact that "no sooner has it disappeared into its own fulfilment than it makes itself felt again in the press toward a next" (Massumi, 2014, p. 56). Much like the unconscious in psychoanalysis, the virtual has effects in the world but does not appear as such. Virtuality is a hermetic messenger, invisibly present in all transformation.

The mind, the spirit, and the soul all refer to the human virtual, that dimension of possibility that the temporal opens in our existence. Insofar as the mind is in unstoppable movement and change, it is permeated by absence; it is grounded in primordial, constitutive loss. As Nusselder (2014) points out, it "contains an emptiness or negativity" (p. 74).

That the mind itself is thoroughly permeated by the virtual means human experience is haunted by lack and incompleteness. This intimate relationship between virtuality and absence invokes the existential dimensions of the virtual,

> Virtuality introduces an "openness" (otherness) in human existence: the dimension of infinity and freedom. Because of this "openness" human existence cannot entirely be grasped on an

objective level (as an object). On the ontological plane, this openness or "wound" of the human subject is the condition of possibility of new configurations of humanity. (Nusselder, 2014, p. 80)

Nusselder places at the heart of our virtuality a wound, which we want to identify with mortal contingency and ontological lack. At the very center of the digital there remains an irreducible negativity that constitutes the very possibility of life, and the human meaning we make of it. This is another pivotal area of experience that we want to keep an eye on as we probe the kind of virtuality that arises out of the digital. What does it do to our wound, to our lack, to that which is imperfect and incomplete in us? And do the new configurations of humanity that arise from this age open or close us to that wound? Do they serve as a balm or poison?

2 Digital life

We find ourselves today in a perpetually fracturing set of discourses around the question of technology. Some will see what is happening in the digital age as a further stage in a continuous progression of civilization, as simply one more (giant) step in the single path of technological progress toward an enhanced humanity. According to that view, the new digital technologies extend our power, enhance our faculties, as technologies have always done. But although they do so with ever greater sophistication, they still remain on the same plane as what came before. Others, however, will see that "progress" as an illusion, the sophistication brought about by each new technological discovery merely amounting to new faces behind which lurks the familiar; in other words, the deeper fact beyond any apparent advance always comes back to the same incorrigible human nature. So here also there is no incommensurable difference with anything that has passed before. Others, on the contrary, see the digital indeed as a world-defining leap, as the beginning of a glorious potentiation of the species, as the transhumanists, with their expectation, for example, of escaping organic life by uploading the human mind into computers. Still others, also affirming such a quantum change, will see in it instead the seeds of human demise, a dangerous and regressive experiment that fundamentally threatens our very nature or is even the beginning of the end of what we have known as human.

We bear witness to the stubborn propensity to polarize in the adamant advocacy of any one of these positions, perhaps the most pernicious obstacle we face when considering technology. It is difficult to have a conversation about the impact of the digital world on our psychic lives without quickly falling into one of these camps, replacing dialogue with argumentation, often leading to frustration or a narrow manicheism. We become tendentious and are forced to choose between one side or another, contributing, among other things, to the generational divide where adults are confronted by the passionate opposition of youth. Typically, parents will rebuke their children, "Look at what is happening to you. You live inside your phone" and their children will disdainfully dismiss them, convinced that they will never understand. One must admit, as one strives to keep an even keel, that sometimes it seems undeniable that we are making progress, that just as the scribal culture enriched orality, the digital is also opening new horizons to the human and therefore enhancing our faculties and experience. But then, at other times, when we see how humans respond to each new technological advance, the same hybris and misjudgement rear their ugly head, and all changes suddenly become nothing but cosmetic. We confess however, that we are inclined to believe that the digital, in opening a new dimension of reality, i.e. the virtual world, is bringing with it a radical transformation, a quantum leap that is changing the kind of creatures that we are as well as our place in the world. It is hard not to see these changes as unprecedented in the history of mankind, giving us the power to determine the future of the planet. But this too may be a mirage, as everyday life has suddenly become so inundated by the new virtualities of the digital that we cannot see clearly anymore. Thus, we must shed our certainties and keep the question open considering the possibility that we are indeed entering a posthuman time. As Žižek lucidly writes,

> ... one should abandon the old humanist idea that, whatever happens, a certain form of human dignity will be maintained or reasserted. This is simply cheating. Such a perspective assumes dogmatically that a basic notion of humanity will somehow survive all these socio-technological transformations. [...] What I am convinced of is that if these tendencies continue, then the very status of what it means to be a human being will change. Even the most elementary things, like speaking language, emotional sense and so on will be affected. Nothing should be taken for granted and it would be inconsequent to be either optimistic or pessimistic. (Žižek and Daly, 2004, p. 85)

Žižek is resisting as folly any judgment that rests on our present humanist conception, but it is that very folly that causes the polarization that infects our current discourse on technology. In that light, we intend to approach the uncharted territory opened by virtual reality with full receptiveness, and neither optimistically nor pessimistically.

No matter how you understand the meaning of digital technology and the virtual for life today, the insistence upon advocating for one particular view over another inevitably blinds us to the utter complexity at the limit of discourse. Any book that addresses the question of digital technology in our current era (and there are scores and scores of them) faces this immense difficulty. Very few accounts of digitality demonstratively stay open in the face of that tension.[2] Instead, they take a stand and stubbornly defend it at all costs. Alternatively, we intend to enter into a broader and more comprehensive dynamic that reflects the primordial tensions of the digital age, never wholly represented by any one systematic discourse or any one certain position. We hope rather to articulate these tensions performatively, in a language attuned to what is inevitably uncertain and ultimately unknowable.

Our assumption is that serious psychological and philosophical engagement will help to overcome this powerful tendency toward dichotomization. We thus offer a different approach to these questions. Whether emancipatory or regressive, optimistic or pessimistic, our method for breaking through these polarizing positions is to give careful and equal voice to all stances, so that their dialogue can speak out of the many-stranded tensions between them. We will be suspending the dialectic to counter the splits that binary logic seems to impose on us and the demand for closure. We aim instead to enter phenomenologically into the thicket of contradictions and indeterminacies that always shadows and shapes whatever tentative conclusions we may draw about the digital.

In an age when everything is so rapidly changing, it is essential to provide a framing of the issues that allows us to encounter the complexity of technology. We use the word *encounter* deliberately to distinguish argumentation about the effects of the digital (which pushes us onto one side or another) from existentially entering the question, addressing what is happening at the level of our being. We explore the intersection of the virtual world with the thinking/feeling body and psyche, and drawing together philosophy and psychoanalysis, we enact a mode of writing in which thinking, affect and lived experience are held alongside each other in their own complicated and often conflicting realities. In our best (and of course imperfect) attempt to relinquish any side, we are not only addressing the problem of foreclosure, but also resisting the impulse to split thinking and affect that weighs down so much academic writing.

In our view, the Luddites who bury their head in the sand and refuse to engage with what is happening, because they don't like it and won't have any part of it, are as confused and problematic as the techno-liberationists who unthinkingly turn toward technology to avoid having to bear the limitations of embodied life in a world that seems to be out of control. There is always something unconscious in any one perspective, as any single approach to the question of technology implicitly negates another. Perhaps it is our very human inclination for closure, as well as an implicit need to preserve a single foundational substance (whether it be the real or the virtual), that makes it difficult to live in this tension. Instead of holding it, we polarize and either fantasize optimistically about digital eternity, fleeing from bodily weight, or battle skeptically and tragically against the digital, which we see as a fever raging in our time and numbing us to life.

3 Poison and remedy

The Internet, through its capacity to cut across unlimited swaths of time and space, takes us out of ourselves into a much wider world of people, things, and meanings, engaging a multiplicity of perspectives on the "other." And yet, at the very same time, nothing more dramatically exposes a process of narcissistic inflation than time spent on-line, as it situates the self at the center, radically severing it from what is other. The digital enhances and enriches human experience while at the same time flattening and diminishing it. The Greeks gave this paradox – of being at the same time a remedy and a poison, simultaneously healing us and making us ill –, the name "pharmakon."

Invoking Derrida's ground-breaking essay on the pharmakon, *Plato's Pharmacy*, Does and Clarke (1999) write:

> Like writing or drawing, each virtual-reality technology is a pharmakon – cure, remedy, potion, drug, poison, magic, etc. They reli(e)ve memory and enhance experience and sensation, but in so doing, they facilitate forgetfulness, dis-ablement, and sensory deprivation. (p. 264)

Our investigations follow what we accordingly characterize as a pharmacological method; we attend simultaneously and systematically to both the shadow and the light of the digital. The pharmakon will serve as a guiding principle for holding the tension of these opposites. Like a discipline of double vision, a contemplative exercise in paradoxical thinking, the pharmakon will help us situate and explore our thought about the digital and all its related phenomena – from video games, and social media to robots and Internet pornography, consumerism and the ubiquitous presence of the smartphone, etc. – from within this paradox. There is a logic to the pharmakon that we will be on the watch for, "according to which what supplements or supports at the same time weakens, what cultivates at the same time undermines..." (Russell, 2020, p. 104).

We do not intend to provide practical guidelines for dealing with digital life. We are convinced instead that the kind of understanding of technology we aim for should be existentially demanding as well as transformative. The reader might experience in confronting this text, at times, a sensation of vertigo, but that is the very nature of what we are proposing to do. We seek not only an intellectual exercise of understanding, but also a concrete encounter with the paradox at the root of the digital, which is increasingly permeating our everyday. We don't intend to defend a theory or to take a position, as much as make evident the pharmacological complexity of the virtual and our digital lives.

All technologies of communication and information poison us with the illusion of permanence but also cure us from that illusion by exposing the inherent spectrality of passing time. They may simply be forms by which we confront the ephemerality of temporal existence, and try to deal with its passing or evade it. They express our need to manage loss and oblivion and are all symptoms of our complex and evolving relation with mortality.

In light of our technologies, the mythological figure of Pygmalion provides a fitting image for reflecting upon our relation with death and mortality. The mythic sculptor is said to have replaced Aphrodite, the object of his love, with a perfect sculpted image of the goddess, just as we secretly hope to replace our imperfect world with the concoctions of our ever more sophisticated genetics, neuroscience and cybernetics. And just as Pygmalion avoids emotional commitment and vulnerability by fabricating a perfect version of his love through his art, we too attempt to escape contingency, up to the point of overcoming our own mortality. Technology is Pygmalionic.

In our Western tradition, we habitually deny time and death. We feel a need to make every change predictable, and hence controlled through scientific theory, political ideology, medical science, and so on, since each unpredictable change always prefigures death. In this sense, we could say that Western culture has been anchored in the melancholic replacement of the ephemeral passing present with the sedimented past. We call this intrinsic melancholy "the Pygmalionic Impulse," for, just like Pygmalion, our culture replaces fleeting experience with mental representations (concepts or images) as if, in fact, intent on preserving the object to avoid suffering its irremediable loss (Krebs, 2004).

But technology is also Promethean: As the fire stolen from the gods earns the reckless titan and his transgression the implacable sanction, technology contains within itself an inner curse that stokes the titanic excess of our nature. In our exploration of the virtual, and in our attempt to grant it its fullest expression, we hope to engender in the reader both the experience of its hermetic paradox, as much as its Promethean ambition and its chastening.

Psychoanalytically and philosophically speaking, we may conjecture that our propensity to closure and rational completeness stems from a tendency in us to control what is to come, unable to deal with the uncertainty or the openness and fragmentariness of life. Here, the virtual is our teacher, provocateur, and guide, since it is an intrinsically open field that resists our systematic tendency to safely encapsulate it in any closed or finished theory. To truly allow the virtual to reveal itself, we must find ways to confront its utter unrepresentability, to open ourselves to the slap it brings to our intellectual profligacy that wants to reduce vital experience to a set of concepts.

The digital throws us into a dynamically changing reality that demands from us a different kind of thinking that explicitly acknowledges death as an unavoidable burden of creatures of language capable of thought; it makes thinking and representing a form of mourning. And yet, because the digital throws us into a relationship with the world that is always mediated, it numbs our relationship to temporality and impinges upon our capacity to more fully embrace the flux of time. Our ability to digitally control and manipulate time blocks our mortal awareness and often prevents us from reaching reality.

The digital modulates in completely original and momentous ways our relationship to the virtual dimensions of our own being. As the new technologies of information and communication continuously thrust us into the particular dance between virtual and actual the digital enacts, it brings us face-to-face with our mortality. But then what effect is the digital revolution having on our relationship to loss and the passing away of things? How does it enhance our relationship to temporality and, conversely, how does it numb us to death?

Coda

At the beginning of the second decade of the millenium it may be time for us to think of technology not so much in terms of the power it gives us to subject Nature to our will, but as an outgrowth of our very life; an outgrowth that is instituting radically new modes of being in the world that respond to the unwieldy forces of the cultural unconscious unleashed by our technological action.

Walter Benjamin (1979) distinguished between technology conceived as an instrument of domination and technology as a means of reflection. As he says, many assume that its purpose is the mastery of nature, but this may be completely mistaken. He reflects thus:

> [...] who would trust a cane wielder who proclaimed the mastery of children by adults to be the purpose of education? Is not education above all the indispensable ordering of the relationship between generations and therefore mastery, if we are to use the

term, of that relationship and not of children? And likewise, *technology is not the mastery of nature, but of the relation between nature and man.* (pp. 103–4)

Technology has as little to do with mastery over nature as the teacher has with subduing their students. If technology is to be mastery over anything, Benjamin suggests, it would have to be over our relation to the world, over how to manage or live with the new nature that it opens around us. But the blindness Benjamin is pointing to is still blatantly clear in our own relation with the world. We should learn to see, therefore, technology as an event of life that speaks to (and from) the deepest levels of human consciousness. Understood in this way, any event in the world – whether it be the roadkill we see on our way back from the country, the burning of the Amazon forests, or the phenomenon of "fake news" – insofar as it involves our technological presence in the world, becomes a sign from which to learn to see technology not merely as a tool we can use for our advantage or even our survival. What this calls for instead is a change in mentality, from the straight-forward Apollonian directness of the scientific ethos, to something more hermetic, like the obliqueness of the virtual itself.

Indeed, Ortega y Gasset (1968) contended that in our time, after more than 2500 years of identifying with reason and submitting sensibility to its demands, we are discovering that reason is nothing but "a tiny island afloat on the sea of primeval vitality" (p. 57). Reason, according to him, with its culture of abstract intelligence, its science and theory, cannot supplant life. Our mission in this era, he believed, is to submit reason to vitality, place it within the life-world, and surrender it to spontaneity. It is culture, reason, and ethics that should be at the service of life and not the other way around.

The real character and import of this digital revolution may be its offering us (or forcing us) into a new perspective that may mark the beginning of that exploration that Ortega y Gasset had seen, as already approaching from the future, so that our gradual withdrawal from the physical into the virtual may in the end serve as a way to disabuse ourselves of the illusory image we have of human being as the zenith of nature.

Notes

1 This propensity of the psyche for dissociation and fragmentation we know from the pioneering works of the early depth psychologists (Janet, Freud, Jung) and their contemporary descendants (Bromberg, Kalsched, Ferro).

2 There are some notable exceptions that we will be citing throughout the book, as for example, Doel and Clarke (1991), Heim (1993), Massumi (2002), Flusser (2011), Murphie (2002), Derrida and Stiegler (2002), Mazis (2002), Bridle (2018), and others.

References

Benjamin, W. (1979) *One Way Street and Other Writings*. London: Harcourt Brace.

Bridle, J. (2018) *New Dark Edge. Technology and the End of the Future*. London: Verso.

Derrida, J., and Stiegler, B. (2002) *Echographies of Television*. Cambridge: Polity Press.

Doel, M., and Clarke, D.B. (1999) Virtual Worlds: Simulation, Suppletion, S(ed)uction and Simulacra. In M. Crang, P. Crang, and J. May (Eds.), *Virtual Geographies: Bodies, Spaces and Relations*. London and New York: Routledge.

Deleuze, G., and Guattari, P. (1987) *One Thousand Plateaus*. Minnesota: University of Minnesota Press.

Flusser, V. (2011) *Into the Universe of Technical Images*. Minneapolis: University of Minnesota Press.

Hayles, N. K. (1999) *How We Became Posthuman: Virtual Bodies in Cybernetics, Literature, and Informatics*. Chicago: The University of Chicago Press.

Heidegger, M. (1977) The Question Concerning Technology. In *Basic Writings* (pp. 283–318). New York: Harper and Row.

Heim, M. (1993) *The Metaphysics of Virtual Reality*. Oxford: Oxford University Press.

Krebs, V.J. (2004) "Descending into Primaeval Chaos": Philosophy, the Body, and the Pygmalionic Impulse. In A. Anderson, et al. (Eds.), *Mythos and Logos: How to Regain the Love of Wisdom*. Amsterdam and New York: Rodopi.

Mazis, G. (2002) *Earthbodies: Rediscovering our Planetary Senses*. Albany: State University of New York Press.

Massumi, B. (2002) *Parables of the Virtual. Movement, Affect, Sensation*. Durham: Duke University Press.

Massumi, B. (2014) Envisioning the Virtual. In Mark Grim Shaw (Ed.), *The Oxford Handbook of Virtuality*. Oxford University Press.

Murphie, A. (2002) Putting the Virtual Back into In Massumi B. (Ed.), *A Shock to Thought: Expression after Deleuze and Guattari*. London and New York: Routledge.

Nusselder, A. (2009) *Interface Fantasy: A Lacanian Cyborg Ontology*. Cambridge: MIT Press.

Nusselder, A. (2014) Being More Than Yourself: Virtuality and Human Spirit. In Mark Grim Shaw (Ed.), *The Oxford Handbook of Virtuality*. Oxford: Oxford University Press.

Ortega y Gasset, J. (1968) *Meditación de la técnica*. Madrid: Revista de Occidente.

Russell, J. (2020) *Psychoanalysis and Deconstruction: Freud's Psychic Apparatus*. London and New York: Routledge.

Weinberger, D. (2007) *Everything is Miscellaneous. The Power of the New Digital Disorder*. New York: Henry Holt and Company.

Žižek, S., and Daly, G. (2004) *Conversations with Zizek*. Cambridge: Polity Press.

Part I
Virtual media

Introduction to Part I

Before we begin our investigations on human virtuality and digital life, we need to provide a genealogy of the technology that has led us to this era. We begin with a short story of the evolution of the media, starting in the emergence of language, and consider the relation between these evolving technologies and what we are calling the human virtual. And we finish with virtuality's different transformations, especially apropos the digital.

1 History of the virtual

[In] a technological world [...] the terms of nature are obscured; one need not live quite in the present or the local.

Rebecca Solnit (2003)

Prelude

Human beings, unlike any other species on the planet, have a sense of history, of living through a sequence of past, present, and future. Animals, on the contrary, do not have our sense of time; they live always in an unstoppable now. They forget as soon as they're done, and then they do it again as if for the first time. Animals immediately forget: not their bodies, that remember in another way, but their temporal consciousness. For them, each moment "sink[s] back into deep night extinguished forever," as Nietzsche (1980, pp. 8–9) poetically says. Their life is condemned to (or blessed with) an eternal present. But humans are freed from this sentence. They suspend the world from the actual present and virtualize it into a representation, a concept, an image, an idea. Images and words are our awakening to consciousness.

According to the Greek myth, we received the gift of thought in the fire that the titan Prometheus stole from the gods as compensation for the precariousness of our natural existence. This titanic transgression curses us but also brings us closer to the gods. In technology, we are given the power to extend reality, to usher the world into the realm of possibilities. It constitutes our "leap into the virtual," which begins the evolution of *Homo sapiens*. Technology generates a history of the virtual, of the many different transformations it undergoes with each new advance. That history has led us – through images painted on cave walls, and words first uttered and then written, through photographic and then moving images – to our latest leap into the digital modulation of the virtual, which we call "Virtual Reality."

The awakening of the intellect, says Wittgenstein (1993), is always accompanied by a rupture from the original ground. Human consciousness involves the loss of the instinctive connection to the world that characterizes the life of animals and human infancy. Every time a new technology arises, it conditions the virtual differently, so that the same dynamic of loss is repeated again. Armed with a new medium, we lose the immediacy of the world we had attained under the spell of the previous one. Our smartphones, for example, capable of carrying an immense memory supplement, begin to displace and obliterate our natural memories, which often no longer remember even the simplest of things. Suddenly, what had been natural for us before, is forgotten with the next technology, which opens a new evolutionary path in its place.

Plato (1980) was the first to warn us about that technological dynamic, especially its particular loss and danger, when he pointed out that the new invention of writing would separate knowledge from experience, doing away with the work of memory that transforms information into understanding, and so leads us to mistake information for wisdom. As King Thamus tells Theuth, the inventor of writing, in the Phaedrus:

> If men learn [writing], it will implant forgetfulness in their souls; they will cease to exercise memory because they rely on that which is written, calling things to remembrance no longer from within themselves, but by means of external marks. [Writing] is a recipe not for memory, but for reminder. And it is no true wisdom that you offer your disciples, but only its semblance, for by telling them of many things without teaching them you will make them seem to know much, while for the most part they know nothing. (p. 275a)

Writing allows us to handle information without having to assimilate it immediately, as we did before, when we received it orally and had to process it right there and then in our bodies, through our emotions. But with writing, we can learn to repeat the discourse of another and "understand" its meaning, at a distance, intellectually, without really grasping it. (Apollo, the myth says, shoots his precise arrows always from a distance.) In making memory dispensable, scribal consciousness disconnects the oral medium from experience and words lose the depth and power of their grounding in the body.

There is a new loss every time we leap again into the virtual. This has been true with speech and written or printed words, photographs, and moving pictures; it is no different with digital images, hypertexts, and the like. But, faithful to its pharmacological nature, that loss always comes with its gain as well. All technology opens new doors, making new experiences possible, at the same time that it closes others. Writing may disconnect us from the immediacy of oral language and its automatic work of memory, but it also sharpens the reasoning and logical skills without which modern scientific advance, for example, would not have been possible.

1 A short story of the media

a Words: From speech to writing

Technology is the expression of a drive to extend ourselves into the virtual. It reflects our capacity to abstract reality, to remove ourselves from the immediacy of experience in the world, to lift it up "into thought." Its consequences mark the path technology has forged in human history, and the world-changing transformations it has occasioned. In order to explore how this manifests in the digital era, we intend to provide a basic framework from which to understand them, outlining, in broad strokes, a short history of the technology of communication and tracing the primary ways in which each subsequent technology has transformed human experience.

The story we want to tell begins with the appearance of what some might consider our first technology: language. With words, human being was extended into the abstract and ethereal realm of concepts that freed us from the passage of time and the tyranny of becoming. Speech articulates the mental world, extends our experience with virtual possibilities, and re-configures it with ideas and constructed narratives. Articulated in the air of spoken words, behavioral patterns, acquired tastes and tendencies, etc., they are passed on from generation to generation, in "memes" (to use Dawkins' now-trending term), which function at the cultural level as genes do biologically. Thanks to language, human evolution speeds up beyond the biological. As Yuval Harari (2011) observes, since the emergence of language, humans don't live in only one mode of natural life, as animals seem to do, they live in many *cultural* alternatives.

The virtual was first forged by spoken words and images, constituting together a mythical worldview.[1] With alphabetical writing – a particularly Western form of inscription that articulates meaning around arbitrary signs – the mythical thought of words and images was replaced by logical, rational thought. By massifying that technology in the 15th century, the printing press helped intensify this shift away from orality which has prevailed in our culture ever since.

In transforming spoken words and images into logical concepts, writing subordinates our synchronistic, moment-to-moment experience of time to the diachronic progression of history. As Vilém Flusser (2011a) says, "the unidirectional flow of writing" (p. xiv) results in a new experience of time as linear, a stream of unstoppable progress, of dramatic unrepeatability, of framing, in short, history. Past, present, and future, and our conception of time as progressive, are made possible by this virtual extension of experience.

> The invention of writing made it possible for stories to reach farther across time and space than their tellers and stay more stable than memory; and new communications, reproduction, and transportation technologies only continue the process. (Solnit, 2003, p. 11)

But as we know, every gain brings a loss with it. As McLuhan (1998) pointed out in his seminal book, *Understanding Media*, the advent of any technology involves not just an extension but also an amputation of experience. When our calculating capacity is extended by an electronic calculator, for example, we stop adding or multiplying in our head. The mental activity of calculating is amputated. When we extend our motility with the car, we amputate our legs so that we hardly consider it a possibility to walk even short distances. When we extend our memory with the Internet, we begin to depend so much on the technological extension that we stop committing to memory the information that is stored there now.

In their battle against spoken language, Flusser (2011b) writes, "the characters of the alphabet suck the life of the language up into themselves: letters are vampires" (p. 37). And, as Havelock (1986) points out, with writing, "the acoustic flow of language contrived by echo to hold the attention of the ear has been reshuffled into visual patterns created by the thoughtful attention of the eye" (p. 13). Writing displaces bodily interaction: the sonority of the voice that the ear receives gives way to the intellectual sharpness of the seeing eye and the spontaneity of speech yields to the deliberateness of reason. The analytic, sequential way of thinking and perceiving fostered by the linear logic of the alphabet pointedly contrasts with the thought and perception that characterized oral culture. The richness of the image and the associative thought it promotes is replaced by the exactness of the concept and rational way of thinking. We thus begin to live as we read, logically and sequentially, as if in a fixed line towards a goal. But, of course, this transformation did not take place immediately.

The printed page, in placing the object before us in inert signs, extends our capacity for concentration, objective analysis, and representational memory. That shift transforms language and modifies the way in which we had traditionally modulated the virtual. Whereas in the oral tradition, the expression with which words were delivered was inseparable from its content, so that they were literally an extension of our tongues, in the new scribal tradition content becomes more important than expression, and so language is transformed into a tool. The industrial revolution's emphasis on production and efficiency, and the pragmatic expeditiousness of that era that is occasioned by writing, turns language into a mere "vehicle of information," what Benjamin (1978) called a "bourgeois language" (p. 318).[2] Its clear concepts, sedimented on the page, simplify the complexity of oral language and its aesthetic dimension. We begin to experience reality through the objective concepts of reason, and gradually become more insensitive to the pregnant opacities of actual experience, unable to see the meanings that opened up through the spoken word and its images.

So, although bourgeois language achieves an aesthetic detachment from sensible experience that is, of course, responsible for many scientific achievements in these past centuries, it involves also the kind of sensible impoverishment that Plato warned us about, when he pointed out that writing would affect the capacity to interiorize what we learn and end up confusing information for wisdom. Once we begin to read the world through the thinking head rather than the resonating body, concepts are divorced from their live, performative contexts. They abstract us from time and disconnect us from its flow. Spontaneity yields to regularity, contingency and the unknown are systematically disavowed, and our vital circle narrows. While written language provides a precise, technical tool and expedites communication, it also takes away its existential depth.

If technology is, as McLuhan (1998) observed, an extension of human being, then images and drawings, concepts and words, each constitute a different extension of experience with its own particular modulation of virtuality. With the spoken word we leave the mute privacy of wordless experience and enter into verbal interaction with actual others that help forge a public world of shared meanings. By suspending temporal movement and casting events into abstract signs (i.e., writing), we substitute the immediacy and fleetingness of experience with a permanent, objective, atemporal, visual trace. No longer subject to the transience of passing voices in a conversation or fleeting thoughts, with writing the world is sedimented into objective, atemporal meanings.

The illusion of an orderly world and of a world with a rational telos, at the service of humans, is only possible with a language turned into a tool of reason, understood as pure or as instrumental. The excesses that this will incur are anticipated, for instance, by the image of Goya's famous etching – of a man crumpled on his desk asleep upon an open book – "The sleep of reason produces monsters."

b Images: From photography to digital image

i Photography

But let us not forget that the word originates in the image. Concepts anchor our world, as Nietzsche (2017) so poignantly puts it, "by means of the petrification and coagulation of a mass of images which originally streamed from the primal faculty of human imagination like a fiery liquid" (p. 22). Despite the prevalence of scribality, words and images both are inscribed in our psyche; both are different openings to the human virtual and stand always in a dialectical relationship. Each marks a different psychic domain and holds a perennial tension within ourselves.

Between the 17th and 19th centuries, printed reproduction spread slowly but steadily, and with the invention of the daily newspaper, it placed itself at the center of culture. The prevalence of the word continued, however, despite the introduction, in the 20th century, of the electronic media. The telegraph, the telephone, and the radio, since they are linked to the voice and articulated language, were still compatible with writing. But with the invention of photography in the mid-19th century, the rupture with scribality begins with its re-introduction of the image. Its extensions in television and film are then powerfully potentiated with the advent of digital technology, which massifies the image in the same way that the printing press did with writing.

Like the written or spoken medium, the trace on the photographic plate continues the technological modulation of virtuality, freezing time and abstracting from experience, but now through the image. Before photography, the past was preserved in memory and brought back in words; but every experience, every object, and every event was unique and unrepeatable, an ephemeral and passing moment. With every photograph, however, we are able "to snatch a moment from the river of time," as Rebecca Solnit (2003, p. 17) puts it. We are able to bring the past back, but no longer just in abstract mental concepts, as language does, but again, as in pre-scribal times (when humans painted on the walls of caves) in an actual two-dimensional visual trace of the empirical experience.

In the otherwise image-dominated history of human consciousness, scribality and linear texts had become primary bearers of important information in the West for a relatively short hiatus.[3] With the photographic camera, a return to the image becomes imminent, and it has important consequences for our relationship to time:

> Opposed to the unidirectional flow of writing, and its unrepeat-
> ability that determines an inscription of time as progressive, the

image now introduces a new temporality that does away with the linear sense of movement and introduces an "all-at-onceness." (Flusser, 2011b, p. xiv)

The photograph extracts experience from its temporality so that we can hold its image completely in our consciousness, just as we do with concepts. But the photograph, unlike the concept, is a physical image that, because it impresses our senses, involves our body and elicits an affect. Being the result of an actual impression of what is photographed, there is a material continuity between the photograph and what it is a photograph of; it works within the logic of the visual image, which unavoidably engages our imagination and the capacity to make connections that go far beyond the actual. A new plasticity emerges, and hence a myriad of possible new connections and meanings that go beyond the rigid sedimentation of concepts. Again, unlike concepts that constitute what we grasp in the ethereal context of the mind, the perception of the image, being a bodily phenomenon, brings in the issue of spatio-temporal experience that is absent in the mental construction of meaning that takes place with writing.

The camera captures mechanically not only what we saw, the partial perception of our senses and our limited attention, but also what we did not see but lay open in the actual event. It brings to awareness, in other words, in the "all-at-onceness" of its image, what Benjamin (2008b) calls "the optical unconscious" (p. 278).

> It is possible, for example, however roughly, to describe the way somebody walks, but it is impossible to say anything about that fraction of a second when a person starts to walk. Photography with its various aids (lenses, enlargements) can reveal this moment. Photography makes aware for the first time the optical unconscious, just as psychoanalysis discloses the instinctual unconscious. (p. 278)

The density of time, its endless flux, the many aspects it hides from us in its movement, are immediately available to the camera. The range of what is seen is broadened, and with it also the range of what can be known. That is why the most interesting detail in the photograph, as Barthes (1981) points out,

> occurs in the field of the photographed thing like a supplement that is, at once, inevitable and delightful; it does not necessarily attest to the photographer's art; it says only that the photographer [...] could not *not* photograph the partial object at the same time as the total object. (p. 47)

The contingency of actual experience slips in through the image, something impossible through the static nature of writing, and awakens us to temporal movement in its recovered loss. Barthes (1981) calls that wound or scar that evidences chance and tears through the framed image the *punctum,* which, as he puts it, "rises from the scene, shoots out like an arrow and pierces me" (p. 26). The *punctum* is that unexpected or unintended detail in the materially captured reality of the photograph that escapes its intentionality and evidences its *having been* there, in space, in moving time.[4] That ghostly effect of the punctum, that affect, tears through the representation and exposes us, making us suddenly vulnerable to the shadow of time; it unfixes, opening us to time's phantasmatic flow, to its radical absence. The image not only brings to presence something now absent, but also intimates something that is no longer here, something missed. Because photographs engage our body, as images normally do, they are more able than words to evoke and bring temporality to experience by physically presencing an absence, in the actual impression of the *punctum.* That paradox confers on the photograph its particular numinosity.

Being a paradigmatic pharmakon, even though it poisons us with the illusion of permanence that its image creates, photography also cures us of that illusion as it exposes us to the ineluctable spectrality of the passage of time.

ii *Film*

> The vision of a celluloid tape with a series of moving images telling a story to millions. Millions anywhere. Millions seen and unseen. Millions seeing the same story without ever knowing each other. Without even having to be together. Affecting their dreams and actions. Replacing their books. Replacing their families. Replacing religion, politics, art, conversation. Replacing their minds.
>
> (Sam Shepard, *Angel City*)

Film inherits photography's material connection with its object, what (following C.S. Peirce) has been called its "indexicality."[5] It therefore also shares the issues of time and temporality that we have seen arise in the photographic capture of the passing moment. But with film, we don't so much freeze time as register its movement. Film introduces the unheard-of possibility of extracting *the actuality* of time from actual time, and of replaying its movement, literally, at any time. In that register, we can see details that, when within the temporal flux, we pass over, but that now serve, in the cinematic image, as a new medium to contemplate, express, and communicate. With film, a whole new level is added to our experience of time, and a new dimension of temporality is given to human experience. As the genius of Russian film Andrei Tarkovski (1994) writes:

> Time, printed in its factual forms and manifestations, such is the supreme idea of cinema as an art, leading us to think about the wealth of untapped resources in film, about its colossal future. (p. 63)

The movement of time that we could only experience in the unstoppable flow of our present awareness before this technology, now becomes a possible object of detailed inspection. Film lifts the seeing eye from its own temporality, and allows it to study time in movement from outside its actual flow. In setting the captured image in motion and then liberating it from the present, film dissolves the static rigidity of the photographic image into the flux of actual becoming. Instead of hiding contingency, embalming time, as Bazin (1971) puts it, film liberates it. While in the photographic image the actuality of time only appears in the "glitches" of its capture, in Barthes' (1981) *punctum*, in film temporality bursts forth upon the screen. It doesn't just pierce us with a static evidence of temporal movement, as the photograph does. The single beam of time that leaks in surreptitiously from the *punctum* now radiates from the immersive flow of moving images on the screen. Temporality floods and inundates here.

In its beginnings, not quite understanding its potential and submitting to the prevailing scribal rationalism, film was constructed following the criteria and standards of representation that it inherited from writing. As Bazin (1971) explains,

> Classical editing separated reality into successive shots which were just a series of either logical or subjective points of view of an event ... [in its] ordering of the shots [it is a] conventional analysis of the reality continuum that truly goes to make up the cinematographic language of the period ... [and] introduces an obviously abstract element into reality. (p. 28)

That abstract element that habitually slips into classical filmmaking in the sequential parsing out of the captured event is a residue from the prevailing medium of writing. In its traditional narrative, film subjects the presentation of reality that the moving image performs to the abstraction of rational thinking. Instead of bringing us closer to reality, this imposed sequentiality in its structure distances us from the density of concrete experience, placing it within a familiar and preconceived framework. This tendency to abstract thinking is, of course, a symptom of the scientific mentality that the printed word spread through modernity.

But eventually film discovered the new relation to reality that it could forge, the real power of its technology. That tendency toward abstraction is precisely what film is to overcome as it moves toward a more embodied experience than traditional film had yet seen. The movement of Italian neo-realism in the 1940s, for example, – with films like *Bicycle Thief* or *La Strada* and directors like Rossellini, Visconti, De Sica, and Fellini – seeks in its newly emerging methods to come closer to reality, to bring film down to concrete experience. This new virtual space requires an intensified sensorial involvement of the spectator with the image.

Whereas initially, then, film images were used to construct fields of perception along rigid rails of logical thinking, modelled after the linearity of writing, and working with our expectation of sequential action in a narrative plane, the cinematic image eventually breaks with the scribal model and begins to respond instead to "a new form of reality [which] is felt to be dispersive, elliptical, errant or wavering, working in blocks, with deliberately weak connections and floating events" (Deleuze, 1989, p. 1). In these new developments, the film image marks its independence from conceptual thinking and appeals to our own experiential discernment.

In departing from the sensory-motor expectation of movement that classical film automatically followed, the cinematic image now traces a virtual space that, even as it works with the discontinuity and fragmentariness of the subjective – what Deleuze (1989) describes as a "dispersive, elliptical, errant or wavering" reality – it presupposes its underlying invisible continuity. The film image now subverts the hold of the prevailing scribal structures of memory that order experience along logical tracks and rational narratives and opens film into a whole new mode of experience of time. It relies no longer on an *a priori* conception of reality, but instead delivers us to an underlying whole from which the image now comes forth. As Bazin (1971) writes:

> The traditional realist artist ... analyzes reality into parts which he then reassembles in a synthesis the final determinant of which is his moral conception of the world whereas the consciousness of the neoreality director *filters* reality. Undoubtedly, his consciousness, like that of everyone else, does not admit reality as a whole, but the selection that does occur is neither logical nor is it psychological; it is ontological, in the sense that the image of reality it restores to us is still a whole. (p. 98)

Whereas in traditional cinema the reality of objects and setting was functional, strictly determined by the physical and psychological demands of the situation, in neo-realism and independent films, it now becomes a protagonist itself. Reality is represented not as a synthesis of elements according to a given continuity, but as the selective filtering of experience by subjectivity. No longer married to the logic of action, film rather flirts now with the openness of (audiovisual) contemplation and imagination. Just as everyday reality is unitary without it depending on a continuous, linear, sequential experience (even if we are often inclined to construct it or narrate it in that way), the cinematic representation of reality appears as a disrupted and discontinuous, though at the same time unitary, whole. So, if the landscape in a film is "bare and confined," this reflects the limitations of the consciousness of the protagonist without falsifying the landscape. What the neo-realist film shows is not false; "it is [...] a mental landscape at once as objective as a straight photograph and as subjective as pure personal consciousness" (Bazin, 1971, p. 98).

The moving image begins to modulate the virtual itself in accordance with the organic way of the image, no longer in subservience to the logical structures of writing. It re-engages our body in the perception of the world, harkening back to the spontaneity of sensible perception that defined oral culture in its appeal to intuition and imagination. Film no longer seeks to represent or replicate an already deciphered real, but "aims at an always ambiguous, to be deciphered, real [...] between the reality of the setting and that of the action," Deleuze (1989) writes "it is no longer a motor extension which is established, but rather a dreamlike connection through the intermediary of the liberated sense organs" (p. 4). Their liberation from scribal strictures generates a freedom of associations and connections that transforms reality into an oneiric landscape.[6]

With the new technologies of photography and film, therefore, the image re-emerges in the 20th century, reclaiming a central place in the collective imagination and forcefully reinstating elements of the magical world that were banished with writing. The advent of the analog (photograph or film) image brought the bodily imagination back into scribal culture. As Sartori (1998) points out, enhanced by television and film, the spectator becomes more a seeing than a symbolic animal, a *Homo videns* rather than a *Homo sapiens*.

> For [Homo videns] things represented in images count and weigh more than things said in words. And this is a radical change of direction, because while the symbolic faculty distances Homo sapiens from animals, the fact of seeing brings him closer to his ancestral capacities. (our translation, p. 33)

iii Digital image

The beginning of the 1990s marks the time – 150 years since the photograph displaced painting – when the digital image on the screen started to displace the analog image on a photographic plate or celluloid. It was no longer the light that came from the object that produced the image, but an array of binary digits obtained from a scanner, which a computer could then process algorithmically into digital images. Every point in a grid is made to correspond to a point of color in the scene or object photographed, which together constitute the mathematical elements from which the image will now emerge. The analog representation of reality is thus digitized. William J. Mitchell (1992), in his now classic book, *The Reconfigured Eye*, writes:

> Just as the elementary operation of painting a picture is the brush stroke and the elementary operation of typing a text is a keystroke, the elementary operation of digital imaging is assignment of an integer value to a pixel in order to specify (according to some coding scheme) its tone or color. (p. 6)

Whereas the (analog) photograph captures a continuous reality, the digital capture is rather constituted by discrete points; it is from these that an image of reality is arithmetically constructed. Mitchell explains the difference between the continuous capture of analog media and the digitized image in the following metaphor: "Rolling down a ramp is continuous motion, but walking down stairs is a sequence of discrete steps – so you can count the number of steps" (p. 10). The continuity of the analog image results in an amazingly precise record of every detail, which is made up of an unbroken sequence of gradations that go from the absence of light (black) to plenitude of light (white). You can magnify analog images indefinitely, and you will always find more information captured from (continuous) reality.

The classic movie *Blow-up* (1966), for instance, is predicated precisely on that fact. A discovery of the murder that triggers the whole plot results from the detail that shows up when an image is magnified while developing a film. Whereas the analog photograph carries the actual impression of the light and shadows emanating from its object, a digital image is a mathematical reconstruction of that impression as it is captured and numerically converted in a grid, and so will only show as much as that conversion will allow. The digital image is not the exact reproduction of the original, therefore, but merely the best approximation according to the available matrix.

A digital copy of a painting, for example, would be faithful, not to the original object but to the conditions of its reproduction. A digital photograph is the result of the capture of all the object's points of light in the field of the image.

But once we decide what the focal field is, as well as the depth and speed from which reality is reconstructed, the act of interpreting those points of light is algorithmically fixed. This places limits on the capture of the actual event, insofar as the optical limitations of the apparatus arbitrarily determines the depth and scope of the representation. Its limits are fixed in that first capture, so that it can never reveal more than it has registered.

The digital object, being discrete, inevitably loses the continuity of the analog, but whereas the analogic object will suffer deterioration in its reproduction, the digital object, no longer a copy but a clone, recreates itself anew every time. Each new copy would be a variation on the digitized data beyond the limits of which it can render no more information.

There is an irreducible ontological difference, therefore, between the continuity of reality transmitted from its material impression (i.e., from actual contact) and the discontinuity of the digital register that is wholly managed in the abstraction of numbers and silicon circuits. No matter how high the resolution of the digital image, gaps will always remain insofar as digital captures break up continuous tonal gradients into discrete steps made up of numerically assigned points. The continuity of curves and fine details are approximated to the grid. Nothing can close the space that separates each discrete digital unit from the other. "As waves dissolve into drops, judgments into bytes, actions into actemes" writes Flusser (2011a), "a void appears, namely the void of the intervals that hold the elemental points apart [...] and so [the] impossibility of measuring the points themselves" (p. 15). The void that appears with the digital betrays the digital images' generation from numerical calculation instead of from an empirical connection with the world. The digital image is fundamentally detached from the real. We see on our screens not an impression but a reconstruction which results from calculation and not from physical contact.

Benjamin (2008a) had noted at the beginning of the 20th century, a difference between the mechanical reproduction of a work of art and the work of art itself. When substituting it with an infinitely reproducible replica, the object loses its unique connection to its original creation, which Benjamin relates to the atmosphere emanating from its material origin – what might be seen as the spiritual or aesthetic depth of the object – which he calls "the aura" (p. 23). The question now is whether the experiential loss of digitization in its disconnection from the reality it pictures, is analogous to the impoverishment of experience Benjamin diagnosed in the technically reproduced image.

In the concept of the aura, Benjamin is trying to capture the resonance that the work of art derives from its unfathomable origin. This quality is absent from the mechanical reproduction, the flatness of which derives from an origin that is no longer inexhaustible; there is no material resonance for the reproduction to carry. For Benjamin (2008a), nearly a century ago, that loss was a sign of his times.

> Every day, the urge grows stronger to get hold of an object at close range in an image [Bild], or, better, in a facsimile [Abbild], a reproduction. And the reproduction [Reproduktion], as offered by illustrated magazines and newsreels, differs unmistakably from the image. (p. 23)

Benjamin is pointing to an ethos that is familiar to us also in our 21st-century culture, where the pulsating opaqueness of living matter is reduced to rational controllable criteria, where the distance between sensible experience and conceptual understanding is eliminated, where singularity is replaced by homogeneity, archetype by stereotype, and the dynamic living thing by static inert matter. It is significant that the very same ethos that occasions that loss in the field of perception in Benjamin's time with mechanical reproduction and its penchant for statistics, is also seen in our dealings with the world in this century; it is echoed in the compulsive need to quantify and measure all things, that seems to have grown with digital technology and its will to digitization.

In the digitization of the image, the object is detached from empirical continuity and transported to a world of pixels, where reality is thus sanitized and disconnected from the body and sensible experience. The sharpening of digital information demands, for example, the systematic suppression of silent pauses or background noise. But as Sheryl Branham (2017) observes:

> [R]emoving [silence or noise] while a speaker is talking [... first] makes correlated noise, such as echo, more pronounced and jarring to the listener. Second, it diminishes a sense of social presence, of *being with* another. [...because] the background noise [that it intends to eliminate] isn't really just noise under normal circumstances. It's a form of information, providing feedback that someone is still there. (p. 147)

But beyond the disconnection that results from the digital modulation, reality and the analog image undergo even further modifications in digitization. What we are perceiving on the screen is always a modified version of what is on the other side, so that our perception is always compromised. Brahnam (2017) explains:

To increase band-width efficiency, some codecs[7] encode only areas that change in a video frame and not the entire frame [...] As quality matters, video and audio errors are detected and corrected, and enhancements to signals are made throughout the transmission process. At the source and at the destination, signals are sharpened, colors heightened, noise adaptively suppressed, silence suppressed, and missing data and other aspects of the signals synthesized and augmented. ... (p. 147)

On Skype (or Zoom or Facetime), we can readily recognize not just a loss but a distortion of what is transmitted, so that what is received is never completely aligned with the reality that is projected. It is not, however, a matter of a loss of quantity of information that happens in digitization, as is generally thought. As Lev Manovich (2001) observes, digital technology has already developed so much that this logical consequence of digitization no longer holds. Digital images can now provide as much information as analog images can. That difference no longer matters, for by the beginning of this century, a digital image already could contain more information than anybody would ever want. The resolution of scanners now provides an exactness that allows the stored image, even if it is comprised of a finite number of pixels, to contain much finer detail than was ever possible for analog photography. The problem is that digitization involves also – beyond the distortion and manipulation necessary for its sharpness – the loss of a particular kind of information that connects the object to its original ground.

With the analog image, as Stiegler (Derrida and Stiegler, 2002) put it:[8]

we know that the luminances that come to touch my eye [the photons that come to imprint and *physically* touch, from out of the nineteenth century, *the photosensitive* silver halides], *really* touched what the photograph renders visible. (p. 152)

But the digital image "breaks the 'umbilical cord'" that grounds the materiality of the process responsible for the ghostly effect of the photographic image, i.e. of something that once was but now is not, irretrievably no longer there. Whereas the photographic plate, we could say, shines back at us an image from a moment past, in the digital image nothing shines back at us from any past:

With analog light, the silver luminances still have to do with touch and with life – with a past life. With the digital photo, this light, from out of the night [...] doesn't come from a past day that would simply have become night (like photons emanating from a past object). It comes from Hades, from the realm of the dead, from underground: it is an electric light, set free by materials from deep within the belly of the earth. An electronic, that is to say, a decomposed light. (ibid, p. 153)

The digital image emerges from a darkness that has no past; it is not a footprint of anything, but an algorithmic phantom of something that has never been there; it merely mimics the indexical character of the traditional image. The digital image becomes an assemblage of computer data that may, furthermore, be permuted and interlaced in ways that need no longer hold any relation to actual reality. The *this was* of the photograph that gave it its truth, becomes now essentially *doubtful*. This discretization, this turning the continuity of reality into a series of discrete points, radically "affects the chain of memorial light" (Derrida and Stiegler, 2002, p. 154). Disconnected from space, the digital image is unmoored from all familiar ports. The indexical connection between the image projected on the screen and the event it represents is done away with, and so our "natural" belief that the image bears something that makes contact, or is actually linked, to an actual moment in time and space, is shattered.

According to Laura Mulvey (2018) this is what distinguishes digital images from analogic (photographic and film) images. The *this was* that sustains the analogic image, she argues, is no longer there for the digital, and the link to an actual origin that guaranteed the representational accuracy and authenticity of the analogic image no longer exists. "The digital as an abstract information system," she writes, "made a break with the analogue imagery, finally sweeping away the relation with reality" (p. 18).

The digital data captured is an approximation of reality, always limited to the possibilities of the equipment available. A digital capture of data is converted into an archive that will become an exact copy, but its exactness corresponds to the sampling rather than to the object itself. As Flusser (2011a) says, traditional images "are observations of objects," while technical images are "computations of concepts." The resulting digitized image will always lack the continuity of the analog because the collected data is discrete. Even if the sampling ends up collecting much more information than we experience (as Manovich points out is already the case), for instance, more visual data than human beings can process or more audio data than even dogs, with their wide auditory frequencies, can hear. In other words, concepts can never be objects, so despite the abundance of data, the discontinuity that distinguished the digital from the analog is never bridged; it may seem, therefore, that we have lost the aura once again. But perhaps it is not so much lost as transformed, and the digital object rather inaugurates a new dimension of experience, drawn from "the night of a past that was never present."

What is interesting is that although it is affected, the chain of memorial light, as Stiegler calls the material connection with the original, may be *not broken*, just "knotted in a different way" (Derrida and Stiegler, 2002, p. 154). Other relations, intertextual and cross media, begin to emerge that while leaving behind the indexical connection may still provide "the chance of a new intelligibility of light, which has always already been [...] the night of a past that was *never present*" (ibid, p. 155). In other words, being cut loose from the causal logic of reality, a different kind of connection and sense-giving logic opens up, which is now defined by the multimedia possibilities introduced by the digital. And thus we touch down again into the oneiric landscape Deleuze found in neo-realism, where the actual and the virtual begin to merge into one single reality.

In digitization, the uniqueness and singularity of the original object is homogenized for the sake of exact replication and so detached from the tradition, which gives it its temporal and material depth. In its binomial reduction to 0s and 1s, the qualitative movement of the analogic image is transformed into the quantitative states of the digital.

As Stiegler points out, a similar revolution was caused by the institution of writing that also discretized and so made the continuity of speech analytical, and hence also analyzable. Prior to writing, the speaker was not aware of any discrete objects in her thought process until the sign system made possible the play of analyzable, diacritical combinatorial elements. Similarly, the digital discretization of the image makes its elements also analytical. But unlike writing, we are ordering something that has never been there.

The digital image is constructed from those discrete elements, even though they do not come from the objects themselves. This means that the possibility of *not having been* is essential to the digital photographic image. But this characteristic, as Stiegler points out,

> inspires *fear*, for [...] at the same time that it is infinitely manipulable, [it] still *remains* a photo, so it preserves for us something of the *this was* within itself, and the possibility of distinguishing the true from the false dwindles in proportion as the possibilities for the digital treatment of photos grow. (Derrida and Stiegler, 2002, p. 150)[9]

Representation gives way to the production of reality in the digital, where accuracy begins to lose importance beside technical dexterity and perfection.

... in-person communication and distant communication resemble each other as much as whole foods resemble highly processed foods—about as much as a real blueberry muffin, for example, resembles a processed blueberry muffin that contains not a single blueberry but rather artificial flavors and textures that taste and feel in the mouth just like a blueberry should—or, as some might say (and this is the ultimate goal), "better" than any blueberry could. (Branham, 2017, p. 147)

We become "[m]ore concerned with questions of technological magic ('How'd they do that?')," as Everett (2010) says, "than with believable representations of reality as markers of success" (p. 32). This, of course, has the consequences we are living with regarding the phenomenon of post-truth, about which we will have more to say in the following chapters.

Imagination, which had been displaced in the act of representation by writing and alphabetical reasoning, comes back again with the digital. So just as with the discretization of language that took place with the invention of writing we learned to analyze the continuity of spoken language and began to construct its meanings in unheard of ways, with the discretization of the image that happens in the digital we are bound to learn new ways of seeing it. And because the discrete image is now lifted into the collectively shared space of the Internet, where new possibilities of interaction introduce a different set of conditions, we might just be witnessing the birth of new forms of belief.

Notes

1 Depending on how we understand the irruption of the virtual in human consciousness, or the play of images and words in its advent, our first technology could be either the tongue, or the drawing hand. We could in this latter case conceive of the painting on the walls as inaugurations of the virtual. Virtuality would have broken into human existence with the ability to articulate the world pictorially before it did through the spoken word. Vilém Flusser proposes this interpretation of technology, as we shall see below.

2 Here we are emphasizing technical writing, holding in mind, of course, the many other forms of poetic and literary writing that do not fall into this deadening trap but which had to be learned during the following centuries following its inception.

3 It's only for about 4,000 years that linear texts (i.e., scribality) became the dominant bearers of important information. As Flusser (2006) argues, before that, image-thinking bore the first modulation of the virtual in human experience, which continued in the margins of culture in the history of painting and the plastic arts. Photography, however, places the image again at the center of experience to modulate virtuality, and forges a path towards

the digital that brings images together with words in a new virtual hybrid whose consequences we will be exploring here.

4 "Punctum" designated in Latin "th[e] wound, th[e] prick, th[e] mark made by a pointed instrument: [it] ... also refers to the notion of punctuation [...] Photographs [...] are in effect punctuated, sometimes even speckled with these sensitive points; precisely, these marks, these wounds [...]" (Barthes, R. 1981, p. 27).

5 The philosopher Charles Sanders Peirce coined the term "indexical," to refer to the gesture of pointing, as this applies to signs that point at something. "I," "now," and "here" are indexicals for they point to what they mean. Photographs and paintings seem to be, in that sense, both indexical, whereas digital images we would have to say are not, insofar as they give visual appearance to numerical codes rather than represent reality.

6 Of course the work of cinema verité and the French nouvelle vague are as important or more important than Neorealism for our purposes. We are, however, not so interested in being faithful to film history as we are in using this particular case as an illustrative example.

7 A codec is a device or program that compresses data to enable faster transmission and decompresses received data.

8 Talking about Barthes' example of a photograph of Baudelaire.

9 Metz (2019) writes: "Deepfakes – a term that generally describes videos doctored with cutting-edge artificial intelligence – have already challenged our assumptions about what is real and what is not." But isn't it ironic that Google scientists are using the very same technology that created them to now detect and uncover deepfakes (NYT, Nov 25th 2019).

References

Barthes, R. (1981) *Camera Lucida: Reflections on Photography*. New York: Farrar Straus & Giroux.

Bazin, A. (1971) *What is Cinema?* Berkeley, CA: University of California Press.

Benjamin, W. (1978) On Language as Such and on the Language of Man. In *Reflections. Essays, Aphorisms, Autobiographical Writings* (pp. 314–332). New York: Schoken Books.

Benjamin, W. (2008a) The Work of Art in the Age of Its Technological Reproducibility: *Second Version*. In *The Work of Art in the Age of Its Technological Reproducibility* (pp. 19–55). Cambridge, MA: Harvard University Press.

Benjamin, W. (2008b) Little History of Photography. In *The Work of Art in the Age of Its Technological Reproducibility* (pp. 274–298). Cambridge, MA: Harvard University Press.

Brahnam, S. (2017) Comparison of In-Person and Screen-Based Analysis Using Communication Models: A First Step Toward the Psychoanalysis of Telecommunications and Its Noise. *Psychoanalytic Perspectives*, *14*(2), 138–158, DOI: 10.1080/1551806X.2017.1304112

Deleuze, G. (1989) *Cinema 2*. Minneapolis, MN: University of Minnesota Press.

Derrida, J., and Stiegler, B. (2002) *Echographies of Television*. Madlen, MA: Blackwell Publishers.

Everett, A. (2010) Digitextuality and Click Theory: Theses on Convergence Media in the Digital Age. In P.K. Nayar (Ed.), *The New Media and Cybercultures Anthology* (pp. 29–45). London: Wiley-Blackwell.

Flusser, V. (1991) Referat am das Gottlieb Duttweiler Institute, at: https://www.youtube.com/watch?v=dAeH1S60utA

Flusser, V. (2006) *Towards a Philosophy of Photography*. Trowbridge: Cromwell Press.

Flusser, V. (2011a) *Into the Universe of Technical Images* (N.A. Roth, Trans.). Minneapolis, MN: University of Minnesota Press.

Flusser, V. (2011b) *Does Writing Have a Future?* Minneapolis, MN: University of Minnesota Press.

Harari, Y. (2011) *Sapiens. A Brief History of Humankind*. New York: Harper & Row.

Havelock, E.A. (1986) *The Muse Learns to Write: Reflections on Orality and Literacy from Antiquity to the Present*. New Haven, CT: Yale University Press.

Manovich, L. (2001) *The Language of the New Media*. Cambridge: MIT Press.

McLuhan, M. (1998) *Understanding Media: The Extensions of Man*. Cambridge: MIT Press.

Mitchell, W.J. (1992) *The Reconfigured Eye: Visual Truth in the Post-photographic Era*. Cambridge, MA: MIT Press.

Mulvey, L. (2018) *Death 24x a Second. Stillness and the Moving Image*. London: Reaktion Books Ltd.

Nietzsche, F. (1980) *On the Advantage and Disadvantage of History for Life*. Indianapolis: Hackett Publishing Company, Inc.

Nietzsche, F. (2017) *On Truth and Lies in a Non-moral Sense*. Hastings, U.K.: Dephi Classics.

Plato (1980) *Phaedrus*. In *The Collected Dialogues of Plato* (pp. 475–525). Princeton: Bollingen Series LXXI.

Sartori, G. (1998) *Homo Videns: La Sociedad Teledirigida*. Mexico: Penguin Random House.

Shepard, S. (2006) *Angel City, va. Fool for Love and Other Plays*. New York: Dial Press.

Solnit, R. (2003) *River of Shadows: Eadweard Muybridge and the Technological Wild West*. New York: Penguin.

Tarkovski, A. (1994) *Sculpting in Time*. Austin: University of Texas Press.

Wittgenstein, L. (1993) On Frazer's "Golden Bough." In J. Klagge and A. Nordmann (Eds.), *Philosophical Occasions 1912–1951* (pp. 115–155). Indianapolis: Hackett Publishing Company, Inc.

2 Dimensions of virtuality

1 Modulating virtuality

a From image to digital image

> Photography does not create eternity as art does, it embalms time, rescuing it simply from its own proper corruption.
>
> André Bazin (1967)

According to Vilém Flusser (2011), while animals are "immersed in an animate world," human beings break away from that "four-dimensional space" (p. 6) when the hand intervenes in the world and makes it an object distinct from the subject that holds it.

> Unlike animals, even primates, human beings have hands that can hold the immediate world at bay, bring it to a stop (so that the environment is no longer relevant). This extension of the hand against the world can be called an "action." With this designation, the lifeworld falls into two areas, the area of the fixed, understood objects and the area of the "one who understands", whose hand abstracts the subject from the lifeworld, brackets it out, leaving a three dimensional universe of graspable objects. (p. 8)

The original, pre-conscious unity is thus lost to the new space that opens with the separation of a subject from the things now abstracted from their context and placed where deliberate human action becomes possible. Without human consciousness, the world of animals is bound up with what is seen; there is no separation between what is experienced and what experiences; they are one and the same. It is in that sense that the animal lives in four dimensions, enclosed, sealed within them. But becoming conscious, a human subject breaks off from its embeddedness in the world, and the three-dimensional world of visible objects is now before him, available for contemplation and control.

The same human hand that holds the world at bay, that manipulates it and molds it to the subject's will, turns next to "extending" the world in images. In the movements of the hand, the image-maker transmutes his experience onto flat surfaces, giving birth now to a new, two-dimensional world. As phenomenologists point out, the process here consists of a spontaneous response, an aesthetic expression of the "intertwining of vision and movement" (Merleau-Ponty 2007, p. 353), that takes place in the resonating, perceiving body. As Merleau-Ponty (2007) explains, it is by "lending his body to the world that the artist changes the world into paintings" (p. 353).

> Immersed in the visible by his body, itself visible, the see-er ... approaches [the world] by looking, he opens onto the world [...] Things are an annex or prolongation of itself; they are encrusted in its flesh [...] Since things and my body are made of the same stuff ... their manifest visibility must be repeated in the body by a secret visibility. "Nature is on the inside," says Cézanne. (p. 355)

The image is not, however, the result of "an operation of thought that would set up before the mind a picture or a representation of a world" (p. 333). The process antecedes rational thought. It is not "a decision made by the mind, an absolute doing which would decree, from the depths of a subjective retreat" (p. 354); it is not, in other words, a "representation" but the spontaneous response of the body to the world. This is how the virtual irrupts in human experience, without the mediation of language or thought, as the result of an aesthetic expression. The virtual brings forth another layer, a further depth to the world. As Merleau-Ponty (2007) writes:

> the animals painted on the walls of Lascaux are not there in the same way as are the fissures and limestone formations. Nor are they *elsewhere*. Pushed forward here, held back there, supported by the wall's mass they use so adroitly, they radiate about the wall without ever breaking their elusive moorings. I would be hard pressed to say *where* the painting is I am looking at. For I do not look at it as one looks at a thing, fixing it in its place. My gaze wanders within as in the halos of Being. Rather than seeing it, I see according to, or with it. (p. 355)

The bison painted on the cave wall is not a replica but an extension of the world, executed by the play between eye and hand. Even though it is a thing, it is a peculiar sort of thing. What makes it an image is not the actual physical markings, but what those markings open up for us. They not only imitate the appearance of the event (and hold it in time for us to revisit once the event is no longer there), but also trigger the imagination that transports it beyond the actual fact thus depicted. The potency of what we perceive resonates once more in the painted image, embedded as it is in the body. That distant echo ushers us into the virtual space of human consciousness. In the image that the hand draws, the three-dimensional space of action becomes the two-dimensional space of pictures on flat surfaces, a new "space," a play-ground for the (human) mind.

> Images are intended to serve as models for actions. For although they show only the surfaces of things, they still show relationships among things that no one would otherwise suspect. Images don't show matter; they show what matters. And that allowed the hand to probe further into the circumstances than before [...] they had to be made accessible, intersubjective, and they had to be stabilized, stored [...] "published." (Flusser, 2011, p. 11)

Pictorial inscriptions manage to capture experience in static forms, something writing will also do later, to stop the world in space and subject it to the human gaze, infusing it with our growing con-sciousness.

Simon McBurney (2011), talking about Werner Herzog's doc-umentary on the world's oldest surviving paintings writes that these artists live in a time where everything was connected:

> They lived in an enormous present, which also contained past and future. A present in which nature was not only contiguous with them, but continuous. They flowed in and out of a continuum of everything around them; just as the animals flow into and out of the rock. As if the rock was alive, so were the animals. Everything was alive. ("Herzog's Cave of Forgotten Dreams: The real art underground," *The Guardian*, 17th March)

In that two-dimensional rendering of the world anything can be connected to anything, for everything can always mean something, as the primitive mind knows. What emerges, then, is a space of magic, a space of promiscuous proximities and viable resemblances that in-flames the imagination. The painted image fuels what Benjamin (1978) calls the "mimetic faculty," which he defines as "a rudiment of the powerful compulsion in former times to become and behave like something else" (pp. 333–336); it creates order and fashions mean-ings.[1] In that primordial virtuality, "[o]mens and maledictions can appear everywhere ... that become unpredictable and frightening [in] a world full of meanings, full of 'gods'" (Flusser, 2011, p. 13).

Freed from the onward march of time, the image virtualizes actual experience, rendering all its possible relations surveyable. The caveman sees the original scene in the image again, but he is now freed from the immediacy of reflex action and so able to ponder and deliberate between the multiple options that he can invent in the new virtuality of the image.

With the technology of writing, another form of inscription appears, that further advances the evolution of the human virtual. Meanings and representations are torn from the magical context of the original pictorial surface and translated into concepts. They are "lifted," as it were, from the surface of the walls by the same fingers that used to draw, which now begin to write. Pictorial two-dimensional surfaces are unraveled into scribal lines. The two-dimensional image is now condensed into a linear one dimensionality by this new gesture.

We could say that the virtual that is first modulated by the bodily imagination in the production of painted images (and in the production of concepts in oral language) is now modulated again, and again by the hand.[2] This time, however, the modulation is not a result of the body's spontaneous response in painting (or in words), but of a cognitive grasp of the world now deliberately articulated in writing. Oral language is thus superseded too by writing, which institutes a new level of abstraction in the human mind. The result is a conceptual universe of texts, calculations, narratives, and explanations (Flusser, 2011), which the invention of the printing press further expands, thus establishing the scribal form of Western culture for the past 400 years.

But, as we have seen in Chapter 1, with the invention of the photograph in 1839, the image comes back to the center of cultural consciousness. The one-dimensional, linear, hierarchical, process-oriented, historical way of thinking instituted by the scribal sequence, now has to compete with the two-dimensional way of the image, as surface, context, scene – a space of connections and associations. The invention of film strengthens the return of the imaginal in the collective. The virtual there, as in the photograph, is no longer simply ideas that we think, but also images that we perceive and feel; moreover, in the cinema our experience is not static but also kinetic; it is immersed in moving time. The virtual now can cause us to experience a feeling of vertigo, for example, whereas in the scribal form we were protected from such emotional or physical immediacy. With the image, the bodily dimension with its sensuality comes back. The virtual is now not only rationally but also affectively modulated. Because of the reinsertion of the image into culture by the photograph and the movies, we no longer experience, perceive, and value the world and ourselves in a dramatic, linear plot, but in fields of relationships, networks of meanings, and random associations (cf., Murphie, 2002, p. 192).

In the reshuffling that took place with the advent of the broadcast voice in the radio at the beginning of the 20th century, as Havelock (1986) observes, there was no return to the oral but a "forced marriage, or remarriage between the resources of the written word and of the spoken, [...] reinforc[ing] the latent energies of both parties" (p. 33). Likewise, what happens with the advent of photography, is by no means merely a reversion back from writing to the image either. Half visual image, half writing – more a product of blueprints and manual instructions, than of the world – the "technical image" is a hybrid, behind which the written word is always lurking. "As apparatuses themselves are the products of applied scientific texts," Flusser (2006) explains,

> in the case of technical images one is dealing with the indirect products of scientific texts [...] Television and cinema are on a different level of existence from caves and the Etruscans. (p. 17)

After scribal culture's long marginalization of sensibility, the body and the imagination return to the center of culture with the technical image. This strange symbiosis, however, in which the image enters with writing, threatens to disconnect it from the actual experience it purports to signify.

In mechanically restructuring the sensory stimuli, the camera compromises or diminishes the physical continuity between object and perception that characterizes the traditional (drawn or painted) image. The technical image emerges now, not according to the spontaneous whim or creativity of the painter but according to a preconceived format. Whereas traditional images signify phenomena, we could say, technical images signify instead concepts. With the camera we focus on the world not as we do on an object of vision, open to the live interaction between my spontaneous, attentive body and its senses, subjectively impressionable, but to the recording or compiling of information by a technical device. Mechanically grasped, received, and taken, the scene before us lives only within the confines of a predetermined set of possibilities in the camera. The world through the camera is no longer a world of objects but, more and more, a world of mental constructs of codified images played on our screens. "Instead of representing the world, [technical images] obscure it until human beings' lives finally become a function of the images they create" (Flusser, 2006, p. 17).

The tourist that sees New York through her camera lens is indeed having an experience, but it has little to do with her actual perception of New York. Her experience becomes a function of her images rather than the other way around. A mechanical take from reality is translated into a photographic representation that is, however, (partially) disconnected from her own subjectivity. What she will get from it when she sees the photograph will be external to the original experience, even if because of its similarity, the photograph may evoke it.

In this hollowed-out image, mediated by the automatic camera program, nothing needs to be about the world any more. The photographic representation lacks, therefore, a certain type of existential depth of experience for, as Flusser observes:

> Human beings cease to decode the images and instead project them, still encoded, into the world 'out there', which meanwhile itself becomes like an image – a context of scenes, of states of things [...] Human beings forget they created the images in order to orientate themselves in the world. Since they are no longer able to decode them, their lives become a function of their own images: imagination has turned into hallucination. (Flusser, 2011, p. 10)

As Flusser pointed out already in the eighties, it is increasingly true that everyday activity now aspires to be registered, whether in a photo or a video; it has to be translated into a screen, converted into a technical image in order to be operative or functional in the social world today, even in order to acquire experiential legitimacy. Insofar as its origin has been displaced or, in this case, intervened by an apparatus, there is in the technical image a loss of depth or (to use Benjamin's words again) of the aureatic.

In potentiating the photographic capture by means of computational calculations, digitization dramatically brings back the hegemony of the rational and completes the path of abstraction that had developed up to this point. Moreover, as we saw in Chapter 1, the empirical connection that still provided the analog image with a foothold in the world, despite its being mechanically modulated, is now completely severed. The digital image ends up being as distanced from the sensible world it supposedly represents as the concept in writing was.

As photographers (analogical or digital), we begin to attend to reality in a very different way than we did when our images were not technologically mediated:

> If [photographers] look through the camera out into the world, this is not because the world interests them, but because they are pursuing new possibilities of producing information and evaluating the photographic program. Their interest is concentrated on the camera; for them, the world is purely a pretext for the realization of camera possibilities. In short: they are not working,

they do not want to change the world, but they are in search of information. (Flusser, 2006, p. 26)

By turning from writing to the technical (analogic and digital) image, we are not going back to the initial two dimensional space of traditional images. As Flusser (2006) sees it, we are making one more step in a trajectory of increasing abstractness or withdrawal from concrete reality:

> Humanity has climbed [a] ladder step by step from concrete toward higher and higher levels of abstraction: a model of cultural history and the alienation of human beings from the concrete. (p. 6)

The one-dimensional world inaugurated by writing is now left behind as we enter into the zero dimensionality of 0s and 1s. The apparatus now finally breaks altogether with the sensible contact of the world; the light that touches the photographic paper that reacts to it due to its material properties and the laws of their relation to light rays is replaced by the coordinates assigned to each point in space in the digital grid. The image that emerges from this process is artificially extracted from it. Nevertheless, the magic of the traditional image, that had been shattered by the linearity of writing, comes back to life in the digital. At the same time that, as we have said, it reinforces the rational order, the digital image in the end also subverts it.

From one perspective the photograph enriches us, insofar as it brings back to collective consciousness the sensuality of the image, and so complexifies our scribal world. But there is also a sense, as we have just seen, in which the digital takes away precisely the connection with the sensible that the analog photographic image brought by virtue of its direct contact with empirical reality. It is completely gone with the digital. It does not receive the image and modulate it, but recodifies it, translates it into a language that has nothing to do with the sensual, and so breaks the physical bond that images had traditionally enjoyed and promoted. We see with the digital a reinsertion of the image but a further distancing from the sensoriality of the body.

As we move on with our explorations, we will continuously witness this oscillation in how we perceive the digital image, which insofar as it is an image in some sense reconnects our body to the sensuality of the world, but insofar as mathematically operated becomes instead a modulation that moves further along the path of disengagement from experience for the sake of rational abstraction.

b *From the virtual to virtual reality*

"What has God wrought?"

(first telegraphic message)[3]

Every new technology modulates the virtual differently. Speech modulated the virtual in the intellectual space of discourse, where it takes shape primarily through the logical associations between words, their syntax and grammar. The first human who drew a picture on a cave wall, or a pictogram on a stone tablet, was further modulating the virtual in the aesthetic space of perception, where it takes shape through the associations suggested to the eye by the inscriptions. Scribal logic prevailed in the West, after the invention of the alphabet, because of the simplicity and easy dissemination of writing. But with the invention of photography and film in the 20th century, the collective rational discourse that determined Western culture, with its stress on logical reason, gives way again to the thought of images in the qualified sense in which we have just seen.

Whereas photography suspends moments of time from actual experience in images, film liberates the image from the constraints of physical existence. For the first time in human history, the virtual is modulated as light projected on a screen. Just as with writing, experience is also embalmed, but now in an ethereal form and movement that is beyond the material. Photographic images bring together both the presence and absence of what they project in singular phantasmatic entities, that both are and are not in the empirical. But film, as we have seen, which is photographic images in motion, further modulates time, lifting the image out of actual flowing experience creating a second track of temporal movement. Time is no longer just the necessary condition of experience, the flowing river of consciousness that accompanies all our perceptions. Contrary to Heraclitus' proclamation that we cannot enter the same river twice, we can say that we can step into the same river as many times as we want with film.

In the concrete images of the caveman, in pictograms on a stone tablet, in written signs and photographic images on paper, the virtual is placed/materialized outside our minds. If we take the virtual to be the potential kept within everything that we perceive, then in the representational act of writing, drawing, and photography, that potential is sedimented in its actualized form. With the film screen – and even more with the digital screen – a further development takes place in the modulation of the virtual.

When we look at pictures in a physical album and rearrange them in different orders, for example, in terms of different criteria than those that had previously determined their order (instead of chronologically, we might arrange them geographically, in terms of the places where they were taken), the actualization of the alternatives forged by the imagination takes place at the expense of their virtuality. Once I arrange them in this order, the multiple other possible arrangements that were virtually present have settled upon one option, so that the virtual is materialized and sedimented into one actual ordering. But in the virtual world, on the contrary, any actualization remains potential, pregnant with further possibilities, pulsating in its virtuality. On the digital screen, the actualized virtual, though actual, remains permeable, always open to change. This fusion of actual and virtual that takes place in cyberspace – this hyper-presence of the virtual, as we might call it – makes experience incessantly fluid and changing, and susceptible to unlimited manipulation. In other words, its plasticity makes reality susceptible to either distortion or enhancement.

2 Virtuality and experience

a Post-truth

In the virtual world we are able, then, to isolate the pieces of past living experience that have been captured by film, and – because they are still pulsating with movement and alive – to bring forth from them their yet unrealized possibilities. In the digital screen, paradoxically, the virtual is actualized while still remaining virtual. This constitutes its irresistible temptation, for options are never exhausted by any particular actualization; what is actual always remains virtually alive. Virtual hybrids of past moments can be generated, which, in their newly edited arrangements, allow us to re-live them in novel ways. We can now not just change the order of experience and create new patterns and meanings, but also play with past, future, and present time, and so generate events that, although non-existent in the physical world, add a novel virtual dimension to our experience. As Stiegler put it, "it is an electric light, set free by materials from deep within the belly of the earth. An electronic, that is to say, a decompos[ing] light" (Derrida and Stiegler, 2002, p. 153).

This newly acquired capacity has enormous potential, even though it begins to wreak havoc in our normal perception of the world and our experience of time. Whereas the scribal tradition is married to truth and ideology, the digital is instead open to a plurality of points of view, seeing ever-new aspects and connections. So the digital does away with ideology insofar as "ideology is about the truth, one truth, my truth" (Flusser, 1990). The more points of view it can collect, the better the picture.

Just as writing changed the way in which we thought of and perceived the world, constituting both in terms of rational logic and sequential orderings, the virtual image does away with the scribal world
of theories and explanations. This technological wizardry threatens
"objectivity," as Mitchell (1992) pointed out already at the beginning
of the nineties, anticipating phenomena as familiar to us today as
deep fakes, catfishing, fakenews, etc.:

> Naive enthusiasm for the almost magical possibilities of this new
> electronic medium soon gave way to alarm. It was a short step, we
> began to realize, from innocuous enhancement or retouching to
> potentially misleading or even intentionally deceptive alteration
> of image content. And that step would put us on a slippery slope:
> the smug apartheid that we have maintained between the
> objective, scientific discourses of photography and the subjective,
> artistic discourses of the synthesized image seemed in danger of
> breaking down. (p. 16)

James Bridle (2018) poignantly illustrates this breakdown between the
objective and the subjective when he tells of a man that, returning
from a holiday with his phone full of photos, noticed an anomaly
while browsing through them:

> In one image, he saw himself and his wife at a table in a
> restaurant, both smiling at the camera. But this photograph
> had never been taken. At lunch one day, his father had held the
> button down on his iPhone a little long, resulting in a burst of
> images of the same scene ... [He] uploaded two of them to see
> which his wife preferred. In one, he was smiling, but his wife
> was not; in the other, his wife was smiling, but he was not.
> From these two images, taken seconds apart, Google's photo
> sorting algorithms had conjured a third: a composite in which
> both subjects were smiling their "best." The algorithm was part
> of a package called AutoAwesome (since renamed, simply
> "Assistant"), which performed a range of tweaks on uploaded
> images to make them more "awesome"—applying nostalgic
> filters, turning them into charming animations and so forth.
> But in this case, the result was a photograph of a moment that
> had never happened: a false memory, a rewriting of his-
> tory. (p. 152)

The seamlessness of the digital in our everyday experience is increasingly such, that the difference between virtual and real becomes
ever more difficult to discern, and the valences of our world come out

of joint. Guy Debord (2012), talking about what he called the Society of the Spectacle, wrote in 1967:

> Images detached from every aspect of life merge into a common stream, and the former unity of life is lost forever. Apprehended in a *partial* way, reality unfolds in a new generality as a pseudo-world apart ... All that once was directly lived has become mere representation. (p. 12)

This emphasis on the apprehension of reality as appearance or re-presentation eventually involves the displacement of truth as a ne-cessary element of communication. The world we live in begins to change in initially imperceptible ways, which may in the end have significant consequences, as we can witness in our time with the phenomenon (or cultural condition) of post-truth, where the blurring of the borders between what is real and what is falsely represented as real, confuses the public into whatever new reality it is possible to weave on screen. In that way, we may find ourselves in a world where there is no reliable order, or where different orders acquire their va-lidity and status in terms of their utility, their persuasiveness, or anything else, and not for any truth they stand for.

"In a world that has been really deranged," writes Debord (2012), "the truth is a moment of falsehood" (p. 14). And, indeed, only in a such a world could one affirm, as some politicians actually have, that "truth is not the truth," or that there are "alternative facts" that ap-parently establish a parallel world where one operates according to criteria that are alien to the truth. And in the confusion that begins to reign in our culture between these parallel worlds, the edges that distinguish the true from the false, fiction from reality, the virtual from the real, are blurred, and a new order begins to emerge, or rather a disconcerting disorder, where lies are viralized and where sentiment and opinion begin to displace truth and fact everywhere. Post-truth is, in this sense, the symptom of an effectively deranged culture; de-ranged by the emergence of social networks and the advent of the virtual world, where the effect of what is said is worth more than what is said, and where the emotional impact of the image, how it stirs the passions, displaces reality.

Stiegler (Derrida and Stiegler, 2002) observes that when we start living in the world mediated by all kinds of technological prosthetics, or through a screen, the very conditions under which we have ac-quired our beliefs up until then are altered. In digital virtuality, these are grounded indifferently in real events and "alternative facts," on realities as well as in mere opinions or assemblages. Our life has spread into the virtuality of the screen to such an extent that if someone says that something happened and builds a narrative in the media powerful enough to represent it, then it happened. In the same way, if I say that something did not happen, and point to the inconsistencies or irregularities of its virtual presentation, sowing doubt about the veracity of the image, then maybe it did not happen, or did not happen the way it is being presented. Faced with the epistemological promiscuity of the virtual screen, the objective criteria of truth become obsolete in the new digital order.

If I can imagine how something could happen, and present in video form a realistic representation of that fantasy, it can be difficult for the mind to sort through whether it happened or not. We see this all the time in our late night political satire where video images, manipulated for comic effect, show, for example, a political figure or a celebrity saying or doing something that is in stark contrast to what, in real life, he or she would actually say or do. This leaves us disoriented, as the video presentation of the occurrence imprints in our mind a sense of truth even though we know at another level it is only a wishful fantasy, a joke.

Since we associate the computer screen with the transmission of real events occurring in real time, nothing escapes digital representation. We automatically accept what we see without distinguishing the live transmission from its deferred edition, the actual fact from the virtual event. We accept the representations as if they were the truth, although it is possible that they no longer correspond to anything "real" outside their own creation.

Not only can the virtual image surreptitiously distort our perception of reality; sometimes it is the virtual image that determines reality beyond the facts themselves. Just consider, for example, the diminishing authority of the sports referee in the age of instant replay, to see how the image on the screen becomes reality and our perception its inaccurate copy. As Doel and Clarke (1999) observe, "what until now represented the real is increasingly subject to the hyperreality of real-time recording" (p. 270). And the power to manipulate reality, to create "truth" as such, is a byproduct of the digital era. In a very concrete sense, everything becomes a game of images, where the value of what is said does not lie in its correspondence with any reality, but in the effect it produces at this moment, in the impact that it is capable of provoking through social networks, in their exposure in the virtual world.

What we call post-truth is the displacement of truth by a hybrid that is validated by very different criteria than those we know, that are sometimes even contrary to what is reality. Perhaps more importantly: it is no longer just ideas, nor thought sequences, nor arguments, nor discourses that build the world, but rather images, panoramic visions, totalizing representations that appeal to our feelings, our fears and desires, and incite our false opinions and ill-founded beliefs. The digital fusion of text, sound, and image, which occurs in the virtual screen, and the possibility of immediate reproduction and the ease and speed of communication in virtual networks, provide the perfect means to replicate the virus of post-truth more and more effectively.

Beyond disrupting the normal criteria that distinguish fact from fiction, virtual and real, the concoction of digital images we are subjected to in this post-truth era seems to replace one dimension of reality with which we are familiar with an incommensurable and disconcerting other which, unmoored from our reliable references, suspends us in a void. Truth and falsity, fact or fiction, real and virtual seem to merge and in this indistinct space all polarities become mute. However, from below this opaque limbo of rising uncertainty, an entirely new horizon may yet emerge.

It is worth noting that the screens of our smartphones place at our entire disposal, at the minimum cost of a single click, a universe of infinite possibilities entirely designed to please and anticipate, often even provoke, our desires. It therefore becomes obvious that post-truth is something more complex than the mere devaluation of truth. It challenges us to assume a reality in which truth no longer counts, and where passions and emotions override it. Now, our moral resistance to this devaluation of truth, strong as it is and justified as it seems, may be ignoring that what is happening calls forth a reconsideration of the very nature and purpose of communication, of life in society.

When the scribal mind confronts and is challenged by the digital, all the structures that had until now guaranteed stability and safety, protecting us from the adversity of the world, shudder. The vital forces that had been channeled and contained by reason's sedimented notions, dogmatic principles and laws, are set loose by the onset of the rhizomatic nature of the digital so that repressed psychic forces break free and run amock, bringing chaos and disorder to the world. The troubling phenomenon of post-truth becomes, in the beginning, the breeding ground for the darkest passions and the lowest human intentions that express themselves in the destruction and disorder that we are witnessing, greatly potentiated today by the onset of digitality.

But perhaps it is now in this darkness that the occasion presents itself to move precisely in the direction pointed to by Ortega's premonition that ours is the time for the exploration of human sensibility and vitality. As Nietzsche once proclaimed, "everything [...] we call today culture, education, civilisation will have to appear [...] before the infallible judgement of Dionysos" (Ortega y Gasset, 1961, p. 58).

b *Laboratory of subjectivity*

Thanks to virtual spaces like Twitter or Snapchat or Instagram, TikTok, blogs, and podcasts, there are now many more and different ways of relating, communicating, and expressing than ever before; ways that, quite apart from their undeniable perils, also broaden our world and open yet unexplored dimensions of human experience. In the communication that takes place on the web, thanks to the invisibility with which we might cloak ourselves in our interactions, thoughts and experiences are expressed and articulated that used to remain trapped in mute, individual private experience. These now become not just shared and public – enhancing one's own personal awareness in the emerging intersubjective discourse – but they also begin to constitute a new collective. Feelings and actions seem to open, in novel and complex ways, to whole new areas of interactive meaning and possible aspects of relating (to) things, which may be recovering connections and modes of awareness once lost to what was repressed by tradition.

Whereas in reality, space and time limit our possible experiences and our visual perception under the weight of various kinds of prejudice, insofar as the virtual world can be color-blind, these limitations are done away with for the identity of who presents themself to us is never guaranteed; we can, for instance, develop very strong feelings about another person without ever being sure of who they are, or even knowing their gender, ethnicity, or culture.

In earlier times, talking about intimate experiences was very uncommon, except in confession or with our closest friends and family. Doing it publicly was inconceivable. Today, this reticence gives way to the unprecedented phenomenon of virtual life, where we are driven to publicly share even the most private and personal thoughts, feelings, beliefs, and images.

The breakdown of what Mitchell (1992) calls the "apartheid qualities" of our scribal world have many unforeseen possibilities. When Facebook, for instance, provides us with a video of our Saturday, with the images of the activities we have been capturing during the day on our smartphone (playing with the kids, walking the dog, jogging, visiting the market, etc.), by amalgamating them into a video clip, our virtual life expands our perception and memory of the day. The memories randomly captured through the digital suddenly become autonomous and provide us with a new string of associations that are affectively alive, producing new perceptions that expand our reality. Or when an algorithm begins to bombard us with memories from the past, there is no telling how many unexpected consequences that may have on our sense of our day, in our sense of time, especially as the past is now becoming so blurred with the present. The virtual temporal flow, its pace and rhythm, begins to erase the distinction between reality and fiction and undermines our notions of truth and authenticity. What we see belongs in a parallel plane of virtual spatio-temporality that, insofar as it is integrated with our experience, confuses or muddles the actual spatio-temporal coordinates that hold it.

We don't even have to generate these virtual moments; they are generated for us (and usually for no pure motives), thickening our existence with layers of virtual residue that can change the course of our days.

Consider Emily Witt (2016), who interviewed several women who found sexual satisfaction performing for strangers on various webcam sites. Internet sexual women, as Witt calls them, in some cases lived in small towns where the dating pool was limited, or they were victims of sexual trauma. As she writes, "digital sexuality allows for possibilities of anonymity, gender-bending, fetish play and other modes of experimentation with a degree of safety and autonomy that's not present in the physical world" (in Williams, 2019).

The digital medium offers us the power to articulate what can be an extremely personal experience, which, digitally encoded, ceases to be a simple personal testimony and becomes exemplary for the collective. The *personal* revelation, in a node of plural and public interactivity, becomes a universalized concept. The virtual world generates, in other words, blueprints of psychic constellations, systems of possibilities where the individual in virtuality is able to come closer to experiences and facts than she was able to consider or even articulate in her world before. In digital life, she recognizes the contours of feelings that she can explore in a practical and ludic way in order to open herself to new experiences. Whereas it is habitual for us, especially in the Western world, to replace experience with our conceptual grasp of it, in the virtual world, the concept is incarnated in the actuality of digital life. We no longer just think our thoughts and fantasies. We live them out in the virtual world. In this way, feelings and sensations, intuitions and images, projections and the work of self-articulation become available in the full range of possible digital interplay that makes them susceptible to experimentation and reflection. The virtual world thus becomes a laboratory of subjectivity, where a new kind of self-knowledge is forged.

People nowadays collect in their smartphones images of their surroundings and of other people. They will dwell on them, magnify them, reduce them, inspect them, fantasize, share, and talk with others about them. They may never see the object of their exploration again, but that is not important. What is important is the opportunity that is offered by the digital capture to explore the empirical world and convert it into a screen upon which to project the resonances that arise from this virtual contact.

Of course, there is the danger of addiction, of feeding one's obsessions or generating new ones that may affect our lives negatively. But in essence the process plays the same role as what took place in pre-digital times, when adolescents spent the day listening to their vinyls, again and again, totally immersed, undergoing an experience that, even though solipsistic, was transformative. The lyrics of their songs became ways of articulating their emotional lives, of making conscious what they otherwise could not have, with the subsequent increased awareness. The difference, however, lies in the way the virtual is modulated in the digital, and how it enables the public sharing and bringing to collective awareness otherwise private experiences. They are submitted in the virtual platform to others, whose responses – as if from a spectral choir, tragic or dramatic, lyrical or humorous – help us discern and make common unexplored dimensions of our subjective life.

i San Junipero

In his iconic television series, *Black Mirror*, Charlie Brooker offers us, in the episode "San Junipero," an illustration of the experimental potential of the virtual. There, in that virtual "beach town" called by that name, people are "downloaded" for a full immersive experience of their youthful days. It's your typical role-play game, except the character you play is nobody else but you, young and in the past. We soon learn that the "San Junipero System" of virtual reality is used by terminal patients for what they call "immersive nostalgia therapy" to help them cope with their bodily demise. But it is also considered, by some, as an afterlife option, a sort of virtual heaven where you can "pass over" – after the death of your body – to live your youth endlessly.

There are two characters in the episode: Kelly, who we first see as a dashing young woman in her 20s, and Yorkie, a curious and rather nerdy-looking bespectacled woman, in the same age bracket. They are in San Junipero, *virtually* there, in 1987. In their real life, which is sometime in our very near future, they are both in their late 70s. Yorkie is quadraplegic, bed-ridden since her 20s, and Kelly is dying of terminal cancer. They "visit" San Junipero for a few hours every weekend. Yorkie is exploring it as a possible permanent virtual destiny, to "pass over" when she dies, whereas Kelly visits to have fun and do all the things she never dared before she dies. They meet there and become erotically involved. Yorkie lives out her sexuality for the first time and falls in love with Kelly, but Kelly resists the emotional pull of the relationship, because of her belief that this virtual stuff is just for fun. As she tells Yorkie, she does not do feelings. But the loving feelings she starts to experience for Yorkie lead her to question the actual attachments in her life and her relation to this virtual world. Eventually, Kelly visits Yorkie in real time, at the clinic where she lies in bed motionless, and mute. Moved by her visit and Yorkie's story, Kelly offers to marry her in order to sign the euthanasia papers Yorkie needs to legally disconnect her body and "pass over" to the virtual heaven for good.

As the story develops, Kelly is visiting Yorkie for the first time since she "passed over" and became a permanent resident. Visibly exhilarated, Yorkie brushes her feet on the sand and, shrieking in delight, bangs the car with her hand to prove it's real. She pleads with Kelly to consider passing over too, so they can live together in San Junipero forever. But Kelly resists. They begin an argument that ends in a terrible fight. Yorkie's puerile analysis of what she takes as Kelly's dilemma (whether to stay true to her dead husband or "pass over" to be with Yorkie), judging her marital bond with the immaturity and naïveté of the 21-year-old she must still be emotionally, enrages Kelly. She forces Kelly to weigh her feelings, now, in the virtual, against her total life, which is no longer just about her but also about her husband, her daughter, and their shared grief over their child's early death, and the arguments and feelings they had had around their afterlife. The virtual reality of San Junipero suddenly leaks into the real, and Kelly is forced to confront her belief in the difference between them.

Can the youthful, vital excitement she is experiencing in her virtual 20's outweigh the trials and tribulations of married life, her 49-year bond with her husband? For Yorkie, who has had no experience or attachments for practically her whole life, San Junipero has been very important to her. Kelly, on the other hand, has always seen it as merely an "immersive nostalgia therapy," providing her with the entertainment of a virtual reality experience of her own memories that diverts from her ailing body. She has never taken it as a serious afterlife alternative, but her skepticism seems suddenly shaken by her growing feelings for her virtual lover.

Our subjective life, our feelings and emotions, seem not to discriminate between real and virtual. The arrows of Eros move freely between them, traversing both. What we imagine frequently finds its way into our reality: We plan our life in this way, and whatever we achieve or don't achieve is a matter of our success in actualizing the virtual; our fears may have a completely virtual source and yet they are actualized in our actions and attitudes in life; when we imagine that we can change the world and embark on the many enterprises that will carry us probably for the rest of our lives, we actualize virtuality, which infuses our thoughts and actions in reality. Or when we dream and try to make our dreams come true, or fall in love and weave the web of fantasy, it inspires us to hold our desire and make it grow.

The real and the virtual do not seem to be opposites, but quite to the contrary interdependent, complementary, porous to one another. We don't need to stick to the story in San Junipero to validate this claim. How many couples have we not heard about or known that have met on the web, fallen in love, then met in real life and lived happily ever after? Brooker's fantasy points merely half a step ahead, where full immersive virtual experience can be seen as nothing but a further technological way to do what we have always done with our minds: to tell stories and compose narratives that help us to articulate ourselves to others and give direction to our lives. The virtual serves Yorkie in her new self-discovery and becomes, for Kelly, too, a place where she finds herself experiencing new feelings, moved to compassion for Yorkie's septuagenarian quadriplegic self, trapped in the real world just as she also feels real passion and joy with her, as the young woman she has met in San Junipero.

Reality and virtuality, in other words, have never been too far from one another in real life. We have always, ever since we learned to speak, navigated from one to the other, nurturing one with the other. Until the advent of the mass media, we have lived their intersection privately by withdrawing into our own subjectivities. Now, with virtual reality, we can not only introvert into ourselves, but into the intersubjective, digital world. Although we tend to consider the virtual as a fake copy of the real, a mere representation of reality, it has become a virtual playground that complements and enlarges our reality by introducing a new possible real, where the virtual does not merely copy or repeat, but engenders wholly singular and novel creations.

San Junipero, regardless of whether it is possible or not to download our souls into a digital chip, conceives the virtual as that space of transit, where the imagination is free from the bonds of sedimented concepts and identities. Insofar as the virtual and the real interact, what happens in the virtual is actual experience; it is not just a simulation, but something that is woven into the fabric of life and complicates or complexifies it.

The question that lurks in the background is the question about the truth of our virtual experiences, the existential status of the virtual copy, which we will be addressing in what follows (Part II). It directly pertains to how we begin to live and slowly to understand – both individually and collectively – the relation between real and virtual, their connection, and interdependence. Perhaps more poignantly than ever before, digital technology, in the advent of the virtual world, confronts us with the complexity of this question, and with how it bears, ultimately, on our difficult relationship with death and mortality.

Notes

1 The advent of writing and the prevalence of the scribal mind has brought about the demise of that faculty, and it is a question for the digital, as we will see, if it resurrects or simply transforms it.

2 Although it is a question whether the expressive nature of language is not primordial, and itself inseparable from the body so that – even in words that weave a theoretical space – the body is not always ultimately involved at its basis. Benjamin (1978) suggests that there may be no higher human faculty where it does not play a decisive role (p. 333).
3 Sent by Samuel Morris to Alfred Vail, on May 24, 1844, over an experimental 40-mile line from Washington, D.C. to Baltimore, taken from the Bible, Numbers 23:23.

References

Bazin, A. (1967) *What is Cinema?* (vol. 1, p. 14). Berkeley: University of California Press.

Benjamin, W. (1978) On the Mimetic Faculty. In *Reflections: Essays, Aphorisms Autobiographical Writings* (pp. 333–336). New York: Schoken Books.

Bridle, J. (2018) *The New Dark Age: Technology and the End of the Future.* London: Verso.

Debord, G. (2012) *The Society of the Spectacle*. Cambridge, MA: MIT Press.

Derrida, J., and Stiegler, B. (2002) *Echographies of Television*. Cambridge: Polity Press.

Doel, M.A., and Clarke, D.B. (1999) Virtual Worlds: Simulation, Suppletion, S (ed)uction and Simulacra. In M. Crang, P. Crang, and J. May (Eds.), *Virtual Geographies: Bodies, Space and Relations* (pp. 261–282). London: Routledge.

Flusser, V. (2006) *Towards a Philosophy of Photography*. Trowbridge: Cromwell Press.

Flusser, V. (2011) *Into the Universe of Technical Images* (N.A. Roth, Trans.). Minneapolis, MN: University of Minnesota Press.

Flusser, V. (1990) *Lecture on Photography*, Budapest, April 1990. https://www.youtube.com/watch?v=ZWcX3XQyukg

Havelock, E.A. (1986) *The Muse Learns to Write: Reflections on Orality and Literacy from Antiquity to the Present*. New Haven, CT: Yale University Press.

McBurney, S. (2011) Herzog's Cave of Forgotten Dreams: The Real Art Underground. *The Guardian*, 17th March.

Merleau-Ponty, M. (2007) Eye and Mind. In T. Toadvine and L. Lawlor (Eds.), *The Merleau-Ponty Reader* (pp. 351–378). Evanston, IL: Northwestern University Press.

Mitchell, W.J. (1992) *The Reconfigured Eye: Visual Truth in the Post-photographic Era*. Cambridge, MA: MIT Press.

Murphie, A. (2002) *A Shock to Thought: Expression after Deleuze and Guattari*. Brian Massumi (Ed.). London: Routledge.

Ortega y Gasset, J. (1961) *The Modern Theme*. New York: Harper Torchbooks.

Williams, A. (19 January 2019) Do You Take This Robot … *New York Times*. Retrieved from https://www.nytimes.com/2019/01/19/style/sex-robots.html

Witt, E. (2016) *Future Sex: A New Kind of Free Love*. New York: Farrar, Straus and Giroux.

Part II

Evolving conceptions of the virtual and the real

Introduction to Part II

It is thought that with the advent of digital virtuality, we have entered into a new era where the virtual dimension is radically transforming the way we live and perceive the world. However, as we have already seen in our exploration of virtual media, virtuality is not a feature belonging exclusively to the digital, but rather it is an intrinsic dimension of the real, always active, always impacting our experience. Even if it is true that the omnipresence of the digital has brought it to prominence for us today, as we will see in this second part of the book, we can better grasp the revolution and crisis we are living by examining the dynamic and puzzling relationship between the virtual and the real, that ultimately defies any fixed categorization.

Embedded in any particular perspective on what technology means to us is a set of assumptions about the interrelationship between material reality – the world of things and objects that we encounter outside ourselves – and virtuality, that dynamic sense of potentiality and possibility that is inherently immaterial. Whether and how the virtual and real line up or don't line up, or are in opposition with one another or in creative play, these are assumptions that resolve themselves into very particular stances that attempt to fix their meaning.

Entering into the singular phenomenology of these stances, we will draw from their distinct intelligence the philosophical and psychological assumptions embedded in them. The radical interchangeability between real and virtual makes it nearly impossible to definitively determine them. And we take that fact as something to be contended with, not explained away. We will deliberately resist the impulse to take sides, faithful to the complexity that is revealed by their tension. Only by holding together each stance's voice and their critiques, will we prevent the polarization that occludes their pharmacological nature and allow their utter unresolvability to strike us.

Moreover, each particular perspective on how the virtual and the real relate to one another always casts a shadow, always leaves something out. But being attuned to their play and allowing their differences to remain in generative dialogue, we will see how one stance can suddenly change into the other, thus enacting a tendency of words and things, when taken to their extreme, to revert into their opposite, what the Greeks called an *enantiodromia*. Thus, as we probe each stance and each critique, we will experience together, as writers and readers, a certain kind of vertigo. We believe that the discourse around technology must be situated in this fracturing, boundary-unsettling dynamic.

Psychoanalysis is thoroughly attuned to the highly complex set of interrelations between fantasy and reality, terms that have the same kind of metonymic play as the "real" and the "virtual." Hence, in its theoretical elucidation of the intrapsychic and intersubjective dimensions of unconscious life, psychoanalysis can shed its own unique light on the nature of the virtual. The perilous dance of the pharmakon, between healing and poisoning, resonates with the psychoanalytic idea that an important aspect of treatment involves the analyst allowing herself to be infected by the patient's illness (Ogden, 2001). Only by taking it inside herself, knowing it from within, can the analyst make genuine, existential contact with what the patient is suffering, thus making it more real to both. One cannot get to the remedy (i.e., therapeutic growth) without carefully working one's way through the poison.

We intend similarly to enter into our technological issues by allowing ourselves to be infected by the poison of the profound contradictions in the force field between the virtual and the real that we are living in contemporary digital culture. In an even more dramatic image from psychoanalysis, our goal is not to heal or cure, but to keep open the wound that is pushing us full force into a digitally permeated life-world (LaPlanche, 2015). We are certainly not aiming at some kind of premature closure that suggests we know where any of this is headed; rather, we steadfastly embrace the utterly contradictory uncertainties that form the unconscious backdrop to all of our positive knowledge about digital life. At this stage of the book, we want to invoke a mode of thinking that, being disposed to affectively charged, lived experience, draws us closer to this wound and challenges the dominant contemporary discourse on technology which, in pursuing clean and clear-cut divisions between virtual and real, always ends up in a polarization that freezes thought.

3 Two stances on the virtual and the real

1 Stance one: The inherent fakeness of the virtual

What we will call "the first stance" is a view that understands the virtual as a false approximation of the real, a copy or simulation, merely an imitation of reality, that never reaches the ontological status of "real." As Doel and Clarke (1999), whose incisive essay we will draw from, express it:

> [T]he virtual is to the real as a copy is to the original: it is nothing more than a reflection, a representation, and a reproduction... [It is] secondary, derivative, and supplemental. Superficial, decorative, and accessorized, it has nothing essential about it. It participates without belonging. (p. 262)

A strict ontological split between the virtual and the real is assumed here. Moreover, that ontological separation is conceived of quantitatively. The virtual is less substantial than the real: not different but lesser. It hovers over events, mirroring them without ever actually belonging or attaching to them. It is a simulation that lacks the vitality and authenticity that arises out of an encounter with the real. The virtual user is removed from the fullness of "real" human existence.

This conception of the relation between the virtual and the real emphasizes how the quality of sensory experience is lessened by the virtual; the aesthetic intensity of the encounter with concrete reality is diminished in that simulation. If, as Kant (1992, I, §6) sees it, the liveliness of aesthetic experience is a function of the play between reason and imagination, then in the virtual that play has been annulled, the tension dissolved or broken and the quality of experience flattened. Virtuality, taken as a simulation of reality, not only eliminates the essential tension in that play but also diminishes imagination, creating a state of indifference and tepidity in us.

Moreover, we become psychologically invested in our virtual simulations because they provide a defensive shield against the messiness and intractability of reality, the time-space drag of the real, that impedes the expeditious fulfilment of what we want, when we want it (Doel and Clarke, 1999). Reality is reduced to the controllable and predictable nature of the copy that is perfectly designed to fulfill our wishes, thus liberating us from the obdurate density of the real. No longer slowed down by the exigencies of matter, space, and time, desire and its fulfilments live in the unbroken circuit of virtual relations that overcomes the frustrations and obstacles attendant to everyday life.

We are increasingly living in a time when simulated realities mediate our access to the real. The moment we switch on, we enter a phantasmatic world that obviates the disjointed and fragmentary nature of life and experience. Just as the Lacanian infant constructs a false image of wholeness by gazing at herself in the mirror (Lacan, 1977), simulated reality – ontologically severed from those dimensions of existence that come about through an actual encounter with the real – also creates an alluring illusion that deceives us. When we are so immersed in the virtual world, we can easily neglect our most vital physical needs. We become trapped in a delusional and pathological fiction, where the objects of the world are divested of their material density, and the tension necessary for the integrity of life collapses.

Insofar as the first stance assumes that the virtual inevitably deceives us into mistaking a copy for the real, that deception can begin to take on a sinister quality as the world becomes flooded with simulations that we can no longer distinguish from the real. This theme of the dystopian effects of simulated reality is portrayed in the *Black Mirror* episode "Be Right Back," which explores the possibility of virtually simulating our presence after we are dead.

The protagonist of this story, Martha, in attempting to overcome the loss of her boyfriend, Ash, who has unexpectedly died, signs up for a website that can virtually re-create her lost partner by extrapolating his digital footprint from his past social media use.[1] This is achieved first with Ash's voice, and eventually, as she develops a closer relationship to the digital version of Ash, with a clone of his body. On several occasions we witness her gradual disappointment and frustration with the clone's lack of spontaneity and inability to respond in a fully human way. At one point, when he fails to react to her emotional prodding she begins violently hitting him in frustration and mounting rage, and then reproaches him for not responding to her violence by hitting her back, as Ash would probably have done if he were alive. He tells her that nothing in Ash's history, the history from which he has been built, includes anything that would have him ever be violent to her or could justify his reciprocal aggression. But if he were human, she realizes, he would go beyond the bounds of his program.

Replacing a "real" object of the world with a virtual copy raises the whole issue of what it means to substitute a spontaneously living object with a digitally replicated copy or clone. With the clone, Martha has someone who looks, talks, and acts exactly like Ash, but someone with whom she is unable to make an affective connection; in their intimate experience, she struggles with the haunting realization that the cloned version of Ash lacks the essential vitality of her living boyfriend. "It's like the old Marx brother's joke," as Žižek (2003) writes, "where Groucho is seducing a typical dowager and says, 'Your eyes, your nose, everything of you reminds me of you... everything but yourself!'" (p. 94). And with this realization, Ash's clone becomes monstrous for Martha and has to be hidden away in her attic for life.

The clone, as we would expect from the perspective of the first stance, will always be inferior to the original. With virtual fireplaces, for example, the experience of the actual fire is replaced by a re-presentation that clearly caters to the more conceptual senses (audiovisual images), but lacks the physical properties that make up for the existential density that is left behind. Virtual pets, moreover, allow for bonds of affection that are from the very beginning un-rooted, lacking real commitment and devoid of relational depth; the on-line avatars through which we engage with others in virtual reality, also do away with the need to relate to their humanity.

A gardener most poignantly articulated this impoverishment. At the apartment building where he worked, he immediately noticed that the tree in the lobby that everyone had praised for its beauty, was in fact artificial. For him, it looked, as he said, "tall, stupid, and dead," and he continued, "I live from my plants, they are my companions. I wake up to them in the morning at home and then in every other folks' homes. I laugh with them, I talk to them, I cry with them. But it makes me so sad when I realize that even though that thing they have brought is a fake, they still want it here; that everyone is just in-different, unwilling to put the time and care needed for real things."

Since any object today can be so flawlessly copied, we become de-sensitized to the real, and so are tricked into believing that we are interacting with something real when in fact we are not, thus losing something vital about the world of objects. Ash's (virtual) identity is algorithmically constructed from past information. Its repertoire is limited to that which has been given to it, so, like a digital simulation, it lacks all vitality. Martha's confining Ash to the attic represents a kind of melancholic withdrawal from the object. But that loss and increasing alienation from the life-world may also be registered un-consciously, resulting in a desperate psychic need to make contact with the real by breaking through the simulations. That was the case, according to Frankel (2002) in the violence of the school shooting at Columbine in 1991, which has become the horrific prototype of an increasing number of school shootings in its wake.

When we interact with any kind of virtual clone, we frequently risk becoming aesthetically and ethically numb to its fakeness: for example, in the recordings of nature music that we listen to in order to soothe ourselves in the middle of the frenzy of our contemporary lives; or, in the electronic voices with which we, more and more frequently, enter into simulated human conversations, habituating ourselves to the hollowness of electronically simulated sounds with the muffled echo of the digital; or with the multiple new forms of artificial intelligence (Siri, Alexa, etc.) whose daily interactions begin to blunt our perception and reaction to the living bodily human presence. We become so used to interacting with a machine, perceiving the world by means of it, that we begin to respond in the same way with their human counterparts and so become blind to the difference. Sherry Turkle (2012) tells of a 16-year-old boy who uses texting for everything that once told her "… someday, someday, but certainly not now, I would like to learn how to have a conversation …" (https://www.youtube.com/watch?v=t7Xr3AsBEK4).

Perhaps we begin to lose our affective and bodily connection to the world; it is little by little disappearing, becoming a thing of the past. Some may call that simple nostalgia; others may want to recover what is being forgotten. As we will see in Chapter 8, that loss brought about by the digital was already anticipated by those philosophers whose ontologies become useful for us now as we face the technological advances of our era. For Benjamin (1979), for example, it was foreshadowed in the loss of the mimetic faculty and the aura of objects; for Wittgenstein (1980), in the disconnection in our materialistic, contemporary lives from what is most important to us; and for Heidegger (1977), in the withdrawal of being that happens with technology.

Many areas of our collective life today have become infected by the simulating effects of the virtual: politics, economics, sex, and war. We are now agitated with the emergence of virtual politics, where the reality of the claims made rely no longer on factual truth but on fleeting reference to "virtual facts," the validity of which depends no longer on their accuracy, but on the immediate impact they have. All is momentarily up for grabs as there is no instant objectivity by which to measure any one truth-claim. The dispensability of truth is emboldened because by the time we have it settled, the moment has passed and the damage done. We see it too in economics, where brick-and-mortar buildings, non-corporate town business centers, bookstores, and so on are increasingly a casualty of e-commerce. The urban world of concrete structures is de-realized by the virtual, so their actual location in space becomes irrelevant, and the physical interaction between people that takes place in such spaces is neglected. Virtual sex is another example where the actual encounter with a real other becomes secondary to its representation. Or take virtual wars, where in striking targets with drones, the pilots are insulated from the risks and dangers of combat, and in that distance, there is only indirect accountability for collateral damage. War becomes a virtual occurrence on the screen wholly separate from the physical, lived reality of a soldier's life.

The virtual liberates us from our situatedness in time and space, which ordinarily serves as a constraint to fantasy and desire. What could not or did not happen in the real happens in the virtual. Take the following case as an example: As we were writing this a few years ago, in January 2016, the coldest day of the year thus far, in Harvard square, in that miserable American Trump-Clinton political season, Harvard students were being summoned by a loudspeaker, like in a call to prayer, to come inside a "virtual reality booth" – a huge tent set up in the center of the public space of the square – where one could go and sit on a sunny beach, go sailing, high-diving, and the like, all of it *virtually*! The real is cold and uninviting, so "come on in and have the virtual-real." It is of course merely a substitute, but if you really let yourself go and give yourself over to how good of a substitute it is, you can create within yourself what used to be called a willing suspension of disbelief. But here's the rub: Whereas previously from the willing suspension of disbelief we entered into the potential space of art and imagination, in virtual times, that willing suspension of disbelief becomes effectively a willing disavowal of reality and a deflation of experience.

One can always counter that those students are just taking a break, that they know it's a cheap trick. Sure enough – but if an increasing portion of social and political life today enacts this unconscious clarion call into the virtual as a response to the disenchantment with the world, our actual relation with the real, both individually and collectively, is severely impoverished. For even if it is our nature to wish for an impossible world, free from contingency and restraint, the digital exacerbates that desire, and so also contributes to the disenchantment. It would seem that we enter the virtual reality booth at the expense of real life, real sensation, real memory, insulating the other fibers of perception that are in the body, always involved with an enrichment of experience. People are now manifesting this loss, for example, in their newfound preference for vinyl over the digital register, "for the richness of music," as they put it. Or the experience we are having more frequently these days, that even when the resolution of the digital image is ever sharper and more precise, it ends up that "realer than real" becomes unreal. Instead of "watching" television we feel as if we are on the "artificial" set itself.

That richness is what we lose, and we lose it not because it is no longer there, but because we have turned from reality without even noticing and started to live in an artificial world that while comfortable and predictable and well under control (we think), involves the forgetfulness and eventual disappearance of another register of experience. Rather than an evolution there may be a pauperization here that should be avoided. Memory will not help, for when we become sensorially habituated to the same perceptual range, we shall not experience the loss nor remember the difference in quality.

The mediation of digital technology ushers us into a new realm of experience where a disconnection (perhaps even an amputation) from the body becomes necessary. And this means that the empathic element that grows in density and depth with the participation of the body diminishes in the flatness of the virtual screen, so that we forget to actually listen to the undertones and nuances of words; or, unable to hear them any longer, we become despondent, melancholic, literally haunted by the shallow emptiness of a virtualized world. Digitization allows us to efface from everyday experience the opaque, the unknown, the uncertain, the unformed; it involves, in other words, a flight from the real. As simulation becomes the order of the day, what used to be naturally, spontaneously implicit and acknowledged now requires to be made explicit, as if vitality were being won over by representation.

a Critique of the first stance: The alleged inherent fakeness of the virtual

There are several implicit assumptions about the virtual behind the first stance that need to be examined. The virtual is seen as an inferior copy of the real, so that when we succumb to it, we lose our ground, and therefore our bodies, our senses, and our genuine experience of the world. This denigration of the virtual creates a powerful dichotomy, a dramatic opposition, between the authentic real and the artificial virtual. In positing such a drastic division, we become obsessed with authenticity. Prioritizing the original over the copy we end up adhering to a correspondence theory of re-presentation, where "the virtual … .must be [...] anchored in and [...] subservient to that which it re-presents and or dis-places" (Doel and Clarke, 1999, p. 264). Allowed to function on its own, the virtual automatically involves us in disavowal. "In short, and for the sake of appearances and experiences, the virtual may seem real and vice versa, but in their respective essences, never the twain shall meet" (p. 263).

This conception of virtuality is Platonic in the traditional sense. It so dichotomizes the virtual and the real that it ends up making the real an immutable and essential form. The virtual tears us away from our ground, and we lose our fundamental orientation toward reality. Embodied, historical memory ceases, and our sensorial awareness breaks down, throwing us into confusion. Encapsulated in the cocoon of virtuality, we start living vegetative existences, where the sensuousness (*aisthesis*) of the world becomes imperceptible to our anesthetized consciousness.

Contrary to the first stance, however, the digital clone or simulation is not simply a degraded version of the real. We see this in "Be Right Back" when Martha directs the clone to jump off the cliff and commit suicide – because his machinic limitations have made him repulsive to her – and he pretends to be scared of jumping, shedding simulated tears, evoking such a powerful emotional response from her that, despite her initial impulse, she is unable to let him destroy himself and is forced to live with him forever, as a ghost in the attic. This is also evident in the case of virtual pets. Even if their sounds, gestures (and even tears) are algorithmically generated, they are still capable of provoking empathy, as we know from the powerful emotional bonds that children and the elderly develop in relation to them. It seems that indeed we can form "real" attachments to these digitally animated objects, which challenges the conception implicit in the first stance that living creatures are necessary for the development of authentic attachments.

To return to the issue of virtual wars, we had emphasized the video game quality of making war, where the "operators–pilots as they are called–sit behind computer terminals outfitted with joysticks, monitors, interactive maps, and other cockpit gear, remotely controlling drones on the other side of the world" (Rushkoff, 2013, p. 120). Here was an image of the distancing effects of virtual simulations: The pilots are being shielded from the real-world consequences of their actions, as well as the ways in which the targets of the attacks became dehumanized, and thus unreal, by their appearance on a digital screen. But, in fact, as Rushkoff points out:

> the levels of clinical distress in drone crews were as high, and sometimes even higher, than those of crews flying in real planes. They were not desensitized video-game players wantonly dropping ordinance on digital-screen pixels that may well have been bugs. They were soul-searching, confused, guilt-ridden young men, painfully aware of the lives they were taking. (p. 121)

This stirring example illustrates the limitations of the first stance, for even though it picks up on real losses incurred by our digital life, in assuming that the virtual is a degraded copy of the real, it misses the power of the virtual to significantly impact one's relationship to reality.

The first stance conceives of the real as some kind of Platonic Idea that stands above the everyday as a supra-reality, without shadow, and ever more vulnerable to the supposed tarnishing influence of the virtual. We must then always be on guard against the virtual and its seductions of degraded reality to protect and preserve the authenticity of the real. Ironically, however, this hyper-idealization becomes even more disconnected from the real than the virtual it had rejected. It seems, therefore, that we are engaged in a dance where the real and the virtual switch places. The idealized, authentic real, floating above the experience of everyday life, takes on the character of what we were previously calling the virtual. And the virtual, that which was so powerfully guarded against, becomes the new real. Thus, when we take the first stance to its limits, it dissolves into its opposite: an *enantiodromia*! This unexpected, and sudden reversal, where the virtual is now seen as more real than real, lands us in what we will explore next as the second stance.

A great deal of the anti-technological literature, from Carr's *The Shallows* (2011) to Turkle's *Reclaiming Conversation: The Power of Talk in a Digital Age*(2016), can be read, perhaps uncharitably, as manifesting a kind of paranoid vision of the virtual intruding and overtaking the real, where we must, at all costs, protect ourselves from its seduction and protect our children from its encroachment. There is a strong sense of nostalgia that underlies this first stance, a yearning for a by-gone time, where experience was unmediated and untarnished, conversations and connections between people transparent and benevolent, a time when reality had no trouble presenting itself to us in the full promise of what it was and what it could become. Inevitably, for those of us who grew up in a world without the digital, there is a yearning to recover those aspects of life and experience that are degraded by our virtual life. But the trap, of course, is our unconscious tendency to idealize the past, and forget, that all of the same problems that we struggle with in a virtual world i.e., the superficiality of conversations, the lack of presence we bring to relationships, how we objectify the other, the rapacious desire for cheap entertainment, etc., were all there before the digital, albeit in a different form and with a different rhythm. Stance one, in its unceasing disdain for the virtual, can then become a way to hide and seek shelter from all that is changing. But as we will see, there are other considerations that need to be taken up if we are going to arrive at a more nuanced view of the matter.

2 Stance two: The virtual as an upgrade of the real

As a counterpoint to the first stance, our second stance conceives of the virtual as an improvement over the deficiencies and imperfections of the real. "The virtual is to the real as the perfect is to the imperfect," as Doel and Clarke (1999) put it.

> Here, it is the real that is figured as partial, flawed, and lacking; whilst the virtual promises a rectification and final resolution to come. [...] The virtual exudes wonderment by 'correcting' defects in the real; by surpassing the constraints, inadequacies, and limitations of the real – particularly the drag of (real) space-time. (p. 268)

Guattari (1995) points out that for Aristotle the goal of technology was to create what nature found it impossible to accomplish, thereby rectifying what is flawed in the real. Overcoming lack and inadequacy, virtuality substantiates a world of repletion and fullness. It offers, in religious terms, redemption from a fallen world.

The ways in which our technologies seem to surpass the limits and constraints fundamental to the everyday experience of space and time explains the appeal of this second stance and the wonderment that it inspires. With each technological advance, we are dazzled by the new possibilities they provide for registering and sharing with each other the passing moments of our lives. I place a GoPro Hero on my ski helmet, for example, and as I swoosh down the slopes on my snowboard, I can re-create, as never before, for anyone who wants to witness it, what it looks and feels like to actually be immersed in what was once a wholly personal experience, now doubled and rendered accessible to all.

Pre-digitally, we had all sorts of devices, each with a different function, to register the many dimensions that constitute lived experience: tape recorders for sound, cameras for images, and all sorts of gadgets (TVs, VCRs, etc.), to play it all back to us. But with the digital revolution, we don't have to wait for someone else to make the capture, we can make it ourselves, whenever we choose; and the same is true of our music, which we can make and have whenever we want. Moreover, we can have it all immediately, at the moment of its happening. All pre-digital functions are now unified in a portable device that is always ready and at our disposal, exhilarating us with the ever-present possibility of quickly and efficiently capturing the ephemeral everyday.

We can now playfully disassemble and reassemble the historical sequence of life events into an intensely personal and idiomatic bricolage. We can then experience, in communion with our friends and family, our world as we have digitally woven it together. This digital extension fosters our artistry in creatively giving form to our relationship to the temporality of events and provides us with a freedom to shape and reshape experience, desire, and memory that significantly transforms the way we operate. Our relation with others is radically transformed; virtually connected, we are able to experience the depths of emotional intimacy, even without physical proximity.

At the individual level, social networks provide a platform for an expression of emotional life that flows from the interior to the social in a creative interchange between what has taken hold of our consciousness at any given moment, and the receptive subjectivity of our intimates. Collectively, the ever-expanding circles of contact in the social web grant us access to larger aggregations of individuals with whom in the pre-digital past we would never have had any opportunity (or perhaps the desire) for real exchange. The virtual thus inaugurates new circumstances and contexts that transform the very nature of friendships and love relationships.

Selfhood expands in the virtual. The immediacy of what is happening in the world arrives at its threshold, up close and personal, giving birth to new configurations of collective life. Social and political happenings, ordinarily outside the range of everyday consciousness, become transformed into events, lived out in the directness of individual experience. A strongly felt creative interchange takes place between what we are thinking and feeling with those on the other end, who are perpetually in an active, responsive witnessing role to what we are experiencing in the moment. Social networks provide a platform for the expression of our emotional lives that freely traverses the border between the interior intimacy of the self and the exterior collective world.

Our devices become smaller and ever more precise as they mediate our physical and psychological engagement with the world, offering not just instantaneous access in words, images and sounds to the events of the day, in real time, but also enriching and broadening the palette of social and cultural experience. Our screens are filled with consciousness, meaning and affect, as they open us to the happening of the world, in its immediate "now" moments. And all those "nows" – all those important and significant events, personal and collective – are also instantly retrievable from the personal flux of our own temporality, which flows more intensely in our own creative digital reconstruction, liberated from ordinary space and time.

We each carry today a personal, a collective, and a cultural memorial archive, a remarkable library of human culture. Digitally, we not only are able to hold on to nearly every event and experience that has significantly impacted us, but also – and unlike the photo album of the past – we are able to do so in a living, three-dimensional inter-activity that creates endless, mind-boggling possibilities for contemporary thought, art, and experience. The power of the virtual to overcome the constraints of physical space and the inexorability of time captures our imagination and persuades us of the unlimited benefits of the digital.

a The virtualization of everyday life

The drive toward an increasing virtualization of everyday life that we are experiencing today is behind the enhancement of reality that our new technologies achieve. As Lévy (1998) so enthusiastically writes:

> [The virtual] is a fecund and powerful mode of being that expands the process of creation, opens up the future, injects a core of meaning beneath the platitude of immediate physical presence. (p. 16)

That "core of meaning," that universe-expanding virtual power, eclipses the alleged importance of physical presence. The fecundity of virtual interconnectivity not only overcomes the physical limitations of sense perception, thus extending our knowledge of the world, but also transforms and expands the world there is to know. As Noura Aleisa and Karen Renaud (2017) write of the virtual interconnectivity in "The Internet of Things":

> a tool could measure heart rate and body temperature, and then communicate with the energy management system to adjust room temperature depending on the individual's physiological status. Other tools activate smart streetlights, monitor surveillance cameras and control traffic lights. Collected information can be shared with different stakeholders to improve business intelligence (p. 1)

Reality is augmented and transformed by technological devices into this broad network of connections that produces ever-increasing amounts of data and information. We can instantly acquire information about things and people absent to our sense experience, in ways that extend, surpass, and even do away with our ordinary perception. In his book *The Internet of Us*, Lynch (2016) imagines what that virtual realization might look like:

> Imagine a society where smartphones are miniaturized and hooked directly into a person's brain. With a single mental command, those who have this technology – let's call it

neuromedia – can access information on any subject. Want to
know the capital of Bulgaria or the average flight velocity of a
swallow? It's right there. Users of neuromedia can take pictures
with a literal blink of the eye, do complete calculations instantly,
and access, by thought alone, the contact information for anyone
they've ever met. (p. 3)

In the *Black Mirror* episode "The Entire History of You," a world is
envisioned in which most people have a small chip implanted behind
their ear that records everything they do, see or hear. Memories can be
played back at will, either in the privacy of one's mind or on a screen,
in a process known as "re-do."[2] Want to know how that woman sitting to your left responded during the presentation you gave at work?
Re-do the scene you have digitally registered in your mind. Your answer is right there. The limitations of human experiential memory are
gone. Everyone in society can possess inside their minds what was
otherwise only registered outside it, making immediately accessible
what had to be externally accessed before. Our minds become nearly
omniscient and we acquire a new power of intelligence, with which
we can more easily grasp and control the complexities of the world.
And as the advances in Artificial Intelligence promise to better capture
the intrinsic properties of the biological substrate of intelligence –
especially with the adoption of the connectionist model, inspired by
neural networks – we can expect a progressively more accurate simulation of our intuitive and aesthetic capacities, over and above the
more abstract cognitive and symbolic thinking that it has already
potentiated, and so an even greater technological expansion of the
human mind.

But the virtual not only enhances the powers of intelligence, it also
aids in the creation of a more perfect sense of self, as Aleisa and
Renaud (2017) also point out. The virtual amends what is lacking –
from the limitations of one's developmental history – in the very
structures that constitute the self. Freed of the inhibitions that plague
it in the real world, the self is broadened and expanded in virtual
space. If I lack energy and motivation, or have a hard time sticking
with something because of my low frustration tolerance, I may well
discover a new source of agency in the plentifulness of virtuality.
Think of the way children, for example, can more easily engage in
musical creativity or train in a new language, once they can relate to it
digitally. The virtual offers compelling short-cuts to certain kinds of
experiences that I may have unsuccessfully sought to attain in my
everyday world. This is certainly true in the realm of friendship and
romance, but also in learning and education, and in the buzz and
excitement of on-line life that outstrips the ordinariness of quoti-
dian life.

The approach to the virtual that evolves out of *stance two* professes a genuine faith that the digital revolution is ushering humanity to somewhere and something better. In its triumph over the defects in the real, digital virtuality is of unquestionably great benefit to us, making everyday life more interconnected, more comfortable and pleasurable, and ultimately more meaningful. It is no surprise, therefore, that from this positive regard for all the good the digital revolution brings, we are unafraid to allow it to continue to unfold unimpeded, without restraint (and perhaps almost cheering for it) till the end.

b Critique of stance two: The virtual as an alleged upgrade of the real

One cannot help but note that there is a triumphant note to stance two. The world, in its digital dimension, becomes transparent to us as a revitalized object of knowledge and experience. Its frustrating insufficiency, its obdurate muteness, is finally overcome. The digital gives us the power to make it speak. But the temerity of leaving the actual for the virtual warrants further scrutiny.

For Plato, traditionally understood, the sensible world of everyday experience is imperfect, a mere copy (*simulacrum*) because the senses only provide us with imitations (*simulacra*) of perfect, ideal forms. The first stance, as we remember, sees the virtual as a false copy of the real in the same way that for Plato the sensible is a false copy of the Ideal Forms. But the apotheosis of that position is when the ever more idealized real itself becomes perfect. And, just as the Platonic forms themselves are threatened by the sensible, this pristine reality is threatened by the debasing virtual.

So, whereas in the first stance, the virtual seduces us into thinking that we are encountering the real (when we are actually caught up with a false and inferior copy), in the second stance, the drive to perfect what is lacking in the world, on the contrary, ends up overtaking the real and leaving it behind. This is precisely the critique advanced by Jean Baudrillard, who observed, that while modern societies organized around production, postmodern societies organize around technological "simulations" (e.g., television, movies, and computer screens). In our current moment, the acme of all technological simulations is the promise of the Internet of Everything to overlay upon the world a self-correcting digital upgrade.

Western culture up until modernity has conceived knowledge and perception as a matter of representation, and relied primarily on models of truth as correspondence. It is through the representational capacity of the mind that knowledge is possible, and philosophy's central concern has been to provide it a reliable foundation, and to spell out criteria to discriminate those representations that did, and those that did not, succeed in accurately rendering the world. The underlying dualism – of a mind that knows and a world that is known – was articulated by both rationalists (Descartes, Leibniz, Spinoza, et al.) and empiricists (Locke, Hume, Hobbes, et al.) in modernity. Contemporary philosophy may be understood in terms of the rejection of this dualism. On the one hand, coherentist theories of meaning in the Anglo-American philosophical tradition (as in the pragmatism of James Dewey and William James, for instance), conceive knowledge as a function of the coherence between beliefs rather than any correspondence with reality. On the other hand, post-structuralism in Continental philosophy (as Barthes, Lacan, Derrida, Foucault, et al.), are also instances of this rejection of the representational model and its reliance on a correspondence theory of truth.

In so radically breaking with the representational model, these "postmodern" or contemporary positions go too far, according to Baudrillard, for they call forth a world of unmoored signifiers, each referring to the other in an endless cascade of drifting and disrupted meanings. Baudrillard understands our media-saturated, consumer society as reflecting this epistemological crisis where we find ourselves caught up in endless loops of images that have little connection to an outside, external reality. Inside the virtual world, surrounded by mere simulations, we become narcotically self-absorbed, and hypnotized, by our absorption in the screen. The existential reality of embodiment is severely disrupted (Baudrillard might say, wholly obliterated) in this unending labyrinth of mirrors reflecting only mirrors. Thus, the ultimate price we pay for the virtual world is the disappearance of the real, as the world itself becomes, in Baudrillard's (1994) poignant term, the "Desert of the Real."

Simulated reality empties out the world, forcing us to seek life, animation, and vitality by fleeing to the virtual. Entertainment, information, and communication technologies generate intensity and immediacy, and thus overcome the dullness of everyday, ordinary experience. And yet, this turn away from the world only increases our desire for the real, for what we end up encountering in the virtual is not the real, but its digital double, the hyperreal.

Baudrillard, in the 1980s, located the hyperreal in places like Disneyland, malls and consumer havens, and TV sports and large-screen blockbuster movies. For us, the situation is very different as hyperreality has taken on wholly new forms and is now all-pervasive. Today, even our most sacred cultural spaces are turned into commercial simulacra, into Disney Worlds, that fuel the voyeuristic madness of tourism, for example. Living in the digital age, as opposed to the postmodern age that Baudrillard was describing, provides instantaneous access to intensified experience, which seems to touch just about everything. This overflowing well of hyperreality affects our sexuality, our politics, and just about every other aspect of human experience.

As we continue to develop our critique of the second stance, "hyperreality," "hyper-consumption," "hyper-connectedness," "simulation," and "simulacrum" will serve us as orienting concepts to explore the digital developments of the last decade, since the introduction of the iPhone in 2007. In a world of iPhones and iPads and recording and tracking devices everywhere, as well as our everyday social interactions mediated by automated processes, Baudrillard's reflections on the idea of hyperreality are more pertinent and familiar now than when he wrote at the beginning of the digital revolution. Ironically, he died the very year the iPhone was made publicly available.

It is our contention that even though Baudrillard's ideas were clearly prophetic, digital culture has taken a whole new and unpredictable turn since he first wrote about it in the 1980s. The use of technology as an upgrade of reality – correcting its defects, overcoming its gaps and voids – has taken on an unprecedented force in the digital era. It has become part of the very fabric of our experience, which has resulted in a near total embrace of the hyperreal. The porousness of everyday life, its existential complexity, is substituted with an experience that feels more real than real, and bestows upon the events of our lives a quality of fullness and presence. But that filling in, that overflowing of meaning and experiential immediacy that is granted by digital hyperreality, casts its own shadow. The exhilaration of hyperreality fizzes out, becoming a one-dimensional, monotone sameness. Too much of everything turns into nothing. The world is stripped of its animation and vitality, life is flattened out and divested of meaning. In other words, hyperreality, as we will explore, partakes of the logic of the digital pharmakon. So, although inspired and forever indebted to Baudrillard's thinking, we will at the same time attempt to freely encounter the hyperreality of our own era as opposed to his.

3 A contemporary phenomenology of digital hyperreality

What we intend to do in what follows is less to go beyond a critique of the second stance and more a reflection of the present state of our hyperrealized society. It is no longer a speculation with regard to the value of the virtual, but a meditation on what it actually means to be now traversed by the virtual everywhere. In the end we will be able to recognize the pharmakon, which advances us to consider the nature of the virtual, rather than to arrive at a third "position."

We are living in a period of history when the hyperreality of the digital virtual thoroughly permeates the institutional, cultural, and psychological structures through which we apprehend the world. Given the rapidity of these transformations, we lack adequate concepts to understand, as well as metabolize, the effects hyperreality is having on our experience of the world, and our relation to ourselves and others. In the following passage, Giegerich (2007) describes what it feels like today to be living with these changes.

> Surfing [the net] goes along with thrill. Thrill is that state in which the individual is absolutely in the Now. Here we have to come back to [...] the indispensability today of the stimulation of the emotions and the importance of the sensual impression something makes on people over against what it is that makes the impression. [...] It is the intensity of the impression or affect that really counts [...] The sheer affective intensity creates a Here!, Now!, This!, and I. Absolute immediacy is the goal. (p. 327)

This intensification of experience that Giegerich calls "absolute immediacy" transforms reality into hyperreality; "hyper," as in having a lot or even too much of something, in this case, reality. The digital speeds up and dynamizes its analogical counterpart and brings a heightened, electric feeling that enlivens experience. The faster they speed up and speed by, the more real and alive things feel. And when things move that fast, time can be suspended altogether, allowing its movement without the loss it implacably exacts in the real. By generating a subjectively intensified, ongoing register of the movement of our own experience in time, our devices enable us to escape the costs of human temporality. The hyperreality effect!

It's not only that we can now stop the very thing that resists any stopping, namely the movement of time. We stop it *in real time*, as historical time is set in the background. Think again of the use of instant replay in sports, where we place before us a past moment and make it a center of attention in the midst of flowing time. We sense the growing tension between the real happening of the game that continues to progress and our fixation on the frozen moment.

With this newfound capacity to bracket a moment of real time, temporal movement is suspended, and we find ourselves in a new (virtual) space of collective experience that disarticulates the coordinates of analogical spatio-temporality and complexifies our conception of what is real. Whereas traditional film memorializes our historical and collective life, the cyber-register hyperrealizes and personalizes it. The digital register of experience gives each one of us control over the archiving process of our own life. What we register is inherently autobiographical – it is ultimately about what is happening and what has happened to me: "Here!, Now!, This! and I." Memoir, a more subjectivized version of the classical autobiography, has become the dominant literary modality of our time.

As time, truth, and meaning become hyperrealized, a vertiginous buzz permeates our experience of being in the world, our ethics, and our politics. We now live in an era where we can no longer distinguish the real from the copy, fact from fiction, objectivity from subjectivity. In our global, interconnected lives we don't have just digital presidents, but hyperreal ones. The far-left French presidential candidate, Jean-Luc Mélenchon, for instance, appeared in 2017 at seven rallies simultaneously, thanks to the wonders of hologram technology. Is it worth asking anymore for the real Mélenchon to stand up?

a The hyperrealization of meaning: Limits, addiction, and the incapacity to metabolize experience

We are flooded today by an unstoppable torrent of unruly and world-shattering forces that burst forth from the digital, undoing the balance and rhythm that structured the analogical world. As we try to digest the personal and cultural events that relentlessly swirl around us, our very capacity for making sense of what is happening, both personally inside and socially, is being hyperactivated. This is evidenced in our dramatic obsession with the present moment. As Rushkoff (2013) observes:

> Everything is live, real time, and always-on. It is not a mere speeding up, however much our lifestyles and technologies have accelerated the rate at which we attempt to do things. It's more of a diminishment of anything that isn't happening right now – and the onslaught of everything that supposedly is ... It's [...] why email is giving way to texting, and why blogs are being superseded by twitter feeds. It's why kids in school can no longer follow linear arguments; why narrative structures collapsed into reality TV; [...] If the end of the twentieth century can be characterized by futurism, the twenty-first can be defined by presentism. (pp. 2–3)

Rushkoff's notion of presentism captures that sense of unceasing attunement to the immediate moment where events are presented simultaneous to their actual occurrence. In this regard, we remember being struck when first hearing about – what has now become a very common phenomenon – the particular ways in which a young man was staying in touch on his smartphone with the events of his girlfriend's life, while she was away at school in another city for a semester. Whatever she was doing – going to a party, studying for an exam, watching a documentary, hiking with a friend, eating, taking a shower, etc. – was posted in video form on her Instagram story feed so that this young man, watching from his digital perch, was able to immerse himself in the present happenings of her daily life. He was there as witness, even if not as a direct participant, commenting in "real time" despite the asymmetry of their electronic interaction as well as the thousand-mile span that separated them. Given the immediacy of his virtual presence, he was able to outmaneuver the feelings of sadness he had for her leaving, his lonesomeness, their not "really" being together.

In our hyper-connected world, the other is unceasingly present, always available, perhaps even more available than when they are in the same physical space. That constant availability of the object clearly affects our relation to separation and separateness, being alone as opposed to being alone with the virtual other.

The present moment, always being on, everything always available and within our reach, creates an ever-churning river of meaning. In our unceasing engagement with the personal, political, and cultural events of the day, as they appear on our phones, and computers, in text, or video form, we experience the overflowing of that perpetual scroll. An infinite realm of possibility opens to us – every book ever written, every song ever recorded, every fetish ever imagined – all in standing reserve, ready to be actualized. This sense of unending digital potential inspires a feeling of boundlessness that taps into the primordial roots of our earliest omnipotence, when our most ardent wishes and their actualization were one. This spawns the digital fever of contemporary life.

The wishing self, in front of the screen, has free rein over the realization of its fantasies without delay. It is no longer a matter of simply viewing a movie, seeing a play or watching a television show, where the beginning, middle, and end occur in a time-bounded frame of predictable duration. That framing of experience is a feature of the sequential temporality of the analog world that stands in marked contrast to the haphazardness and freedom that is possible in the digital (where there are no temporal constraints). One can now watch multiple episodes of a series, or movie after movie, in rapid succession, allowing oneself to be carried away by the hyperrealized narrative world that comes alive on the screen. "Binge-watching"[3] is that fully immersive experience that feels like it never has to end, as the dull routine of everydayness and its slower, more methodical and exacting rhythms of time are displaced. When we are finally ready to stop the story – say, after watching the entire season of a show in one sitting – we are surprised, even shocked, by how much actual time has passed.

But you can also see different episodes simultaneously, or skip through them to only the parts that interest you. In this world, beginning, middle and end make no demand upon us. Surfing, gaming, and Internet pornography are all examples of activities in which digital selves exist in a span of time that readily dissociates from the rhythms of the body and its historical time. Rushkoff's (2013) "presentism" is a hyperreality effect of the digital, that fundamentally changes our relationship to those aspects of reality that occur with a different temporal pacing, for example, things that move slower and require patience, the fact that something ends, or that something has a definitive beginning, and the sense of a pause or break between them, and so on.

If in our delineation of the second stance we emphasized the wonderment and creative potential of this immediate access – for instance, the ability to connect virtually to a distant friend, somewhere on the other side of the globe – here we must consider what hyperreality may be doing to ordinary, everyday, localized experience. Is it creating an undue dependence on a certain intensity of meaning, without which things begin to lose their sharpness and focus and fade from our mind? Bursts of reinforcing dopamine aside, is that why we can't stop ourselves from looking down at our phones? And does it not lessen our interest, blur our vision of things, when we check our timelines, messages, and texts, no matter where we are or what else we may be doing? Are we then not less able to bear the experience of emptiness or indeterminateness in the everyday? These seem like legitimate yet very uncomfortable questions to raise in a hyperrealized world.

i Digital addiction

Hyperreality covers up the lack inherent to the real (i.e., the fissures and disjunctions in experience) with the infinite potential for anything to become animated at any moment in time. And we, in turn, are unconsciously driven to fill in the moments of absence, loss, and the passing away of things that haunt the everyday with the unceasing plenitude of virtual presence. This is most clearly evident in the panic that sets in when someone loses their phone, for instance, or the gaming system of an adolescent is precipitously taken away by their parents. It is symptomatic of an impending dread of the gray dullness of life. Or, in Freud's hands, it is the return of the repressed, now as the ever-present lack in the real.

Emotional experience, of all stripes and varieties, often contains a painful dimension. According to Bion (1983), a crucial part of human development involves the capacity to bear psychic pain, and in fact, its development is essential for the growth of the self. This idea that there is psychic work to be done with one's painful emotional experiences is expressive of the unyielding realities of a person's existential situatedness: what has vanished and must be mourned, the inevitability of suffering, both bodily and psychically, and, of course, one's inescapable attunement to loss and finitude.

But in a hyperrealized culture that so well shields us from these gaps and indeterminacies, we may no longer be able to learn how to metabolize the kind of psychic pain that is an essential part of how we process our emotional lives. Or, in other words, if we cannot find a way to bear the ever-present lack inherent to the real, what the philosopher Charles Scott (1999) calls "time's losses," a good deal of our psychic resources then have to be devoted to holding that lack at bay. The ego, with its own particular set of needs and desires, is now armed with a potent meaning-creating device that can overcome the void of life's emptier moments by situating the self in something much more immediately compelling. The tedium of the world, which can, paradoxically, generate its own harvest of creativity and spontaneity, is mindlessly dismissed.

Because every event can be experienced, and re-experienced in its now-moment, digital addiction becomes, in essence, an addiction to this permanently available and ever-emerging immediacy. Hyperreality, this heightened enhancement of experience, is the drug that feeds our digital addiction. It is what underlies the craving for more, whether it be through pornography, gaming, shopping, or the compulsive search for facts and knowledge. And in our need for the hyperreal, just like with any addiction, the everyday world of non-hyperrealized reality becomes increasingly empty, tedious, and often unbearable.

The digital media tries to compensate for this growing gap by making the simulations themselves feel ever more intensely personal and engaging. The more hyperreal our simulations become, the less they are connected to the real. The less we are connected to the real, the less we can resist the urge to turn, ever more frenetically, toward hyperreality to compensate for this lack. This is its addictive circle, and brings us back to the undecidable logic of the pharmakon where "the needed remedy is also the poison that generates the need" (Russell, 2020, p. 105).

Given the power of digital simulations to so accurately mimic reality, we become entangled in a confounding maze where it can never be "real" enough, because the yearning for more "realness" is created by the fact that it is not real at all. We are seduced into believing that if we can just keep more of our life and our mind immersed in them, we can finally find full satisfaction in our simulations. Madness, as Einstein said, is doing the same thing while expecting a different outcome. Since it's the nature of a wish to clash with what is actually possible, a gap opens between what is there for us in the virtual world and what is not in the real. Because this gap remains unconscious, we are forever prodded to return to the virtual to overcome it. But because it is impossible to reach what we are seeking there and yet we are convinced we can, our virtual life is sustained by a dire illusion.

ii Loss of quality

Hyperreality seduces us with its profligate offerings, and in the rush of the addiction, it is no longer what it offers, but *that* it offers which matters; just as Don Juan, in his unsatisfiable desire for conquest, no longer cares about the particularities of the woman who comes next, but just that it is another one. Quality yields to quantity, and the excessive need to measure displaces everything else, even desire, thus becoming an undeniable symptom of the digital age. As a result, obsession and compulsion overtake us, and reality is spurned for the thrill and satisfaction of quantification. A walk in the park, for instance, is no longer a walk in the park but 3372 additional steps to add to the 2678 already taken, in the quest for a daily total sum, with the euphoria of its completion. And if we think back on the experience of the primitive artist that painted the animal images in ancient caves, as McBurney (2011) says, what truly separates us from them is "not the space of time but the sense of time. In our minute splicing of our lives into milliseconds, we live separated from everything that surrounds us" (*The Guardian*, March 17, 2011).

We are no longer connected to our bodies through the sensual resonances of the inner, but through the external measurements of our gadgets. When we put in our AirPods to silence the external world, we cut ourselves off as well from the internal. When we wear them on a jog, and immerse ourselves in music, it becomes more difficult to listen to the signals emanating from within. The breath, which normally marks our step, is muted. Oblivious to our rhythm and endurance, we fail to mark an even step or run at a good pace. And if to AirPods we add Fitbits, Apple Watches, or any other wearable, we track our workouts but are estranged from the lived experience in our flesh, numbed to everything inside and outside us. Obsessed with our digital attunement, we can't stop looking, we can't stop checking, and the entire experience of the jog is narrowed to the appearance of small numbers on our screen, and the tracking of our progress, where we compare today's run to yesterday's and anticipate tomorrow's.

If behind all digital addictions there is a hidden desire for omnipotence and control, then we may be exacerbating our all-too-human disavowal of the unpredictability of bodily life by making its processes something that needs close monitoring and supervision. All that quantitative scrutiny of our frail, contingent bodies (and remember, our wearables are now with us even while we are sleeping, measuring our heart, our pulse and our REM cycles) makes us obsessively hypervigilant about what is going in and what is coming out. Our oral and anal predispositions to the world are over-stimulated by the digital.

Like any addictive substance or behavior, the shot of hyperreality – whether it takes the form of closely inspecting what is happening inside our bodies or giving ourselves over to the intensified experience of reality that happens when we enter a virtual world – can never truly give us what we actually want or, perhaps more importantly, need. Hyperreality and its addictive circle jettisons us back to the assumptions of the first stance, where the simulation is always inferior to the real. But, in a further twist to the problem, because our simulations have become so "real," they feed our unconscious yearning to possess and ultimately domesticate reality. Instead, however, we must learn to accept the uncalculable dimensions of bodily experience and tolerate and bear its psychic demands. To recover from digital addiction is therefore to recover the real.

iii The narcissistic excesses of hyperreality

As Ian McEwan (2016) points out:

> We are now just past the sort of toddlerhood of the digital age. Millennials certainly take it for granted that we live in a new era, mostly of self-expression, but not so much of listening. We are not Hamlet so much these days. We are broadcasters of the Self. Selfhood is extremely important of course, who can deny it. But when you make the self the outer limit of your politics, you then begin to ignore a great deal of the attitudes, situations, dilemmas, misery of others. [...] Listening, that is abandoning the self, and abandoning yourself to another's point of view is what the Internet has not given us. It has given us trolls, it has given us tsunamis of opinion, but not listening. Perhaps it will take a bend in the future that we cannot yet foresee.

The self is innately vulnerable to narcissistic inflation, grandiosity, and its own aggrandizement, and the digital capitalizes upon this primordial predisposition. If, in the inner recesses of the psyche, the self is as radically unfixed as depth psychology asserts, narcissism functions as a strong compensatory impulse to oppose that flux by firming it up, countering its indeterminateness through strong identifications. The growth of the individual is a dialectical process between the creation of narcissistic structures that fortify the self by keeping out what is not-me and yet at the same time are permeable and flexible enough to make transformative use of what is other.

Neither overly sealed and buttoned up nor too permeable and open, the goal is to stream the self with just enough narcissistic libido that it can hold in some kind of workable tension the inevitable clash between the me and not-me worlds.

From the perspective of our critique of stance two, the digital milieu has the power to wreak havoc on that uneasy tension, generating pathological forms of narcissism that shut down access to otherness. As McEwan points out, by its ceaseless broadcasting of who it is, what it believes and how it desires, the digital self may hamper the possibility of a certain mode of self-abandonment necessary to empathically enter into another's point of view. An important effect of the narcissistic inflation of hyperreality is that the Internet becomes an algorithmically defined echo-chamber ("filter-bubbles" as they are called) relaying information that only reinforces our own views, hemming us in and making us oblivious to the other. The self has little resistance against this plunge into its personalized digital space of resonance. There is nothing more involving and gratifying than having our own sense of the world, our proclivities and idiosyncrasies, expanded and amplified.

The ultimate aim of this narcissistic expansion is the immortality of the self. The urgent need in our species to rescue it from its temporal impermanence, to outstrip our human limitations, is exacerbated by technology's promise of overcoming death. As O'Gorman (2015) points out:

> This promise comes in many shapes and forms, from medical technologies designed to extend life, to artificial intelligence research that seeks to transfer human consciousness into machines, to highly immersive video games and the identity-morphing spaces of the Internet. This false promise of immortality is facilitated largely by our technologically mediated ability to vanquish space and time, to reproduce and extend ourselves electronically through transmission and storage. (p. 9)

Indeed, the self's desire for enhancement and expansion spurs on the growth of technology and the digital magnifies this essential impulse. Conversely, technological extensions promote the self by constantly making its life easily accessible in images. As we scroll through our digital files, it is the snapshots of the self that we cannot stop looking at. They are the undeniable proof of our existence, a bulwark against the thrust of time and its movement. In this regard, consider the selfie phenomenon: Inversely to how Dorian Gray's hidden painting portrayed his true self, ravished by the degenerative effects of time and social debauchery, our public selfies preserve an unchanging, static, posed, and well-fashioned self.

As we go through the day, with all of its many tasks, the digital makes it possible for us to permanently register everything that we do, thus offering the self a kind of immortality. By overcoming its geographical limitations and facilitating its expressiveness, the presence of the self is augmented and expanded. Each person can then indeed become a broadcaster of herself, the events of her life, the people and places she encounters, the food she eats, even her most private moments, delivering a veritable personal daily to all of the world. The ordinary narcissistic strivings to be liked, to have friends, to be known, are transformed into an insatiable demand for thousands of friends on Facebook or followers in Twitter and Instagram, constant gratification through likes and comments, and the permanent attention from the inexhaustible audience in the web. The virtual exaltation of the human desire for closeness and connection turns a basic psychological need into an unquenchable desire.

In the virtual world, the "I" is propelled into the center of action. The digital capture of an event that fixes it outside of time inevitably inflates the self's importance, and turns it into an idol. This individual narcissism becomes a cultural titanism that demands everyone to behold and bear witness to a psychologically intensified and overly libidinized self that knows no bounds. Digital narcissism is of an entirely different order than anything that has ever occurred.

The self's narcissism is hyperrealized by the voyeuristic desire of its virtual audience (i.e., nearly all of us), engaged as we are with digital culture. It is of little importance whether our voyeurism results from admiration or denigration, for it is driven by impact, not substance. Winnicott famously said of the developmental process that there is no such thing as a baby, only a baby and its mother. We could say of our current social predicament that there is no such thing as the self, only the self and its digital feed.

That desire for permanence has spread beyond our representations of the self to infect also our relation to the objects we encounter every day. When at the museum, for instance, surrounded by works of art, we are now often overtaken by an urge to capture the objects and the moment, so as to make them available whenever, even if we never look at the photographs again. A substitute mind lives in our devices, a proxy memory, an ever-expanding archive of the self and its objects, furthering its expanse and reach. Once the event is captured, the shot snapped, we can rest easy and maybe, if only for an instant, actually look at what stands before us, before we repeat the same vicious cycle. The power the digital grants us to outwit impermanence transforms the way we are actually living. The art and cunning genius of digitality lies in its effectively responding to our panic about the ephemerality of the moment; it serves as a shield against change and becoming.

b Digitally induced death anxiety

The compulsion to turn to the virtual world to escape the ravages of time intensifies as everyday reality becomes an increasing object of technological control. No moment is lost anymore because we can bring it back, instantly. Unlimited and infallible memory now exist alongside a permanent and eternal archive of the past. We experience a sense of omnipotence and grandeur, as uncertainty and unpredictability are all but vanquished. The conviction that we are able to so effectively ward off dispossession and disappearance feeds the feeling that ultimately we have the same power against our mortal condition.

These pocket-sized disavowing devices can endlessly forestall the inevitable, promising us a refuge from death. Yet, at the same time, in a peculiar kind of rebounding effect – a return of the repressed, as it were – that which we so desperately want to vanquish finds its way back. A key feature of digital life entails this unceasing and unstoppable oscillation, this haunted relationship to mortality, as we are drawn closer to it at the very same time that we drive it away.

We use our phones and computers and tracking devices to stay in touch with those we care for, bolstering the illusion that if we can just keep an eye on them, nothing bad can happen. And indeed, the invention of the smartphone has actually, to a certain extent, made that possible. If someone is endangered, we will know, and know fast. And maybe we can help them. Many emergencies have been averted because we have our phone and nearly instant access to the other, no matter where they may be. As a result of this intricate network of connections, many lives have been saved. Given this incredible power to always know in an instant, where someone is – and even, if in tracking and surveillance mode, what they are doing – it's not a far stretch to see how we become convinced that as long as the other is connected to me through their phone, no true ill is to befall them. The unconscious fantasy that so pervades digital life is that we somehow insure, with this constant monitoring, that our loved ones will be safe.

The terrible irony is that in safeguarding ourselves against loss, dispossession, and ultimately death, we are also unconsciously enacting a perverse and stultifying relationship to mortality. Our phones, at any moment, day or night, are on the ready to alert us to the injury or disappearance of someone dear to us, someone we love and care for. This contributes to the feeling today of a persistent underlying death anxiety, as our worry about the other – we haven't yet heard from them, are they OK? did they get to where they were going? – only intensifies. We compulsively turn to our phone for reassurance even though, paradoxically, we know deep down it could also be the potential bearer of bad news. This relationship becomes our modern era's *amor fati.* Drop it, break it, lose it, and you are cut off from fate. This explains why our devices can take on more importance than our friends, lovers, and family. This dynamic underlies an existentially rooted fetishism that keeps us desperately tied to them in a simultaneous avowal and disavowal of death. We monitor, we wait, we worry.

Coda: A brief reflection on the interrelation between the two stances

In the first stance, the virtual is fake trickery, seducing us into believing that we are experiencing the real when we are merely experiencing the falseness of virtual simulation that is distinct from and degrades the real. In eschewing the virtual, what is sought from the perspective of the first stance is the reality of unmediated pure presence that can only be found in the real. It is only by staying with the non-virtual darkness and opaqueness of experience that the real can be encountered.

The reality of unmediated pure presence that is being sought in the first stance is, ironically enough, exactly what is being sought in the second stance. But whereas the first stance achieves it by separating the virtual from the real in order to save the real, the second stance seeks that same unmediated presence in the virtual, which is set apart from the time/space drag of the real. It is in the pure presence of the virtual that the world is repaired.

For the anti-technologists of the first stance, we enter pure presence in the realness of the world, where its material limits awaken us to our embodiment and our mortality beyond the virtual. For the pro-technologists of the second stance, however, the ontological maladjustments of the real are fixed by the virtual copy. Instead of degrading the real, the virtual creates another, perfected world, where we transcend the restrictions of material life. There is an uncanny surprise, then, as we think about the interrelationship between our two stances. Those who are committed to creating a virtual upgrade of the real are claiming for themselves the very same territory that the anti-technologists claim to have found outside or beyond or before the virtual. But both are committed to the One-All of unmediated presence – an essential reality in its own right.

Each stance, in its own way, attempts to split off a dimension of the world in seeking out its conception of this unmediated reality. Pure presence in the first stance has no traces of the virtual and pure presence in the second stance has no traces of the real. The anti-technologists' commitment to unmediated presence, as that which lies beyond the virtual, and the pro-technologists' contention that we can only reach pure presence by creating a perfect double, ironically articulate the same suspicious utopian vision of reality.

Indeed we may conclude that the problem with these stances, as compelling as each one is, is not what they hold but the presupposition that they stand on opposite sides. In other words, the problem is having to choose. There is not one or the other bank that we need to take, but the river itself, to which we now turn.

Notes

1 There is a feature in Facebook called "legacy contacts" that allows you to nominate an executor of your personal page, responsible for keeping it active after your death, as a virtual tombstone for your social network. The appointed can choose photos of yours to greet visitors, write messages on your behalf and even select the friends who can view your memorial page. Eter9 is an actual website that further develops this idea of virtual survival. Brooker merely takes this fantasy one step further into the digital reconstruction of the person.
2 This is already a patented product in 2018 that Sony intends to put in the market in the near future.
3 It is now widely known that there are certain formulas that content producers like Netflix use to make their series "binge-worthy," ways of manipulating the telling of the story (e.g., hooking the viewers by ending early episodes with cliff-hangers), or concentrating in the marketing of the show, say, for example, on four central characters, two evil, two good, to keep the story simple and keep a viewer watching. Media critics speak of this as a reduction in how we now tell stories.

References

Aleisa, N., and Renaud, K. (2017) Privacy of the Internet of Things: A Systematic Literature Review (Extended Discussion). Retrieved from https://arxiv.org/ftp/arxiv/papers/1611/1611.03340.pdf

Baudrillard, J. (1994) *Simulacra and Simulation*. Ann Arbor, MI: University of Michigan Press.

Benjamin, W. (1979) *One Way Street and Other Writings*. New York: Harcourt Brace.

Bion, W. (1983) *Learning from Experience*. New York: Jason Aronson.

Carr, N. (2011) *The Shallows: What the Internet Is Doing to Our Brains*. New York: W. W. Norton & Co.

Doel, M.A., and Clarke, D.B. (1999) Virtual Worlds: Simulation, Suppletion, S (ed)uction and Simulacrum. In M. Crang, P. Crang, and J. May (Eds.), *Virtual Geographies: Bodies, Space and Relations*. London: Routledge.

Frankel, R. (2002) A Winicottian View of an American Tragedy. In L. Caldwell (Ed.), *The Elusive Child* (pp. 153–176). London: Karnac Books.

Giegerich, W. (2007) *Technology and the Soul* (vol. 2). New Orleans: Spring Books.

Guattari, F. (1995) *Chaosmosis: An Ethico-aesthetic Paradigm*. Sydney: Power Publications.

Heidegger, M. (1977) The Question Concerning Technology. In *Basic Writings* (pp. 283–318). New York: Harper and Row.

Kant, I. (1992) *Crítica de la facultad de juzgar*. Caracas: Monte Ávila.

Lacan, Jacques (1977) *Écrits: A Selection*(Alan Sheridan, Trans.). New York: W. W. Norton.

Lanier, J. (2018) Social Media is Ruining Your Life. Retrieved from https:// www.google.com.pe/search?q=jaron+lanier+interview+on+how+social +media+ruins+your+life&oq=jaron+lanier+interview+on+what+soci&aqs= chrome.1.69i57j0.10424j1j7&sourceid=chrome&ie=UTF-8

LaPlanche, J. (2015) *Between Seduction and Inspiration: Man* (J. Mehlman, Trans.). New York: The Unconscious in Translation.

Lemma, A. (2017) *The Digital Age on the Couch: Psychoanalytic Practice and New Media*. London: Routledge.

Lévy, P. (1998) *Becoming Virtual: Reality in the Digital Age*. New York: Plenum.

Lynch, P. (2016) *The Internet of Us: Knowing More and Understanding Less in the Age of Big Data*. New York: W. W. Norton.

McEwan, I. (2016) Interview with Jane Clayson [radio]. *On Point*, September 21. Boston: WBUR.

McBurney, S. (2011) Herzog's Cave of Forgotten Dreams: The real art underground. The Guardian, 17th March, 2011.

McLuhan, M. (1994) *Understanding Media: The Extensions of Man*. Cambridge: MIT Press.

Ogden, T. H. (2001) Reading Winnicott. *Psychoanalytical Quarterly*, *70*(2), 299–323.

O'Gorman, M. (2015) *Necromedia*. Minneapolis, MN: University of Minnesota Press.

Rushkoff, D. (2013) *Present Shock: When Everything Happens Now*. New York: Penguin.

Russell, J. (2020) *Psychoanalysis and Deconstruction: Freud's Psychic Apparatus*. London: Routledge.

Scott, C.E. (1999) *The Time of Memory*. New York: SUNY Press.

Turkle, S. (2012) Connected but Alone? (https://www.youtube.com/watch?v= t7Xr3AsBEK4).

Turkle, S. (2016) *Reclaiming Conversation: The Power of Talk in a Digital Age*. New York: Penguin.

Wittgenstein, L. (1980) *Culture and Value*. Chicago: University of Chicago Press.

Wittgenstein, L. (1993) On Frazer's "Golden Bough." In J. Klagge and A. Nordmann (Eds.), *Philosophical Occasions 1912–1951* (pp. 115–155). Indianapolis: Hackett Publishing Company, Inc.

Žižek, S. (2003) *Conversations with Žižek* (S. Žižek and G. Daly, Eds.). Cambridge: Polity Press.

4 The inexorable flow

At the still point of the turning world. Neither flesh nor fleshless;
Neither from nor towards; at the still point, there the dance is,
But neither arrest nor movement. And do not call it fixity,
Where past and future are gathered. Neither movement from nor
towards,
Neither ascent nor decline. Except for the point, the still point,
There would be no dance, and there is only the dance.

–TS Eliot, Burnt Norton, Four Quartets (1980)

Prelude

We want to advance in this chapter a third interpretation of the virtual, but it would be a misnomer if we called it "a third stance." It
could imply that we have arrived at the synthesis – an overcoming, a
sublation, a Hegelian *Überhebung* – of the previous two stances. But
this third reading of the virtual does not synthesize; instead, it re-
pudiates the dynamics of polarization that the first two stances enact,
and battles against the utopianism that underwrites them.

As we advance this new position, we will draw heavily from Deleuze
(1994), who proposes we consider the virtual as opposed, not to the
real as we usually do, but to the "actual." In his famous words, "the
virtual is fully real in so far as it is virtual" and "the virtual [is] '[r]eal
without being actual …'" (p. 208). In the previous chapter the real and
the virtual were seen dualistically as "immutable and inalienable
forms" (Doel and Clarke, 1999, p. 270), each separate and protected
from the "degrading" effects of the other. Here, however, the virtual
and the real are in a constant inter-flowing. No dualism is operative.
And so this new reading of the virtual dislocates the previous two
stances, for neither real nor virtual is more originary or more authentic; they don't compete or threaten one another. Here, real and
virtual amalgamate in the Heraclitean embrace of Becoming.

The virtual does not reside outside of the real but dwells at its very
heart. For example, fantasy and imagination are virtual dimensions of

the mind that although not actual name something real in our experience. "Real" therefore is not only the actual but at the same time the virtual. The real is no longer synonymous with the actual, and the virtual is not opposed to the real.

Splitting what is virtually there from what is actually there, to declare that only what is actual is real, evidences a desire to sediment the real; it amounts to a resistance to change. For if the virtual informs the real even before it is actualized, if there is no originary model that the virtual copies (whether distorting or improving it), then everything is potentially changing all the time; the virtual inseminates and is inseminated by the actual.

Deleuze describes traditional Platonic philosophy as "the dogmatic image of thought" because of its *rigor mortis*, its resistance to all change; in taking all thinking to be representation and not leaving any room for other modes of thought, Plato's conception of thinking is excessively constraining. It thus subordinates mutable sensible experience to an immutable and transcendent (intelligible) reality. So Deleuze envisions instead, an ontology of movement and continuous transformation, where reality is an inexorable flow of virtual and actual that opens room for the acknowledgement of temporal movement and change. Deleuze's ontology is not wedded to permanence and immutability, but is committed to the quickening of becoming. Heraclitus unhorses Parmenides.

Once we free ourselves from the dichotomy of real and virtual, it becomes obvious – as was implicit in our discussion on the emergence of the virtual in Chapters 1 and 2 – that the virtual is an essential dimension of *all* human experience. We mistakenly think that with the advent of Virtual Reality, the virtual is for the first time transforming the way we live and perceive the world; that thanks to our technological advances, we are now finally in full control of the virtual. But digital technology simply provides us new ways of engaging or modulating the virtual; and as today we are tempted to identify the virtual with its specific digital instantiation, we need to explore virtuality's embeddedness in the real.

1 The Deleuzian simulacrum

Whereas the Platonic simulacrum (or simulation) is always conceived as a mere copy of an original, the Deleuzian simulacrum rejects the assumption of a stable immutable original that is opposed to the copy. By rejecting the implicit dualism involved in that conception, the simulacrum is freed from the demand for sameness and identity and welcomes instead the acknowledgment of difference and change. It moves us beyond the polarity of real vs. copy. As Doel and Clarke (1999) put it, the Deleuzian simulacrum is "without original archetype or prototype" (p. 282).

> We [...] begin, then, by simply casting off the denigration of virtuality as a dubious and duplicitous xerography. Hereinafter, it is acceptable to love the simulacrum; and to love it all the more for departing from re-presentation – for turning the 're' of representation from just another one of the same to a wholly transformative production of something other than the same. (Doel and Clarke, 1999, p. 266)

Whereas for Plato a copy is defined, as Massumi (1987) writes, "by the presence or absence of internal, essential relations of resemblance to a model," in other words, it is tied to a commitment to sameness.

> The Deleuzian simulacrum [...] bears only an external and deceptive resemblance to a putative model... [that] envelops an essential difference. (p. 91)

There is a different agenda, then, than to copy an original. Without anything to copy, its identity is autonomously forged, independent of any permanent model. Rather than a reflection of something else, it is a *sui generis* interaction of horizontal vital intensities – of what Deleuze calls vectors and lines of force – that are always active behind the sedimented identities.

> The thrust of the process is not to become an equivalent of the 'model' but to turn against it and its world in order to open a new space for the simulacrum's own mad proliferation. The simulacrum affirms its own difference. (Massumi, 1987, p. 91)

Our first response to a dream of someone familiar to us, say a dream of our mother, is to equate the dream image with the actual person, as if the image were merely a copy or simulacrum. But working with the dream, it soon becomes clear that this outward appearance is hiding a difference, for the "mother" in the dream, as a spontaneous product of the imagination, has an autonomy of its own that breaks from its referential origin. As Hillman (1979) says:

> The persons I engage with in dreams are neither representations (simulacra) of their living selves nor parts of myself. They are shadow images [...] they are personae, masks [...]. (pp. 60–1)

As he says elsewhere, they are "the deep, subjective psyche in its personified guises" (p. 98).

The simulacrum becomes indeed, as Doel and Clarke put it, "a transformative production of something that is other than the same" (p. 266). It does not re-present something through resemblance and sameness, but merely *presents* the ever moving flow of experience, a vital force that will emerge in new constellations, bringing forth difference instead.

Now, for Plato and the subsequent tradition in philosophical thought, knowledge was possible only by reference to a stable identity, to an external and unchangeable model, and difference, as he declared, is "unthinkable in itself" (Deleuze, 1994, p. 145). The Deleuzian simulacrum, on the contrary, rejects the paradigm of sameness to which Plato and the tradition adhere; embracing change and movement, the simulacrum becomes a center of new formations, opening the floodgates to the prolific creation of new identities that constitute sensible experience in time, thus bringing change back to the fore of human consciousness. Deleuze sets the task of finding a way to think the difference that Plato declared unthinkable, but which is inevitable if we are to come to know anything in the ever flowing river of temporal experience.

Because the metaphysics of presence since Plato is predicated on the centrality and prevalence of being, sameness and permanence, it invents a still and unchanging structure, a crust as it were, that replaces the vitality of temporal experience and the pulse of becoming with the illusion of an unchanging world. It provides a scaffolding by which, detained in thought, the contingent can be made an object of intellectual knowledge.

We are, indeed, living in a time where digital entities enter our world (holograms, avatars, memes, gifs, etc.) not as copies that downgrade or upgrade reality, but as virtual simulacra (i.e., as spontaneous and creative emergences) active from within themselves and not in terms of an external or transcendent original. Given the impact our technological gadgets are having on how we experience the world, we need a new ontology that instead of covering up, or sedimenting, opens up to the aliveness of experience and its differential complexity.

2 Differentials and microperceptions

Behind our stable perceptions, there is the evershifting multiplicity of the sensible, which is composed of what Deleuze calls "microperceptions," that is, fuzzy or unconscious perceptions beneath our "macroperceptions." It is from these constellations of different intensities that freely circulate under our awareness that clear perceptions will eventually emerge into consciousness. What we normally consider to be perception is in fact, as Murphie (2002) writes, "a differential operation at the threshold of perception" (p. 199).

The virtual is an immanent presence that underlies the real, a pulsating energy, "a pure a-subjective current" (pp. 3–4), an indeterminate vitality, an open-ended power of reorganization that "is made of virtualities" (Deleuze, 1997, p. 5). Massumi thinks of them as a "pressing crowd of incipiencies and tendencies" (Bennett, 2010, p. 57) underlying matter; they interact as "a set of speeds and slownesses between unformed particles" (Deleuze and Guattari, 1987, p. 262) that flow at the edge of conscious awareness. They actualize the virtual, not by repeating (the same) but by negotiating the mesh of differences, the microperceptions that generate "a wholly transformative production of something that is other than the same" (Doel and Clarke, 1999, p. 266). For Deleuze and Guattari (1987),

> Every constellation of singularities and traits deducted from the flow—selected, organized, stratified—in such a way as to converge [...] artificially and naturally [...] is a veritable invention. (p. 406)

As Jane Bennett (2010) explains, "we are talking here of a materiality that is *itself* heterogeneous, itself a differential of intensities, itself *a life* [... where] there is no point of pure stillness. No indivisible atom that is not itself aquiver with virtual force" (p. 57).

The virtual is however not merely possibility. The possible is a mental construct that lies within the abstract structures of thought and theory, and only becomes real when it enters the immanent field of perception, whereas the virtual is always already real as a differential. Bennett (2010) calls it a "peculiar 'motility' of an intensity," "a vibratory effluescence that persists before and after any arrangement in space" (p. 57). The virtual is there always as the "minute, obscure, confused perceptions" (Deleuze, 2015, p. 86) from which conscious, clear, and distinct macro-perceptions eventually emerge; it does not await some event to become real.

This distinction between the possible and the virtual is crucial for understanding how the digital-virtual can precipitously devolve into a hypostatization of the possible. We need only think of the experience we might have had when we first got a digital music service like Spotify that put all songs ever recorded at our immediate disposal. In our excitement, our desire is ignited, and we thrill at the possibility of playing through any song we could think of. The virtual has been awoken. But after a while, the thrill subsides and the zero dimensionality of digital possibility freezes something. The music is drained of its uniqueness, everything starts to sound the same. A deadened feeling creeps in which causes a further plunge into a more intense search for that elusive song that would redeem it all, if we could just keep looking. If there's one thing the digital excels in, it is in offering us to make real, at any moment we choose, the endless possibility of novelty. But, in the end, what at first awakened the virtual, now causes it to flee. The excesses of digital possibility drain out the liveliness from experience, like water squeezed from a sponge.

When these forces of flux constellate into a perception, they inject temporality into the real. The simulacrum is not to be conceived as a static object, somehow reflecting, duplicating something else but as an animated center of emergence. Simulacra stand at the threshold of perception. Every simulacrum then, is a constellated set of micro-perceptions that obeys no prior model, but rather constitutes a radical transmutation.

Perhaps we can understand the mechanism or process of this transmutation by considering what goes on in the following stanza from 'Être': a composition by the Chilean musical artist Nicolas Jaar:

It's a body floating into the land
No, it's a body swimming out into the water
No, it's the land itself here that's a body
A body of land
It's the water itself that's a body of water[1]

In this text the frontiers between identities, or territories demarcated by definite concepts, are de-constructed, subjected to the movement between possible different aspects of a perception, transforming a description of a (static) object to the expression of a dynamic constellation of forces in movement.

By deconstructing the ties between model and copy, or doing away with a model altogether, Jaar creates the experience in which the si-mulacrum is traversed by the fluidity of time. When time is injected into something sedimented, microperceptions are activated that be-cloud our perceptual experience, causing new zones of perception to emerge, new aspects to dawn, as Wittgenstein says.

This diffusion of the world into microperceptions and differentials becomes even clearer in the video that attaches to Nicolas Jaar's poem, where one is never quite certain whether they are seeing a body, land, a reflection of a body in the water, or the reflection of land on the surface of the water. Or, perhaps more precisely, where what one is seeing is not separable from the uncertainty of these different modulations of perception.

We begin to perceive and experience no longer in terms of sub-stances, but in terms of processes; we leave behind hierarchies and move on to networks, from considering things in terms of quantities we begin to see them as qualities, or as Deleuze (1992) says, objects become objectiles. The objectile (i.e., the object conceived of as moving entity) as an event discloses the simulacrum's grounding, no longer in some ideal atemporal realm but in an immanent world of temporality, a flock of differentials.

The way the act of remembering is described by Matt Bluemink (2020) in his *In memoriam* of the famous philosopher of technology Bernard Stiegler, after his recent death, clearly illustrates what we are describing above. Bluemink tells the story of Stiegler in a French prison for bank robbery in the early 80's making his way through the prison library, chock full of the great works of 19th- and 20th-century philosophy, where he fell in love with the discipline. As he read and reread and took notes from these texts

> he found that his present interpretation was not identical to the one he had presented previously, or the one he remembered. He came to realise that what he had read the previous day had modified his memories. In other words, the exteriorisations of consciousness [...] that were laid out on the page in the form of letters and words had fundamentally changed his perception and interpretation of those memories. This led him to demonstrate that our memory is never static—it is constantly being changed [...]. Matt Bluemink. In Memoriam. In *#am Magazine*, August 13th, 2020. https://www.3ammagazine.com/3am/bernard-stiegler-in-memoriam/

The contents of memory are not static unities; they are "a flock of differentials" that are being permanently touched by what we perceive and experience, and so transformed into what they are now, where "now" is an indexical, always referring to this present moment and its current movement. Memories are indeed not objects but objectiles.

The Deleuzian simulacrum thrives in a logic of becoming, populated not by the full presences of external things, but by ghostly presences and hauntings. Like the image provided to us by Jaar, it is the very fluidity of everything that impregnates us with its irreducible ephemerality. The call to love the simulacrum involves, therefore, an acceptance of our permanent uncertainty, our connection to non-being, our standing on the edge, where we can "begin to feel, or ought to feel terrified that maybe language (and understanding, and knowledge) rests upon very shaky foundations – a thin net over an abyss" (Cavell, 1979, p. 178).

Deleuze and Krauss (1983), quoting Nietzsche, drives this same point home:

> Behind every cave ... there is, and must necessarily be, a still deeper
> cave: an ampler, stranger, richer world beyond the surface, an abyss
> behind every bottom, beneath every "foundation." (p. 53)

The event is a force of movement along many different and imperceptible dimensions. The passage from minute, microperceptions
to conscious perceptions is not a quantitative, measurable matter. It is
a kind of bricolage in motion, unmappable, stripped of Cartesian
coordinates, not to be understood in terms of a totality or a sum of
homogeneous parts, but as a function of particles in motion, waves
and beams of light, and sudden flashes. It results in a particular non-
linear, non-hierarchical, non-causal manner of being that introduces
us to the order of resonances and echoes, and horizontal connections.
This is how James Hillman (1979) describes, for example, the
dreamwork, when he compares it with the activity of a bricoleur:

> [T]he dream bricoleur is a handyman, who takes the bits of junk
> left over from the day and potters about with them, tacking
> residual things together into a collage. While the fingers that form
> a dream destroy the original sense of these residues, at the same
> time they shape them into a new sense within a new context [...]
> Imagination works by deforming and forming at one and the
> same moment. (pp. 127–128)

Representation gives way to expression or performance, and the sedimented objects of the scribal mind implode and begin to flow,
constituting meaning not from linear, logical linkages but from intensive tides, pulsations, and forces of attraction and repulsion.
Quality is introduced where quantity had been the rule. It is propelled
not by a rational need for totality but by affective impressions and
attractions that are inwardly charged, in dynamic tension. Those
animate forces are responsible for the passage from vitality to consciousness. An "infinite sum of minute perceptions that destabilize
the preceding macroperception while preparing the following one"
(Deleuze, 2015, p. 86) produce a conscious perception. The task of all
perception, Deleuze says, is "pulverizing the world, but also [...]
spiritualizing its dust" (p. 87).

3 Rhizomatic play

In the move from substances to processes, from objects to objectiles
that we have been illustrating with Jaar's song, a new logical framework arises. Whereas the guiding metaphor for the traditional logic
that deals with substances was conceived in terms of the arboreous (as
in Descartes' tree of knowledge), in this new logic, Deleuze and

Guattari (1987) refer to the image of the "rhizome," which in contrast to the hierarchical and sequential mode of thought, is characterized more by circulations than by lines and angles:

> [U]nlike trees or their roots, [the rhizome] connects any point to any other point, and its traits are not necessarily linked to traits of the same nature; [...] It is composed not of units but of dimensions, or rather directions in motion. It has neither beginning nor end, but always a middle (milieu) from which it grows and which it overspills. (p. 21)

The rhizomatic deconstructs the scribal order, insofar as it goes against its logical hierarchical structure, thus making the very notion of representation idle. The inherence of a system of referentiality that binds the simulacrum-as-copy to an original is abolished. It explodes the static model that provided fuel to the original-copy relation, creating a multiplicity of forces that in fluid horizontal interaction result in wholly new self-originating, autochthonous meanings.

This shattering of the familiar framework and rebirth of the rhizomatic that characterized the oral is illustrated in the word play that takes place in Blossom Dearie's song "Rhode Island Is Famous for You":

> Copper comes from Arizona/ Peaches come from Georgia/ and Lobsters come from Maine/ The wheat fields/ are the sweet fields of Nebraska/ and Kansas gets Bonanzas from the Grain// [...] /Pencils come from Pennsylvania/ Vest from Vest Virginia/ And Tents from Tent-esee/ They know mink where they grow / Mink in Wyo-mink/ A camp chair in New Hamp-chair / That's for me. (Blossom Dearie, "Rhode Island is Famous For You" by Arthur Schwarz and Howard Dietz)

In this portion of the lyrics of this song, sameness in sound becomes the alibi for the reconstitution of new interrelations that connect layers of meaning that were previously unconnected. "Kansas' bonanzas from the grain" are well within the literal meaning with which the song begins, but by the end, when we arrive at "Pencils from Pennsylvania" and then from "Mink to Wyomink," or "a camp chair with New Hampshire" it is the sound and rhyme that counts, no longer the truth of the facts or the information about the places discussed that those words represent. Suddenly there is play. The words in the song slide from representational to acoustical meaning, as the "meaning" of the words becomes secondary to the sound that prevails. New connections are distilled from petrified meanings, weaving new relations in an alternative web of virtuality.

Another illustration of the rhizomatic shift we are explicating is found in the work of the French performance artist ORLAN. In a live Internet transmission, she subjected her face to reconstructive surgery and had a second mouth opened on her cheek. Her surgical intervention disrupts the connections that are active in our normal perception. The mouth becomes something very different when it is seen as part of one's cheek. The face no longer looks like the face but is dispersed in new infinitesimal differential relations, that evoke – at both the conscious and unconscious level – new (and perhaps, here, shocking) perceptions.

An example from James Baldwin's *Giovanni's Room* (2000) reinforces the same occurrence:

> I was in bed upstairs, asleep. It was quite late. I was suddenly awakened by the sound of my father's footfalls on the walk beneath my window. I could tell by the sound and the rhythm that he was a little drunk and I remember that at that moment a certain disappointment, an unprecedented sorrow entered into me. I had seen him drunk many times and had never felt this way – on the contrary, my father sometimes had great charm when he was drunk – But that night I suddenly felt that there was something in it, in him, to be despised. (p. 21)

Here we see again a new and unexpected impression displacing what is familiar, cracking open the crust that covers up the virtual differentials, setting them free as fragments from which new ways of seeing spontaneously arise. A conscious perception is therefore not the result of the ordinary object or its familiarity, but rather arises from the minute and unconscious perceptions quickening beneath it. The simulacrum is not a mirror that reflects the world but, we could say, a black mirror that absorbs it, sucks it into a field of yet unformed forces, a dark vitality that can now come to light in new constellations.

In the Deleuzian simulacrum the meaning and reality of the event is determined from within its own occurrence and not by any external model or criterion. The simulacrum, in other words, is not a reproduction but an emergence. Differentials weave opposites together into a rhizomatic psychic and physical space, and the images produced by the virtual resemble nothing other than themselves in their own movement. As Deleuze (2015) puts it, "Resemblance [here] is equated with what resembles, not with what is resembled" (p. 96).

Abstract painting, for example, results from the dismantlement of the representational scaffolding of normal perception by the forms and colors emanating from the canvas. The "reality" that emerges in abstract art is independent of any model; it owes allegiance to nothing but its own autonomous occurrence.

But when the simulacrum is understood as a false copy (first stance), its own originary differential virtuality is denigrated as inferior; and when it is seen as perfecting the real (second stance), that perfection overshadows its living immanence. From this new perspective the simulacrum involves neither denigration nor idealization. It evidences the fact that the actual is permeated by the virtual, which goes all the way down, in these minute perceptions, inexhaustibly. More than a mere possibility, it is invisibly active, always and forever able to emerge.

What the simulacrum does in its state of severance from an original is to usher us behind the scene of the representational, beyond the mimetic contract of sameness that the traditionally understood Platonic model imposes on us. As Deleuze and Krauss (1983) see it:

> Plato, by dint of inquiring in the direction of the simulacrum, discovers, in the flash of an instant as he leans over its abyss, that the simulacrum is not simply a false copy, but that it calls into question the very notions of the copy ... and of the model. (p. 47)

By rendering the simulacrum free from its commitments to representation, Deleuze's ontology opens us to the abyss over which Plato leans.

As we have said, it is the masked difference behind the surface similarity and its rhizomatic play that constitutes the depth of the simulacrum. In Deleuze's (1983) words:

> The simulacrum [...] contains a positive power [...] It sets up the world of nomadic distributions and consecrated anarchy. Far from being a new foundation, it swallows up all foundations, it assures a universal collapse, but as a positive and joyous event, as de-founding (effondement). (p. 53)

Whereas a copy merely stands for its model, the Deleuzian simulacrum instead generates different circuits of connections and associations that break the rigidity of representation.

4 Modulating modulations

In the digital age, we awaken to a new ecology of the virtual, where the actual is not only permanently open to, but also inseparable from it. The Deleuzian simulacrum is not a mimesis, but a "modulation." It liberates experience of the world from the paralyzing expectation of stability by temporalizing it. As Murphie (2002) points out, it is not that virtuality itself has been increased with the digital, but rather that it is our ability to modulate it that has been dramatically enhanced. With each new technological advance "modulation is no longer a filter for a stable world, but is applied to modulation itself, so that everything is taken up within this modulation of modulation" (p. 191).

We can screen in or screen out, speed up or slow down, intensify or block out different dimensions of the real, regulating the many ways the world is open to us – ontologically, perceptually and affectively. The virtual is nothing other than the permeability of the real to these modulations. The digital provides the tools for modulating that permeability, in ways that – for the first time in history – put the human totally in charge.

As we have already seen in the first part of the book, we can understand the history of the virtual as a history of its successive modulations. The oral articulation of the virtual, we could say, constitutes its first modulation, making private experience shareable in our verbal interaction. The written word modulates that modulation, extending the public realm beyond its actual living context, traversing space and time. The virtual is further modulated with the moving image, which insufflates time into virtual space. The flow of actual experience becomes shareable, not just its conceptual or photographic modulation, but also the sensible dimension that had been previously suspended.

The digital modulates these modulations of the virtual, not just by new representations, but by the creation of a new virtual public space where – differently from the space of the moving image – it becomes interactive and independent of our physical location. Indeed, it doesn't only duplicate or represent, but begins to merge with physical experience. We begin to inhabit, together, a common spatial and temporal situation other than the one we are empirically occupying.

> VR creates a totality which (potentially) both overwhelms present perceptive thresholds and creates, rather than represents, a "total *enough* world" within the world(s) at large. (Murphie, 2002, p. 193)

These new modulations bring to the fore dimensions of the virtual that had remained below the threshold of conscious perception. Insofar as we can now extract time from personal, subjective temporality, we become also able to modulate it – accelerate, decelerate, and stop it – reconstituting experience by virtually reassembling its original order, merging different temporalities to our own experience of time. In the example we already considered in the introduction, replaying in slow motion the capture of our peeling an orange, the pressure of our fingers against the peel is evoked in the experience of the screen images, where the conjunction of our bodily memory and the audiovisual feed unveils aspects of our subjective experience that usually go unnoticed. The fleshiness of the fruit, the precise movements of our fingers in interaction with the orange, and so on, all aspects which would otherwise have remained buried in the darkness of unconscious oblivion now open into consciousness, providing in this encounter, the rudiments of new vocabularies and common discourses that can broaden the range of lived experience.

VR brings in front of us something that we have always ignored, i.e., the movement behind what we saw as stable bodies and fixed states of affairs. Murphie (2002) writes that it

> brings to an end the regimes of separation which would, through the operation of certain representations, deny the *interactive* reality of the virtual and the actual in favor of a simple facticity of *stable* bodies and *fixed* states of affairs. (Murphie, 2002, p. 192)

As a consequence, we are able now to begin to see the world beyond those sedimented perceptions that had constituted our familiar predigital world and deliberately affect it, modulating the virtual that had previously remained unconscious.

In instituting a new *public* interactive realm beyond the bounds of ordinary space and time, new modes of intersubjective experience enter our social lives in the digital world. Human relationships are dislocated from their ordinary and everyday time-space coordinates so that the kinds of things we say, the forms by which we speak with others, the bonds we make, are all transformed.

We learn to combine and integrate, or separate and distinguish different aspects of our lives. With those captures we effect further modulations that open spaces of relating where we begin to live beyond empirical life. The committed partner, for example, can be in touch, through Facebook, with their first high school boyfriend or girlfriend. There can be contact, play, active reminiscing, and so on and yet, because it is held in virtual space, it does not necessarily threaten the partner's actual relationship with their husband or wife. The experience of intolerable tension and conflict that an empirical encounter produces in actual life, can be muted or dissolved through the digital modulation – through Zoom conversations or Instagram lives – and so wholly transform or complement the empirical relationship. By being able to better filter what we show to the other of ourselves, digital virtuality softens something, sharpens or invents something else, in other words, it greatly expands the psychological possibilities of relating. Adding texture to our relational lives, and drawing out in original ways the intersubjective virtuality that is always already at play, the virtual staging offers a new medium for containing the inherent tensions endemic to human relationships.

Freed from spatiotemporal locality, our whereabouts become irrelevant, and so the virtual may complement the present actual context, our everyday life, with unexpected possible connections. In that ethereal space of virtuality, many different dimensions of experience and temporalities crisscross, potentially creating constellations that escape the exclusive one-track sequence of fixed identities or logical meanings. Thus, we construct from what we see and read about people on social media, identities that no longer correspond to the actual time and space in which each person lives, unveiling possibilities of relations that are non-existent in our mere physical interaction. How often do we learn about someone's activities that belong to the past in our virtual screen, yet we ignore that temporal constraint, treating it as if it were happening now, with no real consequence. Past moments may be woven together with the present in different ways than they do actually in reality. For example, someone might comment on a trip we took last year, as if it were a recent event, without our correcting them but simply taking these dislocations in time as new routes of shared experience, alternative historical sequences, new or unexpected topics and discourses that change and diversify our original experience. The virtuality of the space in which we are relating makes any discrepancy with actual fact irrelevant to the dynamics of the relationship and, to the contrary, mines those discrepancies for unexpected meanings and relations.

The a-historicity of events in the virtual world creates alternative realities where we are free to participate and shape them as sequences in a playful blending of actuality and virtuality that may, in the end, have actual consequences. When Facebook gives you back images from the anniversary of an event, say, by reposting them on your wall, stories are relived outside their actual temporal contexts, virtually re-experienced. With the historical havoc wreaked by this muting of chronological time and experience, and the constant delivery of automatic (timeless) images from the digital media, our memories are stratified and layered together in unforeseen ways.

Our new digital apparatuses allow us, therefore, as Murphie (2002) puts it, "to shift the gears on the thresholds of perception, operation, and expression more powerfully than ever before" (p. 188). The digital-virtual offers, beyond social interaction, a new way of modulating the play between fantasy and reality, thus providing novel spaces for the expression and strivings of the self.

In the second season of the HBO comedy *Crashing*, we find an amusing illustration of this. The main character, played by Peter Holmes, who has been living in his friend's garage, in one particular scene is sitting on a couch, his computer on his lap, getting ready to masturbate. He types in the word *boobs* into Google Images and gets a screenful of pictures of women with tight dresses, showing their cleavage. Not satisfied, we see him remove his Google Filter, which had been set on high (to screen out explicitly sexual material), and now he gets a series of very salacious pornographic pictures of breasts as well as vaginas and penises and people engaged in a surprising variety of sexual acts. As this becomes too much for him, he then changes his filter back to medium and a new series of pictures of woman's breasts suddenly appears on his screen that are just right for what he wants. As this character successfully discovers the exact level of explicitness he needs to satisfy his onanistic urges, we witness the modulation of modulations in action.

A masked difference, we have seen, lays behind the surface similarity of the Deleuzian simulacrum, constituting its creative power. When we construct a self from the representations of someone's digital footprint in the virtual world, that construction's depth is grounded on the differences that such variations, free from their dependence on a "real" and fixed model, are able to uncover, and not on the supposed identity of the subject.

From the perspective of the conventional self, what would seem fragmented here instead makes it possible for us to see an aspect of that person that was previously unseen. No longer subservient to the person we know (yet still connected to him or her), this new identity acquires a validity that relies on the intensity or expressiveness of what is virtually emerging. The constraints of objective truth are thus lifted, as they are in fictional narratives (oral, written, photographed, filmed). Playing with temporality, undoing linear developmental assumptions about how an individual life unfolds, we constellate different and diverging identities. Although fragmented and partial, there will be a multiplicity of qualities ascribed to a person and recognizable beyond her so-called "real" identity. They won't represent anything essential, but – more imagistic, associative, intuitive – they become containers of previously inoperative potentialities, now actualized in the vitality of the digital.

Breaking thresholds, ushering suprasensible similarities, "internal relations" between things, the inexorable flow between the actual and virtual awakens in us a new sensibility by which we may begin to construct a reality more attuned to a range of differences that did not exist before the advent of the virtual world. Beyond its enriching our experience by providing us with the possibility for new connections, the digital taps into a spontaneity from which the "mad proliferation" beyond the constraints of an already established reality can arise.

With the virtual world we are learning to live with simulacra and their reckless and unforeseeable promiscuity. Resonances with the passions and emotions begin to reverberate rhizomatically. Emotional expression in the web (sometimes sponsored by the cloak of invisibility available there) is opening realms of shared meaning that before never passed the walls of a family setting, or the closet of one's own inhibited mind. As we will see in Chapter 8, when we discuss the loss of Benjamin's "mimetic faculty," we will see how modes of thought that have been relegated to the fringes of modern culture start to be activated in this inversion toward the non-referential Deleuzian simulacrum. And the potentiation of spontaneity in whichever form it takes – be it natural or artificial or a hybrid of the two – may well serve as a training ground for what is becoming our post-human future. The question again is whether this shaping is not just another step in a sequence, but a quantum leap in human consciousness.

Coda

In our digital ecology, a new spectrum of experience opens up that challenges the hierarchical power-structures of traditional thinking. This becomes intelligible to us from the perspective provided by what we have been calling the Deleuzian simulacrum. But true to its pharmacological nature, these new technologies also seem to be reinforcing the dualistic conception of the Platonic simulacrum that Deleuze was so forcefully criticizing. Through a repression of difference, these same technologies seem to promote sameness and identity, pushing us further into our old power arrangements, freezing the world rather than freeing us to the rhizomatic play of digital life. As Murphie (2002) points out:

> This increased ability to operate the virtual is by no means immediately ethically positive. It is not until we answer the question, each time specifically, of what manner of living it implies, of what passions can break up the trademarks we increasingly live through every time we boot up. (p. 192)

So what manner of living does this new digital age imply? Does the breakdown of referentiality and self-dissemination in digital virtuality adhere to the spirit of Deleuze's post-Platonic metaphysics, or is it a mere bastardization of it? Does virtual reality deliver us to the immanent field, or is the flash/bang of digital impregnation merely window dressing, disguising a further deepening of the fissure between the virtual and the real that Deleuze is so intent on deconstructing? Does cyberspace instantiate rhizomatic play or does it further disavow it? Or is it instead, that it does both?

Note

1 To listen this soundtrack: https://vimeo.com/55793775 (0'23"–0'42").

References

Baldwin, J. (2000) *Giovanni's Room*. New York: Random House.
Bennett, J. (2010) *Vibrant Matter. A Political Ecology of Things*. Durham: Duke University Press.
Bluemink, M. In Memoriam. In *#am Magazine*, August 13th, 2020. https://www.3ammagazine.com/3am/bernard-stiegler-in-memoriam/
Cavell, S. (1979) *The Claim of Reason. Wittgenstein, Skepticism, Morality and Tragedy*. Oxford: Oxford University Press.
Deleuze, G. (1992) Postscript on the Societies of Control. In *October*, vol. 59 (Winter), pp. 3–7.
Deleuze, G. (1994) *Difference and Repetition*. New York: Columbia University Press.
Deleuze, G. (1997) Immanence: A Life.... *Theory, Culture and Society 14*(2), 3–7.
Deleuze, G., and Krauss, Rosalind (1983) Plato and the Simulacrum. In *October*, vol. 27 (Winter), pp. 45–56. Cambridge: MIT Press.
Deleuze, G. (2015) *The Fold: Leibniz and the Baroque*. Minneapolis: University of Minnesota Press.
Deleuze, G., and Guattari, F. (1987) *A Thousand Plateaus*. Minneapolis: Minnesota University Press.
Doel, M.A., and Clarke, D.B. (1999) Virtual Worlds: Simulation, Suppletion, S (ed)uction and Simulacrum. In M. Crang, P. Crang, and J. May (Eds.), *Virtual Geographies: Bodies, Space and Relations*. London: Routledge.
Hillman, J. (1979) *The Dream and the Underworld*. New York: Harper and Row.
Massumi, B. (1987) *Realer than Real. The Simulacrum According to Deleuze and Guattari*, Copyright No. 1 (pp. 90–97).
Murphie, A. (2002) Putting the Virtual Back into VR. In B. Massumi (Ed.), *A Shock to Thought. Expression after Deleuze and Guattari*. London: Routledge.

Part III
Depth psychology in the digital age

Introduction to Part III

The Deleuzian simulacrum, in not having a source outside of its own becoming, is resonant with the unconscious psyche that underlies our affective lives. They both allude to a source of alterity and otherness, out of which perceptions and meanings arise, that traverses the human subject. If indeed we want to explicate in what ways digitality ushers us into the rhizomatic, we have to examine how it opens or forecloses access to the non-representable aspects of our being. Depth psychology can help us wrestle with these questions. With its own unique renderings of how we psychologically live out our virtual nature, it sheds an important light on the agonizing tension between immanence and transcendence that entrenches itself in everything digital.

Deleuze's radical ontology opens into a temporal world that resonates with the frenzied activity of digital life. But what if, unconsciously, we make use of this newfound power to further something in us that undermines the creative expansion that revealed itself to us so compellingly when we saw the digital through Deleuze's eyes? Possessed by power, greed, and hubris, our technologies seem indeed to pull us in the opposite direction toward a fixed and ossified world. Can we hold the tension between the virtual world as rhizomatic and the virtual world as mimetic, between the virtual as presentation and the virtual as representation? This becomes the underlying theme of what is to follow, in particular, as we explore the implications of what it means today to be endowed with the digital powers to modulate, in unprecedented ways, the actualization of our innermost wishes and desires.

What happens to the real in an age when the very stuff of our fantasy lives is so effortlessly actualized in the virtual world rather than in the empirical? What, in other words, lends itself to falsification or mere replication, and what opens in fact new doors to experience and reality? By exploring what might be provoked in our unconscious life by these new tools, we can better assess what of digital virtuality is faithful to the Deleuzian vision and what betrays it.

5 The virtual within

Prelude

One central idea running through the depth psychological tradition is that fantasy and reality live in a rich and complex set of dialectics.[1] This underlying dualism has far-reaching implications, and spawns a powerful set of dichotomies, whose dynamic tension generates the very contours of our psychic lives: the inner world and external reality, internal objects and real objects, the unconscious and conscious mind, self and world. The mode of virtuality that arises from our new technologies, what we have been referring to as digital virtuality (as opposed to its human counterpart), unsettles these well-entrenched dichotomies, destabilizing the ways in which we have come to make sense of our psychology. Digital virtuality is a singular space with its own unique dynamics. It turns the inner (and often private) world of fantasy and imagination outward, as psychic life is now lived collectively in the social media; simultaneously it turns the outer world of material reality (including, of course, the body) inward, as it now appears on our screens in the form of virtual simulations.

The possibility of digital virtuality arises from the technological innovations of the 21st century that have allowed us to code reality, and thus virtualize the events and processes not only of the organic, material world, but of our minds and our bodies as well. As Zuboff (2015) puts it: "As a result of pervasive computer mediation, nearly every aspect of the world is rendered in a new symbolic dimension as events, objects, processes and people become visible, knowable, and shareable in a new way" (p. 77). Indeed, the very term "virtual reality" has now become one of the most important and critical, even though still opaque and ill-defined, signifiers of our contemporary technological discourse. We will employ this term, and its counterpart, the digital virtual, in the broadest, most open and encompassing way possible to describe the realm of human experience and interaction produced by the digital. We understand digital virtuality as a new way in which life and mind are virtualized, and the border between the virtual and the actual radically reconfigured.

But, at the same time, we want to distinguish it from human virtuality here defined as the psychological and existential play of fantasy and reality that grounds our embodied existence. Compared to its digital counterpart, human virtuality is located inside the coordinates of our identities as psychological beings. And thus, our term of choice, the virtual within, becomes a moniker for the mode of virtuality that is native to a depth psychological perspective, a virtuality out of which we maintain an inner sense of self while living in the world with others.

The very project of depth psychology is one that traces how the actual becomes virtual: how trauma, loss, the implacability of the real, as well as the affectively-charged events of human life, become de-literalized, de-substantialized, and thus transformed into psychic realities. Hillman (1979) contends that movement along this path from the actual to the virtual, from concrete reality to the symbolic, is one of the central functions of our dreaming life.

> [T]he dream is less a comment on the day than a digestive process within the labyrinthine tracts of the psyche. The dream-work cooks life events into psychic substance by means of imaginative modes ... This work takes matter out of life and makes them into soul, at the same time feeding soul each night with new material. (p. 96)

Indeed, as we proceed, one of the primary ways that we will compare human and digital virtuality is from the perspective of the existential coordinates that constitute our dreaming lives. Here we concur with Ogden (2009) that dreaming is "the most free, most inclusive, and most deeply penetrating form of psychological work of which human beings are capable" (p. 104). Dream life is rife with what is most other in the psyche, i.e. its a-subjective and non-representable dimensions, and, at the same time, with what is most personal, distinctive, and familiar. Our dreaming minds, our capacity for fantasy, reverie, and imagination, the very source of psychological virtuality that makes us who we are, will be the tableau against which we want to examine the virtuality endemic to the digital. Each is replete with a fantastic freedom of action and "transformational fluidity" (Scott, 1999), yet, what is different in their occurrence – the fact that in the digital, this freedom of action is under the control of the self, whereas in the dream, it seems to arise from an other-than-me source – leads us to ask how the virtuality of the digital age is impacting our relationship to the virtual that comes alive in dreams. What is it doing to the intuitions of the non-representable inherent to our dreaming minds? What is it doing, in fact, to the human virtual?

The digital unleashes the private experiences of the self into the collective and networked spaces of contemporary life. For example, in the past, the experience of birth and death involved rituals kept sheltered within our most intimate circles. The digital has radically transformed these rituals, as today, these events (and indeed practically all aspects of our emotional lives) occur in a much more public and visible way. It is no longer uncommon to set up webcams in hospital rooms for the dying and memorial websites for the deceased, where everyone who has ever had any contact with the person (and even those who did not) can publicly comment on and interact with the mourners; websites that remain active with users long after someone's death and continue on in perpetuity. Long before we are able to download our consciousness into machines, the digital is offering us a new kind of immortality.

This sudden obliteration of a private and personal space forces us to reconsider our sense of boundaries, and the importance of modesty, discretion, loyalty, and so on. These changes rattle our beliefs about the individualistic self and its values. They represent a new privileging of the external over the internal, the public over the private.

Some insist that this dissolution of the self into the maelstrom of collective forces has the negative effect of foreclosing many, if not all, of the values that practitioners of depth psychology (in whatever of its many forms) tend to affirm, such as the freedom of imagination, "negative capability" (Li, 2009, p. ix), interior depth and the privacy of the self, and so on.[2] This anxiety about the possibility of such foreclosure speaks to the concern that something essential is being lost because we no longer consider it worthwhile to preserve the difference between psychic interiority and collective exteriority. Or, to put it another way, we have become so enthralled by the participatory immediacy of the collective-self provided by our everyday devices that the other portals for unconscious psychic life that require privacy, solitude, slowness, and stillness are gradually starting to recede. The exteriorizing that is inherent to the digital self seems to thwart the development of interiority that requires a certain degree of protection for the privacy of self-experience in the face of collective impingement. Some therapists experience that recession acutely. Perhaps that's why the presence of the smartphone, perched comfortably in the patient's lap during a session, is so threatening. They think (and sometimes even say): "Put that away, at least just for this hour, so we can focus on just you and I and what is arising both inside and between ourselves!" And the patient, especially if he is younger, resists this opprobrium, retorting, "What do you mean interior and exterior, private and public? They are the same." The smartphone even breaks down the temporal conditions under which therapy has traditionally been practiced, infecting the field with virtual time. Text, facetime, and email extend in a nearly unlimited way the scope of therapeutic contact.[3]

This eruption of the digital into what was once considered the most private and hallowed of all spaces, the therapist's consulting room, gives us pause, as we seriously consider whether the interiorized self's historical moment has passed. Is it a pre-digital relic, a now archaic and untenable potential for selfhood that in the contemporary era is replaced by a digitized self that only dreams collective – no longer private, hidden, and interior – dreams (Giegerich, 2007)? Have we come indeed to the collapse of the project started by Freud a little over a century ago?

A world pervaded by digital virtuality challenges our modernist constructions of selfhood, making obsolete the notion of an inter- iorized object-relational world that lives in a creative and dynamic tension with the outward demands of social, familial, and cultural life. If we are truly near the endpoint of this experience of the self, do we resist the challenge wrought by the digital and try to go back? Or is the digital revolution offering us a desirable option to the individualistic subjectivity that has dominated our psychological outlook and our conception of the human since the Romantic era?[4] Should we simply let the principles and insights of depth psychology be displaced, or should we protect and preserve them as a necessary compensation for the losses that we are incurring in the digital era?

The depth psychologist makes the claim that there is always going to be an essential need to come to terms with forces inside the self that are distinct from the collective. The internal object world that en- genders the complexity of our emotional lives is a reality that cannot so easily be dismissed. The psyche, contained within each of us, has an indispensable metabolizing function. It is responsible for trans- forming the raw, undigested materials of psychic life into structures that form the architecture of the developing self. Indeed, the very existence of an inner apparatus for the psychological processing of experience is what enables us to come to terms with the existential and emotional realities of life (Bion, 1983).

But what the digital suggests is that, on the contrary, there might be other ways of arranging things to deal with these emotional com- plexities. Perhaps the psyche is even more vitally engaged and better contained when we allow ourselves to dwell in the interfluidity be- tween digital virtuality and the real. As explorers of this present-day world, we are being offered wholly new and distinct ways of bearing the affective contingencies of everyday life, cooking life events into "virtual" substances by means of the digital vessel.

The depth psychologists' first impulse is to stand in judgment of digital virtuality, seeing it as false and inauthentic. It is nothing more than a delinquent attempt to mimic the true source of the virtuality emanating from the inner recesses of unconscious life. But this assumes, as we saw in the first stance, that the virtual is inferior to the real, that the spontaneity and creativity that it generates is no more than an unconscious investment in the expansion of our narcissism and its desire for unending gratification. From this vantage point, the virtuality of digital life is seen as reifying the world, reducing its existential possibilities rather than furthering them. Experience is deadened, its metaphorical resonances obviated. This adjudication of the digital as negative and regressive seems to enact a foreclosure of its own, preventing a dialogue with the technological world that has the potential to revision the traditional dichotomies fundamental to our conception of psychic life.

In virtual space, the things of the world and the processes of the mind penetrate one another differently than they do in the ordinary, off-line life of the mind. That difference points to the unique play of the digital, the way it can so seamlessly engineer a cross-over from mind-fantasies to their actualization in the virtual, freed from both the encumbrances of the body and the materiality of the world. This rhapsodic intertwining of fantasy, imagination, and virtual reality places our much beloved and well-theorized psychological metaphysics on the chopping block. It disrupts and confounds our first principles, the basic set of metapsychological assumptions that have been determinative for our understanding of how we live as psychological beings and our relationship to embodiment, other people, and the external world. The entire mind-body, self-world, inner-outer organization (i.e., the criss-crossing, two-channel system that is foundational for depth psychology) is subverted. Digital virtuality is a third term that forces depth psychology, and its binary structures, back on its toes.

If indeed we have to go back and rethink everything, and envisage a way of seeing the psyche that is in tune with the digital age, we are confronted (again) with the very virtual, in all of its unpredictable wildness, dwelling under the rubric of unconscious psychic life, which, for over the past 100 years, depth psychology has been grappling to understand and articulate. We are entering an era in which the self that arises out of the digital leaves us struggling to find a new framework that can bear and contain the novel modes of virtuality that are opened up with the advancement of these startling technological changes. The worldview presupposed by the digital age, as much as that of depth psychology, determine our stance toward the unfathomableness of human virtuality.

One important vantage point for catching sight of these transformations is the consideration of how each new technological advance modulates our relation to temporality. Depth psychology and its metapsychological framework arose out of the scribal era. Derrida (1995a) remarks that if it wasn't for the very particular temporal rhythms of its early founders sending and receiving letters, psycho-analysis would never have evolved in the particular way that it did. The digital age, in contrast, is not only speeding up the exchange of ideas and information, but, in its unparalleled ability to capture human experience, grants us a new kind of dominion over the passing away of things. The digital offers a defensive refuge from the ravages of time contemporaneously with the possibility of a more originary experience of human mortality. In its extraordinary capacity to stop time, the digital is haunted by the specter of death. This signals an essential link between digital virtuality and our mortal condition. If we are to contend with the virtuality of our era, then we must come to terms with this paradox. If indeed we are experiencing a shift away from depth psychology, we not only have to embrace those dimen-sions of the virtual that had been previously foreclosed and are now opened, but also come to terms with the foreclosure and loss of what earlier was open and available.

1 Digital mind in search of a soul

If, for Jung, modern man searched for his soul in the interior cham-bers of the individual psyche, today, as inhabitants of the digital era, we turn outward, toward the collective psyche, to discover our depths. We live less inside ourselves and our own bodies and more in the virtualized spaces that arise out of the interchange between smart-phones, social media networks, and the Internet of Everything that connects them. This has a wide-ranging impact on how we experience psychological reality. The unconscious, that internal place of depth and otherness, is, for the digital man in search of a soul, wholly ex-teriorized by our technologies. Jung used to say that, in our modern age, our gods were found no longer in the heavens but in our pathologies. We might say that today they are found not in the heavens but in the Cloud, not in our pathologies but in the devices we carry with us everywhere.

In an age where self-display and network connectedness have be-come the norm, where there are to be no secrets anymore, no hidden crevices of the psyche immune from exposure, and self-confession has become a cultural imperative, it is an edgy time to be practicing psychoanalysis and psychotherapy. It is as if we are living in a digital Panopticon; everything about us is on perpetual display, as what was once internal to the self is now voluntarily (and almost compulsively) laid bare for all to see. This collapse of privacy and internal space is revealed by the pace and mode in which people speak about their symptoms and tell the stories of their lives in therapy. The fact that it is less metaphorical and more literal, and that there is less capacity for self-reflectiveness (to say nothing of how taboo it is becoming for there to be moments of silence), is evidence of this collapse. There is a pressure to get to the next thing and the thing after that, as if therapy provides another opportunity for binge watching, this time a show exclusively about the self.

The speed and self-assurance that the digital life inspires bleeds into the consulting room. It is so difficult to disconnect, even for the hour, that whenever a patient's smartphone rings or vibrates, he is incapable of silencing it without first looking to see who is beckoning. It's not only the impingements to therapeutic intimacy perpetrated by the smartphone that poses such a great challenge. There is also little room for opaqueness; issues must be clarified quickly, and thus we find ourselves as therapists unwittingly rushing to make meaning out of the patient's material at the pace of a Google search. The digital has so habituated us to immediate answers that the pressure to do something, to know something, to solve the problem, in a nearly automatic fashion, often drives the dialogue. Perhaps this need for quick solutions is a reflection of how, for patient and therapist alike, it is increasingly difficult to tolerate uncertainty and not-knowing, which is essential for grounding therapeutic work in the life of the unconscious. Today, we are desperate to escape the inferior feelings that come when something is not quickly known and made clear. This has the effect of impeding the process of allowing something to arise of its own accord from within, spontaneously and unexpectedly, rather than its being imposed from the outside, narrowing the scope of psychotherapeutic practice.

The move to slow down, to think and feel something from the inside, is counter-intuitive as today both patient and therapist are possessed by chronic impatience. This urge for a quick fix has always dogged psychotherapy, especially in its contemporary, positivist forms. However, that pressure for rapid solutions seems to have intensified, especially since the digital life of the patient – his text messages, dating profiles, Facebook and Instagram postings – have now become the *prima materia* (the prime matter) of the therapeutic work. The unconscious, no longer extracted from the interior reaches of a private self, springs forth from a fecund and proliferating superabundance of digital images, sounds, and narratives that we have become more and more porous to in our intensified virtual life. The internal object world, once the sacred province of depth psychology, has now suddenly become populated with the characters of the "shows" and tv series we are watching such that we find ourselves preoccupied with the fictional lives of those we identify with in our screens. Of course, we have always been susceptible to this with novels, movies, soap operas, etc., but there is something uniquely penetrating about the way these streaming services deliver their content that accounts for this new form of psychic inhabitation. Psychic life and digital life have become so intertwined that the psychodynamics of the everyday are not easily distinguished from the cyber-dynamics generated by the digital. This is why very often a good deal of what happens in any one session involves metabolizing the patient's digitally saturated everyday experience.

In an age of digital openness, where the sharing of intimate images and narratives about one's life in an extended virtual space with others has become one of our newest and most valued cultural institutions, self-coherence is now dependent upon self-display. We know ourselves best, we feel most whole and put together, when we broadcast the events of our lives to the world as they happen. The acknowledgment of our words and actions by a receptive other (how many likes, how many followers) helps us hold on to who we are, and makes us feel relevant and coherent. The development of self-awareness, a common goal of nearly all forms of psychotherapy, takes root now in how we are seen, known, and approved of by others in virtual space. This poses a challenge to the psychological conception of identity as a matter of inner depth. How does psychotherapy reconceive its own task under these new and changing circumstances?

2 Digital narcissism

While contemporary digital practices seem to be ushering in a distinct conception of a self that casts aside its own interiority in the name of collective recognition, we return again to our working assumption that the concepts of depth psychology have a unique contribution to make. Undoubtedly, given all that we have just laid out, this is quite paradoxical. On the one hand, the digital age is forging a new conception of selfhood that fundamentally deconstructs the privacy and interiority of the depth psychological self. And yet, on the other hand, these very same psychological notions about the nature of selfhood that the digital so powerfully challenges, can also shed a revealing light on the unconscious complexes that haunt it. For instance, the concept of narcissism, which is so central to the psychoanalytic discourse, powerfully illuminates how the digital is structuring the contemporary psyche. Technology and narcissism are inextricably bound. Technology feeds our narcissism just as much as narcissism drives our uses of technology. Still, the very suggestion that technology may be unwittingly fostering a new kind of narcissistic omnipotence makes us recoil, as does the idea that the technological impulse itself is inherently narcissistic.

Healthy and pathological narcissism are generally distinguished by psychoanalysis. Healthy narcissism is the basis for personal agency and autonomy, that internally generated sense of positive self-regard that allows us to take action in the world with resolve and confidence. Pathological narcissism, in contrast, traps us in a self-aggrandizing bubble that constantly needs mirroring reinforcement from the outside, cutting us off from any authentic contact with the other (Kohut, 1971). In attempting to clearly and cleanly distinguish one form of narcissism from the other, our psychological theories are vulnerable to over-simplifying what is a decidedly complex and confounding phenomenon.

In popular culture, narcissism has become our default lens for making judgements about the words, actions, and character of those close to us and those in public life. When we call someone "narcissistic," the language surrounding these judgements often takes on a one-dimensional and overly moralistic tone. For example, by commenting on someone's unbridled grandiosity and exhibitionism, we take them down a notch. We accuse our most intimate partners of being narcissistic when they do something that we perceive as being selfish, something that counters our own self-interest. We use it to wound the other, forcing them to once again pay attention to us and our own narcissistic needs. But we also use it to praise a certain kind of self-confidence and fruitful hubris that we respect and celebrate – "She's narcissistic, for sure, but at least she goes for what she wants." The word is thrown back and forth, like an exchange of daggers: self-absorbed and impervious, yes, but highly magnetic and effective. It is an endless and vexing see-saw.

With equally sweeping pronouncements of praise or damnation, depending upon which side is up and which down, this same kind of see-sawing effect occurs in how we talk about the digital. If we listen closely to the many claims that are made about its redemptive or destructive qualities, we hear tones and inflections that evoke the discourse on narcissism: Is the inflation brought about by the digital revolution a positive, life-affirming type, or does it also need to be taken down a notch in order to come to terms with something beyond it? Technology extends the reaches of the self, feeds its generative expansion, and offers it a unique platform at the center of the action. And yet, at the same time, nothing inflames the narcissistic impulse more than a smartphone in one's hand or a computer on one's lap. And when we are fully absorbed inside that mini-universe of the self, there stands, outside of us, the narcissistically wounded friend we have abandoned, imploring, "Why did you leave? Why aren't you placing me at the center of your attention rather than your device?" In both cases, thwarted or realized, narcissism is infused in every aspect of our digital lives. We must confront this narcissistic dynamic that is always there running behind the scene if we are to truly come to terms with the paradoxical effects of technology upon the psyche.

Narcissism is perhaps the most vulnerable feature of the human soul. It is the place from which we first begin to love, and thus it holds our most primary wounds and greatest ambivalences. There is no avoiding the fact that there is a narcissistic investment, very often concealed, in nearly everything that occupies our mind. By dint of having a desiring self, narcissism always has us in its grips. But, as Derrida (1995b) explains, there are different ways of being gripped by it:

> There is not narcissism and non-narcissism; there are narcissisms that are more or less comprehensive, generous, open, extended. What is called non-narcissism is in general but the economy of a much more welcoming and hospitable narcissism, one that is much more open to the experience of the other as other. (p. 199)

He goes on:

> I believe that without a movement of narcissistic reappropriation the relation to the other would be absolutely destroyed [...] The relation to the other, even if it remains asymmetrical and open, must trace a movement of reappropriation in the image of oneself for love to be possible. Love is narcissistic. (p. 199)

Through this idea that love itself is narcissistic, Derrida is emphasizing a fundamental ambiguity in the relation to the other. Or, in slightly different terms, he is emphasizing the inherent and enduring conflict between our self-interest and our investment in the well-being of the other (Slavin and Kriegman, 1992).

The myth of Narcissus, a core image for depth psychology, contains within itself all of the rich and evocative complexity that we have been discussing. The beautiful young man, leaning over the pond, enraptured by the sight of his own reflection, suggests at least two very different readings. The view of classical psychoanalysis contends that what we are witnessing here in its purest form is an image of self-love: a solipsistic absorption in a beautifully magnified reflection of the self at the expense of one's investment in the other. In the myth, this other is portrayed by the figure of Echo, who is in love with Narcissus, but has to come to terms with how his self-absorption makes him unresponsive to her love. This self-absorption accords with Freud's (1914) vision of "primary narcissism," inherent to early infantile life: A baby, at the very earliest beginnings, finds itself in a state of nearly totalizing self-satisfaction that has no need for an other.

Hillman (1983) offers a second reading: "Narcissus leans out and over and into the image; he is not wrapped up in his own feelings, his own self. He has forgotten himself, subjectivism completely gone, no narcissism whatsoever! The image fills consciousness and his desire" (p. 182). For Hillman, Narcissus is an exemplar of the imagination as an a-subjective, autonomous dimension of psychic life. Lou Andreas-Salomé, a neglected yet important early follower of Freud, drives this point home by pointing out that what Narcissus is really enraptured by is not his own image, but the world reflected back in the pond.

> Narcissus [...] looked not into a man-made mirror but into a forest pool, the mirror of nature, so that what he saw was not just his own face, but his face in union with the outer and boundless world of nature. That union, that entirety was what he was in love with. (Livingstone, 1984, p. 185)

Narcissus falls in love with the world; in peering through the self, he experiences union with what is outside of himself. This second reading offers a very different way of envisioning the narcissism at the core of love, supplanting the inwardly turned love of the solipsistic self with a love that opens toward the beauty of the world. Rather than manifesting a frenetic desire to stamp itself everywhere, this is a narcissism that supplants its own face with the face of nature, an image that speaks to the dissolution of the self into "the outer and boundless world of nature." As Hillman says, "subjectivism completely gone." Narcissism is thus transformed in its encounter with its opposite, the a-subjective, which lies outside the mind and its constructions.

In light of this second reading, we can see how digital narcissism, in connecting with so many people in so many ways, encourages an existentially expansive opening of the self toward the world, a more welcome and hospitable stance toward "the other as other." However, it can also galvanize us to turn back on ourselves, in ceaseless self-absorption, blocking out the world. In the demanding speed and buzzing confusion that make slowness and quiet reflection impossible in the digital, we are barely conscious of these opposing forces.

Think about how this tension collapses when our relationship to a digital device is challenged: For instance, how, when we are asked to justify the amount of time we spend online, or on our phones, or playing video games, we deflect and mis-direct, anything to divert the charge, refusing to acknowledge them as the narcissistic objects that they have become for us.

We are very vulnerable to becoming completely absorbed in them, often at the expense of our more immediate connection to what is occurring around us. A well of shame is opened up when this self-absorption is censored by the other. In our own wounded narcissism – the profound lack at the core of our being – that we seek to hide from ourselves and keep hidden from others, we cannot bear to acknowledge the pleasure we take in our gadgets. The digital helps us ward off the lack by ceaselessly inflating the narcissistically delighted self.

The psychological origins of this lack are the love, understanding, and care that we desperately needed when young, but could never get enough of. The creative potential for love and attachment to help us contain this lack has its own conflicted history, rooted in one's earliest emotional experience. In its most extreme and pathological forms, it becomes a narcissism whose only mode for bearing its own lack is through the exploitation of the other. Unable to love, it becomes a malignant narcissism.

Heidegger (1996) takes it one step further by speaking of an ontological lack, the nullity of existence, that haunts us all our lives, evoking an existential shame we all feel for having a null void at the center of our being: the shame, in other words, of being mortal. Weaving together this psychological and ontological shame in whatever ways we can (conceptually, emotionally, experientially) enables us to see inside each of us the workings of these twisting poles of shame as they wind their path through the maze of digital life. Why are we so stubbornly defensive about our digital practices? What are we most afraid of having exposed?

Well, one way to put it would be to say: We cannot ever truly come to terms with the fact that in our desperation for the enhancement of self, and the emboldenment of our narcissistic drives that forms the basis of the digital impulse, there lies a shameful act of recovery, an attempt to obtain the love that has always eluded us by using the digital to fill in lack and loss and gap. We cannot bear to see, operating behind the scenes, the hidden promise to repair our broken narcissism.

As an answer to the powerful yearning of restoring what has been traumatized, abandoned, and left behind, the digital blends together self-importance, omnipotence, and a feeling of union with the world. In other words, the digital enacts a powerful unconscious fantasy that we can become whole again, and that what was lost in the potential fullness of ourselves can now be regained.

This deeply buried narcissistic wound is at the core of what could be called the digital unconscious. Each of us, in our own particular and idiomatic ways, are driven to exploit the digital, where our insatiable hunger can eventually lead to a virtual life that lacks "nothing." Beyond simply being defensive about our attachment to our gadgets, there is a nearly involuntary resistance to reflect upon the origins of our digital narcissism. We know so well from psychoanalysis how the unconscious resists exposure, so it is not surprising how very arduous, even agonizing, it can be to examine our libidinized narcissism and its hidden investments. We just want to indulge in our devices and be left alone.

3 Digital illusion and the virtual-real

Psychoanalysis offers a unique vision of the psyche as an intricate yet ultimately indeterminable dance of polarities. For example, desire and sexuality, as a fundamental source that animates psychic life, encompasses an astonishing mixture of opposing tensions: love and hate, tenderness and aggression, intimacy and distance. Freud's conception of how these polarities structure our lives helps us to understand not only how human behavior is driven by unconscious forces, but also the staggering degree of self-deception that goes on in the mind when it comes to understanding why we do the things we do. Psychoanalysis as a practice involves learning how to live amidst these tensions, how to contain them well enough within oneself so that one can continue to stay in an open relationship with the world.

Keeping in mind these key features of psychoanalysis, we want to push further the dialogue between depth psychology and digital virtuality by way of Freud's (1974) "Two Principles of Mental Functioning." The Pleasure and Reality Principles describe a primary tension between the instinctual drive for pleasure and the impulse toward immediate gratification, on the one hand, and the facts of reality that demand a necessary delay of gratification, where we have to face, rather than disavow, reality, on the other. Our ceaseless search for pleasure is always bumping up against the exigencies and obstacles of a world that does not simply bend to our wishes.

In order to realize the full force of what is at stake in these two opposing principles, it is necessary to move away from the attempts to bind the primal energy of the psyche into normative paths of progressive growth and development – what Bersani (1986, p. 112) calls "the teleological thrust" in Freud's theories. But, remarkably enough, alongside his theoretical attempts to funnel desire into socially respectable and normalized channels, there is a counternarrative in Freud's writing that acknowledges the non-teleological a-directionality and ungovernability of desire. This bifurcation in Freud strongly parallels the dynamics we have already seen, between the Platonic move to ground the simulacrum in representational structures and the Deleuzian approach that leaves it unmoored, open to its own vital movements. Following this spirit in Freud's work, we intend to stay closer to the latter Deleuzian approach in our continuing exploration of the virtual within.

This move echoes the important broadening of classical psychoanalytic theory into the rich post-Freudian literature, where the opposition between pleasure and reality is transformed into an outwardly expanding set of lively dialectics, as, for example, the creative tension between the internal (object relational) world of psychic reality and the external demands of communal, intersubjective life. This broadening also happens in continental philosophy, as the dualisms of inner and outer reality, as well as mind and body, are fundamentally deconstructed. We see this particularly in the Deleuzian ontology of immanence, which aims to do away with the traditional splitting of self and world. As we proceed, we will use these ideas to help us draw out the implicit ontological and existential registers embedded in Freud's work that will become useful for our on-going exploration of virtual life.

A common feature that runs from Freud to the post-Freudians to these contemporary philosophical discourses is the assumption that the play of illusion and reality (virtual and real) ontologically structures our psychic lives. We cannot bear too much reality, so we turn to illusion as a creative shield, protecting us from that which is unbearable. But when our inner resources are exclusively devoted to keeping reality out, and we are left without the capacity to process psychic events (and thus make the unbearable bearable), that shield is unwittingly transformed into a fortress, and our illusions become calcified, numbing us to the sense of our own aliveness.

A primary function of psychoanalysis, and perhaps implicitly of all forms of therapy, is to help a person move beyond the traumatic (and the neurotic) in order to facilitate new ways of organizing the self so that it can both bear and be enlivened by the suffering from our encounters with the primary oppositions of life and death, fantasy and reality, virtual and real. Psychic destructiveness and psychic emergence stand in a dynamic tension with one another. When the drives are wholly unbound, a person is subject to psychological destruction. Early trauma, for instance, can be seen as premature exposure to an overwhelming drive energy that causes the psyche to split and turn against itself for the sake of self-protection (Kalsched, 1996). But something destructive also happens when the drives are too tightly bound, as when so vigilantly defending against them one is cut off from the creative potential of one's own life force. In the encounter with what is "other," therefore, the psyche can either be creatively transformed or destructively overwhelmed.

Between creativity and destructiveness, illusion is an essential mediator. As Stephen Mitchell (1988) points out, illusion, which he describes as the overvaluation or idealization of a person, a thing, or an experience, can be seen in two contrary ways. When the experience of something becoming larger than life, vitally important and compelling, is used to conceal or disavow some aspect of reality that we have failed to come to terms with, illusion becomes defense, an attempt to escape the real. The view of the virtual as an upgrade of the real would be an example. We seek comfort in its offer of a cleaned-up, perfected reality, because reality itself is too harsh to bear. By bringing the things of the world so close in that they feel alive, compelling, and important, the digital fuels this over-idealization of experience. But this can easily veer in a pathological direction, especially when it hooks our narcissism. In order to maintain its illusion of omnipotence, the all-important self needs to ward off an awful lot of the world that does not fit into its idealized image of itself. It's easy to see, then, how these new opportunities to simulate reality unconsciously compel us to steer our virtualities toward what we want and who we think we are.

When the virtual is not seen as opposed to the real but inseparable and always embedded in it, our view shifts. The virtual becomes a life-potentiating wellspring for our creative response to the world, allowing us to embrace it in its full dimensionality. In being able to temporarily escape the heaviness of material and psychological reality, illusion allows us to play and can become the growing edge of how we come to know ourselves. The digital virtual is a prime example of how we deepen our experience of the real through creative illusion. The networked connectivity that surrounds us everywhere fills us with possibilities that bring an almost magical aura to ordinary life.

But it is this very "magic" that is in question as we consider that the digital is the greatest fabricator of illusion that has ever been created. It can make us believe, body and soul, that we are living in one kind of reality that can stand in absolute contradiction to our actual life circumstances. The homeless man sitting on a city bench staring into his smartphone (an image not uncommon today in a large metropolis), dreaming that he is living a very different life becomes a poignant metaphor for this condition. Every time we log on and start clicking we enact that dream. What in actual life can only be one way, in the virtual can be any way. But how is that trick performed, and how does it differ from our ordinary experience of imagination, daydreaming, and fantasy?

What is "illusory" about the digital-virtual is that it seduces us into believing that we are experiencing something real, not virtual; the very same illusion that underlies our conviction that we are awake when dreaming. The virtual-real entices us with the promise that we can have all the real we want, always ready and at our disposal. Because of our vulnerability to self-deception, we can trick ourselves into believing that we are indeed experiencing something real when in fact we are, on the contrary, desperately resisting it. It can draw us into that rapture of self-absorption, into what can become, unchecked, a trance-like state. Oliver Sacks (2019), mourning for an era that is apparently being left behind, describes what has become a common contemporary scene that exemplifies the ubiquity of this enthrallment:

> I cannot get used to seeing myriads of people in the street peering into little boxes or holding them in front of their faces, walking blithely in the path of moving traffic, totally out of touch with

their surroundings. I am most alarmed by such distraction and
inattention when I see young parents staring at their cell phones
and ignoring their own babies as they walk or wheel them
along. (p. 28)

Whereas fantasy or the creative immersion in illusion used to be held
in check, it is now becoming unbound. The permanent accessibility of
the virtual-real is making whatever was outside limiting it, irrelevant.
Its enticements are dramatically restructuring our relationship to the
phantasmatic dimensions of psychic life that Freud called primary
process. This free-flowing, always on-tap, digitally-generated virtuality
is a new presence on the world stage that in its very occurrence
conceals our relationship to those other sources of virtuality that have
nothing to do with digital realities. Today, we can have as much of it
as we want, with little risk or exposure. The massive outpouring of
virtual-real is bedeviling human virtuality. Something fundamental
about our desire is changing.

The digital age, in a very short span of time, has created astonishing innovations in our most bedrock cultural institutions: politics, media, education, economics, to say nothing of child-rearing,
dating, sexuality, consumerism, and our everyday experience of
human (and non-human) relationality. The illusion of the virtual-
real potentiates life as it bolsters the self. But, at the very same time,
it holds within it the promise of an endlessness that has the potential
to carry us away into a frenzied state. We can only continue to
partake of its riches by fundamentally disavowing key aspects of
material and psychic reality. The Hikikomori who cease to bathe, eat,
and drink until they literally fall over, exemplify this disavowal. The
virtual-real satiates a profound hunger for more intensity, more life,
while at the same time leaving unaddressed the demands of our
bodily existence.

How much illusion is necessary to make bearable the undeniably
painful dimensions of existence? In the recesses between pleasure and
reality, the virtual-real creates a space where our most primordial
desires can manifest themselves in a medium that transforms mind-
fantasies into virtual immediacies. What is conjured up from the recesses of the psyche is virtually presented to us as real, in unlimited
supply, at whatever intensity we choose. But the central issue (and
this refers as well to the implicit question of narcissism, which remains lurking in the background) is whether having such immediate
access to all the virtual-real we want tips the scales (in either
direction), thereby collapsing a necessary tension between these two
sides of illusion, defensive or creative, narrowing or expanding life,
which touches the very core of who we are psychologically and
ontologically.

In the spirit of "pharmacological" thinking, we want to hold our discourse open to both sides of the ledger: There is something about the phantasmatic nature of the virtual-real that is creative and enlivening and furthers our capacity for imaginative living. And there is at the very same time a strong unconscious pull to use it to block out what we refuse to bear.

The core Freudian tension between pleasure and reality can be read existentially, as the distinction between subjectivity and world occurrence, i.e. what happens in our mind as opposed to what happens in the world. The mini-universe that arises from the virtual-real is limited by the ontological reality of our everyday life-world. Scott (1999) suggests that it is the very eventfulness of human embodiment that sets these limits, when he writes:

> There is something not at all virtual in the inexorability of a singular event [....] It is "real," we are inclined to say, not imagined at all, quite beyond the reach of the perceptions that grasp it, imagine it, and name it. There is much that is not virtual in a child's sickness, a realization that brings many new parents out of a cloud of romanticism and imagination when they see that their child, burning with fever, can die. Not virtual, real. It is one thing to see a car wreck on film. It is quite another to be in a wreck, to feel the shock of the accident, the impact, the radical movements, out of control, twisting and rolling with you tossed and thrown in them [...] I knew a 13-year-old boy who ran a very painful first marathon. Afterwards he said, "I always thought that in the movies, if I were the guy on the ground, wounded, reaching for the gun, that I would do it. I would move two inches more, get the gun, and shoot the other guy. Out there I got to where I couldn't move any more than I was moving. I thought I was going to die. I tried, but I couldn't do any more. You know, you reach a point and you can't go farther." The nonvirtual reality of limits. (p. 189)

The extraordinary access we have to the virtual-real, in its fluid capacity for infinite transformation, shields us from the unyielding nature of life events. As it becomes so seamlessly assimilated into the texture of everyday life, our awareness of how much of the real we are allowing to be replaced by the virtual-real is slowly eroding. When our technologies provide too much assistance in holding at bay what is unbearable in the real, and, at the same time, give us such immediate access to its vitality, we become unable to use our own imaginative capacities to bring to life the things of the world. It's easy to imagine us soon walking around with our VR headsets, immersed in virtual reality, increasingly numb to those moments in everyday life that

Scott calls the "nonvirtual reality of limits," like sadness, boredom, loneliness, and emptiness.

Yet what from one perspective appears to be withdrawal and escapism, warding off the hard realities of material life, may, from another, be seen as a liberation from the rigidity of culture. Our new and emerging virtualities can expand and deepen our experience of the concrete world, and change our attitude toward non-human others; they can unshackle our erotic energies, and deconstruct the binaries of gender and sexual orientation. What emerges is an ethos of multiplicities that are no longer ruled by or originate from a central structure – an overturning of the Law of the Father, an overcoming of sexual difference.

Trauma often entails a premature exposure to psychic and/or physical impingements, where the ego is overwhelmed by the aftershocks of severe loss, abuse, and bodily disintegration. This causes a breakdown of the capacity to metabolize psychic pain (Bion, 1983; Ferro, 2007). Because unguarded exposure to life's contingencies has the potential to unconsciously re-invoke the traumatic experience, the victim of trauma must live a restricted existence. What results is the "frozen" child who is unable to play, or the adult survivor who cannot bear anything that hints of the unpredictable and unknown, and thus is cut off from the spontaneity of psychic life and its richness.

Now let us imagine what it would be like for a traumatized person to have a certain amount of control in a medium where the play of illusion and imagination can be enjoyed, relatively safe from the impingement of others. The experience of omnipotence without limits, pleasure that transcends the boundaries of the real – all features of life online – creates a potential space for psychic exploration of tremendous promise for recovering what has been foreclosed by one's developmental traumas. The virtual-real helps repair the damage done to the virtual within, by offering "safe play" for the enactment of fantasy and desire, helping to generate the building blocks of a psychic capacity that may never have had the chance to be borne.

Young people nowadays take for granted the relatively "safe play" made available by the virtual. There they engage in psychic explorations that are dynamically open to the currents of the imaginative psyche that flow in sexuality, friendship, video games, art, music, fashion, and more. There is an immediacy of connection and a vibrancy of communication in those spaces, an "instant of sheer youth, an order where everything is pending, where what is no longer possible historically remains always possible" (Scott, 1999, p. 231). The virtual-real thus becomes an ahistorical moment of pure possibility.

The instant of sheer youth made possible by the virtual suggests that the digital age instantiates a puer psychology, where the experience of "now" is given supreme value. Always seeking, always wanting, always chasing after the new that lurks just ahead, life is lived in an unceasing quest for the unattainable. The *Puer Aeternus* of Greek Mythology gives us an image of this high-flying youth, who, longing for the unattainable, seeks to escape the grounding limits of reality:

> Phaethon, Apollo's son, tries to drive his father's Sun-chariot straight up in the sky. Icarus, in his desperation to escape the starry-eyed bull at the center of Minos' labyrinth flies upward toward the sun on waxen wings constructed by his father. Both figures fall to their death on a reverse traversal toward the earth. Vertical flight and free falling characterize this aspect of the puer spirit. (Frankel, 1998, p. 183)

The puer-like dimension of digitality inevitably evokes its opposite, the senex – the low and leaden-footed old man or woman – that signifies the dramatic descent that forcefully grounds it.

With the ever-present possibility of the virtual-real, one never lands anywhere definitively, everything stays open ... until the inevitable fall. From the senex perspective, being always up in the air, open to every and all possibility, is nothing other than an avoidance of material life, superficially skimming its surface. Here we find ourselves swept up again in yet another instance of the paradoxical dichotomy embedded in our technological discourse, although this time in the image of the puer-senex. Hillman (1998) and López-Pedraza (1990) have written convincingly of the tremendous psychological work involved in not polarizing these two figures. We are contending that the permanent availability of the virtual-real that flows from the digital, in its turbulent extremes of wide-eyed optimism and dark pessimism, embody that very polarization, a splitting of two vital life orientations, that are in desperate need of a pharmacological intervention: learning to stand in-between the sprint toward the future and the new, on the one hand, and the slow walk backward into the past and the old, on the other.

4 Digital virtuality and the pleasure principle

The digital challenges the assumption that pleasure, fantasy, and illusion need to be firmly bound in order to adequately heed the call of the real. As an agent of unbinding, digital virtuality releases us from the stultifying binaries that repress non-normative desires and orientations. With this incredible liberation of desire, imagination, and a newfound fluidity in our sexual lives, there stands Freud, in full senex regalia, declaring that the digital virtual is nothing other than the adult re-creation of the pleasure principle inherent to early, infantile life. Were he around today, Freud might describe the Internet as a narcissistically regressive device – a wish-granting machine, as it were, in its hallucinatory-like ability to bring to life the object of our desire. Indeed, the transformational malleability of the virtual eerily echoes the primary process world, where wishes are instantaneously gratified without the need of a real "other"; the virtual-real condenses an entire scene into an extensionless point.

Just as the hungry baby hallucinates the milk-filled breast, the virtual creates an immediate path from desire to its gratification, overriding the necessity of the circuitous path of secondary process – Freud's *Umweg* – where, in order to actually be fed, one has to emerge from the solipsistic world of wish-fulfillment and take into account the reality of an "other," separate from the self. In the mode of primary process, the infant is granted control over the breast. It is there and then gone, but when mother leaves, the loss evoked by her absence is overcome: The breast is hallucinated back into presence. The digital places in the hands of the ego that selfsame power to overcome absence through the "virtual" re-creation of the object.

The hermeticism of the infant's world is ruptured when she has to acknowledge the difference between her desire and its object, between her subjectivity and the external world. Coming to terms with that gap is what ultimately delivers her from infantile fantasy into reality. The digital provides a magical means to go back to the hermeticism that existed before that acknowledgment. The virtual world and its objects, a repository of our desires and projections, returns us to the psychic womb. Digital representation seals us off from the other, re-creating the very solipsism of the infant.

Digital life, with its totalizing access to an infinite world of virtual objects that are there, ready, at our immediate disposal, be they sexual, aesthetic, consumerist, or informational, is wholly bound up with desire's lack at the heart of the pleasure principle. We are placed in the same situation as the breast-hallucinating infant with one essential difference: now these hallucinations are digitally materialized in a virtual space that is public and collectively accessible. Wishes, which had before solely remained in the inner spaces of the mind, are now made tangible as "objects" in the virtual world. Moreover, we have acquired experience that forces us now to deal with these new virtual objects, not solely from the mute solipsism of infancy.

The role of pleasure and desire in our daily digital duties, though often unconscious, infuses them with sexual energies that represent the primary investments of our affective lives. This hidden erotic sphere explains why, even in the midst of our most intimate relationships, we cannot wait to get back to the screen. When our experiences with real others fail to give the right dose of pure pleasure output, we rush to make contact with the virtual, where the eroticized omnipotence of self (a real "turn-on") can always be relied upon. We are drawn away from what is before us as we long for what is there waiting for us. The pure potentiality of the virtual is the source of this powerful seduction, where fantasy and desire are activated through the promise of seeing and thus "having" whatever it is that we want.

It's not that we love our digital devices more than, for example, our children, or that what is happening there is more important than what is happening around us. Rather, the bond that grows between us and the digital overrides the bonds we have to empirical reality and those closest and dearest. It is an attachment to a material object unlike any other. It's not like loving your car, even obsessively loving it. Or loving your house or even your dog. A shockingly large quantity of narcissistic-libido pours forth from our devices, carrying an electric-like psychic charge that overcomes the tedium that we experience in our everyday being. Take that away, and we are catastrophically faced with a powerful shock of negativity that is caused by the return of the repressed emptiness. Suddenly, and without warning, we stand on the precipice of a lack that we no longer know how to deal with. This may be why our digital devices have become as indispensable to us as, say, our hands or our mouths. Once all our information is lost and our pocket-sized representational universe has vanished, we have the feeling that something fundamental to our subjectivity has been erased. One's machine crashes, and what has become an essential part of the desiring self's experience is suddenly obliterated. The digital fills us up, overflows us with the dynamism of its hidden erotics, and when it ceases, our world is emptied and we are driven into a state of panic.

Whether it be in the desperate compulsiveness of online shopping or Internet pornography, or in our mindlessly surfing the web or checking for the likes we have or the chats pending, the virtual provides us with the unceasing novelty of its offerings which is meant to banish the void and transport us away to somewhere else. We are in an endless quest to avoid desolate spaces, to reconnect with liveliness and desire, to lose ourselves again and again in the erotic.

According to Plato in the *Symposium*, Eros is the child of the mythic couple *Poros* (plentifulness) and *Penia* (poverty). The digital is well-attuned to Poros, as it so effectively fills us up, but what happens to our relationship with Penia, that sense of poverty that haunts our digital ministrations? If indeed the digital erodes our capacity for metabolizing emptiness, lack, and loss, then, paradoxically, the diminishment of that capacity increases the powerful seduction of the digital's overflowing fullness. Penia is the gap between what we imagine and what we get. She's the non-representable dimension of language, which communicates despite its failure to communicate. And most poignantly, she is the null center of subjectivity, that vast reservoir of nothingness out of which the self emerges. We keep grasping for more virtual-real, using it as a glue to fill in the gaps of reality, in order to forestall an encounter with Penia. The operations of the digital-virtual covers over the gappiness inherent to our own occurrence. They bring precision, uniformity, and full presence. No holes. No empty space. Nothing to fall through.

At times, when we are really gripped by it, we want to be rid of anyone or anything that stands in the way or interferes with our engrossment in the digital. Think here of the fights that ensue at dinnertime or bedtime when the exasperated parent is struggling to get a child or adolescent to close down the game, put the phone away, shut off their iPad. Or when a friend asks another to put down their phone and listen to what they are saying. Or when we refuse the darkness of sleep and dream in the name of the eternally illuminated screen, never to be extinguished or perhaps not until that very last moment, just before we fall into sleep, the moment of our own self-extinguishment. And when we awaken in the middle of the night, amidst the darkness of the dreaming self, we once again crave its light.

Lacan tells us that love is giving what you don't have (i.e., giving to the other what you lack). Thus in order to love, we have to come to terms both with our own lack, as well as the lack in our beloved. So what happens to that lack when our love lives are suffused with the overflowing digital? On social media, we seek out love with the strategy of Poros – fires are lit, matches are made, and passions burn. In searching for love on the Internet, we present the perfection of our digital identity, which covers up all inadequacies and vulnerabilities. Our attractions resonate with a digital fullness that conceals lack and inverts the grammar of Eros.

5 Sexuality hyperrealized

The digital has brought about a dizzying expansion of the erotic imagination, calling forth a vastly wider range of sexual possibilities than ever before. In the age of Tinder, Grinder, Bumble, Match, and the like and the numerous and diverse forms of cybersex, sex has become accessible in an entirely new way. Along a broad spectrum of options – from the digitally mediated partner behind a screen to the digitally searched and sorted partner lying next to us – we can have what we want when we want it, with a single swipe. Sex in the digital age is nearly instantaneous. No more waiting around. Deferral and delay have all but been eliminated. We can have sex with our partners in virtual space, and even with people over the Internet that we don't ever have to meet in the real world.

By removing the many and varied obstacles between what we wish for and what we can have, the virtual creates a hyperrealization of desire, often pushing us toward its omnipotent edge. Hyperreality fuels the erotic charge of the sexual images and situations that unfold before us. The digital register of sexual experience, the brilliant realness of its image, its rapid change of angles, objects, and perspectives and its capacity to zoom in and scrutinize, places before our very eyes what was once only possible in art and imagination. As the digital brings pornography to its ultimate evolution, the greatest turn on may very well be hyperreality itself. The still photo culminates in the porn videos of today, as the sharpness of the digital representation reveals the erotic right down to its most minute gradations, all now captured in stunning high definition reality. Although pornographic images date back to the earliest days of human history, with the advent of film there has been a progressive intensification of the erotic imagination in barely a century. The digital makes the experience of watching simulated sexual acts no longer a form of voyeuristic vicariousness but real-time virtual interaction.

What we are witnessing today is nothing short of an erotic revolution. In this light, the digital can be seen as a dynamic force that has lifted the cultural prohibitions and repressions that have tried to regulate and normalize human sexuality. Today, everything is open and available, freeing libido, liberating desire.

With its focus on unruly and disorderly drives that seek satisfaction independent of their objects, Freud's *Three Essays on the Theory of Sexuality* reveals what in sexuality cannot be domesticated. As Bersani (in Bersani and Phillips, 2008) puts it, Freud articulates a

> sexual desire [that is] indifferent to personal identity, antagonistic to ego requirements and regulations, and, following a famous Freudian dictum, always engaged in group sex even when the actual participants are limited to the two partners of the socially approved couple. (p. 43)

This unbinding of Eros that occurs in Freud's original drafting of the *Three Essays* parallels the hyperrealization of sexuality that is opened up by the virtual. When erotic fantasy becomes real through its actualization on the web, we can now see and experience whatever it is we can dream up. The Internet maxim mysteriously referred to as Rule 34 states that "if you can imagine it, there is porn of it"; Now, whatever sexual act we fantasize instantly materializes. We can get as close up to the action as we wish or keep it safely distant, as is evidenced by the increasingly common practice of couples and groups filming themselves while having sex (and often posting it for others to see). And increasingly, with the sophistication of virtual reality technologies, Internet pornography is becoming a three-dimensional immersive experience. The virtual actualizes what is truly polymorphously perverse in our nature, creating an inexhaustible combination of the sexual instinct's "source," "aim," and "object" (Freud, 1905). In enabling us to bypass the encounter with a separate other, the digital reinforces a turning away from the actual object, which is crucial to Freud's definition of sexual excitement. More and more of our erotic life takes place amidst digitally constituted, virtual objects that we can use at our own discretion to give shape to the drive.

Breaking free of the analogical structuring that tethers the self to its own unique history, the digital is an invitation to enter into one's own radical multiplicity. In virtual space, we are temporarily relieved of the burden of having to hold ourselves together as a somewhat unified self in order to negotiate the vicissitudes of worldly experience. In this move from one to many, an affective intensity is ushered in, making space for the many different dimensions of self that get little play or everyday recognition. In terms of one's erotic life, what does not happen in ordinary social experience can happen in virtual social space. We can say or see or enact anything we want, buttressed by the anonymity and distance of the digital. Playing at different genders and sexualities, we are free to experiment with our identity and desire in whichever directions it may take us.

Faced with the problem of the unruliness, disorder, and multiplicity brought about by sexuality, we may choose, as Freud does, to see sexual repression as the compromise we make for an orderly, civilized life. But the digital offers an alternative solution by creating a space free from the constraints of the reality principle where we can realize dimensions of our sexual drives that have no place in civilized society. Our primitive desires, aggressive and erotic, which threaten social norms through the voyeuristic and exhibitionistic tendencies of the self, for example, can now happen virtually, thereby preserving civilization, and perhaps even transforming it.

If the domestication of our sexual and aggressive drives is the price we pay for civilization, is there any price to be paid when these very same drives can live out a relatively undomesticated life in the virtual world? The digital makes sexuality more fluid and accessible, opening us to the expressive freedoms of an undomesticated Eros; however, if there is a cost to these new freedoms, it may very well be a certain kind of disconnection from everyday, embodied sexuality. Bionic sexuality is rapidly advancing into the culture, as sex with love dolls and sex with avatars becomes commonplace, and, just around the corner, sex with robots (Danaher and McArthur, 2017). As Knafo and Bosco (2017) point out:

> The sex-doll industry is burgeoning, and high-end silicone love dolls are being manufactured in the United States, Japan, and Germany and sold briskly on the Web. There are even sex-doll

brothels and escort services [...] David Levy, a well-known AI expert, boldly claims that in less than 40 years, marriage to robots will be legal in some states. (pp. 14–15)

Just a little over a decade ago, there were a couple of films that depicted the fictional occurrence of human sex-doll relationships (Lars and the Real Girl (2007), Kūki Ningyō (2009)). Nowadays, these fictional stories have become real life occurrences, perhaps a little odd to some, but unsurprising to many. Indeed, this new mode of sexual behavior is becoming so normalized that it is not uncommon to find that, for example, in his Instagram account, a Russian man is constantly posting photographs, videos, and commentaries about his love life with a doll, rhapsodizing about her as an actual (human) lover. As we increasingly rely upon a world of non-human objects to sustain our sexuality and begin to live out our primordial drives in the digital world, we contemplate the prospect of a post-human future.

Another potential cost is just how addictive digital sexuality can become. The disembodied engagement and permanent availability of unending erotic possibilities helps to explain this, as there is always something new and exciting that promises more in the next click. It's a way of dealing with desire and finding pleasure with little cost or emotional or psychic investment. The object of our desire appears before us and engages us scopophilically, hyperactivating our fantasy while our increasingly aroused body remains mute, passive, and invisibly participating. We can have the object we want as close as the screen can bring it, but never beyond. The session eventually ends when it finds release, but only as the inexhaustible call of sexual possibility hyperactivates again the draw toward something new, something not yet seen. Our desire is unable to penetrate the real. As Zizek (1997) sees it:

> My cyberspace sexual partner is...over-present, bombarding me with the torrential flow of images and explicit statements of her (or his) most secret fantasies. Or, to put it another way: [the real other] is the cut of the Real, the traumatic obstacle, which again and again unsettles the smooth run of my self-satisfying erotic imagination, while cyberspace presents its exact opposite, a frictionless flow of images and messages – when I am immersed in it, I, as it were, return to a symbiotic relationship with an Other in which the deluge of semblances seems to abolish the dimension of the Real. (p. 156)

The intensification of sexuality, while unbinding and broadening may, at the very same time diminish and flatten the erotic. Hyperrealized sexuality intensifies things, makes them hotter, but at the same time may cause Eros, in his ineffability, to flee. Here, we bump up against the paradoxical ambivalence of the erotic, as it plays itself out digitally.

The drive toward the cyber-realization of desire aggravates our relation to desire's lack. Because of the unending virtual availability of what we most desire, that we can have as much of exactly what we want, without interference, we are tricked by the seductive promise of the erasure of lack, that desire can be truly and finally satisfied. We can't stop looking. We can't stop searching. We can't stop believing that we will ultimately find the right combination of sounds and images that will fully extinguish our desire. But in the end, we are entrapped by the masochistic search for the ever elusive object.

In *Being and Time*, Heidegger (1996) describes what happens when we make the world into a repository for our wishes:

> Being-in-the-world whose world is primarily projected as a wish-world has lost itself utterly in what is available, but in such a way that in the light of what is wished for, what is available (all the things at hand) is never enough. (p. 182)

In the episode of *Black Mirror* that we have already mentioned, "The Entire History of You," there is a scene that shows the husband and wife, in bed, having sex. As the excited and passionate moments subside, each partner uses the re-do button to stimulate themselves as they approach climax by replaying the previously impassioned moments. It is not clear whether they are playing back what just happened or past fantasies with other lovers, but in that turning back toward a moment that has (just) passed, they become impassive and disconnected from the living reality of each other's body, but sexually stimulated by and fixated on their own representations.

Sex with a real other involves this back and forth movement between intersubjective sexual contact and interiorized fantasy, whether we are imagining and remembering what just happened, or fantasizing about a different lover, or different parts of someone else's body altogether. The re-do button literalizes the virtualizing of sexuality in the act of making love, something that is usually private and concealed. This scene thus stages the phantasmatic, virtual dimensions of sexuality (i.e., the hallucinated, real/not real play that constitutes it). But the scene also raises an important question about the effects of the digital on sexuality. By providing an instantaneous replay of past sexual memory come to life, the self, clicking away at the re-do button, hyperrealizes fantasy. The sexual imagination is handed over to the cyber-ego in the form of on-demand instant replay pornography. Even though the "real" other, the real relationship, is not completely eclipsed, it is displaced by this artificially intensified fantasy now made manifest as a virtual reality.

When the cyber-ego takes control of Eros, sex becomes an ever-narrowing expression of what the ego wants. The digital brings in so much of the agentic self and its strategies of perversion (which no doubt inflame sexuality), and thus becomes so tied up with narcissism, that the other is just out of reach, and the possibility for establishing a different kind of intensity – more welcoming of the other as other – is elided.

Sex is one of our most forceful reminders that desire ultimately flows from loss and lack. What is truly pornographic about the digital is that it literalizes the wish for unending and unlimited satisfaction. Who can resist its call to the enduring youthfulness of life? The compulsion to use the digital to solve the problem of lack in sexuality is just one more instance of the same drive behind the use of our pocket sized machines to disavow lack in the world. If emptiness evokes the negative, virtual life evokes its opposite. Mortal existence itself is always pervaded by absence, darkness, and the passing away of things. But we must reckon with what we are missing when our digital lives are fueled by the promise to banish death and contingency, and full presence becomes the order of the day.

Notes

1 By depth psychology, we are speaking of those psychologies that orient themselves around the concept of the unconscious, thus including not only psychoanalysis and the post-Freudian tradition but analytical psychology and post-Jungian thinking as well.
2 Negative capability is a term adopted by Wilfred Bion (1970), who takes it from Keats, to refer to a capacity to bear "uncertainties, mysteries, doubts, without any irritable reaching after fact and reason" (p. 125).
3 Of course, since the pandemic, psychotherapy has all but transferred to the virtual, as most sessions now take place on a digital platform, so that the very issues we are exploring here have been magnified and exacerbated.
4 As we will see in the fourth part of the book, the issue of whether the notion of an individual self will survive seems to announce the dislocation of the concept of the human and lead to the idea of the post-human.

References

Bersani, L. (1986) *The Freudian body: Psychoanalysis and Art*. New York: Columbia University Press.

Bersani, L., and Phillips, A. (2008) *Intimacies*. Chicago: University of Chicago Press.

Bion, W. (1983) *Learning from Experience*. New York: Jason Aronson.

Bion, Wilfred R. (1970) *Attention and Interpretation*. London: Tavistock Publications.

Danaher, J., and McArthur, N. (2017) *Robot Sex: Social and Ethical Implications.* Cambridge, MA: MIT Press.

Derrida, J. (1995a) *Archive Fever: A Freudian Impression.* Chicago: University of Chicago Press.

Derrida, J. (1995b) *Points: Interviews 1974–1994.* Palo Alto, CA: Stanford University Press.

Ferro, A. (2007) *Avoiding Emotions, Living Emotions.* London: Routledge.

Frankel, R. (1998) *The Adolescent Psyche.* London: Routledge.

Freud, S. (1905) Three Essays on the Theory of Sexuality. In J. Strachey (Ed. and Trans.), *The Standard Edition of the Complete Psychological Works of Sigmund Freud* (vol. 7, pp. 125–243). London: Hogarth Press, 1974.

Freud, S. (1911) Formulations on the Two Principles of Mental Functioning. In J. Strachey (Ed. and Trans.), *The Standard Edition of the Complete Psychological Works of Sigmund Freud* (vol. 12, pp. 218–225). London: Hogarth Press, 1974.

Freud, S. (1914) On Narcissism. In J. Strachey (Ed. and Trans.), *Standard Edition* (vol. 14, pp. 67–104). London: Hogarth Press.

Giegerich, W. (2007) *Technology and the Soul: From the Nuclear Bomb to the World Wide Web* (vol. 2). New Orleans, LA: Spring Journal Books.

Heidegger, M. (1996) *Being and Time*(Joan Stambaugh, Trans.). New York: SUNY Press.

Hillman, J. (1979) *The Dream and the Underworld.* New York: Harper and Row.

Hillman, J. (1983) *Interviews.* New York: Harper and Row.

Hillman, J. (1998) *Puer Papers.* Dallas, TX: Spring Publications.

Kalsched, D. (1996) *The Inner World of Trauma: Archetypal Defenses of the Personal Spirit.* London: Routledge.

Knafo, D., and Bosco, R.L. (2017) *The Age of Perversion: Desire and Technology in Psychoanalysis and Culture.* London: Routledge.

Kohut, H. (1971) *The Analysis of the Self: A Systematic Approach to the Psychoanalytic Treatment of Narcissistic Personality Disorders.* Chicago: University of Chicago Press.

Kūki Ningyō (2009) Dir. Hirokazu Koreeda, Japan.

Lars and the Real Girl. (2007) Lars and the Real Girl (dir. Craig Guillespie, 2007, USA).

Li, Ou (2009) *Keats and Negative Capability* (p. ix). Continuum International Publishing Group.

Livingstone, A. (1984) *Salome: Her Life and Work.* New York: Moyer Bell Ltd.

López-Pedraza, R. (1990) *Cultural Anxiety.* Einsiedeln: Daimon Verlag.

Mitchell, S. A. (1988) *Relational Concepts in Psychoanalysis: An Integration.* Cambridge, MA: Harvard University Press.

Ogden, T. (2009) *Rediscovering Psychoanalysis: Thinking and Dreaming, Learning and Forgetting.* London: Routledge.

Sacks, O. (2019, February 11) The Machine Stops. *The New Yorker.* Retrieved from https://www.newyorker.com/magazine/2019/02/11/the-machine-stops

Scott, C. (1999) *The Time of Memory.* Albany, NY: SUNY Press.

Slavin, M., and Kriegman, D. (1992) *The Adaptive Design of the Human Psyche: Psychoanalysis, Evolutionary Biology and the Therapeutic Process.* New York: Guilford Press.

Žižek, S. (1997) *The Plague of Fantasies*. London: Verso.

Zuboff, S. (2015) Big Other: Surveillance Capitalism and the Prospects of an Information Civilization. *Journal of Information Technology, 30*, 75–89.

6 The virtual as potential space

There was a child that went forth every day,
And the first object he look'd upon, that object he became...
-Walt Whitman

Prelude

As we have indicated, although formulated in significantly different concepts, the issue of the virtual (and its relation to the real) is paramount for psychoanalysis, in its elucidation of the complex and dynamic tension between the inner world and outer reality. Pleasure vs. reality, fantasy vs. trauma, transference vs. the real relationship, are all expressions of this fundamental tension. In Lacan, it manifests in his tripartite division between the symbolic, the imaginary and the real. The individual's growing capacity to differentiate the virtual from the real, fantasy from reality, traces a progressive path toward separation and individuation that we find in psychoanalytic developmental theory from Freud to Winnicott to Klein to Bion.

In all of the many and varied guises in which psychoanalysis takes up these issues, Winnicott's work is most profoundly oriented toward the virtual dimensions of psychic life. He offers a developmental framework from which to understand its earliest origins in infancy as well as the continuing role it plays in child, adolescent and adult development. In our continuing effort to differentiate an existential-psychological virtuality from the virtuality that arises from digital technology, Winnicott is the perfect foil, for his writing and thinking took place in the mid-20th century, an era that saw many significant cultural and social changes, but one clearly preceding the changes brought about by the digital revolution. Not only does he provide us a framework for understanding the developmental origins of human virtuality, but, when held up against what is happening to the mind in a 21st-century digital culture, his work shines a bright light on the many effects, both positive and negative, that the digital is having on this trajectory as it develops throughout the lifespan.

For Winnicott, psychic life is potentiated when fantasy and imagination make creative contact with the outer world. Such moments of potentiation, when experience feels most alive and real, cannot be located simply as wholly inside or outside. *Potential space* is his term for a third area of experience, an intermediate area in which this vital mode of psychological engagement takes place. It is the point of contact between the inner world of fantasy, where things are fluid and idiosyncratic, and the outer world of reality, where things appear to be fixed and unchangeable. Potential space provides a dynamic scaffolding, "a resting-place for the individual engaged in the perpetual human task of keeping inner and outer reality separate, yet interrelated" (1971a, p. 2).

Potential space is an area of illusion, but this term is used in a positive sense to point to the place where things come creatively alive with meaning. If we think of potential space as possibility and emergence, there is then an implicit link between what is potential in human life – the mode of experience that occurs in potential space – and the concept of the virtual. Indeed, potentiality is the base definition of the virtual in philosophy, as we have already seen. As Massumi (2014) explains:

> What is in potentiality may come to be; and what has been, already was in potential. The virtual must thus be understood as a dimension of reality, not its illusionary opponent or artificial overcoming. The virtual, as allied to potential, belongs specifically to the formative dimensions of the real. It concerns the potency in what is, by virtue of which it really comes to be. (p. 55)

Winnicott's (1971a) definition of potential space as an intermediate area of experience, "to which inner reality and external life both contribute" (p. 3) strikingly maps onto the dynamic tension between the virtual and the real that has been the object of our study.[1] By exploring in what follows the dynamics of Winnicottian potential space – "this potency in what is, by virtue of which it really comes to be" – we are offered a unique pathway for differentiating the virtual as a mode of potentiation inherent to virtual reality technologies from a mode of potentiation belonging "specifically to the formative dimensions of the real" (Massumi, 2014, p. 55).

A significant struggle for us as psychological beings (pre- and post-digital) is to find life-affirming ways to engage the many polarizing tensions that result from the virtual/real dichotomy. Fundamental to the task of bearing the human condition is keeping inner and outer reality separate yet intimately related, or, in other words, finding ways to creatively stand in these tensions. Yet, it is not always so easy to discover this "resting-place." Potential space is difficult to sustain and very vulnerable to collapse. We are prone to cutting off or ridding ourselves of one side or the other, eclipsing the scope of our experience in the world.

The possibility of losing or collapsing potential space in a digital age is what is at issue in this chapter. This resonates with the idea that we have been developing throughout the book that, paradoxically, there may be an attenuation of the virtual in the age of digital virtuality. Yet, as always, we will try to stay open to both sides, and, as we will come to see, especially in our exploration of adolescence, the digital may also be creating new kinds of potential space, new forms of life, that uniquely re-envision the encounter between the virtual and the real.

1 Three senses of the virtual

Because Winnicott was first and foremost a developmental theorist, our method will be to examine three critical moments in his work with an eye toward what they reveal about the emergence and maturation of human virtuality. We will start from its earliest origins, in the primary relationship between mother and infant, move to the phase of transitional phenomena, when the infant begins to negotiate the process of separation, and lastly turn to adolescence, when the whole question of virtuality comes to the fore again in surprisingly new and unfamiliar ways.[2] The question of the virtual will be explored against the backdrop of how, in each of these moments, an originary contact with both the externality of the world and the otherness of the psyche is accomplished by the evolving self. Three distinct, yet related aspects of virtuality arise in the context of these particular developmental moments that offer new insights into many of the topics that we have touched upon up to this point.

The first sense of the Winnicottian virtual gives expression to how the imagination (play, illusion and fantasy) aids the developing psyche in mediating otherness and difference.

> The mother, at the beginning, by an almost 100 percent adaptation affords the infant the opportunity for the illusion that her breast is part of the infant. It is, as it were, under the baby's magical control [...] Omnipotence is nearly a fact of experience. (1971a, p. 11)

Here, the illusory aspects of the virtual are prominent, establishing the earliest foundations of the mother-infant relationship. This "opportunity for illusion" constitutes a nascent virtuality which grants the world a high degree of malleability that accords with the wants and needs of the baby. For example, "... there is opportunity for the feeling of oneness between two persons who are in fact two and not one" (Winnicott, 1987a, p. 7). The breast is not an object coming from the outside, but is experienced as part of the infant himself, engendering a foundational sense of omnipotence. This essential link between omnipotence and our nascent experience of virtuality will become central to our analysis when we begin to explore the resonances between the baby's feeling of having magical control over the breast and the ascendancy granted to the self as a result of digital virtuality.

In modulating the relationship between illusion and reality, the virtual keeps certain facts about the world at bay, thus granting the infant time and space to grow. This modulation is best captured by Winnicott's (1987b) deceptively simple phrase, "the world in small doses," which describes the necessity of protecting the vulnerable infant from the psychic destruction that can happen when the world rushes in too quickly. Being careful to safeguard the infant from those aspects of the world that she is not ready to take in, aligns with a view of early trauma as the premature intrusion of a world not given in small doses, but rather in large and traumatically overwhelming ones that fracture the developing psyche. There is a fragility to self-world relations in early development, and the self's inner implosion and collapse is the result of externality's premature impingement that brings a tide of pathology in its wake. The virtual, in its capacity to modulate reality through the "opportunity for illusion" provides a sheltering function that helps to protect the infant from untimely exposure to the world.

Alongside this protective and mediating virtuality, we also find Winnicott articulating that aspect of the virtual that imbues life with psychological meaning and makes our experience in the world with others feel real. It is the force underlying the potency and creativity of the psyche. And indeed, for Winnicott, the very question of whether or not life is experienced as being worth living centers on "whether creativity is or is not part of an individual person's living experience" (Winnicott, 1986, p. 39). He goes on to say:

> Creativity is then the doing that arises out of being. It indicates that he who is, is alive ... [It] is the retention throughout life of something that belongs properly to infant experience: the ability to create the world. (pp. 39–40)

Creative living, which Winnicott at this point wants to distinguish from being artistically creative, involves an encounter with externality that is lived out, experientially, on multiple psychic stages: the dream stage, the fantasy stage, the stage of instinctual drives. Each marks a larger psychic surround that envelops the self with its own cast of characters, as the virtual makes it possible for the figures of our inner psychic life and our actual objects – those that we love and depend on – to live in an intimate, psychically animating transference.

A third sense of the virtual appears with Winnicott's contention that there are private and hidden aspects of the self which do not accede to representational knowing. In fact, not wanting them to be found at all, what is hidden in the self resists communicating and being communicated with. This inner otherness evokes the unpredictable and ungovernable arising of psychic life that seems to bypass human intentionality all together; this non-personal force of emergence permeating all experience accounts for the electrifying spark in the virtual, whose origins lie in something beyond human subjectivity.

And if there is one central message of the whole Winnicottian oeuvre, it is this: We should not prematurely force upon these un-formed, non-communicating dimensions of the psyche our need for representational knowing. They should ultimately be respected and left to be. Undoubtedly, one very important aspect of psychological maturation involves learning how to allow the non-representable aspects of our psychic lives to be available to us without having to be made transparent and fully understood. The way, for instance, you can let the images of the dream you wake up with remain present as you move through your day without having to *know* what they mean. Letting the unrepresentable stay unrepresentable yet still inform ex-perience is no easy matter, and we infer it has something to do with bearing that primary ontological tension that constitutes us.

A certain degree of emotional openness to uncertainty and in-determinacy is required so that the unconscious can become a source for enlivening experience and animating the world virtually. In this view, Winnicott becomes a guide for potentiating our unconscious life. To be in potential space is to be fed and nurtured by this un-representable undercurrent, allowing it to pulsate as something felt, yet still unknown, as one lives in the world as an active subject. The collapse of potential space is the loss of access to that psychic other-ness which we have been characterizing as our inner virtuality. For Winnicott, early environmental conditions, when *good enough*, allow for emotional openness and so rightfully set the stage for releasing the virtuality of the self into this world-potentiating force. But when conditions are not *good enough*, life becomes deadened, things no longer feel real, and we are forced to seek symbolic substitutes that ironically cause further restriction, barring access even more.

We might then see the allure of technological hyperreality as an unconscious compensation for the collapse of potential space, the loss of existential access to the potentiation of psychic reality. It's as if the digital takes charge of potential space and says to the self: "You can now have this whenever and wherever you want. And though we cannot exactly give you the feeling that comes with an internally generated virtuality in loving dialogue with the world, we offer the next best thing, a substitute mode of hyperreality that simulates its immediacy as best it can. And if you stick with it long enough, you will never miss the real."

This is illustrated by the recent attempt to aid a grieving mother in South Korea whose daughter died of leukemia at the age of 7.[3] Using new virtual reality technologies, an avatar of the child was created as a composite of her digital photographs, the registration of the mother's memories and the movements of a child actor. Donning a VR headset, she was able to see and hear her daughter again, move with her in space as if she were still alive. In being able to bring the child back, there is the hope that this mother can better work through her grief. There she is again, alive and lively as she ever was, so the mother is offered another chance of being with her, even talking to her in this strange new ghostly medium. What kind of potential space is this? It's as if the gap between life and death is being filled, holding at bay the reality of loss, which remains only potential, through this spectral re-encounter with the object.

We are only beginning to consider how this might affect, positively or negatively, the process of mourning. The promise is that the virtual representation will help the mother come to terms with the abrupt loss by lessening its finality. But we could imagine that it might instead (and here we are on very shaky ground) become an obstacle for her working through her loss, as the avatar replaces the non-representational depth of the real with a hyperreality that erases it.

This reveals yet another aspect of our digital dependency, where our use of virtual technologies short-circuits the psyche's relation to the non-representational, making us ever more reliant upon our simulations to compensate for that loss. Winnicott's ideas serve as a gauge to our growing digital addiction, reminding us that there is another way of potentiating experience, dreaming reality into being. Can we see the Winnicottian virtual as a response and compensation for the hyperreality of our time?

2 The psychological origins of virtuality

We have noted Freud's weariness of the omnipotence that characterizes the infant at the breast, as he perilously retreats from the world of real objects to seek out the hallucinatory satisfaction of his desire. The solipsistically self-satisfied infant at the *virtual* breast is a foundational image, for it reveals the invincibility of the pleasure principle in its precipitous dismissal of reality. In its hallucinatory re-creation of the real, the virtual offers a substitute satisfaction that simulates "actual" satisfaction.

But one cannot dwell there too long. Sooner or later, the infant will have to pull himself away from the virtual breast and seek a breast that can offer "actual" nourishment. It is a matter of survival. But we also know that early developmental trauma can give rise to individuals who adhere to their simulations at the expense of a *real* life.[4]

For Freud, the virtual is dangerous because its seductive charms cause us to mistake illusion for reality. The self-enclosed Freudian infant has not yet turned toward a *real* other for satisfaction; he is trapped in the illusory belief that he can receive all the satisfaction he needs from the virtual itself. In pointed contrast, Winnicott's focus is on the interceding m(other).[5] Winnicott conceives of a different beginning, one that already presupposes her active presence in creating a holding environment that enables the infant to actualize the experience that he has indeed created the world. "[T]he mother makes her breast available (or the bottle) just as the baby is preparing to conjure up something, and then lets it disappear as the idea of it fades from the baby's mind" (1987b, p. 73). Here, the inner imagination about what is most ardently desired (the breast in fantasy) meets up with the actual breast that satisfies that desire.

> [T]he breast is created by the infant over and over again out of the infant's capacity to love or (one can say) out of need. A subjective phenomenon develops in the baby, which we call the mother's breast. The mother places the actual breast just there where the infant is ready to create, and at the right moment. (1971a, p. 11)

This profound synchrony between a fantasy in the mind and its actualization in the world elucidates an originary or foundational experience of the virtual, where mind (that perplexing admixture of fantasy, desire, and selfhood) and world temporarily fuse, and in that emergent state, the distinction between self and other fades away. The world comes alive as mind, and mind is embodied in the world.

> In nine months the mother gives about a thousand feeds, and look at all the other things she does with the same delicate adaptation to exact needs. For the lucky infant the world starts off behaving in such a way that it joins up with his imagination, and so the world is woven into the texture of the imagination, and the inner life of the baby is enriched with what is perceived in the external world. (1987b, pp. 73–74)

If things go well enough between mother and infant, this early experience of desire potentiating reality is woven into the subjective fabric of one's being. As an important counterpoint to the solipsism of omnipotent hallucinatory satisfaction, Winnicott highlights the thoroughly intersubjective nature of the origins of the virtual, challenging the overly restrictive lines Freud drew between psychic reality and the external world. Winnicott's virtual gives rise to a self-expansive turn toward the experience of aliveness in relation to objects that engenders the development of an inner psychic capacity to amalgamate fantasy, desire, and imagination with the actuality of the world.

In considering the earliest exchanges between infant and mother, Winnicott is evoking a time when fantasy and reality are not yet differentiated, and the infant experiences a world that is wholly receptive to his innermost virtuality. In the abundant fullness of its ever-expansive, possibility-granting fluidity, the virtual gives shape and expression to the infant's dreams, thoughts, and desires. Thus, this first stage of Winnicott's developmental story finds the infant dreaming up the world without any question that it will reciprocate in a total and all-embracing responsiveness.

Because there is someone else there offering her caring and protective attention, the infant can safely venture in a non-defensive way toward the aliveness of the world. The risk is being able to bear its open and fluid nature, its "cavalcade of emergence" (Massumi, 2014, p. 55) well enough to be transformed rather than damaged by it. Mother mitigates this risk for the infant, as the therapist, in a parallel way, does for her patients. Inside a therapeutic holding environment the patient can risk breaching the self, turning toward its transformative possibilities; opening, in other words, to its inner virtuality, as it becomes, in the presence of another, a space safe enough again to engage with.[6]

Winnicott's work can be read as a testament to his continuing elucidation of states of being in which these two distinct orders – self and world, inner and outer, reality and fantasy, body and mind – can interpenetrate one another, for it is in their overlapping points of contact that virtuality is borne. Like our use of the word *psyche*, virtuality becomes the third term that bridges them, suggesting that the very mode of the real that underlies Winnicottian potential space is an immanent virtuality, which does not split self and world, but unifies them.

In our dreaming life, we return to this immanent virtuality, reconnecting with a state of mind that parallels the infant's originary act of dreaming up the world, as the sharp divisions between subjective and objective experience, self and other, fall away. But when we awaken and begin to remember the dream, there is always something ineffable of the experience that cannot be recovered, that does not return. The virtuality that infuses the dream is ungraspable, slipping through our fingers the moment we try and pin it down. The digital, in the full force of its technological potentiation, seeks to simulate this originary virtuality, offering us a non-divided world that is wholly receptive to our wishes and desires. Anything we conceive of can be grasped there, the moment it comes into our mind.

For instance, let's imagine that when you are spending time with your teenage daughter, a particularly stirring song from your past all of a sudden pops into your head. You are so excited to share it with her that you impulsively rush to find it on YouTube, abruptly click the link, and there it plays, just as you remembered it. The digital now allows you to potentiate, in a parent-child relational space, all of the associations and fantasies you had while hearing that song as a teen-ager, as you listen to it alongside your daughter as an adult. But when she seems to be immune to the meaningfulness of the song, you notice that something is awry. While you expected the vital memory lodged in your mind to shift in the flash of a moment into an inter-subjective event of the present, you suddenly realize that YouTube failed to translate the inner imagination you had of the song, without which it loses its poignancy. Just as with the residues of the dream that we are left with upon awakening, it does not bring back that ungraspable quality of the past that made it so vibrant when you first thought of it.

What contributes to the false hope that there could be such a perfect transfer from the past to the present is the speed by which we are able to actualize that fantasy. Its instantaneousness evokes the feeling of "[t]he mother plac[ing] the actual breast just there where the infant is ready to create it, and at the right moment" (Winnicott, 1971a, p. 11). YouTube becomes the stand-in for the maternal function, for as it has become so adept at simulating that originary desire-creating-the world moment, we expect things of it that it cannot really provide.

The digital plays a bit of a trick on us, making us believe, for that second, that there is no loss, that the time and context of my ex-perience of that song (or person, or event) is not really in the past. In the virtual everything that has passed is suddenly back in our grasp. Nothing is lost to time. And as we enter into that aspect of the illusion, the ineffable is erased, just as with Benjamin's mechanical reproduction the aura is abolished from the work of art, and we be-come immune to its absence. Experience is, indeed, literally flattened, for all depth (spatially and temporally) in our perception is lost. "The digital society of transparency," Byung-Chul Han (2018) writes, "de-auratizes and demystifies the world" (p. 7).

Yet, dwelling in the full presence of what has passed but now re-turns, in an immediate and graspable way, also opens up a psychic playground for self-exploration. We have detailed the many sig-nificant ways, therapeutically and otherwise, that these new virtual spaces offer unique and powerful opportunities for growth, self-expansion and healing. The illusory sense that nothing is actually lost may be an important part of what contributes to the potentiating power of that dynamic.

At the same time, we must acknowledge the regressive shadow that haunts the speed and brilliance with which the digital recovers the past. For in protecting us from exposure to certain essential, and here we might say, non-virtual dimensions of experience – especially those dealing with loss and absence – we become unpracticed in bearing change and the passing away of things. If we return to the concept of an immanent and embodied virtuality, a virtuality that comes alive in its contact with the world, we must come to terms with the fact that something is forsaken when that immanence is replaced by its digital simulation (we might say, ironically, that the missing is missing). That which cannot wholly be captured in simulated form, what Heidegger calls "the worldliness of the world" or "the thingness of the thing" is sacrificed.

We can now see further into the existential dimensions of this virtual regression, for as more and more of our life is enchained to the circuits and devices that constitute the everyday digital, there is a turning away from the world. Where virtual and real are locked in a deadly opposition, the virtual kills the world, and in the end, we fall in love with our simulations rather than with each other and certainly no longer with the world.

There is a very human tendency to take asylum in the merger states endemic to those earliest desire-creating-world moments, where the innocence of the self meets up with the innocence of the world. This is the very stuff that gives such poignant vibrancy to our dreams and fantasies. Perhaps we are so taken in by Facebook because it emanates a nostalgia for this originary condition. Our desire to (re)experience that lost state of innocence (often an innocence that most of us never got much of in the first place) pulls us further and deeper into the labyrinths of digital virtuality. A game like Second Life represents this yearning to once again have at one's disposal a world that is relatively free of risk and harm, one that wholly bends to the impulses of the self. But there is concern, as we have seen, that a world without risk has drawbacks of its own. Something grows there, and at the same time, something else cannot grow.

Our current digital practices tend to deny the fact that the kind of merger state that was foundational for us as infants is no longer germane in the same way when we become adults. By losing sight of the developmental vicissitudes of the virtual, we force it into serving our own regressive psychological and emotional demands, using its potentiating power to covertly recapture that originary virtuality. When we place into the hands of the adult ego the means by which our wishes, in one fell swoop, can be turned into realities, we inevitably invoke that hidden will to power that seeks to eradicate otherness, a theme we will explore in the next chapter.

And let's remember here that for the Winnicottian infant, otherness was not something that had to be expunged in order for the virtual to emerge. Indeed, just the opposite. When otherness is fed to the infant in small enough doses by a sensitively attuned caretaker, he has access to a non-disavowing virtuality. As Adam Phillips (2019) writes:

> In Winnicott's account we can only bare and enjoy the fact that we didn't create the world as we wanted it to be after we gain the conviction that we did create the world, and that it was as we wanted it to be [...] The reality principle is only what Winnicott calls an "insult" to the child if it impinges prematurely. (p. 37)

The virtual surround of the digital world, as it occurs for us today, is not often fed in small doses. It becomes harder to protect ourselves, at any stage of development, from its overpowering and often over-whelming impingements that flood in and overtake the potential space of an emergent self. The digital then takes advantage of the very situation it helps to create with its injunction: "The only safe place left for you is inside here. Come on in, and shut the door behind you. Let us join together and banish the world."

3 Virtuality and transitional phenomena

In his reading of Freud, Lacan (1978) envisions an unrecoverable gap at the center of subjectivity, resulting from the initial cut that severs the unity of mother and infant. Our original connection, gone for-ever, creates a state of self-alienated and compulsive object-seeking that haunts our psychological lives. Lacan's account stands in marked contrast to Winnicott's conception of transitional phenomena, which envisions a very different way of bearing "the cut in the real" in-evitable in the separation from mother.

As the infant develops and the mother no longer perfectly adapts to his needs, a gap opens up between what is wanted and what actually arrives, between desire and its fulfillment. As the infant is faced with a space of difference between a "me" and a "not me," something is needed to help him negotiate and bear this emerging gap. Transitional phenomena mark the passage from being merged with mother to being separate from her, when the infant turns to the outer world and uses a transitional object, say a bit of a blanket or a soft toy, to help bridge this difference. The separation that would have occurred be-tween mother and baby does not actually occur. There is only potential space between them, not actual space.

The transitional object is a creative solution to the original separa-tion. The baby takes this bit of the emerging "not me" world that reminds him of mother, a particular touch object, one that is soft and smells of her body and uses it in place of her. It carries the meaning of that which is, yet is not mother and that which is, yet is not self. Winnicott describes this paradoxical state of holding on and letting go (to mother, to self) as a non-compliant resolution to the infant's inevitable loss of omnipotence.

What ensues, then, with transitional phenomena is a whole new dimension of the virtual based upon the creative deferral of the actual. It gives rise to a potential space in which separation, loss, and the otherness of the world remain in potential form, while, at the same time, there is contact with something real, an actual object. The tattered blue blanket that must never be washed provides a "resting place" in which an infant can gradually come to accept the reality of an outside world that is not simply fashioned from his own mind, but stands outside of it, with its own separate existence. "I am here staking a claim for an intermediate state between a baby's inability and his growing ability to recognize and accept reality" (Winnicott, 1971a, p. 3). Or, to put it another way, transitional virtuality offers the developing child an original way of mediating the difference between his subjectivity and the occurrence of the world.

The importance of the material (technical) object in the constitution of human virtuality is something Stiegler (2013) points out. As Roberts (2007) explains:

> For Stiegler, philosophy is both founded on and founders on the exteriorization of the human, or, as he calls it, 'technics.' Technics encompasses everything from primitive tools through systems of writing to modern telecommunications. For him, 'technics is the condition of culture, and it would be absurd to oppose technics to culture.' Technics, thus understood is not merely instrumental, a means to an end, where the 'end' remains a resolutely human need or desire. Rather technics shapes what it means to be human, and the 'human' in this sense is constituted always already through technics. Indeed, technics is the 'prosthesis of the human': the human is constituted not by some interior capacity (e.g. consciousness) but by a new prosthetic relationship with matter. (p. 26)

Stiegler finds strong resonance with Winnicott, for whom the transitional object demonstrates "the foundational role that material things play in the generation of the child's psychic life" (Russell, 2020, p. 113). As Russell continues:

> [R]ather than being simply present at birth […] object-relatedness is the effect of the identity of the maternal object and the technical (mechanical/processive) aspects of maternal practice. This identity is what is re-encountered/repeated by the child in the form of the transitional object (…) as something material that can be absolutely manipulated but that is also experienced as animated and mindful. (p. 114)

What he means by the identity of the maternal object and the technical aspects of maternal practice is that the breast itself, as Winnicott tell us, stands for the whole technique of mothering (feeding, holding, soothing, etc.). Object relatedness is not a given, it is acquired through the repetition of these practices.

Stiegler posits a transitional virtuality lying "beyond or beneath" (p. 1) the actual object and startles us with the claim that:

> The transitional object has a distinct virtue: *it does not exist.* Certainly something exists that enables it to appear – for example, a teddy bear or cuddly toy. But what makes this teddy bear or cuddly toy able to open up 'transitional' space [...] is that beyond that part of the object that exists in external space [...] there holds something that is precisely neither in exterior space, nor simply internal to either the mother or the child. (our italics, p. 1)

This transitional virtuality is what reinforces the loving bond between them:

> What takes hold between the mother and child in not existing, but in passing through the transitional object, and which therefore finds itself constituted by it, links and attaches them to one another [...] through a relation of love [...] What holds and is upheld as this link through which these two beings become incommensurable and infinite for one another, is what, by allowing a place for that which is infinite, consists precisely to the immeasurable extent that it does not exist – because the only things that exist are finite things (pp. 1–2).

When Stiegler speaks of allowing a place for that which does not actualize itself in the world as a finite object, "something that is precisely neither in exterior space, nor simply internal to either the mother or the child" (p. 1) he is evoking what we have been calling the human virtual, that space of emergence where the pure potentiality of "that which is infinite," comes to the fore as an animating and life-vitalizing force. Here, it gives rise to the paradoxical situation in which mother and child can differentiate themselves from one another while at the same time being held together in loving union. The virtual, "to the immeasurable extent that it does not exist" holds open a space for the possible as opposed to the actual, an infinite realm that disseminates the finite actuality of their relationship by opening to a larger order of reality that underwrites them both.[7]

But the pivotal gesture that Stiegler finds in Winnicott, which has such importance for how we think the technological, is that this very opening to the infinite, to the possible, to the virtual, happens through a relationship to a technical object, which in early development is linked to the mechanical/processive and temporal aspects of maternal care: the over and over again experience of the infant feeding at the breast, which is "re-encountered/repeated by the child in the form of the transitional object" (Russell, 2020, p. 114). There is something processive, even mechanical, at work in our relationship to the object-world that ignites the virtual. This shows the interdependence between technics and virtuality, and thus any attempt to distinguish human virtuality from digital-virtuality cannot be done by splitting them apart and trying to naively recover a pre-technological world. In Stiegler's framework, there is no avoiding technics as constitutive of what makes us human, whether we embrace digital life with open arms or shun it. It is at our very origins, as Winnicott shows.

Stiegler (2013, p. 3) enables us to understand how it is that the transitional character of the object is responsible for constituting a world. Or, to put it another way, the material world that surrounds us becomes animated and alive through the current of virtuality that runs through everything. That's why when we are cut off from the virtual, a world once bustling with potential is supplanted by a de-realized one, resulting in a diminished connection to a sense of aliveness in relation to things. The mother's job is to convey to the child that life is worth living, and she does so by co-experiencing with the child the current of virtuality that underlies the transitional object, so that the very fabric of their bond is impacted by its animating and enlivening force. This makes very clear for us the connection we have already seen between virtuality and Eros; indeed, the erotics of a life-affirming desire (the very thing mother conveys to the child) is at the root of the feeling that life is worth living. This is the opposite of a

> [r]elationship to external reality which is one of compliance, the world and its details being recognized but only as something to be fitted in with or demanding adaptation. Compliance carries with it a sense of futility for the individual and is associated with the idea that nothing matters (Winnicott as quoted in Stiegler. 2013, p. 21)

The opposition between the feeling that life is worth living and futility will become important again when we explore the pharmacological nature of digital virtuality in adolescence, for it also moves in both directions: on the one hand, it amplifies the sense of vitality that is so intensely stirred during that time, while on the other, it can heighten the feeling of emptiness (life is dead and nothing really matters) also endemic to the adolescent psyche, which can push one into either destructive rebellion or stultifying compliance.

It's perhaps not surprising, then, that for Stiegler the transitional object is the first pharmakon

> because it is both an external object on which the mother and child are dependent (losing it is enough to make this clear) and in relation to which they are thus heteronomous, [and an] object that [...] provides [...] sovereignty to both mother and child: their serenity, their trust in life, their feeling that life is worth living, their autonomy. (pp. 2–3)

The mother protects the child from the threatening aspect of this first pharmakon which manifests as the prospect of the child becoming overly reliant on it, for too long of a period of time. In this regard, Winnicott's (1971a) claim that "most mothers allow their infants some special object and expect them to become, as it were, addicted to such objects" (p. 1) takes on new relevancy. The issue of dependency, as manifest in the impulse to concretize and thus become addicted to our technical objects at the expense of the vital circuit of virtuality that lies beneath them, is so crucially at stake in what we have seen thus far, from Benjamin's loss of the aura to our seemingly insatiable craving for the hyperreal.

It's almost as if Winnicott is providing the directives that the good enough mother already intuitively understands for protecting herself and her child from the negative side of the pharmakon. Russell (2020) provides us with the philosophical scaffolding for her instinct.

> [I]t is crucial that the mother not challenge or denigrate [the transitional object] by insisting on the priority of [...] [the] actual – that she not impose a subject/object structure of opposition but instead provide for an experience in which the thing appears as having been both discovered and created. Doing so generates in the child the feeling of discovery which is met by a world waiting to be discovered – a world that is there. ... (p. 114)

What's so critical in this formulation is that the way the mother protects the child from becoming overly dependent is rooted in her ability to let the object itself stay transitional by not challenging the intermediate space in which it dwells. As we have seen, this requires her own receptivity to the current of virtuality that runs through it. In the end, the threat of fixation fades, as the object loses its significance over time and is eventually discarded. Yet, the child retains access to its world-constituting force, as the transitional object gives way to transitional experience, and the intersubjective, psychic processes, i.e.

the way that virtual transitionality mediated the love between mother and child, now spreads itself over the whole cultural field.

Because the "abrogation of omnipotence" (p. 5) is a feature of the transitional object from the start, there is something foundational about this non-compliant resolution that grants us our initial exposure to a world that is different from the self and stands outside it. The pharmacological tension within the human being is revealed by two radically opposed paths that can subsequently unfold.

> At this point my subject widens out into that of play, and of artistic creativity and appreciation, and of religious feeling, and of dreaming, and also of fetishism, lying and stealing, the origin and loss of affectionate feeling, drug addiction, the talisman of obsessional rituals, etc. (Winnicott, 1971a, p. 5)

In the first case, it becomes the source of play, dreaming, creativity (i.e., all of the activities that enable life to be lived imaginatively, passionately, in fruitful contact with this in-between space) while in the second, it becomes a path toward self-destruction, in the forms of lying and stealing, perversion and addiction.

Transitionality, as a state of being that is characterized by an openness to the potentiality of the virtual, does not disavow the actual but holds it at bay, analogously to how the mother forestalls the ever-demanding complexity of the world, offering it in small doses to the infant. Yes, the infant is no longer all-powerful and mother is no longer completely under his control, but in exchange for that abrogation of omnipotence, the infant gains a newfound capacity to dream the real, to bring together "what is objectively perceived and what is subjectively conceived of" (Winnicott, 1971a, p. 11). This is quite a reward, for it allows us to develop the capacity to play with the deferral of the actual, with the back and forth illusion of things being real and not real. The world of symbol, metaphor and metonymy is thus opened up, without having to sacrifice or disavow the real.

But something entirely different can happen as well. Development can be not quite good enough, and we find ourselves unable to surrender our omnipotence. When this occurs, the deferral of the actual inherent to transitional virtuality becomes a means of disavowal, and our technics are placed in the service of extending our subjective conception of the world beyond its limits. In the name of an inflationary egoic agency, we thus attempt to subdue all that is other to us. This is why Winnicott points to talismans, obsessional rituals and addictions, as the transitional object becomes a fetish, a way of holding onto a world absent of separation or loss. As a result, the virtual can no longer perform its mediating function and difference collapses.

We are most vulnerable to the poisonous side of the pharmakon when we lose our capacity to bear the difference between the object itself and the potential space it opens up. We clamour to possess that potential space, to have it always there at the ready, at our disposal. We try to do so by colonizing the object, but we find ourselves smack dab in a destructive relationship of dependency, as we fear that once we lose it, or stop its incessant use, we will be cut off from the very source of virtuality. This process is now recognizable to us as the pharmacological roots of addiction, one of the great dangers posed by our digital lives. It accounts for the panic we feel when we lose our phone or are for some reason impeded from going online, as if we were being cut off from life itself.

What if we consider all the digital objects that we surround ourselves with today – our smartphones, laptops, tablets, video games, airpods, apps of all sorts that stream video and music and link us to social networks – as derivatives of the first pharmakon itself, which allowed the developing child to discover/create an intermediate space in the name of bearing the loss of omnipotence that inevitably comes in the encounter with the otherness of the world. We would have to consider, as the mother does for the child, how to protect ourselves from the threatening and destructive aspects of our digital objects in order to contend with their pharmacological nature. What are we actually doing with these devices as we move through the most ordinary moments of life?

In this light, let's consider how pervasive transitional moments really are for both children and adults. We see it most clearly in those experiences from childhood that involve a passage from one state to another: the transition from waking up to going to school; waiting for the bus; the end of recess and the return to class; standing in line at a store, waiting for dinner, having to stop whatever it was we were doing and go to bed. It's the wise adult who helps with these transitions by remembering to bring along a little something to eat or a small object to fiddle with, especially when the child is very young and truly requires a hand in learning to manage such moments. The need of something to help bridge those gaps does not end when we become adults, for they do not disappear, but simply change terrain. Now there is driving home from a long day of work and having to enter the very different rhythm of domestic life; or, once back home, trying to shift into a space of relational connection with a family member after finishing a long list of household chores; or moving from a dull and uninspired feeling into something meaningful and even inspired, as we attempt to engage a creative act; or finding ourselves in the hollow between the non-erotic and the erotic when we want to have sex with someone, and the mood is just not there yet.

If we look around today, we see nearly everywhere people (children, adolescents, and adults) using their devices to help manage these endless transitions. We have become very dependent upon the virtual deferral to plug the tiny holes and gaps that emerge in those small moments between one thing and the next. Someone leaves the room, and without even giving it a moment of thought, I instantly flip on my device. I'm hungry, but it's not yet time to eat, and I go directly to Instagram. He breaks up with me, refusing to see me ever again, and I can't stop myself, for months on end, from obsessively checking in on him on Facebook. I miss the bus, I'm late for a train, a flight is cancelled and there's my phone as solace for all of the endless waiting that lies ahead.

One of the great blessings of the digital is that it enables separations, endings, momentary lapses in the action – where we may well register the hauntings of loss and absence – to always remain potential, not actual. I'm bored and have nothing to do; someone is coming but hasn't yet arrived; five more minutes and then I have to leave; red light; stalled car; walking the dog; pushing the baby carriage; eating lunch alone. But is the quick turn to the device to replace the object and ward off these difficult feelings truly a blessing? Or, has the smartphone become – as it makes an appearance today in nearly every single transitional moment – the ultimate fetish object? Does the play between the subjectively perceived and the objectively presented enhance or diminish the vitality of difference? Do our virtual objects, in their play of deferral, open or collapse transitional space? As Stiegler (2013) says, "[t]hings can constitute a world only insofar as they irreducibly proceed from the transitional character of the object" (p. 3). Do we lose or gain the world?

This raises the very serious and troubling question as to whether is it possible or not to have a non-fetishized relationship with these objects. Is there a way to get enough distance or detachment from them so that the virtuality that is awakened through them, that surges beneath and beyond them, can, like the fate of the mother–child relationship, become incommensurate with the technical object so that we can be nourished by its infinite potential without having to reify the object itself? Is there any way to relate to our current crop of technical objects such that the potential for fixation evaporates, and the dazzlement of its technological dimension organically loses significance over time and is eventually discarded. Will there ever be a post-digital period of history?

Recently we heard the story of a psychotherapy patient who, in having to prematurely end a very successful treatment because his therapist was moving away, suggested at the beginning of his last session that she provide him with access to her personal e-mail account, so that they could very occasionally have contact with one another. Here, in this particular fantasy of termination, the attempt to use the digital to defer loss is painfully evident. Is it a creative deferral or a refusal of loss? Does it soften the blow of the end so that it can actually be felt by the patient without overwhelming him, or does it keep him trapped in the fantasy of an interminable relationship, where the end never comes?

As a psychoanalyst of the virtual, Winnicott is showing the gradual progression of transitional phenomena from their incarnation in a specific object into a mode of being that enables us to bring the full force of our psychic lives into creative contact with the world. Taking note of this progression is crucial for our investigation of digitality insofar as we continue to explore how the virtual object, as phar-makon, both opens up as well as blocks access to the real. When are we retreating into our screens to escape the world, and when does the world seem to pour forth from the digital in new and originary ways? Undoubtedly, this becomes a central topic with adolescents as today one of the primary ways they begin to forge an emerging relationship with the outside world is by withdrawing from the outward life of the family into the privacy of their digital screens.[8]

4 The re-emergence of virtuality in adolescence

Winnicott addresses the developmental necessity of protecting the psychic reality of the infant, child and adolescent from external im-pingements, so that what is tacitly growing within can, over time, come to live in harmony with the facticity of the world. We have spoken of this protective sheltering as the mediating function of the virtual, in that its dynamic play of illusion and reality can serve to regulate how much of the world may enter at any one time. But Winnicott (1965) takes this requirement for protection from ex-ternality one step further with his assertion that there is a core to the personality that,

> never communicates with the world of perceived objects, and that the individual person knows [...] must never be communicated with or be influenced by external reality .... Although healthy persons communicate and enjoy communicating, the other fact is equally true, that each individual is an isolate, permanently non-communicating, permanently unknown, in fact unfound. (p. 187)

This need for aspects of the self to stay hidden, unknown and un-found, takes on paramount importance during the tumultuous transformation in identity that happens in the passage from child-hood to adulthood.

Th[e] preservation of personal isolation is part of the search for identity, and for the establishment of a personal technique for communicating which does not lead to violation of the central self.... (p. 190)

Winnicott was writing at a time before our personal technologies so readily served as a "remedy" to the problem of human solitude by providing the contemporary adolescent with a manifold of nearly irresistible opportunities for communicative connection. In sharp relief from the embeddedness in community and fellow feeling that being on Instagram, Snapchat, and TikTok calls forth, Winnicott was making the claim that learning to bear loneliness, isolation and feeling separate from the collective – aspects of being alive that evoke the existential dimensions of having unknown and unfound parts of oneself – are an important element in the adolescent's search for her soul. "Struggling through the doldrums" is his catchphrase for this period of development in which a young person finds himself experiencing periods of impotence and passivity in the face of an overwhelming, and at times, deadened world. Not only is the adolescent, like the infant, essentially an isolate, but his isolation often manifests with depressive-like symptomatology: melancholy, sometimes severe; inaction, at times crippling; and a lack of connection to others that can wear the mask of social anxiety.

In our current era, where there is so little tolerance for depressive affect and social withdrawal, we rush to pathologize the doldrums, treating them as a condition that needs psychiatric intervention. As denizens of a brightly illuminated digital world that so effectively eradicates feelings of isolation and loneliness, what do we make of Winnicott's insistence upon the psychological necessity of this inwardly oriented turn toward the dark opaqueness of one's own being? How does the digital adolescent, with the pressure to sustain a well-crafted online persona, establish a *personal technique* for communicating that does not violate those aspects of her identity that are not ready (if ever) to be known or found? If indeed, as we have hypothesized, the digital is a stand-in for the mothering function (in its role of being a self-object as well as a container and facilitator of originary desires) need it only be seen as an intrusive mother, and as such, incapable of not violating the unformed? Or, as we will come to explore, does the digital also uniquely adapt to the very situation – the psychological necessity in adolescence for concealment – that Winnicott is drawing our attention to?

We need to grapple with that which comes at us from the outside in order to perceive what is expressing itself in a quieter way within. It is only in that stillness that we can come to know the more private dimensions of the self that resist communication with the outer world. Often, it is in solitude – and the forceful confrontation with the psyche that being alone brings with it – that the uniqueness of who one is, different from everyone else, can be discovered and reflected upon.

> People are afraid to find themselves alone, and so don't find themselves at all ... You can't create something without being alone ... What seems different in yourself: that's the one rare thing you possess, the one thing that gives each of us his worth; and that's just what we try to suppress. [Instead] we imitate. (Gide, 2018, p. 30)

The incommunicado self is a fitting image for that acute sensitivity the adolescent has to those aspects of who she is and what she experiences that can never be fully articulated, not to the self, nor to another. When she is lost or alone, without orientation, or carried off by her dreams and fantasies, the depth she encounters there often surpasses the markers of who she knows herself to be. She is thus brought into contact with intimations of her being that have very little consequence for her well-functioning, social self.

Adolescence is a time of flux, where we are very open to the proliferating play of the virtual, as it drives the many and frequent experiments with persona, identity, and the ever-shifting boundary between self and other that are such a prominent feature of this age. By being given space to follow those circuits of virtuality, the adolescent comes to create/discover the uniqueness of his individuality, the idiosyncrasy of his desire. Here again it is incumbent upon the parent to tolerate and endure this intermediate space, even when it flies in the face of adult reason. It is essential in providing the adolescent a resting place from the either/or logic of this age, and thus helping her bet manage the tension between the inward draw toward the private and interior, and the outward pull, in the face of collective pressure, to imitate or be like others. In this light, we can read "Struggling through the Doldrums" as a primer for how to be potentiated by the world in accordance with the exigencies of the incommunicado self. It is a guide for seeking access to a mode of potential space that grounds self-experience in that third sense of an a-subjective virtual, a state of mind that we live but do not make (Scott, 1988).

New urgencies arise in mind and body during adolescence. What had been dormant becomes active, as the sexual and aggressive impulses, heretofore contained by the mind of the child as internal fantasies, now seek expression and contact with the physicality of another body and the materiality of the world. A period of growth is instantiated that is, on the one hand, enlivening and expansive, and on the other, threatening and dangerous. For the adolescent faces in a wholly new way the richness of the world's possibilities as well as its equally real and implacable limits. Like it or not, externality, in all of its radical ungovernability, comes marching up to the adolescent's door, beckoning him or her to step through. We fall in love for the first time, and are awakened to the suffering of erotic life. We are overwhelmed by feelings of alienation and disconnection in relation to the family that once held us. We cast a new and unsettling eye on the contradictions and hypocrisies of the culture that surrounds us. And then there is the inevitable confrontation with an adversary, an enemy, be it a fellow student, a teacher, a parent, or a love rival. Competition, striving to be better, or just giving up and giving in, takes on a whole new meaning, as does winning and the possibility of defeat. It all starts to feel like a matter of life and death.

We want to think of the virtual, in all three Winnicottian senses – as a deferring and protective mediator, a world-enlivening potentiator, and that which gives rise to the unfathomable, a-subjective surround from which the self evolves – as helping to hold and contain the adolescent, as she undergoes these transformations. One's relation to the play of gain and loss, the opening and closing of the world to desire, the dialectic of illusion and reality that engenders experience, that is, one's relation to the very virtual itself, is determinative for how one survives this treacherous passage. One is thrown from the shelter and safety of being a child cared for by parents into the unpredictability and instability that comes with a sexually mature body, facing the uncertainties and hazards of adult life. The adolescent makes use of the mediating, deferring, protective side of the virtual as a safeguard, an internal holding environment, so that the physical and affective intensity of these experiences can be borne well enough such that they can do their psychic transformational work without falling prone to the destruction that can happen if there is not enough containment. That is why making room for, nurturing, and paying heed to the internal psychic space of the adolescent is essential for their psychological health and growth.

The adolescent experience in a virtual world forces us to confront once again the paradox by which the digital robs us of something in our relation to human virtuality that causes a compensatory intensification of our engagement with the digital. This is one way of understanding its nearly magnetic draw on the adolescent of today. Digital virtuality, in all of its raw and ferocious power (and think of that sheer quantum of energy alongside what gets opened up in the psyche during adolescence) tends to override and upset the depth psychological way of imagining the relation between virtual and real which locates one's unique individuality, one's true self, as dwelling deep inside a person's psyche. So what's wrong with challenging that formulation, with all of its inherent proclivities toward dualism and its historical denial of social and cultural realities? The digital is simply tipping the virtual/real/actual scales, coming up with a new equation that gives the adolescent more direct modulating power over the whole operation.

But the worry is, that in so powerfully replacing the internal with the external, the private and interior with the collective, and its demands for representational transparency, there may be less of the inwardly generated human virtual available to protect the adolescent in her confrontation with externality. Its unceasing stimuli tends to drown out what we have traditionally conceived of as space for the emergence of an internal world. And we worry then most, not about the transformations happening as a result of this new digital-adolescent hybrid – in other words, what they are doing in that space, (and as we know it is often physically safer there today than out in the world) – but the lack of psychic protection found there in the name of a diminishing human virtual. Yet, and perhaps this is the greatest paradox of them all, we find ourselves turning today, as the realities of the external world grow harsher and less habitable, to the digital as an unexpected shelter for the adolescent psyche. We can't help but encourage our kids to dwell there when the alternative, being-out-in-the-world, feels so dangerous. Those are the very kind of knots we believe Stiegler was attuned to, as we attend to the pharmacological maelstrom that is going on today with adolescents and their technology.

5 Digital adolescence

Adolescence is a potential space in its own right. No longer a child, and not yet an adult, the adolescent stands on a precipice between what has been and what is to come. But if the quest to hold onto the more opaque and non-communicative aspects of the self wasn't fragile enough in the life of the pre-digital adolescent, it is an even more formidable process for someone growing up in the digital era. In a world where the exteriorized spaces of socially digitized networks encapsulate the adolescent's experiential and affective life, "Struggling through the Doldrums" can seem like an archaic and out-of-date concept. However, if we for a moment dim the beam of digital light, we are forced to confront the fact that for a self that takes root in the collectivity and transparency of virtual worlds, there is little opportunity for inwardness and solitude, less ground for learning to bear the always contingent nature of human experience itself.

> [During] adolescence ... there is a strengthening of the defences against being found, that is to say being found before being there to be found. That which is truly personal and feels real must be

defended against at all cost, and even if this means a temporary blindness to the value of compromise. (Winnicott, 1965, p. 190)

The outward pull toward being seen and validated, something already so engrossing for any adolescent, becomes, for the digital native, a totalizing mode of experience. There is little room left to explore those aspects of self that shy away from attention, and resist premature attempts at representation. As the adolescent is pulled toward a state of near total visibility, the defenses against being found before being ready to be found are breached. All becomes fodder for the posting and profiling of the nascent self.

But we also have to consider that there is an important flipside to the search for identity in adolescence that moves in the exact opposite direction: the growing hunger to make contact with the world, and the people and events in life that feel most alive and real. Given this strong drive to seek out vital and compelling experiences that move one away from the predictability of family life and the trappings of the childhood self, it is no wonder that adolescents are so powerfully drawn to our 21st-century technologies. The digital is a meaning-intensifier; it imbues experience with an emotional immediacy unlike almost anything else in life. It supercharges the virtual's potentiating effects. With video games, for example, adolescents can enter a totally immersive world of excitement and action, where newly awakened sexual and aggressive impulses are given free rein. In these virtual encounters with unknown worlds, where contingency and risk, violence and destruction, the erotics of agency, action, and affiliation can be safely played with, adolescents come to know something more about the authenticity of their self-experience.

Perhaps the digital stages its own solution to this fundamental dilemma of adolescence: not risking premature exposure to the unformed dimensions of the self alongside an equally strong impulse to move outside the self and make contact with the world. Inside the protected space of the digital, two aspects of the virtual that we uncovered in Winnicott's early developmental theory can be woven together, as the digital provides both a mediating and protective force field, offering shelter from premature exposure to the world while at the same time, in its actualizing function, allowing desire to potentiate reality, as the world becomes ripe with possibility. There is an unrestrained quality to this intensification of experience yet it takes place in a very protected environment.

Having transformed the experience of being alone, by making it not only tolerable, but, at times, deeply pleasurable and often preferable, our contemporary technological gadgetry offers the adolescent a unique mode of psychological privacy, a perch from which the interior dimensions of psychic life can be explored. When she closes the door of her bedroom and clicks on the screen, she enters an intensely social and public, yet wholly sequestered, holding environment. In such a space, she can be as anonymous as she chooses, thus modulating how much of herself she reveals to the other and how much is kept hidden. The encounter with social networks and digitally mediated realities provides a means of exploration for her innermost fantasies and reveries, beyond the psychic reality of her mind, as they now appear in virtual worlds, to be shared, shaped, and camouflaged. In this heretofore unseen and puzzling way, the digital allows her to reach inside herself by reaching outwards, thus establishing virtual reality as a sheltered sanctuary for the actualization of her innermost self-experience.[9]

Because it provides both a safe and protected space (its mediating function) and a compelling and enlivening one (its potentiating function), the virtuality inherent to digital life offers the adolescent a platform for the spontaneous unbinding of the self, a loosening of identity that escapes the strictures of a life dominated by the wishes and needs of others. The digital contributes, in its own bewildering and, at times, contradictory ways, to a profound leap into the outer world. There are people to encounter, an endless multitude of things to see and experiences to be had. So much comes alive, erotically and relationally, in the vast and open wilderness it provides for friendship, love, and the sheer excitement of encountering what is new and unfamiliar.

Free from the scrutinizing and judging eyes of one's parents, there is an extraordinary fecundity that happens in the private spaces of digital adolescence. Because it occurs in a relatively safe zone, a contained space (the adolescent is not out in the streets, but in one's bedroom) he can use it to engage in the complex (and of course, lifelong) process of learning to make contact with others without being overtaken by them, to show off the self and hide it at the same time, and to loudly and brashly communicate while holding back what's not ready to be said. If indeed adolescence is a potential space all its own, which holds in tension this confluence of paradoxical and opposing forces, then perhaps we can consider, to an important extent (that must be reckoned with to understand the life world of the contemporary adolescent) that the kind of virtuality that manifests itself in digital space can become an effective vessel for its hard-wrought transformations.

Part of what defines adolescence and ultimately pushes one into adulthood is some kind of collapse, some kind of failure to contain the particular ways in which we are broken in upon by the world. We are not claiming that the digital forestalls such collapses; rather, we want to seriously consider what it might have to offer along the way, as a new kind of container, a profoundly distinct means of actualizing experience that at least partially overcomes certain types of hazards when experience is acted out in the world.

We began with the idea that the digital runs contrary to the psychological tasks of adolescence, as it blocks access to a personal and idiomatic virtuality in the name of an all encompassing, difference-erasing collective virtuality. And we end by saying that digital life can be understood as a rich launching pad for an intensive engagement with the intricacies of the virtuality that comprises the adolescent psyche. So which is it? Or do we have to choose?

Notes

1 Winnicott never explicitly uses the word *virtual* even though the problematic of the virtual and the real is significantly at issue in his work.
2 In the next chapter, we will examine Winnicott's (1971b) essay "The Use of an Object" and explore the difference between object relating and object usage as we come to relate to the other as a separate subjectivity. This analysis will lead us to think about what impact digitality is having on this always already difficult struggle to come to terms with the "otherness" of the other. Without a doubt, this is also a crucial stage in the developmental origins of human virtuality, but we will treat it separately given its centrality to the question of the other.
3 https://www.youtube.com/watch?v=MU38axHhzxM
4 This is akin in adults to what in psychoanalysis is known as a psychic retreat (Steiner, 1993), a protective enclave inside the self that offers temporary escape from the reality of loss.
5 We do not need to take the word *mother* literally here. Whoever is performing the "mothering" function, regardless of gender, is the mother.
6 Cf. Winnicott's (1958) "The Capacity to Be Alone" for his account of how our capacity to be alone begins in the presence of the m(other).
7 … and ultimately gives them their psychic/numinous/ aureatic force.
8 And, of course, this is becoming an issue for adults as well, insofar as the temptation to fetishize knocks at our door at every moment when we must move on from one activity to the next?
9 Just imagine what this means for the new complexity and multifacetedness of the digital adult!

References

Frankel, R. (2013) Digital Melancholy. *Jung Journal: Culture and Psyche*, 7(4), 9–20.

Freud, S. (1917) Mourning and Melancholia. In J. Strachey (Ed. and Trans.), *The Standard Edition of the Complete Psychological Works of Sigmund Freud* (vol. 14, pp. 237–258). London: Hogarth Press.

Gide, A. (2018) *As Quoted in Johnson, F. The Future of Queer* (p. 30). Harpers Magazine

Han, Byug-Chul (2018) *The Expulsion of the Other*. Cambridge: Polity Press.

Hillman, J. (1979) *The Dream and the Underworld*. New York: Harper and Row.

Krebs, V.J. (2013) The Power of Ghosts: Psychic Awakening in the Virtual World. *Jung Journal: Culture and Psyche, 7*(4), 31–38.

Lacan, J. (1978) *The Seminar of Jacques Lacan.* Book 11: *The Four Fundamental Concepts of Psycho-analysis* (Alan Sheridan, Trans.). New York: W. W. Norton. (Original work published 1973).

Massumi, B. (2014) Envisioning the Virtual. In M. Grimshaw (Ed.), *The Oxford Handbook of Virtuality* (pp. 55–70). New York: Oxford University Press.

Phillips, A. (2019) *The Cure for Psychoanalysis.* New York: Wrong Way Publishing.

Roberts, B. (2007) Introduction to Bernard Stiegler, Parallax, 13(4), 26–28.

Russell, J. (2020) *Psychoanalysis and Deconstruction: Freud's Psychic Apparatus.* London and New York: Routledge.

Scott, C.E. (1988) *Boundaries in Mind: A Study of Immediate Awareness Based on Psychotherapy.* New York: Crossroad Publishing Company.

Stiegler, B. (2013) *What Makes Life Worth Living: On Pharmacology.* Malden, MA: Polity.

Steiner, J. (1993) *Psychic Retreats: Pathological Retreats in Psychotic, Neurotic and Borderline Patients.* London: Routledge.

Winnicott, D.W. (1958) The Capacity to be Alone. In *The Maturational Processes and the Facilitating Environment* (pp. 29–36). Madison: International Universities Press.

Winnicott, D.W. (1965) Communicating and Not Communicating Leading to a Study of Certain Opposites. In *The Maturational Processes and the Facilitating Environment* (pp. 179–192). Madison and Connecticut: International Universities Press.

Winnicott, D.W. (1971a) Transitional Objects and Transitional Phenomena. In *Playing and Reality* (pp. 1–25). London: Tavistock Publications.

Winnicott, D. W. (1971b) The Use of an Object and Relating Through Identifications. In *Playing and Reality* (pp. 86–94). London: Tavistock Publications.

Winnicott, D.W. (1986) *Home Is Where we Start From.* New York and London: W.W. Norton and Company.

Winnicott, D.W. (1987a) *Babies and Their Mothers.* New York: Addison-Wesley Publishing Company.

Winnicott, D.W. (1987b) *The Child, the Family and the Outside World.* Reading, MA: Addison-Wesley Publishing Company.

7 Virtuality and the other

And I sneeze into my phone which transcribes this explosion as "you."
(Maureen N. McLane)

How can he be a self and others others since the others too are selves,
to themselves?

(John Banville)

Prelude

We are in the grip today of a powerful instinct to know and be known
by larger and larger networks of people. We are consumed with the
impulse to expand the self beyond the boundaries of where we are
currently situated and be in simultaneously active (and often live)
virtual contact with a multitude of others – extended family, friends,
acquaintances, colleagues from work, people from our past, as well as
acclaimed people, celebrities, sports figures, and the rest. This drive to
immerse ourselves in a collective network of others has a rapacious
quality that we try to quell by passively turning to our news feed, the
updates, photos, videos, and likes of that wildly random, voluminous
assortment of people that we mark as friends or followers. There is
contact, exchange, meet-ups, and so on, that are part of how we satisfy the desires of this digitally expanded self alongside a more passive, voyeuristic mode, where the thrill and pleasure is in checking up
on and watching how others are living their lives. The excitement and
at times, desperation, to receive likes on our postings, to be rated by
the other, or to playfully explore the number of matches we might get
on a dating app (even if we are not really looking for a date) speaks to
the unabashed yearning to be seen, to feel held inside the other's
mind, or to hold the other in ours.

As a result, bolstering that feeling of being connected to the whole
world, our minds become populated with an extensive arrangement
of people and events; no longer the inner objects of the depth psychologist, "the cemeteries of the brain" (Arsic, 2016, p. 71), but outer

ones, brimming with aliveness, vitality, and change that implant themselves in our everyday consciousness. Through this process of taking in so many lives other than our own, the digital is expanding our relational world at an accelerated and unrelenting pace. Yet, this outward focus and attention toward virtual others may deafen us to the rhythms of the inner self and the free arising of its imagery. We have discussed this in terms of the virtual within, portrayed by depth psychology, in its Freudian and Jungian stripes, as an internal world complete with its own universe of characters, whose affectively charged currents of images and narratives, journey beneath our outer lives. Two distinct forms of virtuality, two different virtual reality worlds.

In wondering whether we can still hear the music of our own imagination amid the clamoring roar of the collective, we are impelled to consider the interplay between the virtual as it manifests in the singularity of the individual psyche and its dissemination into the collectivity of a networked mind. This familiar topic can now be illuminated from the perspective of the other. Our internal and external object relational worlds are taking shape today against the backdrop of digital virtuality, in which new modes of both taking in and expunging the other are becoming increasingly prevalent. This destabilizes the assumptions that we have up to now taken for granted about where we draw the boundary between self and other, and has dramatic consequences, as we will see, for the place of otherness in everyday human life.

1 Digital disavowal

"Under normal conditions," as Young says, "dissociation enhances the integrating functions of the ego by screening out excessive or irrelevant stimuli. Under pathological conditions the normal functions of dissociation become mobilized for defensive use" (Young, as quoted in Bromberg (1998)). In the course of everyday life, there is not such a clear distinction between these two – integrative and defensive – instances of dissociation, but more of a spectrum; and even in clinical practice it is often difficult to discern where on such a spectrum someone lies. In our everyday use of digital devices, the distinction between adaptive and pathological instances of dissociation become even more blurred. For example, it is commonplace (and now no longer only with the younger generations) that when people are gathered together in the same communal space, it is considered well within the boundaries of ordinary social behavior to turn away from whatever is happening in the immediate present circumstances and begin interacting with someone else, on one's phone. But some may say we have always done that, in more covert ways, all the time anyway, not on our phones but in our minds. Indeed, in our engagement with others we often find ourselves lost in thought, taken somewhere else, being physically yet not emotionally or cognitively present.

If dissociation can be described as a momentary splitting of the mental from the physical, one state of self from another, does anything change when the dissociative moment of being swept up and taken somewhere else is no longer contained within the boundaries of one's own mind and body? Is the nature of being split different in the case of our smartphone life, when we are physically present with one person while engaging virtually with someone else, somewhere else, at the same time? If we are always already, in the everyday, non-pathological sense, in a mild state of dissociation, if indeed, as Bromberg (1998) claims, this is how the mind functions, is it another instance of the same, or is the digital pushing us toward a more severe, problematic level of dissociative splitting?

The spectrum between ordinary and traumatic dissociation we find in Bromberg is also present in Freud's concept of disavowal. Freud considers it to be a pathological defense that the ego uses to radically deny the impact of an unpleasant or horrifying external perception, by splitting itself into two parts.[1] As a result, two simultaneous paths form in the mind, two independent logics, that do not interact or interfere with each other. At the same time, Freud (1940) also seems to imply that disavowal is an ordinary, non-pathological aspect of the mind, where there is a self-generative back and forth movement between disavowing something and then acknowledging it, a creative and adaptive use of it.[2] We can see this dynamic play in our relationship to our own mortality, and the ongoing oscillation between living our lives as if we are not going to die (disavowal) and moments where are brought face to face with our mortal condition (acknowledgment).

Bromberg (1998) expresses a similar state of play between knowing and not-knowing something when he says that ordinary dissociation is

a basic process that allows individual self-states to function optimally (not simply defensively) when full immersion in a single reality, a single strong affect, and a suspension of one's self-reflective capacity is exactly what is called for or wished for. (p. 273)

We can be acknowledging one reality while disavowing another, not because we are defensively trying to escape from something, but creatively trying to enter it, keeping certain aspects of a situation out of awareness so that we can more fully immerse ourselves in it. This happens with events and with people. Indeed, this play of disavowal and acknowledgment is one of the primary ways by which we regulate our relationship to the other. This is strikingly evident in the paradoxical nature of the therapeutic setup. The business relationship between therapist and patient (you pay me for my services because this is how I make my living) is disavowed well enough in order for both participants to enter into the affectively charged, relatively unguarded relationship necessary for the therapy to work. This play of disavowal and acknowledgement is what holds the tension between intimacy and professionalism that is necessary to both sustain the therapeutic bond and eventually break it, when it is time for the treatment to come to an end.

And finally there is the use of disavowal for psychic survival, as what happens with trauma. Here it is not a creative play of knowing and not-knowing, or a near-psychotic refusal to acknowledge what is before one's eyes, but an active turning away from reality in order to protect the self from fragmenting. Only by being able to disavow the traumatic experience can the victim hold onto another part of himself that continues to exist separate from the trauma. This brings us back to the image of two independent tracks, where the traumatized ego and its non-traumatized part become separate, non-interacting systems that account for how someone who has suffered such experiences survives and continues on with life.

A wide range of digitally induced behaviors toward the other lie on the broad spectrum from interactions laced with ordinary dissociative moments to more severe and, at times, pathologically induced examples of disavowal, where the reality of the other is so erased from the mind that it is as if he or she ceases to exist anymore. The digital provides us with new instruments for regulating contact: We can move in toward the other, very close and quick, or suddenly expunge her, effacing her from memory. In the discourse of our digital times, there are many terms that illuminate the spectrum of these new modes of modulating our relationship to the other: friending, liking, muting, blocking, unfriending, and, in its most annihilatory form, ghosting. These movements along the path from connection to erasure have dynamic effects both on who is acting and who is being acted upon.

"Sorry, I have to take this" was used in the past to excuse the momentary interruption of a phone call, and there was an expectation that the other would come back and re-engage. But that mantra today has transformed into a perpetual "waiting," for with the advent of the smartphone, there is no predicting when someone might take a call, and if they do, we can certainly never know for sure when and if they will return. In psychotherapy, in what was once considered a revered space of intimate depth relating, it has become commonplace for the patient to interrupt the exchange, no matter what is being talked about, no matter how affectively charged, by taking a call or responding to a text and then re-presencing with the quip, "Oh yes, where were we?" If the patient is momentarily dissociated, searching to find their way back, so is the therapist, as their experience of being embedded in a dialogical process has also been breached by the interruption. But again, is this any different from a psychotherapy patient who, speaking to her therapist on the phone from an outdoor park, intermittently interrupts the process by turning her attention to the tweeting bird that lands nearby? Whether the distraction is virtual or not seems to make no difference, for they both have a similar dissociative effect.

The withdrawal from the present moment has no apparent indicators; it can happen at any time, called from the outside by a ding or the inside by an impulse to tweet. It is generally permissible now to ignore whoever we are with in real life in order to respond to the virtual beckoning. This is the unwritten rule of digital social life. In groups, hanging out with family or friends, we simultaneously have a foot in each world, real and virtual, and the virtual is progressively given favor.

We are increasingly intolerant of any lull in conversation, all the many awkward moments of not quite knowing what to say or where to go next. Phubbing, where we ignore our companion by turning to the phone or screen, has become socially acceptable. I'm bored with you, so I phub you. Or your phubbing signals that you are bored with me. Any moment, no matter how intimate, can be interrupted. The digital phub becomes the ever-ubiquitous solution to working our way out of such holes. I stumble over my words, or take too long to say what I want to say, and "poof!" the other is gone. There is the running joke that nowadays people are phubbing even while having sex.

And of course, we are also phubbing ourselves. We may be thinking or working on something, deeply engaged in a task, and thus tempted with the ever-present enticement to click away and go somewhere else. High school and college students report always having to add into the time calculation any one homework task will take the endless minutes or hours spent compulsively searching the web, and often, after the first few minutes, not even enjoying it.

But what effect does phubbing have on the other; what happens in the mind of he or she who is being phubbed? As we saw in our psychotherapy example, the experience of being engaged together with someone and then suddenly dropped, sets off a dissociative process in the mind. Whatever ways in which we might have been present to ourselves, and/or present to the other, is shattered in that abrupt and unexpected experience of being turned away from. It can potentially create a wave of strong affect – upset, anger, outrage, sadness, helplessness, and so on – that is inevitably blotted out, as we are all expected to adhere, without complaint, to this unwritten code of digital conduct. Isn't it parallel to the situation of a child who grows up with a parent whose attention toward her is constantly being interrupted, which results in herself becoming split? Dissociated parents forge dissociated kids. And of course, for us today, dissociated kids also forge dissociated parents. Since the limits of their relation to their children are regulated by the demand that to make emotional contact they must also partake in the virtual, the emotional life of the parent suffers these fissures too. Abrupt shifts in presence and attention are the currency of contemporary exchange.

We shouldn't pretend anymore that our gadgets only serve communicative ends. In our impulse to make them into tools of erasure, there is an imperious urge for dominance, a will to power. I no longer have to bother with the reality of the separate other, for the smartphone in my hand can become a weapon, offering me a quick and efficient escape from her demands. It allows me to defend against the ways in which the uninvited other tries to penetrate my defenses and occupy space inside my mind. And does this remarkable power to psychically expunge the other from our being, help explain our psychological yearning to always be in possession of such a device, especially in moments of great vulnerability?

To understand the nature of these self-other dynamics, we must first face an important paradox contained within them. Because we are social and relational beings from the start, the formation of loving attachments with our early caretakers is a crucial necessity for not only our physical but our emotional survival. One of the primary consequences of forming a close relationship with another person, however, is having to bear the residues of the other's unprocessed and unmetabolized affects. We unconsciously and unwittingly take them in. A mother does it for her baby, as she metabolizes the unthinkable anxieties that the infant cannot yet bear (Winnicott, 1962; Bion, 1983). And we do it, consciously and unconsciously, when we love each other, in that enormously complex, bi-directional exchange of affective chaos that is the life-blood of any significant relationship.

As infants, we just drank in the other. The internal object world disclosed by psychoanalysis is generated from how un-self-consciously and openly vulnerable we were to taking in the unconscious dimensions of their being. And because this process gives rise to the innermost structures of the self, we are forever haunted by this enigmatic stamp of otherness inside us.[3]

With the reverberating echoes from those early experiences where we were once colonized, the boundary between self and other becomes a psychic fault line. In this conception of human development, we are ever vulnerable in our relational lives to the unmetabolized actions and words of the other. Whereas repression is a defense against instinctual demands that arise from within, disavowal defends against the claims of reality, which in this context, amounts to the claims made upon us by the people who inhabit our closest orbit. Nevertheless, there is, as we have indicated, a constructive use of disavowal. It can serve as a protective shield, allowing us greater capacity for bearing the primordial conflict between self and other without having to repress it. By disavowing fundamental aspects of who someone is, we can better tolerate and live in a less-conflictual stance with them. The back and forth of knowing and not-knowing, disavowing and acknowledging, becomes the means through which we dynamically modulate our relations.

So perhaps digital disavowal has a positive potential. It helps to prevent our falling through the many small fissures that are always on the verge of multiplying in our relation to the other. The click that suddenly switches things off can very well be seen as a momentary disavowal that allows us the chance to recoup and gain our footing once again. By temporarily distancing or even erasing the other, we protect ourselves from his unsettling effects. It also helps us bear the otherness that lives within, in the form of traumatic traces of early object ties that, in certain triggering situations, create unbearable affects that threaten the integrity of self-experience. When we live out a wholly new identity on the Internet, for example, we enact a mode of internal disavowal, where we can disregard certain facts about ourselves and our history. In Jungian terms, we might speak of this as a creative disavowal of the shadow. We may find that this digitally constructed persona better sustains the synthesizing processes that knit the self together and keep it whole.

The digital is able to disavow one thing in the name of the next so adroitly that we can exist in multiple realities and diverse worlds without contradiction. This quicksilver passage from one reality to another can be taken up in very different ways. It can become a seductively enticing hide-out for the self, where we can appear to others one way but actually be acting antithetically to it. Here, the digital magnifies the all-too-human trait of self-concealment; it makes us masters of deception. Whatever we are doing on-line, whoever we may be in contact with, can be secreted away from the other, in a mere click, as we return to the report that we were writing or the shopping that we were doing. This quality of being hidden in plain sight – everyone on their laptops or phone, furtively clicking away at something – exacerbates the tendency, so much a part of modernity, to live a compartmentalized life, acting out the conflicts within the self by dissociatively switching between multiple, yet contradictory identities. These disavowing mechanisms help to further repress these conflicts, so we can continue on with things despite them.

But, at the same time, it also offers us the possibility of engaging, rather than repressing, them; a way to hold the mind's multiple compartments in a free play of exchange. As we have seen, the other can be as directly acknowledged by the digital as it can be disavowed. And in-between the two, there is a creative play of knowing and not-knowing things about the other, while letting them know and not know things about ourselves. The unique mix of virtual and actual that happens in digital life offers us the possibility of learning to play, of opening up the very space of "don't act-out and don't repress" that is so central to the psychoanalytic process. The digital enriches and expands the creativity of modulation, that fecund dance of revealing and concealing, which makes our relationship to the other more alive, more bearable, fuller, and richer.

Never in human history have we seen outside the province of our own minds such a quick and totalizing mechanism for disavowal as that which we are given with the digital screen. It seamlessly keeps incompatible realities apart from each other, on separate and parallel tracks. It allows heterogeneous things, with their diverse and separate dynamics, to lodge, conflict-free, inside a person's awareness. Because what is happening on one screen does not impact what is happening on another or in our actual empirical experience, we can go from one to the next, guilt-free, without ever having to look back.

If indeed we are all struggling to bear the ways in which we are inhabited by the traces of the other, then the specific ways we use our pocket-sized disavowing machines expose the innermost aspects of our psychology. If we let ourselves go and truly make full use of the logic of disavowal, we must reckon with the inescapable conflict between a disavowal that empowers us to better bear the otherness in human life, or a disavowal that aggressively erases the other for the sake of self-dominance.

2 Digital eros

Virtual life tends to smooth over the emotionally fraught and un-predictable nature of self-other interactions as they occur in everyday experience. Certain aspects of why, at times, it can be so difficult to bear other people are attenuated by the digital: the physical space of our fellow embodied beings and how much of it they take up, their demanding gaze, the inevitable conflict between their desire and ours, and our aggression towards them.

When we are speaking through the screen, my gaze cannot reach you, that is, I cannot look you in the eye, which is something we can always do in the presence of the other. My gaze does not cross the same space as yours when we are together virtually, nor do my eyes receive the same light from which you are looking at me. Screen-mediated relations create an emotional distance that helps to dampen down affect, diminish conflict, giving us a new kind of control over how we interact and communicate. Nevertheless, our minds already seem to have settled and unconsciously convinced themselves that, when we are conversing with others on the screen we are indeed in the presence of those people.

But while our minds are easily persuaded, our bodies are not. In these virtual interactions, we stop receiving almost all the bodily and physical signals to which we are accustomed, and from which we build our impression of reality. However, our growing dependence on technology forces us to live our relational lives in a world increasingly mediated by screens. Adolescents spend significantly more time now with friends online than in their actual, physical presence. And not only do they not miss much in such virtual interactions, but often they tend to feel more comfortable with them than in actual embodied encounters.

The inherent instability of human relationships is stabilized by a life extended by the virtual. The anxiety of meeting someone new, for example, is vastly reduced by the mediation of the screen. Paradoxically, at the very same time, the other also becomes more accessible, more transparent. When he is no longer there, we can bring back his recorded image and hold it before us, and have as long as we need to take a very close and intimate look at just who he is. We can make a careful study of his facial gestures or the definition of his muscles, examining the precise details of any part of the body that may interest us.

The digital gaze penetrates its object and enlivens it more than photography or painting ever allowed; the still image, now insufficient, is quickened into living video motion by a simple touch. And if we have sent tiny cameras to film our subject from within, we can even look inside the body so we can render visible, not only for the medical eye, but also the artists', what is invisible to the naked eye. As the impulse toward making all representations into some form of a video-like feed has encroached upon us, we barely notice that the once motionless and mute photographs have even become in our phones living moments as well.

The ability to film, edit, and view at will the image of the other offers us a new way of inhabiting him, and holding him in consciousness, often without consent. It is as if today we can safely stalk whomever we want on any of the trending social media, without ever having to cross the line and impose ourselves upon them in real life. Digitization promotes a nearly perfect mode of voyeurism, in that it both holds the other safely at a distance, while at the same time allowing us to see up-close whatever it is we want to see. By obviating the need for physical presence, and thus transcending the opposing force of the other's difference, we can innocuously probe his inner depths. Abolish the body and you are halfway there to taming the other.

Digital voyeurism opens up new pathways into the paradoxical dynamism of approach and avoidance, fight or flight behavior. This new capability for coming in close while staying distant complicates the already intractable psychological issue of intimacy with the other. And since this dialectic is so germane to our sexual lives, the apotheosis of digital voyeurism is virtual sex. When we enter the safe and predictable domain of the virtual, the raw, unpredictable, and affective aspects of sexuality are deferred. Clean and efficient "intercourse" with a virtual image (whether we are watching pornography, sexting, or engaging in cyber or robotic sex) is less emotionally complicated than what happens when two bodies meet. The uncontrollable excess inherent to desire, its wildness and unpredictability, is reigned in; what is so utterly vulnerable about sexuality is expunged. But no longer constrained by the bodily presence of my partner, I can enter an unencumbered sexual flow as the erotic frees itself from the limiting effects of the other and becomes an almost pure act of imagination.

This liberation of the erotic from its rootedness in what is vulnerable and hence potentially traumatic has radically opened the doors of sexuality, freeing it from the prison of repression. The digital has unlocked something fundamental about our sexual lives that, as Freud noted, when bottled up, consumes a good deal of our psychic energy. More than just the significant increase in sexual freedom and expression inaugurated in the '60s, today, thanks to the Internet, there is a new mode of access to the sexual imagination in all of its forms and varieties. A uniquely constituted polymorphously perverse fluidity, in the best and most creative sense of that term, boosts the possibilities for living out our erotic lives.

Freud was always more weary than we are today about the negative effects on culture when sexuality is released too freely. If neurosis is caused by sexual repression, the solution is not simply lifting it with the goal of immediate and unending gratification, but rather reckoning with this energy, facing inside ourselves what it is wanting. In his existential reading of Freud, Jean-Luc Nancy (2008) suggests that coming to terms with how the sexual drive (*Sexualtrieb*) lives inside us is tantamount to facing our fate, thus he provides us with an ontological scrim against which to examine what is happening to eros as it makes a new home in the digital, freed from its repressive confinements.

> Man comes from a momentum [*élan*] or a surge [*poussée*] which surpasses him, which surpasses in any case much of what Freud designates as the "self" [*moi*]. He calls this momentum or surge the *Trieb*.

Instead of translating it as "drive," Nancy uses the French *pulsion* to re-interpret Freud's Trieb, stressing the fact that we originate from

> a movement that has come from elsewhere, from the non-individuated, from what is the hidden archaic state of our origins, proliferating and confused – and that is: nature; the world; the whole of humanity behind us, and behind it what makes it possible; the emergence of the sign and the gesture; the call of all of us to the elements, to forces, to the possible and the impossible; the sense of infinity lying ahead of us, lying behind and amongst us; the desire to answer to this call, and to expose oneself to it. We originate from this movement, from this momentum, from this surge. In the final analysis, it is within this movement and as such a movement that we can grow.

This active momentum inside us that comes from elsewhere, moving us forward as the basis for growth, precisely sums up what in Chapter 4 we were identifying as the (immanent) virtual. Nancy goes on to say:

> This surge comes from elsewhere than us. ... This "elsewhere" is not a "beyond" ... This "elsewhere" is inside us: it forms within us the most creative and the most powerful engine driving this momentum, which is what we are. This is because it is nothing less than our being ... "being" considered in the meaning of the verb "to be": it is a motion, a movement, an emotion, the shock and rise of desire and fear, waiting and attempting, trying, accessing, even crisis and exaltation.

While the particular way of thinking about what is beyond the human in the digital is given form in the externality of the robot, the avatar, the cyborg, the algorithmic transmutation of the mind (i.e., a technical consciousness, freed from the materiality of existence, which exceeds human awareness), here we are offered a non-technological ontology for thinking beyond the human subject. Because the digital is inorganic – even though more and more we try to wear it, insert it under the skin, in our brains, replacing parts of our body, etc. – it is always extraneous to us. But in his rendering of Freud's drive as a surge that surpasses what we ordinarily think of as the self, Nancy – clearly in contrast to the digital – locates this nonhuman beyond inside us. It is an outside inside that allows for an encounter with an elsewhere that is intrinsic to our being. Moreover, in describing that drive as an "infinity lying ahead of us, lying behind and amongst us" (ibid), Nancy is giving voice to that realm of infinite possibility that underwrites human subjectivity, the very virtual itself.

This non-personal surge strongly resonates with the mad pro-liferation of the simulacrum that we saw in Deleuze. Although the digital expands the self, giving it more freedom and creativity, un-leashing desire (sexual and otherwise), in new and unheard of ways, it is of a different order than the virtual that lies within and beyond us i.e., the "non-individuated drive that arises from the hidden and ar-chaic state of our origins, proliferating and confused." This provides a clue about why in the example from *Be Right Back* that we analyzed in Chapter 3, the clone lacked the spontaneity without which it could not respond in a human way.

In Nancy's hands, Freud's theory of the drive seems to veer toward Jung, who equates libido with the psychic or life energy that drives our being. But there's the sense in Nancy that we can only get there by first coming to terms with this confusing, non-linear proliferation of desire that has no inherent organization and thus is at some basic level ungovernable, never completely contained by the psyche, that Freud, in the *Three Essays,* identifies with sexuality. The digital gratification of the sexual impulse seems to be at risk of erasing this non-human elsewhere of sexuality, its very ungovernability, the non-individuated drive that destabilizes the unity and coherence of the self. In the name of a freely flowing digital eros, virtual sex can scale down our erotic lives into something uncomplicated and predictable.[4]

Inside the protective shell of the digital, eros is cut off from the contingency of the world that is the source of its emergence. It is constrained by the flat and frictionless surface of the virtual, where difference and otherness are dampened down, almost to the point of being mute. Thus sheltered, the other cannot truly make contact with us, as the immateriality of the medium evaporates their existential density, numbing us to the separateness of their desire. We are thus sanctioned to pursue the singular quest for gratification. Digital eros gives succor to the pure pleasure principle which is ultimately turned in upon itself, unleashing the selfishness of the drive. Freed from the possibility of harm, we can feel we are living our erotic lives with renewed intensity and immediacy, taking more risks, exploring more possibilities, yet that smoothing over the psychic turmoil inherent to sexuality can cast a very potent shadow that haunts eros in the virtual world.

There is something very difficult to bear about sexuality as it opens us to forces outside our control, unpredictable and unreliable, and never fully known. Together with death, sex brings us face to face with our inherent and unavoidable vulnerabilities, the fragility of our bodies, the demands and strength of our desire. Being vulnerable, being open to risk, is essential to how we love, just as in the Greek myth, in order to unite with Eros, Psyche has to undergo trials and suffering. But digital eros seems to disconnect us from psyche, to be devoid of the very soulfulness of human love. This impoverishment of eros leads us down the well-trodden path of the erotic becoming the sexual and the sexual the pornographic. As Byung Chul Han (2017) puts it:

> [A] sexual object that can be consumed is not the Other. It never calls me into question. .... The pornographic image emanates no resistance to the Other or the Real. It is neither upstanding nor distanced. What is pornographic is precisely the lack of contact and encounter with the Other. Instead, autoerotic contact and auto-affection protect the ego from being touched or seized by the Other. (p. 45)

The virtual world indeed provides us with opportunities to do away with the presence of the erotic other (in the end always an enigma) by replacing it by various easily controlled digital substitutes. Taken up with the transhumanist anticipation of the Singularity,[5] the machinic (robots, cyborgs, technological prostheses, etc.) is no longer separate from our sexual nature. One particularly unexpected and telling instance of this fantasy is found in the glee in which the transhumanists describe the advent of sexbots, robots that we can sexually interact with, who will be able to provide us with "longevity orgasms":

> [Sexbots will] be more desirable, patient, eager, and altruistic than their meat-bag competition, plus they'll be uploaded with supreme sex-skills from millennia of erotic manuals, archives and academic experiments, and their anatomy will feature sexplosive devices ... They'll offer us quadruple-tongued cunnilingus, open-throat silky fellatio, deliriously gentle kissing, transcendent nipple tweaking, g-spot massage & prostate milking dexterity, plus 2,000 varieties of coital rhythm with scented lubes. (Huffpost "Sex robot 'longevity orgasms' may help extend human lifespans, futurist suggests." (http: www.transhumanity.net, Nov 7th, 2012 (found 2019))

In this futuristic virtual world, sex becomes a solo, masturbatory act. There is no need for an "other." In fact, a real other only gets in the way of the intimate relationship that is portrayed between the virtual and the self. The virtual, in the form of a sexbot, is the most finely attuned and acquiescent lover the self will ever have. It can draw out the deepest and most penetrating orgasms, and the self, if it can just agree to fully give over to its virtual lover, can have these orgasms on demand, daily, even hourly, if it so desires. We would be then capable of dosing ourselves with regularly available shots of pleasure, something already pictured in Huxley's *Brave New World* and the social use of Soma.

The seduction of the sexbot is that it ensures a level of predictability and control in our relation to the other. But this may very well result in narrowing the scope and lowering the quality of our subjective lives. The Transhumanist faith in the power of digital technology to transcend the human is nothing but a skeptical response, a refusal to acknowledge the loss natural to human existence but also an attempt to better reality, to replace it. The sexbot is meant to do away with our dependence on the human other that binds together the complicated web of human existence and gives substance to life.

We are nowadays moving increasingly toward that fantasy, inviting the digital into the innermost regions of our sexual lives, thus enormously complicating both love and sexuality. Spike Jonze's film *Her* (2013) strikingly portrays this conundrum. Joaquin Phoenix plays Theodore, a man who, heartbroken after his marriage ends, purchases what in the film is advertised as the first artificial intelligence operating system (OS), designed to adapt and evolve like a human being: an intuitive entity that listens to you, understands you, and knows you. Theodore decides to give his OS a female identity, and he names her "Samantha," voiced by Scarlett Johansson. He is fascinated by her ability to learn and grow psychologically, and as the movie progresses, they fall in love and begin a virtualized sexual relationship.

We remember having experienced the premiere of *Her* with a feeling of disorientation, conceptually and intuitively; it made no real sense, yet it captured our imagination. Little did we know that six years later, as we wrote about it, we would realize that these confusing concepts and images are now for us so easy to digest, because of the new realities we have been confronted with in that time. It is no problem, today, to understand Theodore's circumstance, after learning to share our lives with Siri, Alexa, and so many other artificially intelligent devices, these once unheard of entities that now begin to engage us and populate our world.

Samantha, the cybernetic consciousness, is fascinated with human embodiment and longs to have a body herself.[6] Wanting to actualize her desire in the physical act, she yearns to have non-virtual sex with Theodore. So she contacts Isabella, a young woman who is eager to play the role of a surrogate sexual partner for a human-OS relationship. Theodore does not like the idea; he is content with their wholly virtual, un-embodied love-making, but reluctantly agrees to the plan of allowing Isabella to act as Samantha's body, so as to consummate their love.

When Isabella arrives at Theodore's apartment, she is mute and emotionally absent, as she prepares to completely give herself over to Samatha's consciousness. Isabella is eager to escape her own body and become virtual, whereas Samantha wants to escape her virtuality and become embodied. Theodore can do neither, and as he tries to make love to Samantha's voice, he finds himself unable to surrender to the illusion that it is Samantha's body he is caressing. Isabella's body, in its material reality, keeps breaking in on him, interfering with his attempt to ignore it and thus stay inside virtual space. Things break down on the physical plane and he sends the "real" woman, Isabella, away in tears.

Isabella symbolizes what is other to the virtual, here in the form of an embodied self. Her body obstructs Theodore's capacity for disavowal, exposing the limits of the virtual, frustrating its flow. Before Isabella, Theodore's desire for Samantha was never disrupted. Her disembodiment freed his imagination and opened up his sexuality. But when their communion is mediated by a real body, the body of an other, Theodore finds himself impotent, unable to engage the (virtual) object of his desire.

In bracketing out those aspects of what may be most problematic in our relationship to the other, we open up new avenues and possibilities for encounter. In being able to modulate the scope of how much of the other we are required to contend with, we can see and act in ways that may have been previously impossible. Something flourished in Theodore's sexual imagination with Samantha that never came alive in his former attempts at love and sexuality with a real human being. Yet the need to control and make the other predictable, losing the vibrancy and vitality of the unpredictable, is something we all have to contend with today. New possibilities, new problems.

Freud might say that when sexuality is so turned upon itself that difference and contingency are all but abrogated, we are left in a fairly unstable, perhaps even alarming place. The regression brought about by the digital echoes a time in our development when we had not yet discovered ways of bearing our erotic lives that did not rely upon a primitive form of narcissism that kept at bay what was other to the self. When eros is pirated by the digital, something of this situation is re-invoked, as the reality of the other no longer serves as a check to the pure pleasure instinct. We are then more vulnerable to falling into a purely ego-centered erotics, as we lose our capacity to imagine more expansive and life-affirming possibilities for bearing sexuality.

In order to emotionally evolve as a human being, it is necessary to come to terms with the fact of the other as a separate existence, with a separate center of consciousness and a separate view of the world (Benjamin, 1995). This involves finding good enough ways of binding our narcissism so that we can respect that difference, live with it, and not cross certain boundaries when it comes to imposing our way of seeing the world on the other. And nowhere is this more necessary than in dealing with the ungovernability of our sexuality, and the blinding narcissism that rages inside it.[7] In that realm, we must learn to come to terms with the actuality of a "real" other, whose needs and desires are different than our own. But when that "real" other is re-placed by a "virtual" one, what is there to bind the excesses of our narcissism? What guideposts are left to help us distinguish between a "me" and "not-me" that is so essential for the maturation of our erotic and sexual lives?

3 The absent body

A rather broad and unwieldy question is evoked by the phenomenon of being present with another person virtually, as, for example, when we FaceTime or Zoom, take part in webinars, or when we participate in virtual communities generally, where our relationship with a group of people takes place exclusively over the Internet: Does the absence of bodily co-presence in the same space/time coordinates fundamentally change anything about our encounter with the other? Does it really matter if the body is there, or does something fundamentally change when the body is absent? This is the aporia of the digital era that we must face as we are all engaging in a rapidly expanding collective ex-periment in which more and more of our social, cultural, educational, and professional interactions are happening in cyberspace.

The question of the body is an especially vexing puzzle for practi-tioners of psychotherapy and psychoanalysis, as an increasing number of treatment sessions take place either on the phone or Zoom, and there is an enormous amount of contention in the field as to what kind of effects this is having on clinical practice (Lemma and Caparrotta, 2014; Lemma, 2017; Scharff, 2018)[8]. It also takes on in-creased urgency when it comes to dating and falling in love. Not only have dating apps become the central way sex and love is pursued, but many liaisons that begin in the digital world remain there, sometimes for the entirety of the relationship. When it comes to sex and ro-mance, the need for the other's actual body seems to be significantly declining.

In considering the wide spectrum of human relationships, whether they be between lovers, family members, friends, colleagues, ac-quaintances, or even strangers, a distinctive bi-personal field is gen-erated when two people come together in the same physical space. This is a phenomenon of intersubjective life whose early foundations have been well-mapped out by psychoanalytically-oriented infant research (Stern, 1985; Lachmann and Beebe, 2014). There is a pro-found exchange at the psycho-somatic level of experiencing in the context of the complex and emotionally rich dialogue that happens between infants and parents. We grow and become our unique selves as a result of these early encounters that are grounded in the preverbal intimacy of close bodily relating. Early contact with the other's embodied presence serves as the placeholder for the desiring self.

The kind of relating that we do in the digital world, however, is noteworthy for its absence of embodied contact. We can hear and see the other; indeed, their visual appearance is often brought into sharper focus than in our everyday perceptions. There is still plenty of presence, as the other on my screen is someone we can engage with in conversation, as if they were in the same room, sitting next to us. Yet, at the same time, we cannot touch them, or smell them, or empirically register their physical presence; screened out, it is kept at a distance. We can tell, of course, if they are suffering or in pain, for the camera picks up the obvious visible signs of whatever they might be physically experiencing. Telemedicine, for instance, is a burgeoning field, no doubt, in part, because of the immediate feedback it provides about the state of the other's body, to say nothing of its practicality. With these new virtual developments, that sense a doctor might have of being attuned to a bodily reality that exists beyond words and visual surfaces when sitting in the same room with a patient, is lost.

We would never expect to Zoom with our dog back home and be able to establish the kind of contact we have when sharing a physical space with it. Our relationship with an animal is rooted exclusively in the embodied encounter, as it is between parent and infant. The dog cannot perceive us, recognize our voice, our face on the screen, let alone our smell. So no matter what we do from our side – we can't stroke them, snuggle with them, sense their very discernible smell, or feel the attunement of our breathing patterns – nothing could make that relationship come alive. The absence of our physical bodies to each other, in fact, the virtuality of our presence in this new space precludes any contact with other (non-human) beings. Even a mosquito would not try to bite us!

When we Zoom, although not many of the usual sensations in human relating make it through the screen, there is so much clear and sharp verbal and visual information that the existential pulse of embodied life is not really missed. Rather than an open field of perception, where we are empathically attuned to the sentience of the other, screen-mediated relations take us out of our body and into the visual processing dimensions of the mind where sensations quickly become concepts. In speaking of the primarily visual experience of being in front of a screen, Virilio (1995) writes, "It is the eyeball that now englobes man's entire body" (p. 148). "Come over here and take a look at this," is the plea of whoever is holding a smartphone and wants to show you something. The eyeball establishes itself over the entire perceptual field. Here the eye's dominion parallels the "I" in cyberspace englobing the entire world. The digital subject, as we have seen, can be thought of as existing at the center of a mini-universe, but here we want to notice that part of what makes it easier to hegemonically flow through such a universe is that the body, both ours and the other's, is no longer there, mucking things up.

This absence of materiality is what maintains the frictionless flow of virtual life. We love being able to Skype or text in lieu of actually encountering someone. It makes things run so much smoother. But in that positivity, the awareness of what is so irresistibly appealing about being able to see and relate to someone without really having to confront their suffering body in the same physical space as ours, is repressed. In the name of convenience, expediency, and the wonders of our technological subversions, we are apt to deny that there is another motive at work. Think of the quick, mad-dash entries and even quicker exits the digital affords us. The cumbersomeness of our body in relation to another's, that complicated mixture of intimacy and responsibility, affinity and aversion, is forestalled. At any moment, whenever we want, we can just click off and the "other" instantly disappears. With this act comes an assuaging feeling of being released from her hold on us. The cool and aloof act of clicking or swiping off, ending the session, moving on, has now displaced what used to be the adrenalized charge of hanging up on someone. The digital provides new and more ubiquitous forms for modulating the level of contact we desire.

This set of reflections about the difference between bodily and virtual co-presence ultimately brings us to the question of human aloneness. It has always been the case that to combat the feeling of loneliness, you find people to hang out with and spend time together. That's why we like having families where there is always someone around whose bodily presence engages us and provides a sense of profound and soothing comfort. What does it mean, then, to try to deal with our existential isolation by appealing to the other's virtual presence, where this more familiar way of taking comfort is transformed? The virtual world is changing the ways in which we think about what it means to be alone. Winnicott (1958) saw the capacity to be alone as a developmental achievement rooted in how the growing child learned to be alone in the presence of the (m)other. Does something fundamentally change when it is a virtual other? This question of the relationship between digital technology and human aloneness creates a confounding pharmacological paradox. On the one hand, because of our devices, being by oneself is so much more tolerable; in close proximity to our smartphones, it feels like we are never truly alone. Whether it's Siri's voice answering our questions or the instantaneous immediacy and permanently available connection that happens on our social networks, they keep us company and provide comfort. But on the other hand, we have less and less capacity to be alone. We can't tolerate it. The slightest hint of it makes us panic. And this is especially evident when we are without a device, stranded, as it were, with ourselves, and only ourselves.[9]

In a commercial for Amazon Echo, a family is seen leaving Nana's house, hugs and kisses and sad good-byes: "We're going to miss you so much, I wish you didn't have to go." The scene changes and Nana is all alone, except for her cat. The doorbell rings and she bends down to pick up a box that her family has sent containing the new Echo, which looks like a common desk clock. A card instructs her to tell Alexa to call home, which she does, and suddenly the four family members are there again on the round-shaped clock turned screen. "Surprise!" they yell, and Nana is no longer alone and, we intuit, no longer lonely, as excited, animated voices and faces fill the room. As we watch this brief drama unfold, it's hard not to imagine the next moment, when the conversation between Nana and her virtual family empties out, turns flat, and the family switches off and Nana is left alone again in her house with her cat. In offering her something that has never existed before in human history, the virtual presence of her loved ones now on the screen, is Nana's relationship to her solitude forever changed? Can the Echo, or any other device, solve the problem of human aloneness? Or is it all just a gimmick?

4 Facing the real other

In "The Use of an Object," Winnicott (1971) offers a compelling account of how the infant moves from the position of experiencing the other as a creation of the self (the subjective object) into that in which the reality of the other as a separate center of consciousness can be psychologically integrated (the object objectively perceived). An apt image for precisely framing this issue occurs at the very start of his essay:

> Two babies are feeding at the breast. One is feeding on the self, since the breast and the baby have not yet become (for the baby) separate phenomena. The other is feeding from an other-than-me source. (1971, p. 89)

Here, in bold relief, we are confronted with the question of how, at the earliest beginnings, one makes contact with and takes in what is other to the self. From what is visually present in this image of two nursing babies, it is impossible to know which infant is feeding on the self and which from a source outside of itself. We may well imagine being in the same quandary when we see two young people, side by side, instagramming with friends and being uncertain whether there is a difference in how each of them is relating to the other. How would we know who was narcissistically feeding on the self and who was being nourished from an other-than-me source? This is what makes it so difficult to ascertain, from a purely behavioral standpoint, what kind of relationship any one person has to her device. The internal, emotional dynamics surrounding their use is as concealed to the outside observer as the difference between the two nursing babies.

Early on, in what Winnicott terms "object relating," the infant, in a state of subjective omnipotence, relates to his mother "ruthlessly." The mother here is a subjective object, wholly under the infant's mental control. A transition occurs when frustration at the inevitable failure of the mother to exactly meet the infant's need reaches a certain pitch and the infant damages the internal image he has of his mother by attacking her in fantasy. The mother's task is to hold the situation over time, so that the infant can see, on a moment-to-moment basis, that she is different from the internal mother towards whom his frustration and aggression is being directed. When the object is destroyed internally, in fantasy, and yet survives externally (the actual mother not retaliating or abandoning the baby) the infant comes to the recognition that the object is not subject to his mental control. A new state of "object usage" emerges, which revolves around the infant's dawning awareness of the limitations of his all-out destructive attacks, resulting in a new mode for discovering the externality of the world.[10] Developmentally, the infant breaks out of a state of omnipotent fantasy, where the world is magically under his control, and begins to come to terms with the actuality of a separate object.

In one of the most renowned passages in the psychoanalytic literature, Winnicott (1971) vividly describes this movement from object relating (feeding on the self) to object usage (being nourished by an other-than-me source).

> The subject says to the object: I destroyed you', and the object is there to receive the communication. From now on the subject says: 'Hullo object!' 'I destroyed you.' 'I love you.' 'You have value for me because of your survival of my destruction of you.' 'While I am loving you I am all the time destroying you in (unconscious) fantasy.' (p. 90)

Michael Eigen (1999), in his elaboration of this passage, offers an astute characterization of what it means to make genuine contact with an other:

> What is happening is the 'continuous' destruction of the fantasy objects (the introjective-projective world) and the birth of the real object, the other subject outside all of one's psychic web-spinning.

It is an all out, nothing held back, movement of the self-and-other feeling past representational barriers, past psychic films and shells, a floating freely in a joyous shock of difference. (p. 8)

How is our relationship to the other affected by the kind of virtuality that springs forth from the digital? Could we say it becomes "an all out, nothing held back, movement of the self-and-other feeling past representational barriers, past psychic films and shells, a floating freely in a joyous shock of difference" (Eigen, p. 8)? Surely, we can see it this way when we consider the myriad forms of experience that are available in cyberspace that promote new and expansive modes of relationality. As we encounter the other in the present tense mode of the "digital now", there is a receptive immediacy to the interchange that dramatically breaks down representational barriers. But we must also consider how the digital blocks access to the other. If the self is constantly being created anew by psychic fantasy bumping up against the "real" otherness of the object, and the virtualization of the "other" erodes that realness, then, are we not more vulnerable to being pu-shed back into a world of subjective objects, objects, there to satisfy our needs and sustain the projections of our fantasies?

5 Facing the digital other

If, indeed, one of the vulnerabilities of digital life is the tendency it has to propel us in the direction of object relating, where the other primarily serves a mirroring function for the self, then we must learn to contend with the omnipotence that is intrinsic to this position. The self that relates to the other as a subjective object collapses the tension between inner and outer reality, such that there is a near total ab-sorption of the other into the self, as the mother was assimilated by the infant at the earliest stages (Benjamin, 1995). Bearing in mind the narcissism involved there, let us return to the myth.

Narcissus was transfixed by his own image in the pond, yet he was not aware that he himself was the object of his transfixion. Narcissus could be described as a "monadic self ... encapsulated in a closed system, the omnipotent mind ... [who] cannot reach something outside" (Benjamin, 1995, p. 91). This would accord with the more classical reading of the Narcissus myth, as we saw in Chapter 3 But there is something else at work here, for as Narcissus adoringly gazes at himself in the pond, he mistakenly believes he is falling in love with a real other. He does not recognize that it is he who is the object of his own reflection. Here the false consciousness of Narcissus, this mis-recognizing moment where the self is assumed to be an actual other, exemplifies how our own concealed narcissism is masked by the virtual. This is akin to Freud's (1900) description of the inherent egoism of dreams.

> Dreams are completely egoistic. Whenever my own ego does not appear in the content of the dream, but only some extraneous person, I may safely assume that my own ego lies concealed by identification, behind this other person. (pp. 322–323)

For Freud, dreams are illustrative of the narcissistic illusion that when we think we are encountering or engaging with someone or something that we experience as "other," we may actually only be meeting our own projections. Does the digital exacerbate this fundamentally human tendency to collapse the difference between self and other?

Byung Chul Han, considering depression to be an outgrowth of this collapse, answers in the affirmative when he writes:

> The Internet is a space where above all you encounter yourself. The other person is long gone. Depression is a disease of the narcissistic self that has been set adrift from relationships, that has lost all sense of what is different. The virtual space is a hell of sameness. (Tollman, 2011)

One common denominator of all of the technological devices with which we populate the most intimate spaces of our lives, from Siri and Alexa to our smartphones and iPads, is how they so adroitly reflect back and thus enhance the self. This corresponds to one of the main functions of what Kohut (1971) calls a self-object, crucial to early development, where the parent or caregiver mirrors back to the child her qualities and accomplishments, thus laying the foundation for a healthy source of narcissism in the construction of the self.[11] In other words, in order to arrive later in life with a foundational feeling of self-worth and self-esteem, it is essential to go through a period of development in which the grandiosity and omnipotence of the self is reflected back to the child by a loving parent. Winnicott (1948) gives the example of the young girl who says, "I can fly" and instead of the father saying "No you can't," he picks her up and flies her around the room like a bird. But one cannot remain in this mode of developmentally appropriate illusion forever. Without some kind of transition toward object-usage, what starts off as the psychological necessity of a certain mode of self-expansive omnipotence sours into a narcissistic entrapment where the world has to keep feeding one's illusions for the sake of the self's coherence. The digital, we might say, reawakens those early strivings for omnipotence and the constant need to place one's "self" at the center of all things. In this light, we might describe the ubiquity of mirroring provided by our technologies as a Kohutian world of self-objects run wild.

As we move through our digital days, we are immersed in technologies that offer a ceaseless flood of mirroring, from the specially targeted ads that algorithmically inflame my acquisitive desires, to the messages in my inbox, all tantalizingly addressed to me, to the flurry of likes awaiting me in response to my most recent tweets or Facebook or Instagram posts, to the objects of my desire that come straight from the screen to my front door. Siri and Alexa answer my questions, assuage my concerns, and, in their omnisciently soothing voices, I feel as if they are there exclusively to help me. I turn on my GPS, and the coordinates and location of where I am currently situated become the center of the world. We now rely upon these external devices, as much, and in many cases more than, the actual people in our life, to maintain what Kohut would describe as the functioning of a cohesive self.

Zadie Smith (2015, Youtube) provides a cogent analysis of how this constant need for recognition impacts our relation to the other. She points to the difference between the kind of performativity that occurs in the world of social media and everyday relational life:

> The weird thing about Facebook is that everybody on it is like their own mini-celebrity. That's what it turns you into. You have fans, you are constantly giving them up-dates, you are like a little celebrity. And the relation, no matter what anyone says, is pretty much one way. And then you are voyeuristic about other people's celebrity profiles, and how many friends they have. It's one way. [Yet] while being relational, in real life you have to deal with other people. You have to have some kind of relationship with them and you can't just perform yourself. You have to look at them, look at them in the eye, which has become increasingly difficult for young people. On the Internet it's all self-revelation.

The digital exacerbates our yearning to be seen by the other, to be mirrored by them, intensifying a wholly ordinary need into a frenetic and unquenchable desire. If a parent's face is the infant's first mirror, our phones are the second (and, in many instances that are of a growing concern for the fate of the child in the digital age, the first). Hence, the digital becomes a dynamic reflector of the self that, unlike a parent, never stops giving. It thus aggravates and perhaps hyperrealizes this very basic human need for recognition. Today, we demand to be mirrored with a ferocity second to nothing else in our lives, including how we love. The effectiveness of social media, as a finely tuned instrument for "self-revelation" becomes the means by which we think we can finally conquer this profound and affective hunger for a mirroring recognition that is there from the earliest beginnings and seems now to have become an omnipresent force in our lives.

Searching, checking, updating and posting, and the ubiquitous loving or liking become the dominant currency of all social relations. We are forced to confront the issue of how mirror-hungry we actually are when we consider that the presentation of self on our social media accounts is not really us, but an embellished version of how we want to appear to others so that we can receive the maximum amount of recognition and acknowledgment. This unconscious, at times desperate, drive to be seen spurs us on to craft the perfect persona – sexy, witty, charming, serious, funny, and so on – one that will get us the most likes, the most followers.

There is a very poignant scene in Bo Burnham's (2018) movie *Eighth Grade* in which the young protagonist of the story, a girl who is a week away from her junior high school graduation, is sitting at the dinner table with her father, earbuds plugged in, scrolling through her smartphone. On the eve of this momentous event, her father wants to share some important reflections he has about the positive changes that she has made in her life so he asks her to take out her earbuds so that he can speak. In her initial refusal, we see him desperately entangled in a fight to become a mirroring self-object, as he continues to insist that they talk. She finally relents and listens for a minute or two, but what the scene makes abundantly clear is that there is absolutely no competition between the father's recognizing (albeit awkward and somewhat sappy) words, and the kind of mirroring that she is receiving from her phone, the self-object *par excellence*. She is impatient with his offerings and cannot wait one moment longer to get back to it.

Who can forgo the urge to click on and enter this miniaturized universe in which all of its denizens ultimately circle around *you?* Who can resist that reliable dose of self-recognition that is always there, waiting, that sumptuous gift to the self that never stops giving? But the paradox is that with this intensification of mirroring, we all feel ever more desperate to be seen. It's difficult to discern whether the phone's camera and its link to our social media diet is a symptom of that desperation or its cause. Either way, the digital has become an unruly pharmakon as we carry this insatiable demand to be recognized, while at the same time having a diminished capacity for offering in return the kind of recognition that does not unconsciously enact a pernicious *quid pro quo*, a tit for tat: I recognize you so that you will recognize me.

This is the intersubjective conundrum of a mode of object relating that rests upon an exchange of mutually enhancing recognition, which never gets beyond what I need the other to do for me, and what

I must do for the other to keep the attachment going. There is no way to get outside of myself and no way to get inside what is truly other about the other. What Winnicott calls object-usage, as we have seen, is a way out of this trap. It is the process by which we break through the bubble of self-referentiality and encounter a reality beyond our own mind. In terms of the dynamics of the Virtual Within, the transition to object-usage is that moment when the omnipotence, narcissism, and powerful need to perform the self that forms the building blocks of our inner virtuality is fundamentally pierced by something truly outside it.

Marion Milner (1957), who wrote a great deal about the process of self-development in relation to creativity, speaks about this transition as a re-emergence "into a new division of the me-not-me, one in which there is more of the 'me' in the 'not-me', and more of the 'not-me' in the 'me'" (pp. 154–155). Digital life does very well with the first half of Milner's equation, allowing a surplus of "me" to penetrate the "not-me," but very poorly with the second, because as the "me" expands in the digital, it has less and less tolerance for "not-me" experience, for the other in his or her irreducible separateness. As Zizek (1997) writes:

> What tends to get lost in virtual communities is this very abyss of the other, this very background of undecidability: in the 'wired universe', the very opaqueness of the other tends to evaporate. (p. 166)

And, as we have repeatedly seen, the narcissistic cocoon offered to us by the digital, frequently serves as a place of refuge from the not-me.

Because the virtual "other" is so intimately interwoven with our subjectivity – yet we are hypnotized by its materialization as something outside ourselves – we become blind to the many ways in which our virtual interactions are a reflection of how we want to shape reality, how we want it to conform and bend back toward us. This is what we have been depicting as the hidden erotics of the virtual self, how drawn in we are by the fact that virtualizing the other frees the object to become the ultimate *speculum* of and for the self. If there is an unconscious drive toward the virtual, it may very well have to do with this newly gained "positionality" that conquers the abyss of the other.

Perhaps the critical challenge of our times is to discover new ways of relating to the digital that lead us in the direction of object-usage, thus opening up pathways for bringing more of the "not-me" into the "me," more of the world into the self. This involves learning how to tolerate and bear the encounter with the radical undecidability of the other, somehow holding in check the strong urge that arises today to evaporate that opaqueness in the digital haze of our devices. We spoke of this in Chapter 5 as the maturation of our relationship to the virtual. In surrendering to the "not me," we experience a curtailing of our omnipotence. The virtual is no longer something I subjectively possess; rather, it reflects an openness to making contact with, and be contacted by, its transformative force.

Coda

The *Black Mirror* episode U.S.S. *Calister* poignantly illustrates the impact the digital pharmakon is having on how we bear the differences within ourselves as well as those between us and others. It tells the story of Robert Daly, an introverted computer programming genius, who is portrayed as a psychologically damaged man with a limited capacity to engage with real others. We see him being treated disdainfully by his office co-workers, and cruelly degraded by the man who co-founded the computer gaming company where they work, James Watson. Watson flagrantly bullies and humiliates Daly in front of his peers. But Daly takes revenge on them all by stealing their DNA and creating digital clones of them, which he imprisons inside a simulated Star Trek–like space adventure game. Alone at night, in the isolated chamber of his apartment, he enters the game as Captain of the Starship, leading his crew on sci-fi space missions to conquer the evil enemy. His crew, of course, are the very cloned office workers, including Watson, who have so terribly mistreated him in actual life. The game offers Daly the perfect space for revenge, for not only can he act out his most aggressive and sadistic impulses toward them, but he has them trapped, completely under his control, as clones on the Starship in an infinite, digital forever.

As an alternative to what we might consider the more typical relationship between internal objects (those psychic presences that live inside us, constituting our unconscious fantasy and dream life) and external objects (the actual people that we encounter in daily life), what this episode brings into dramatic focus is Daly's intense psychological engagement with virtual objects that are neither real nor fantasy. The people he interacts with everyday at work are transformed into characters that inhabit his private virtual reality world. What's interesting here is how this portrayal of digital virtuality mimics the virtuality of the psyche. Freud's concept of day residues (*Tagesreste*) – as the impressions of the people we have been psychically involved with during the day awakening in the mind during the night – points to a very similar virtualizing process.

Without having to steal anyone's DNA, our dreams produce psychic clones of the other, the *dramatis personae* of our nightly dreamscapes. So what kind of dream is Daly having when the tumultuous unfoldings of his instinctual and affective life actualize themselves in a realm with many of the same characteristics of his internal object world, which is now populated by virtual clones? The digital-virtual is nothing if not a completely new way of dreaming, a form of imaginative engagement that we haven't seen before, and one that is very hard for us, conceptually, to comprehend.

Jessica Benjamin (1995) delineates the developmental trajectory of how we come to relate to the fact of the other's independent consciousness and how we, as separate subjects, come to recognize each other as equivalent centers of experience. Along the way, there is often a breakdown into what she names a "doer-or-done-to complementarity," where we cannot overcome the impulse to either objectify the other or find ourselves objectified in relation to him -becoming the doer or becoming the done-to. This is a very common form of splitting that can potentially dominate so much of our relational life.

In his real life in the office, Daly always appears in the role of being done-to, a victim of Watson and the others. But on the U.S.S. *Calister*, he flips the script and becomes the towering figure of the captain, doing to the other what was done to him, though now in a perversely exaggerated and aggrandized form. No longer emotionally withdrawn and wounded, he is their supreme commander, completely in charge. Here, we see the pharmacological nature of the digital restructuring the virtual-actual dynamics in such a way that the virtual becomes Daly's compensation for what he suffers in real life. Once ensconced inside his private, virtual world, he becomes the victimizer, overcoming the daily onslaught of victimization he experiences at the office.

The ethics of this script-flipping are extremely knotty; they cast a pall over the "positive" uses of the virtual to make up for what we cannot get in the real, as in the many examples we have explored up to this point. Here, what happens to Daly's mind and behavior, the extreme ways in which his personality changes when he leaves the real and enters the virtual, exposes the potential pathology of this kind of virtual compensation. For example, after Watson tears into him in the office for not completing an assignment on time, Daly hurriedly wraps up his day and rushes back home to re-enter the game. One moment Watson is chewing him out, publicly shaming and humiliating him, and the next, Daly is viciously attacking Watson for failing on the space mission. He kicks him to the ground, savagely beats him and then demands that Watson kneel before him so that he can use his prone body as a footrest. The digital grants Daly total control over the other. Because the crew is trapped in his own secret, self-created, hermetically-sealed virtual chamber, he can do with them what he pleases with no "real" consequences.

The virtual then becomes a territory freed from all ethical considerations, allowing Daly to actualize his sadism without bounds.

Its most extreme expression happens in his cloning of Watson's be-loved young son, Tommy. He brings him aboard the starship and forces Watson to watch, as he launches the boy into space without a spacesuit, to see him freeze to death and crack up like a porcelain doll. Because he possesses his son's DNA, Watson knows that Daly can bring Tommy back at any moment and make him witness again and again, a mad proliferation of scenarios, repeating the torture in in-finitely varied ways. Not daring to step out of line, Watson is subjected to Daly's need to devise ever crueler and more horrible scenarios to remain in control.

Here we can usefully contrast the limits of sadism in everyday life and the limitlessness of its actualization in virtual space. Our sadistic impulses toward others and equally toward ourselves, have a very powerful charge. Even though things can and do, on occasion, get out of hand, there are built-in limits, safeguards against destructively acting on these impulses. Rather than acting them out in shared public space, our interior representational world, the inner space of the psyche, is where we attempt to contain them. For Freud, this was one of the functions of the dream in that it allows psychic expression of our aggressive and sexual impulses so that they do not have to be split-off and projected back into the relational world with others.

Another conception of containment is offered by Winnicott (1945) with his idea that the subjective world of fantasy needs to be brought into balance with external reality:

> External reality has brakes on it, and can be studied and known, and, in fact, fantasy is only tolerable at full blast when objective reality is appreciated as well. The subjective has tremendous value but is so alarming and magical that it cannot be enjoyed except as a parallel to the objective. (p. 153)

Virtual space infinitely expands the reaches of one's individual fan-tasy life. There are no ends to how far we can go in the virtual world. There is no anchor in outside reality, no balancing of the subjective and the objective, because the virtual is freed from any real-world effects. It creates its own self-perpetuating container that collapses that tension, and thus activates in us something that, in this story, takes us to the edge of horror. Watson is extremely abusive to Daly in their interactions at the office; he is a very sadistic man. But nothing he does to Daly even approaches the constant threat of Daly's forcing him to bear witness to his child being viciously tortured.

In the virtual we can always find a precise digital image to intensify whatever we are enraged about in the world, as we are now granted a near total and immediate access to an interactive archive of our shared collective imagination. But it goes one step further, allowing us to live out the most extreme aspects of our impulses with a simple click.

Sadism and masochism, hatred and aggression are magnified in the absence of flesh-and-blood "real" others in the virtual. But it is the face-to-face encounter with the other, to use Levinas' language, absent in the virtual, that is at the basis of our ethical lives. What form of ethics, then, should be required of the virtual self? Does it need to conform to the same ethical standards as any other self? Or, do its actions in a space that does not have any real world consequences, demand that we think of it as morally neutral?

For Daly, it takes a demonic turn, as the virtual frenetically feeds his angry and omnipotent revenge fantasies. We watch the unfolding of what eventually becomes his total identification with a malicious and dictatorial ego that prevents the virtual object from becoming anything other than an evacuative repository for his own hatred and rage. The crew of the starship, these digital copies of his actual office mates, are portrayed as sexless, unthinking and unfeeling beings, who cannot make a claim on their own subjectivity. Rather, they are forced to stay in role and act in limited and predictable ways whenever Daly re-enters the game. He becomes increasingly cruel and punishing, only interested in the continued expansion of his power and aggrandizement. If anyone on the crew steps out of line, refuses to narcissistically mirror his god-like greatness, he zaps them and instantly transforms them into the embodiment of the evil-other they are there to fight, a horrifying and monstrous creature, that becomes both punishment and threat, warning the others of a similar fate if they fail to submit.

The story takes a dramatic turn when Daly steals the DNA of a newly hired programmer Nannette Cole, and brings her into the game. Unlike the others, she continues to think the thoughts and feel the feelings inherent to her actual human self. It is electrifying to watch Cole's refusal to play along the moment she enters the ship. Ultimately, she sees through Daly's game, and exploits her familiarity with his "real" life to defeat him and free themselves from his virtual prison.

The play of virtual and real in Cole's engagement with virtual reality could not be more different than Daly's. Rather than turning it into a cocoon of revenge, she finds a way of relating to this virtual space that does not feed her omnipotence, but instead triggers a series of latent possibilities in herself that, in the end, brings about an empowering psychological transformation. In actual life, she is meek and fearful, unable to tap into her own agency, whereas in the virtual she not only discovers the innate strength of her own mind, but her capacity for leadership and ingenuity.

We see her on her first day at work relating to Daly in an idealizing way, as she so admires his programming genius and the stunningly intricate code he writes. In her deferential awe, she shrinks in her own being, losing sight of her capacities. We learn that Cole was victimized by her former boss's bullying behaviors. When she realizes that she is Daly's virtual prisoner, she is no longer a victim as her reverence turns to rage, and she out-programs and out-foxes him, claiming her brilliance, and renouncing her idealized notion of him.

Daly is interacting in a one-dimensional realm, where objects are denuded of their otherness. In the hermeticism of such a space, he does not have to put anything of himself on the line. Because he is captain, always sovereign, holding the reins of the virtual in his hands, he doesn't have to risk anything. He never has to deal with the consequences and the self-exposure to someone else actually experiencing him behaving in this way. There are no "real" witnesses in his virtual game until Cole comes along.

She, in contrast, has something real on the line that she is fighting for, that is, the fate of her cloned self and the threat of its perpetual suffering in Daly's virtual hell. Rather than demanding false praise from the crew, as Daly does, Cole becomes the legitimate captain, matching her mind against his, as she hacks his code and, at the very same time, exposes the pathological game that he is playing. Cole's engagement in the virtual makes her aware of unlived aspects of her own strength and power, and furthermore, makes the crew aware of their complicity in Daly's demonic virtual world. The digital virtual produces in her a non-disavowing and non self-aggrandizing ego, whereas for Daly it is the very opposite.

Daly's immersion in the virtual world creates an untenable split between virtual life and real life. The further he can keep them apart, the better he can actualize his psychic fantasies. In his actual life, he is completely isolated, deadened in his relation to others, without access to his own thoughts and feelings. Only inside the game can he find himself. This severe splitting is symbolized by the sign on his apartment door which says KEEP OUT. The story of Cole, on the other hand, reveals a profound and intimate connection between virtual and real. Waking up in the virtual, she sees through its dream-like haze, thus avoiding the radical splitting of virtual from real that plagues Daly. Paradoxically, virtual reality allows her to heal that split, as her own inner virtuality is activated and she is able to live something out in the virtual that is not yet possible in actual life.

The effects of the virtual on the structures of our relational lives are both creative and expansive, negating and exploitative. As is so well illustrated in this episode, it is essential that we pharmacologically avoid polarizing and thus splitting these effects into their usual pro and con reductions.

Notes

1 In his paper "The Splitting of the Ego" (Freud, 1900), that horrifying external perception is the little's boy's awareness of the reality of castration when he sees the female genitalia.

2 Humphrey Morris's (2016) cogent analysis of Freud's concept of disavowal in his paper "The Analyst's Offer" has been crucial to our understanding of the term (*Journal of the American Psychoanalytic Association*, 64(6): 1173–1187).

3 "In [Laplanche's] 'generalized seduction theory' all parent-infant communication has its inevitable traumatic edge: passionate, exciting, untranslatable erotic messages from the adult other break into the infant, are repressed or disavowed, and lose their context in any communicative, caretaking exchange: 'they are then closed in on themselves, which precisely constitutes their enigmatic .... and traumatizing ... character'" (Morris, 2016, p. 1178).

4 The most obvious example is the profuse availability of pornographic material in the net. The latest statistics is that Pornhub has nearly 120 million visitors per day, more than Netflix, Amazon Prime, etc., combined.

5 The "Singularity" is a term used by transhumanists to describe the moment in the future where there will be no clear distinction anymore between human and machine. Cf. Chapter 9

6 In Wim Wenders (1987) film *Wings of Desire* this longing is felt by Angels in their contemplation of human existence, suggesting perhaps the difficulty or tension implicit in extricating the concept of consciousness from the bodily.

7 One image, found in Greek mythology, of opening the erotic to the world of imagination and reflection rather than literal action is that of Odysseus blindfolded and tied to the mast of his ship, where he is able to hear and be affected by the siren's call without being able to literally act on it.

8 This debate, of course, has intensified since the pandemic, given that therapy is taking place almost exclusively now on virtual platforms.

9 In the *New York Times*, Richard A. Friedman (2020) writes: "Consider the following experiment: Researchers asked a group of people to spend just 15 minutes in a room and instructed them to entertain themselves with their own thoughts. They were also given the opportunity to self-administer a negative stimulus in the form of a small electric shock. Strikingly, 67 percent of men and 25 percent of women found being alone with their thoughts so unpleasant that they chose negative stimulation over no stimulation (p. 9)."

10 There is always confusion as to why Winnicott speaks of usage as a development progression following relating, since it has such a utilitarian, even machiavellian sound to it. He picks the word to emphasize that we cannot truly make "use" of an object, a person, a thing, that we are invested in, in other words, work with it and engage it in a fruitful way, until we have gone through this process of destruction and survival.

11 Kohut also speaks of idealization and twinship as the two other functions of the self-object, both of which have implications for digital life, but here we are exclusively focusing on mirroring.

References

Arsic, B. (2016) *Bird Relics: Grief and Vitalism in Thoreau*. Cambridge: Harvard University Press.

Banville, J. (2009) *The Infinities*. New York: Vintage Books, p. 8.

Benjamin, J. (1995) *Like Subjects, Love Objects: Essays on Recognition and Sexual Difference*. New Haven: Yale University Press.

Bion, W.R. (1983) *Learning From Experience*. New York: Jason Aronson.

Bromberg, P.M. (1998) *Standing in the Spaces: Essays on Clinical Process, Trauma, and Dissociation*. New Jersey: The Analytic Press, p. 273.

Eigen, M. (1999) The Area of Faith in Winnicott, Lacan and Bion. In S. Mitchell and L. Aron (Eds.), *Relational Psychoanalysis: The Emergence of a Tradition*. New Jersey: The Analytic Press.

Freud, S. (1900) *The Interpretation of Dreams*. S.E. Vol. 4.

Freud, S. (1940) *Splitting of the Ego in the Process of Defence* S.E. Vol. 23.

Friedman, R.A. Is the Lockdown Making You Depressed, or Are You Just Bored? (2020). Op ed. *New York Times*, Aug 21, p. 9.

Han, B.-C. (2017) *The Agony of Eros*. Cambridge: MIT Press.

Kohut, H. (1971) *The Analysis of the Self: A Systematic Approach to the Psychoanalytic Treatment of Narcissistic Personality Disorders*. New York: International Universities Press.

Lachmann, F., and Beebe, B. (2014) *The Origins of Attachment: Infant Research and Adult Treatment*. London: Routledge.

Laplanche, J. (1999) *Essays on Otherness*. Oxford: Routledge.

Lemma, A. (2017) *The Digital Age on the Couch: Psychoanalytic Practice and New Media*. London: Routledge.

Lemma, A., and Caparrotta, L. (Eds.). (2014) *Psychoanalysis in the Technoculture Era*. London: Routledge.

McLane, M.N. (2018) Self-Reliance. *The Paris Review*. Vol. 225, p. 167.

Milner, M. (1957) *On Not Being Able to Paint*. New York: Putnam.

Nancy, J.L. (2008) Freud – So To Speak. *European Journal of Psychoanalysis*. #26/ 27 (Published on-line).

Scharff, J.S. (Ed.). (2018) *Psychoanalysis Online: Mental Health, Teletherapy and Training*. London: Routledge.

Smith, Z. (2015) *Zadie Smith on the Effects of the Internet Revolution*. https:// www.youtube.com/watch?v=3W77NqokMsc

Stern, D. (1985) *The Interpersonal World of the Infant: A View from Psychoanalysis and Developmental Psychology*. New York: Basic Books.

Tollman, V. (2011) The Terror of Positivity: An Interview with the Philosopher and Media Theorist Byung-Chul Han, *Springerin*, Issue 4.

Virilio, P. (1995) *The Art of the Motor*. Minneapolis: University of Minnesota Press.

Winnicott, D.W. (1945) Primitive Emotional Development. In *Through Paediatrics to Psycho-Analysis: Collected Papers* (pp. 145–156). New York: Brunner/Mazel.

Winnicott, D.W. (1948) Paediatrics and Psychiatry. In *Through Paediatrics to Psycho-Analysis: Collected Papers* (pp. 157–173). New York: Brunner/Mazel.

Winnicott, D.W. (1958) The Capacity to be Alone. In *The Maturational*

Processes and the Facilitating Environment (pp. 29–36). Madison: International Universities Press.

Winnicott, D.W. (1962) Ego Integration in Child Development. In *The Maturational Processes and the Facilitating Environment* (pp. 56–63). Madison: International Universities Press.

Winnicott, D.W. (1971) The Use of an Object and Relating Through Identifications. In *Playing and Reality* (pp. 86–94). London and New York: Tavistock Publications.

Žižek, S. (1997) *The Plague of Fantasies.* London/New York: Verso.

Part IV

Philosophical issues of the virtual

Introduction to Part IV

We begin this fourth part of the book with Ortega y Gasset's conception of human beings as *ontological centaurs*, creatures caught between the trascendental and the empirical, suspended between a body that roots us to matter and a mind that extends us to the virtual. Technology emerges from this paradox; it enacts a radically ambivalent impulse to both acknowledge and disavow time, death and mortality. The mythological figure of Pygmalion, who preferred the perfect statue to the goddess he loved, serves as a lens through which to understand how our relationship to the finiteness of human existence is fundamentally shaped by technology.

We examine the recurrent sensation that we have been considering, that the digital modulation involves a flattening of reality, and recognize there the idea of the simulacrum as false copy that we saw in Part II. But we also consider, in detail as well, the many unexpected positive experiences that are already familiar in the virtual, where we are indeed left with the impression that we are experiencing an upgrade of the "real." In the end, it becomes clear that every modulation– digital or scribal, electronic or mechanical – must always leave out and yet depend on the non-representational ground of all modulations from which human virtuality arises.

What our pharmacological stance to the digital brings us to contemplate is a world of incessant change and movement, a flow of virtualities actualized at every present moment, only to be left behind for an equally transitory new emergence. The most surprising discovery is that – once we attain a perspective that does not oppose but holds on to its paradoxical tension – the digital becomes, as in the end all technologies do, a reminder of the illusory nature of every image, whether technical or sensible, virtual or real. The technical representation thus becomes a means to arrive at the limits of representation, and technology a way to face mortality.

8 Ontological centaurs

... suspended between a celestial and a
terrestrial nature, between animal
and human ... his being always
less and more than himself.

—Agamben (2002)

Prelude

If philosophy is a preparation for dying, as Socrates said, its mission
would be to combat our impulse to ignore mortality, and teach us
instead to connect to its reality as often as necessary, to make it ever
more familiar as it approaches. It could counter our impulse to stop
life, detain its movement, and control the uncontrollable, which we
have seen propels the technological drive. Philosophy would then
need to renounce the Pygmalionic search for perfection and its
commitment to permanence and immutability that has shaped our
culture; we might then become able to keep open the unpredictability
of the sensible and acknowledge and embrace mortality as an
ineluctable, constitutive reality.

Upon seeing Aphrodite's bare ankle, stunned and overwhelmed by
the emotions that the vision provokes in him, Pygmalion flees and
takes refuge in his workshop, where he immediately and obsessively
begins to sculpt an image of the naked goddess. Once in the presence
of the perfect image he had sculpted, he falls in love only to discover
her frigid incapacity to respond to him and, as the myth tells us, it is
the ensuing suffering he undergoes that moves the real goddess to pity
and bring the statue to life.

Technology seen as an attempt to protect ourselves from the overwhelming reality of death, enacts Pygmalion's stubborn attempt to
shield experience against temporality and change; and just as the
frigid statue is incapable of returning Pygmalion's love and eventually
comes to life precisely because of his suffering her muteness,

technology too may through the impoverishment of experience and its consequent suffering, lead us also to a transformative experience where we are able to embrace life's imperfection, its fragility, its temporality. Technology may yet become, as Benjamin imagined it, an awakening to the dynamics of the human psyche and its resistance to change; no longer propelled by the denial of death, it may serve as a means of self-reflection and not of power and control. Its blatant triumphalism would deflate once it was grounded in the acknowledgement of loss. It is precisely for that kind of thinking that the philosophers we will consider in this chapter may be seen to have been preparing the way.

While on the one hand thinkers, intellectuals, and artists in the 20th century were experimenting with the limits of writing and subverting in various ways traditional thinking, on the other, the advent of what Marshall McLuhan called the electric media – telephone, radio, television – likewise subverted scribal culture, by gradually bringing in the logic and rhythm of orality back to the forefront of (the collective mind of) Western culture. There were winds of change in those times, when the world became, in McLuhan's famous image, "a global village" and the media our tribal drums. Nowadays that scenario is magnified by the emergence of the social networks which, in their promiscuous connectiveness together with our ability to encounter one another in a common virtual space, annulling all distance, throw us into yet uncharted territories. Finding our way within this new medium seems to be an inevitable task for our time. Ortega y Gasset (1961) writes:

> Pure reason cannot supplant life: the culture of abstract intelligence is not, when compared with spontaneity, a further type of life which is self-supporting and can dispense with the first. It is only a tiny island afloat on the sea of primeval vitality. (p. 57)

Ortega called it spontaneity, but it spans the entire range of sensibility, including feeling, intuition, imagination, and whatever other faculties in our experience that fall outside the capacities of reason. The task of our age involves the immersion into sensibility and the acknowledgement of the reality of bodily existence and mortality; nothing less than a radical transformation of our Western worldview.

1 Beyond the Pygmalionic

The philosophers we are considering in this chapter, – primarily Giles Deleuze, Walter Benjamin, and Ludwig Wittgenstein – anticipated the need to overcome the "metaphysics of presence," that philosophical viewpoint that conceives the world as constituted by substances;

privileging permanence, it valorizes the present now, while shunning becoming and difference. Each in their own distinct way aims at liberation from the consequences of the representational *Weltanschauung* that results from that metaphysics. Their common insight is that the prevailing metaphysics no longer holds; so, whether consciously or not, they prepare the way to the changes that begin to occur with the new technologies.

As we have already seen in Chapter 4, Deleuze and Guattari (1987) are famously known for deconstructing, in *A Thousand Plateaus*, the rational logic of traditional writing, rejecting its hierarchical, "arboreous" conception of knowledge, and occasioning instead the mad proliferation of what they call a "rhizomatic" form of thinking.

> A rhizome has no beginning or end; it is always in the middle, between things, interbeing, intermezzo. The tree is filiation, but the rhizome is alliance, uniquely alliance. The tree imposes the verb "to be," but the fabric of the rhizome is the conjunction, "and... and... and..." This conjunction carries enough force to shake and uproot the verb "to be." (p. 25)

If Parmenides presides over our traditional metaphysics of presence with its emphasis on being and sedentary thinking, Heraclitus, with his stress on becoming and nomadic thought, seems to preside over the philosophy that overturns the Pygmalionic impulse of modernity, and displaces "being" with "becoming." The constant strife between these two paradigmatic philosophies is always present in –one could almost say underwriting – Western thought.

As we suggested in Chapter 1, the invention of the photographic camera during the Industrial Revolution revitalizes the visual order in our experience and processing of reality, complementing – and even at points displacing – the scribal order. Not that images had not played any role in the intervening centuries since the invention of writing (in fact they had been present in the illustrations of the medieval manuscripts, for example), but with the photograph the image attained a much greater protagonism, becoming an increasingly important element in the everyday experience and collective consciousness in the following centuries.

We could speculate that the advent of any new technology responds to a general need of the times that always stands behind it. Tarkovski (1994) believed this was true of the cinema, in its acknowledging the growing importance of time and temporality, but the photograph was, as it were, the prelude to or preparation for that invention. In its case, it was perhaps a general need for freedom from all traditionally imposed (scribal) categories, that prompted the re-emergence of the image during the 19th century, and provoked the many cultural experiments of the earlier part of the 20th century. The imposition of a scribal tradition – sequentiality and consistency, linearity and perspective, hierarchy and order – all came under fire, from all directions. Impressionism, Cubism and Surrealism in the plastic arts, for example, started to explore the irrationality of the unconscious, struggled with the representation of movement and introduced perspectivalism; atonality in music sought to break free of serialism and tonality. They were all experiments in stretching our powers of expression and thought beyond the limitations of the rational and logical structure of the traditional media.

This Heraclitean thrust in the intellectual consciousness of the 20th century also makes its appearance in the writing of literature in authors as diverse as Joyce, Beckett, and Cortázar. But in philosophy as well, as Benjamin and Wittgenstein begin to produce writing that does not follow a logical sequence, and diverts from linear thinking. Benjamin's writing is characterized by Susan Sontag (1981), for example, as "freeze-frame baroque" (p. 129), and Buck-Morss (1999), referring to the writing in his late *Arcades Project,* says it forces us to think in correspondences, to proceed through allegorical images rather than through expository prose. One could even say that Benjamin's text is a proto-hypertext, introducing a logic and dynamic very much at odds with traditional scribality but significantly approaching the rhizomatic logic described by Deleuze and Guattari that we will eventually identify with the digital.

Wittgenstein (2009) points in the same direction in his *Philosophical Investigations,* when he declares in the Preface, that he had failed in producing a book that satisfied the usual criteria of philosophical writing:

> It was my intention at first to bring all this together in a book [where] the essential thing was that the thoughts should proceed from one subject to another in a natural order and without breaks. After several unsuccessful attempts [...] I realized that I should never succeed [....] my thoughts were soon crippled if I tried to force them on in any single direction against their natural inclination. (p. 3)

The confessed failure of his fragmented writing, however, eventually becomes a moment of liberation. In following the inclination of his thought against the grain of linear sequentiality, the disconnection from experience caused by theoretical thinking becomes a topic of his work. Metaphysical idols and fixed ideas are the perils against which he proposes a path of thinking, a methodology, that ultimately appeals to our ordinary language, everyday life and concrete experience instead of to metaphysical abstractions. McLuhan thus identified a "strongly oral character" (Nyíri, 2016, p. 160) in Wittgenstein's work, which harks back to the logic of a pre-scribal era.

Both Wittgenstein and Benjamin are, to some extent or in some sense, returning us, through writing, to a mode of thinking or a type of consciousness that is closer to the oral and which, as Buck-Morss (1999) remarks,

> to the mind that would comprehend intellectual phenomena in terms of a logical or chronological development, wherein one thing leads to another, to use Benjamin's metaphor, 'like the beads of a rosary,' [their] work offers no satisfaction. (p. 7)

The writing of the *Investigations* gave to the Wittgenstein of its preface – who considered it a failure because of its inability to proceed sequentially and logically – as little satisfaction as the logic of the web, with its reticular functioning, rhizomatic nature, and "textual promiscuity" (Murphie, 2002, p. 189) gives the typical 20th-century scribal person.

Without knowing the digital world, Benjamin and Wittgenstein anticipated and prepared us for it. And Deleuze, as we have already seen in previous chapters, introduced concepts that are useful tools to understand better what is happening with our century. Although he died on the cusp of the digital revolution, his thought too is deeply attuned to the changes that have come with technology, even though he says nothing directly pertaining to it. All three thinkers enact in their writing the demise of the scribal paradigm and anticipate the milieu that digital media will institute, providing the conceptual means to understand and move with awareness in them.

2 Losses and recoveries

a The aura

The gradual narrowing of society to bourgeois interests and practices, together with the overestimation of science and its rationalistic understanding were responsible, in Wittgenstein's (1980) eyes, for an alarming existential impoverishment in Western culture. Everything appeared to him as estranged and distant from everything that was important.

Benjamin (1973b) noted, in considering storytelling, that there were less and less people able to tell memorable stories, primarily because "experience has fallen in value":

> Never has experience been contradicted more thoroughly than strategic experience by tactical warfare, economic experience by inflation, bodily experience by mechanical warfare, moral

208 Philosophical issues of the virtual

experience by those in power. A generation that had gone to
school in the horse-drawn streetcar now stood under the open sky
in the countryside in which nothing remained unchanged but the
clouds, and beneath these clouds, in a field of force of destructive
torrents and explosions, was the tiny, fragile human body. (p. 84)

Not just the overwhelming and traumatic experience of the first world
war but also the spirit of the industrial age seemed to have reduced man
to silence and all language into a merely informational vehicle, into
what, as we have seen, Benjamin (1978a) called "bourgeois" (p. 318).

The emphasis on knowledge and reason that characterized the beginning of the 20th century, propelled by an enthusiasm for scientific
novelty, and a frenzy for industrial production and economic profit,
had thus the effect of narrowing our conception of human existence,
divorcing it, as it were, from its root in bodily experience.
Philosophers, moreover, seduced by the advances in formal logic and
mathematics at the beginning of the century, were able to dismiss the
expressive dimension of language as irrelevant to the accurate representation of reality, which they made their true purpose in the
same spirit as the scientific mentality, with which philosophical
thinking identified.

But in the '50s, J.L. Austin in Oxford and Wittgenstein in
Cambridge questioned the exclusive focus on the representational
conception of language which reduced all linguistic communication
to the articulation of verifiable facts and instead proposed a return to
concrete experience. These "ordinary language philosophers" – as
they were derisively called – began elaborating on the expressive and
performative dimension of words, revindicating in this way the
complexity of ordinary language and experience against the objectifying scientific mentality, finding in its neglect of the concrete nature
of human existence a cause of the impoverishment of culture that
Wittgenstein had lamented.

The mass-production of images made possible by the technology of
mechanical reproduction likewise led to the disavowal of the importance of the ordinary, and caused a certain blindness to aspects of
its experience. Gauging its effects on artistic production, Benjamin
(1973a) argued that mechanical reproduction stripped the work of art
of its "aura," which he tried to describe with this image:

If, while resting on a summer afternoon, you follow with your
eyes a mountain range on the horizon or a branch which casts its
shadow over you, you experience the aura of those mountains, of
that branch. (p. 216)

The aura of the mountain range or the branch that casts its shadow

over us in a summer afternoon is the experience we have, in perceiving it, of a temporal and material depth that informs our experience of those objects and recedes into an unknown darkness.
Benjamin was trying to get at the excess in our perception of the
object that makes it point beyond itself. "Not a final determination of
being but an unraveling of its limits," in Agamben's (1993) words, a
"tiny displacement [which] takes place not in things but at their
periphery, in the space of ease between everything and itself" (p. 54).

One could relate that excess, that feeling of something not contained by the object itself as an awareness of the dynamic nature of
experience, and the process-like character of all existence. But what
concerns Benjamin is the obliteration of the aura by a technology
fueled by the desire to subject things to our control; by the desire, as
Benjamin (1992a) has it

> of contemporary masses to bring things 'closer' spatially and
> humanly, which is just as ardent as their bent toward overcoming
> the uniqueness of every reality by accepting its reproduction.
> Every day the urge grows stronger to get hold of an object at very
> close range by way of its likeness, its reproduction. [...] To pry an
> object from its shell, to destroy its aura, is the mark of a perception
> whose 'sense of the universal equality of things' has increased to
> such a degree that it extracts it even from a unique object by
> means of reproduction. (pp. 216–217)

Technically reproduced works of art, detached from their spatio-
temporal origin, Benjamin points out, replace that unique existence
with "a plurality of copies," just as representation reduces language to
the mere statement of facts, discarding everything that does not serve
bourgeois practicality, and literally binding its expressiveness.
Representational language, flattening the liveliness of human communication, and mechanical reproduction divesting the object from
its aura, both precipitate the uncanny depth of things into the existential vapidness of information, sufficient to satisfy our modern
pragmatism but fatally deficient to the aureatic vision. Both moves
instantiate the human reflex that needs to establish and sediment,
resisting movement and change.

Digital reproduction seems to complete the dream of bringing
things closer by producing the illusion that in the digital we may
conjure up the world without remainder. By closing the gaps of
analogical experience we seem to become capable of enfolding reality
without the unrepresentable excess in perception that belongs to the
realm of the aura. It's obvious that this same desire to bring the object
closer is further indulged nowadays, for example, in the high resolution of digital images, or in the invention of 3D printers that make it

possible for physical objects to traverse space and time and reappear right next to anyone, wherever they are. This extraction of the object from its physical singularity is the result of a perception, as Benjamin adds, directed by a need to universalize things.

Whereas for Wittgenstein the loss of aura is without a doubt a lamentable loss, Benjamin resists any judgement in that respect and so adopts what we could call a much more pharmacological attitude. But, regardless of whether they point to the changes as negative or positive, there is here a loss we need to acknowledge and grieve. Disavowing the mourning, however, we lock ourselves in melancholy. Anchored again as we were in the melancholic *scribal*, where the ephemeral passing present is replaced with the linguistically sedimented past, ours has now become a *digital* melancholy (cf. Frankel (2013)). Both cultures, scribal and digital, it seems, trade fleeting experience with mental representations (concepts or images) intent on replacing the loss, and so avoiding its suffering, instantiating the chronic oblivion of (human) mortality.

3 Mimetic faculty, emergence, and seeing aspects

Benjamin and Wittgenstein agree in their respective diagnoses of the impoverishment of experience. But the tendency to homogenize, to pry the object open and do away with its originality, which we have seen characterizes the modern ethos, results not only in the loss of the aureatic dimension of experience; it also brings with it the gradual diminishment of our capacity to imagine, to see beyond mere appearances. It prepares the ground for the eclipsing of the human virtual by the digital virtual, which we have identified as one of the perils of the virtual world: the growing incapacity to connect to that potential space from which creativity arises.

Benjamin (1978b) considers this loss in terms of what he calls "the mimetic faculty." He contrasts the naive modern conception of experience which reduces it to its minimal meaning – as a "reception of perceptions" (Benjamin (2010, p. 163) – to the vision the pre-animistic people had where the world was not simply registered through the senses but also experienced through an affective, empathic resonance with what they perceived. What interests Benjamin (1978b) is the pre-rationalistic world of perception, where things are not fully closed off from the subject by the mechanism of representation, but depend rather on mimesis, as seen in, for example, those who "identify with animals and plants," or insane persons who "identify in part with their objects of perception," or clairvoyants who "can at least claim to receive the perception of others as their own" or to perceive magical correspondences between things (p. 66).

Benjamin (2010) is intent on making room for diverse types of knowledge by broadening the narrow conception of experience of the Enlightenment, which he thought was devoid of spiritual and existential depth (p. 166). And he finds that depth of experience, which seems to escape us, not only in the perception of ancient peoples but in art, where there is also an intelligence that perceives presences (nature's, artifacts', etc.) mimetically and expansively in the identification with them.

> The perceived world (*Merkwelt*) of modern human beings seems to contain infinitely fewer of those magical correspondences than the world of the ancient people or even of primitive peoples. [...] Human beings might have perceived [...] that objects had a mimetic character, where nowadays we would not even be capable of suspecting it. (Benjamin 1978b, p. 66)

This intelligence is responsible for creating a space of similarities or continuities that belongs to the realm of the aura, by which we are capable of revealing what lies right before our eyes but escapes us in the objects of ordinary experience. It is responsible, in other words, for our being able to detect the sublime in the ordinary and the ordinary in the sublime.

In the same way, Wittgenstein's (1993) own critique of representational thinking begins also with a criticism of Frazer's attempt – in his classical anthropological study *The Golden Bough* – to understand magic practices and religion as primitive modes of science. Wittgenstein argues that Frazer was able to understand neither magic nor religion, insofar as he attempted to conceive them from a scientific perspective. Wittgenstein's purpose is to open us to the space of similarities or continuities of the aureatic, that are obviously invisible to Frazer's scientific vision, by breaking with the causal reasoning in his interpretations of the rituals, inciting instead an associative mode of thinking where he appeals to what he calls the ceremonial creature in us. Telling us explicitly that his purpose is to teach us to "see connections" he will do the same that Benjamin's writing did, promoting a mode of thinking that contrasts with the linear and sequential logic of scribality, and departs from the constraints of (representationalism in) scientific thought. Indeed, we see this new mode of thought performatively in Wittgenstein's writing, as we have already noted, where examples and cases proliferate, continuously reminding us of the manifold of experience and the diversity of modes of knowing – imaginative, metaphorical, poetical – involved in our everyday lives.

This critique comes to fruition in his investigation of what he calls "seeing aspects," which is the experience of suddenly perceiving something that has not changed in its empirical presence but does in its appearance of significance to us. We notice an aspect, Wittgenstein (2009) says in the *Investigations*, for example, when "I contemplate a face, and then suddenly notice its likeness to an other. I see it has not changed; and yet I see it differently" (II, xi, p. 193). That experience involves an appeal to elements in our perception of reality that refer us to dimensions of experience that involve modes of association and configuration of the world that are not limited to the causal, rationalistic ways of scientific thought. The phenomenon is well illustrated by another passage from James Baldwin's (2000) *Giovanni's Room*:

> I laughed and grabbed his head as I had done God knows how many times before, when I was playing with him or when he had annoyed me. But this time when I touched him something happened in him and in me which made this touch different from any touch either of us had ever known [...] Then, for the first time in my life, I was really aware of another person's body, of another person's smell. (pp. 13–14)

Benjamin (1997) reflects on the psychological dynamics involved in such experiences of sudden new awareness, from the perspective of memory:

> Anyone can observe that the duration for which we are exposed to impressions has no bearing on their fate in memory. Nothing prevents our keeping rooms in which we have spent twenty-four hours more or less clearly in our memory, and forgetting others where we have passed months. It is not, therefore, due to insufficient exposure-time if no image appears on the plate of remembrance. More frequent, perhaps, are the cases when the half-light of habit denies the plate the necessary light for years, until one day from an alien source it flashes as if from burning magnesium powder, and now a snapshot transfixes the room's image on the plate [...] such moments of sudden illumination are at the same time moments when we are beside ourselves, and while our waking, habitual, everyday self is involved actively or passively in what is happening, our deeper self rests in another place and is touched by the shock, as is the little heap of magnesium powder by the flame of the match. (pp. 342–343)

Something unconscious seeps in between the crevices of our habits and sedimented notions, irrupting into our familiar perception, revealing previously inarticulated or unexpected meanings.[1]

These three thinkers, Benjamin, Wittgenstein, and Deleuze, each in their own way, were interested in conceiving experience more profoundly than what the representational mind allows. And they were anticipating, in their methods, the need to recover the capacity to face a world no longer as static and sedentary, no longer as a unified cosmic substance, but as a series of processes, fragments, intensities, lines of force, in constant flux. As we will soon come to see, what is arising here is a world that anticipates and mimetically resonates with the digital world.

4 Beyond representation

a From scribal to digital

The world of representation is defined by the primacy of sameness and identity. But in a world of change, carried in the unstoppable stream of temporality, repetition is not the same as resemblance. Nothing that repeats ever repeats the same. Repetition in a world of flux is married to difference, it cannot be explained by the form of identity locked in by concepts or representations. When we give identity priority over difference, as we have done traditionally, we are constrained to understand repetition always as a repetition of the same.

It is only when the sedimenting mentality behind the representational framework brackets that movement, that we are able to slip out of the flow of history and live in an objectified world, where repetition is indeed married to the same, change replaced by permanence and immanent time by a transcendental atemporality. Repetition is a matter of sameness only within a metaphysics of presence. Constrained into a Procrustean bed of fixed structures and concepts, the changing, dynamic nature of reality is concealed. Our need to sediment does away with the depth of reality, making us insensitive to its aura.

We have seen how intellectuals and philosophers of the past century were clearing the ground for a rhizomatic perspective on experience. The break from the limitations of representation that underwrites their thinking results in the discovery of the vital forces that swerve under representation, where repetition is divorced from sameness. Identity becomes an "optical effect," as Deleuze (1994) puts it, produced by "the more profound game of difference and repetition" (p. 9). Under those conditions, sameness serves as a disguise behind which difference erupts and dislocates experience.

> Because repetition differs in kind from representation, the repeated cannot be represented: rather, it must always be signified, masked by what signifies it, itself masking what it signifies. ... (pp. 18–19)

Beyond representation, a world opens where what appears as the same, is actually hiding an unexpected difference. Under the re-presentation of the identical, there emerges what Doel and Clarke (1999) have called "a wholly transformative production of something other than the same" (p. 266).

We are contending that the digital materializes this shift, opening up an ontology of flux, that overcomes the optical effect of identity which results from sundering the world and experience from their material-temporal existence. No longer tied down to the rigid logic of the scribal, the virtual world stimulates the kind of associative perception – seeing connections, producing new similarities, making differences – that, Benjamin points out, was powerful in the mimetic faculty in ancient man. Indeed, Benjamin himself had noted a si-milar potential in the cinema which may allow, as he said, a new stage in the transformation of the mimetic faculty in modern human experience. As Buck-Morss (1999) explains, in providing the audi-ence with a new capacity to study modern existence reflectively,

> Benjamin was suggesting that the new mimetic techniques could instruct the collective to employ this capacity effectively, not only as a defense against the trauma of industrialization, but as a means of reconstructing the capacity for experience that had been shattered by the process [of industrialization]. (p. 268)

The moving image schools our mimetic powers since, as Benjamin (2008a) himself noted, "with the closeup, space expands; with slow motion, movement is extended, [and...] brings to light entirely new structures of matter" (p. 36), so that for the first time we were able to analyze the unconsciously interwoven space:

> By its use of close-ups, by its accentuation of hidden details in familiar objects, and by its exploration of commonplace milieux through the ingenious guidance of the camera; on the one hand, it manages to assure us of a vast unsuspected field of action. (p. 37)

That same potential is magnified with the powers of "reflection" that the digital medium provides the common individual nowadays. Indeed, the digital makes accessible to us a world conceived, not from the hierarchical Platonic vision of original and copy that binds the world to a fixed and calcified idea, but rather from the horizontal and fluid environment of the Deleuzian simulacra. Here the world is con-stituted by processes and events instead of by static objects and quali-ties, and experience may be able to recover or recreate the aureatic.

The new environment within which writing and speaking are placed in the digital is no longer conceived as static but as ever-flowing.

The virtual media train us to see the invisible threads of possibility that now connect everything with everything, perhaps re-igniting the mimetic faculty. The vast scope of the virtual world awakens the vital spontaneity titillating from the infinity of possible connections, where simulacra are copies without originals, creations that emerge out of no model, out of nothing except the pure, playful spontaneity that it triggers. This reality, undergirded by an active criss-crossing of forces always in movement, permanently available for the constitution of new and different constellations, becomes the site for the construction of innumerable unique and singular worlds.

Deleuze (1994), 30 years before the digital revolution, in the wake of the failure of representation already envisaged by the intellectuals of the past century, attempts to provide a metaphysics of difference that accounts for our changing perception. He proposes a conception of reality and experience that is liberated from the representational yoke that, specifically, gives up on the Platonic notion of an original model (an Idea) to which everything tries to conform. We learn "to think difference in itself independently of the forms of representation which reduce it to the same" (p. 9) and instead, think of it in terms of expression.

Although it took some time before film liberated itself from the subjection to the linear narrative of scribality to discover its rhizomatic logic, once it did, it became the source of "texts" that had to be read beyond the structures of narrative thought, more according to an imaginal logic of associations and rhizomatic relations. Screened and placed now within a digital virtual realm, where time becomes a crisscrossing of forces always in movement, the digital image can always constitute different constellations, where the recurrence of anything will never be simply a repetition of the same. The sediment, the concept, we could say, is a mask that reality wears.

> There is nothing underneath the masks [... They] do not hide anything except other masks ... There is no bare repetition which may be abstracted or inferred from the disguise itself. The same thing is both disguising and disguised .... (Deleuze, 1994, p. 9)

The creativity that is unleashed by this new digital medium awakens us to what we have been calling (with Deleuze) the simulacrum's "mad proliferation," which establishes multiplicity and diversity as more real than sameness and identity. Representation is but a mask. Rather than imagining ourselves passively receiving inert sense-data, already structured independently of our speech and feeling, we start to see ourselves as centers of energy, multiplicities everywhere in us, intensities running through us, always in contact and in movement together with everything that surrounds them that constitute reality.

As Nancy (2008) said, "man comes from a momentum or a surge which surpasses him."

There is, however, a strong resistance to shifting out of the scribal paradigm; we cling to it and are still intent on preserving it, as if it were indispensable for our very survival. And this resistance manifests itself at the most practical level. For example, we react to the ecological crisis not by considering changing our techno-scientific habits or attitudes, but, because of our attachment to the scientific vision and its demand for control, by attempting to fix it. We then apply our new technologies with the same purposes. Instead of transforming our awareness to leave and change our present course, in other words, we seek to solve the problem through eco-engineering, that is, through the same vision of technology that has provoked the global crisis in the first place. Our resistance stems from our inability to deal with the openness and fragmentariness of life, from our deep need to control what is to come.

b The symptom of "post truth"

Behind the changes we have tried to capture in the ontology of flux that we have distilled from Deleuze, lies the radical subversion that time and space have undergone due to the arrival of the digital virtual. Flusser (2011) claims that these changes can begin to be accounted for in terms of two concepts we have learned from 20th-century science, namely *relativity* and *quanta*. Einstein's theory weaned us from the belief in the absoluteness of space, and because of quantum theory we have learned that the world is "no more than a swarm of tiny particles whirling about at random" (p. 141). From the Cartesian exactness of measured causes and effects we move into no more than approximations, statistics, probabilities. The stringency of physical reality and its logic are dislocated, and space itself, the location of its elements, extended into a larger virtual ecosystem. Physical order is now articulated not in the single realm marked out by Cartesian coordinates but at different levels and in different dimensions, and not independently of time. But from quantum physics we know that it does not stop there; there are further layers of nuclei, hadrons, and quarks:

> As bodies we inhabit the molecular level, but as thinking beings, we inhabit the level of hadrons [...] matter and energy swim in the atomic [structure]; causality comes to an end in the nuclear [...] the hadronic [structure] requires a new mathematics and logic; with quarks, it makes no sense to distinguish between reality and symbols. (p. 142)

In this profusion of levels our world begins to happen, indifferently, in any and all. We already manipulate bodies at their biochemical level, modifying their genetic structure, and we transport them in the virtual images on our screen that knows of no spatial separation, nor density or weight, i.e. its zero dimensionality. Technology is already generating, from the discoveries of quantum science, a myriad of tools and devices: HD screens and microwave ovens, laser beams, resonators and scanners, and so on. And as much as we have advanced our understanding of the multiple dimensions of matter, we are also learning to delve into the various levels of mental activity. In our brains, too, thinking shows itself to occur in processes that involve

> electrons, protons, and similar particles [that] jump across intervals in the astronomical numbers of nerve synapses [...] what we call an idea, a feeling, a wish, or a decision turns out to be a statistical summary of quantum leaps; what we call perception turns out to be a summarizing of quantum leaps into a representation. In the brain, representations are formed from distinct elements, and from these in turn spring (in quanta) ideas, desires, feelings, and decisions. (p. 143)

The digital revolution feeds from these levels of matter and space, and condenses them from what was already the one dimensionality of the linear thinking in scribality, into the zero dimensionality where the world is turned into numerical codes. Everything that can be decomposed into minimal unities – quantities, images, sounds, colors, temperatures, words – can be represented by a numerical sequence. Everything can be translated to numbers, 1s and 0s, lifted from the physical realm and transformed into information that is easily transportable: fast as light, weightless, timeless, ubiquitous, stainless. Everything is transported and stored without occupying any space in no time. Digital reproduction is Benjamin's mechanical reproduction on steroids.

Reality begins to acquire a different density, a different feel, once it is subjected to digitization; it changes the ways in which our bodies and minds interact, perceive and value it. Baricco (2020) says we become lighter, creatures of surfaces rather than of depth.

Depth may seem to us – as it does to Carr (2010), Vargas Llosa (2012), and many others – an unacceptable loss, since we have made it an imperative of our enlightened culture. But regardless, the fact is that the world appears to us now, for the reasons just alluded to, much nimbler and prismatic than before. And the younger generations naturally battle the slower, heavier pace and tempo of the previous world and its concomitant regularity, law, authority and depth. Rooted in the repetition of the same and its resistance to change and difference, pre-digital mentality restricts the mad proliferation that has become today's experiential imperative. In a virtually connected reality, where the empirical is dissolved into information that whizzes by at electric speed, extending itself into the zero extensionless space of the digital virtual, new demands, new expectations, new suppositions come to be. The hybrid reality that results from the digital intervention proves unmanageable for the traditional scribal mindset and the paradigms we have relied on for understanding and predicting reality become fruitless and shatter.

The prolific digital (dis)order begins to wreak havoc on our most established traditions and beliefs, threatening the objective criteria of truth, which proves insufficient to face the hybrid epistemology of the virtual screen. As Weinberger (2007) points out, we have been taught that "everything has its place [...] and we master our world – we know it – by discerning and enforcing those places ...." (p. 177), so that we have measured our progress by how thoroughly we are able to tame it. But with the digital we are forced to learn to think and live with the unruliness, disorder and multiplicity that it produces in nature and experience, where there are no more fixed and secure places, where the whole concept has changed. It is rather like having to swim in water, when all we've ever done is walk on land.

The transition from a static conception of the world to a processual conception – the first consequence of entering the digital – involves a radical undermining of the traditional notion of truth as correspondence between mind and reality (*adequatio intelectus ad rem*). As we already saw in Chapter 2, what we think or say need no longer correspond to the facts. For something to be true is for it to become a #trendingtopic in the virtual media. The spectacularization of culture and the logic of the reality show, both mainstays of the digital, are responsible for the fact that the truth of an assertion takes second place behind its mediatic and rhetorical effect. The speed of the virtual cycle "skips over" verifiability and rushes over the facts, blatantly denying – or even postulating *alternative facts* that will trump – any other fact. These are the new conditions for the era of post-truth.

Free as they are now from the empirical constraints of actual facts, our beliefs are, so to speak, different mental creatures than they were when they resulted from experiences within our actual spatio-temporal context. Now that we are able to modulate the virtual in the virtual world, our hybrid existence has changed the usual conditions for the constitution of our beliefs, challenging all our criteria for truth and meaning and shattering our old beliefs and certainties. Belief is no longer a matter of seeing what is objectively right, measurable by external standards. Since, as Stiegler noted, we perceive through the intermediary postheses of perception, "the conditions in which our beliefs are constituted have entered into a phase of intense evolution" (Derrida and Stiegler (2002, p. 149): Causality yields to free association; temporal actuality is eclipsed by the immediacy of the virtual; truth is displaced by affective resonance and "chemistry." All the conceptual damns we had built since Plato and consolidated in the last three centuries of modern science, are vexed by the changes occasioned in our everyday lives by the incessant technological inventions and advances. The greatest of these is the virtual world, that flows unstoppable.

The virtual has acquired a "materiality" that opens up a new territory for human consciousness and installs a different kind of relation between imagination and empirical experience, fantasy and reality, objectivity and subjectivity, actual and virtual. The virtual world inaugurates a new psychic territory that begins to reveal levels in human interaction and communication that depend, to a large extent, on the random coincidences of a system open to chance and resistant to all natural necessity. It is not so much anymore the *sequence* of events but the *coincidence of events*; less causality than synchronicity that is operative in this new world.[2]

The social media has facilitated the diffusion of instant information and potentiated the capacity of individuals to expose themselves to the buzzing energies of the network, providing them unlimited influence and facilitating the spread of fake news. At the same time, individuals and groups become the target of special interests and fall prey to the collective frenzy that has a tempestuous effect on society. Facebook, for example, with its new and powerful AI systems - that learn from user behavior and cater individually to users according to very detailed preferences gauged from the information to which they have access,- is able to construct *information bubbles* that divide and congregate groups with similar interests and objectives. And YouTube has recently become the social media platform of the Brazilian right, thanks to which Jair Bolsonaro, a once marginal figure in Brazilian politics (but a YouTube star in the far-right community) was able to win the presidential election. The same happened with Cambridge Analytica and the experience with the Trump campaign in 2016, where it was through the very demographic information they acquired from individual voters, that they used to feed them with propaganda of the type that would appeal to each and drive them toward a favorable vote. The rapid spread of practices and companies of the same sort throughout the world is exacerbating polarization and intensifying the social conflicts that are responsible for most of the present day turmoil on the planet.[3]

The phenomenon of post-truth is so confusing because it is completely other to truth as we conceive it in our Platonic framework. But it is also something more complex than the mere devaluation of truth. It is rather a phenomenon that puts into question precisely the moral presupposition that makes truth an indispensable value and its loss a catastrophe.

But words, Nietzsche (2015) says, are nothing but lies that we assume as truths; each concept by which we articulate reality must necessarily betray it, generalize it in such a way that it falsifies what it is supposedly representing. Because it is formed by equating what is not equal, each concept is a lie, but a lie without which we could not be part of a society or indeed even possess a world. So we repeat our concepts by agreed upon conventions. Unconsciously forgetting that they are lies, we arrive at our idea of truth. Language thus establishes deceit at the very heart of human existence.

In that light it may be instructive to read Emerson's (1983) claim that in original and not conventional verses, "the sentiment they instill is of more value than any thought they may contain" (p. 259). Post-truth may be a way of coming in contact with that sentiment, an occasion to cultivate it so as to be able to be impacted by it alongside the assertion of facts. We are already learning to value honest spontaneity over the single-mindedness for truth, which makes us blind to the fascination of multiple aspects and relative significances. We can see in this strange dislocation of truth, the possibility of a revolt against the rational and its representational rule in favor of the new energies, or rather the insistent energies that begin to demand from below, something more than what we know or are yet able to see.

It is of course a fact that the social media can take advantage of the confusion created by the present crisis. Instead of something beyond truth beginning to assert its rightful place in human discourse, it seems to call forth our blind omnipotence that runs over reality, so its first signs are, of course, destructive.

But if instead of fixating on the loss of truth we could learn to contemplate what is actually happening instead, we may find - as we already said in Chapter 2 - a new path towards the exploration of spontaneity and a discovery of the potencies of vitality, traditionally so neglected by our confidence in reason and its lure to sedimentation and stasis. If we collectively find our way to a new consciousness, however, then perhaps that limbo where post-truth delivers us can become the prelude for an opening to a new mode of human life, where the point of utterances is not – as we have assumed until now – to reach some stable truth, but something completely different.

Notes

1 As we saw in 2, Facebook manages this by putting together images of the day in a new way, thus revealing aspects of our experience that had gone unnoticed, as if the algorithmic were able to take over the mimetic function.
2 Carl Jung calls "synchronicity" an acausal principle in which "the coincidence of events in space and time [means] something more than mere

chance, namely, a peculiar interdependence of objective events among themselves as well as with the subjective (psychic) states of the observer or observers (...). Just as causality describes the sequence of events, so synchronicity (...) deals with the coincidence of events." (Wilhelm R, 1967, p. xxiv).

3 More recently, a slide from a 2018 Facebook presentation warned: "if left unchecked [...] our algorithms exploit the human brain's attraction to divisiveness," adding that "Facebook would feed users more and more divisive content in a effort to gain user's attention and increase time on the platform." As Jeff Horwitz and Deepa Seetharaman reported, in the *Wall Street Journal* (26 May 2020), Facebook leadership ignored the findings.

References

Agamben, G. (1993) *The Coming Community*. Minneapolis: Minnesota University Press.

Agamben. G. (2002) *The Open: Man and Animal*. Stanford: Stanford University Press.

Baldwin, J. (2000) *Giovanni's Room*. New York: Random House.

Baricco, A. (2020) *The Game*. Editorial Anagrama. Kindle Edition.

Benjamin, W. (1978a) On Language as such and on the Language of Man. In *Reflections: Essays, Aphorisms, Autobiographical Writings* (pp. 314–332). New York: Schoken Books.

Benjamin, W. (1978b) On the Mimetic Faculty. In *Reflections: Essays, Aphorisms, Autobiographical Writings* (pp. 333–336). New York: Schoken Books.

Benjamin, W. (1992a). The Work of Art in the Age of Mechanical Reproduction. In Arendt, H. (Ed.), *Illuminations* (pp. 211–244). London: Fontana Press.

Benjamin, W. (1992b) The Storyteller. In Hannah, Arendt (Ed.) *Illuminations* (pp. 83–107). London: Fontana Press.

Benjamin, W. (1997) *One-Way Street*. London: Verso.

Benjamin, W. (2008a) The Work of Art in the Age of its Technological Reproducibility: *Second Version*. In *The Work of Art in the Age of its Technological Reproducibility* (pp. 19–55). Cambridge, MA: Harvard University Press.

Benjamin, W. (2008b) Little History of Photography. In *The Work of Art in the Age of its Technological Reproducibility* (pp. 274–298). Cambridge, MA: Harvard University Press.

Benjamin, W. (2010) Sobre el programa de la filosofía venidera. In *Walter Benjamin. Obras, libro II, vol 1.* (pp. 162–175). Madrid: Abada Editores.

Buck-Morss (1999) *The Dialectics of Seeing: Walter Benjamin and the Arcades Project*. Cambridge: MIT Press.

Carr, N. (2010) *The Shallows: What the Internet Is Doing to Our Heads*. N. Carr, New York: Norton.

Deleuze, G. (1994) *Difference and Repetition*. New York: Columbia University Press.

Deleuze, G., and Guattari, F. (1987) *A Thousand Plateaus*. Minneapolis: Minnesota University Press.

Derrida, J. and Stiegler, B. (2002) *Ecographies of Television* (pp. 145–163). Cambridge: Polity Press.

Doel, M.A., and Clarke, D.B. (1999) Virtual Worlds: Simulation, Suppletion, S (ed)uction and Simulacrum. In M. Crang, P. Crang, and J. May (Eds.), *Virtual Geographies: Bodies, Space and Relations*. London: Routledge.

Emerson, R.W. (1983) Self-reliance. In *Emerson: Essays and Lectures* (pp. 257–282). New York: The Library of America.

Flusser, V. (2011) *Does Writing Have a Future?* Minneapolis, MN: Minnesota University Press.

Frankel, R. (2013) Digital Melancholy. *Jung Journal Culture & Psyche*, 7(4), 9–20.

Horwitz, J., and Seetharaman, D. (2020) Facebook executives shut down efforts to make the site less divisive. *Wall Street Journal*, May 26.

Murphie, A. (2002) Putting the Virtual Back into VR. In B. Massumi (Ed.), *A Shock to Thought: Expression after Deleuze and Guattari* (pp. 188–213). London: Routledge.

Nancy, J.L. (2008) Freud – So to Speak. *European Journal of Psychoanalysis*. #26/27. (Published on-line).

Nietzsche, F. (2015) *On Truth and Lies on a Non Moral Sense*. East Sussex: Delphi Classics.

Nyíri, K. (2016) Emerging Media and the Philosophy of Time. In Floyd, J. and Katz, J. (Eds.), *The Philosophy of Emerging Media* (pp. 159–170). Oxford: Oxford University Press.

Ortega y Gasset, J. (1961) *The Modern Theme*. New York: Harper Torchbooks.

Sontag, S. (1981) *Under the Sign of Saturn*. New York: Random House.

Tarkovski, A. (1994) *Sculpting in Time*. Austin: University of Texas Press.

Vargas Llosa, M. (2012) *La civilización del espectáculo*. Madrid: Alfaguara.

Weinberger, D. (2007) *Everything is Miscellaneous: The Power of the New Digital Disorder*. New York: Henry Holt and Company.

Wilhelm R, W. (1967) *The I Ching or Book of Changes*. New York: Bollingen.

Wittgenstein, L. (1980) *Culture and Value*. Oxford: Basil Blackwell.

Wittgenstein, L. (1993) On Frazer's "Golden Bough." In J. Klagge and A. Nordmann (Eds.), *Philosophical Occasions 1912–1951* (pp. 115–155). Indianapolis: Hackett Publishing Company, Inc.

Wittgenstein, L. (2009) *Philosophical Investigations*. Oxford: Wiley-Blackwell.

9 Digital pharmacology

*To reach, not the point where
one no longer says I, but the
point where it is no longer of any
importance whether one says I*

Deleuze and Guattari (1987)

1 Digital transcendence

a Dataism and the mind

When the digital seeks to achieve a perfect world and immortality, it responds to the wish that has fueled technology always and from the very beginning. Each new technological modulation has promised to overcome our natural limitations. Today, when human virtuality is extended into the bounties of the virtual world, the digital is but the latest version of that most human pursuit.

As Yuval Harari (2017) observes, there is a hidden religious ideology behind this most recent technological promise. He calls it "dataism."

> Dataism adopts a strictly functional approach to humanity appraising the value of human experiences according to their function in data-processing mechanisms […] In the XVIII century, humanism side-lined God by shifting from a theocentric to a homocentric worldview. In the XXI century, Dataism may side-line humans by shifting from a homocentric to a datacentric view. (pp. 394–395)

In that datacentrism we find ourselves free to fantasize about leaving the imperfect, frail body behind, in order to enjoy the virtual eternity of the Internet. *Black Mirror*'s "San Junipero," an example we have already mentioned, provides us with a version of the digital in its promise of eternal youth and the defeat of bodily decay. There, the self – identified with consciousness – is considered a measurable amount of data, which is easily codified and transferred from one material to any other. Upon death one enters into the archives where the memories of all the dead are kept alive in memory chips where they become immortal. Brooker imagines cold imposing mausoleums with infinite rows of automatized machines plugging and unplugging the flickering lights behind which the memories of each new immortal soul are uploaded into the San Junipero System of virtual reality. Immortality becomes a matter of digital archiving.

In this religion, flesh may be substituted by silicon or any other matter, as long as it is capable of carrying information. The mind is nothing metaphysical, certainly not the spiritual substance the moderns imagined it to be. Souls are condensed into data from which they can be resurrected and ushered into virtual immortality, through the Messianic power of digital technology. Cartesian dualism is resolved in this technological fantasy, but at the cost of the physical body. Laced with its blinding hubris and ambition, Prometheus' gift, then, may come at a high cost.

In turning the mind into data and replacing the body with silicon, technology enacts a denial of (material) mortality, that numbs us to the inextricability of death in the reality of human existence, obscuring our understanding of what it actually is to be human. Of course it may be argued that it remains a question, whether the physical organic body – the opaqueness of the flesh in all its imperfection and perishability – is not intrinsic to human life; whether reducing a mind to data does not inevitably do away with something essential to who we are. This does, though, appear to be the case with the numinosity of psychic images (as opposed to technical images) and the spontaneity of the body. In both, the depth and unpredictability of the lived body anchored in the dynamic of vital organic forces, immune to digital reduction, is erased.

N. Katherine Hayles' (1999) distinguishes between the codification or conceptual register of the thing – which she calls its *inscription* – from its becoming concrete or embodied – which she calls its *incorporation*. What we are saying is that spontaneity cannot be captured in the inscription, for it (the inscription) is derived from the codification of what has already happened, that is, from the sedimentation of an event. James Bridle (2018) explains this built-in limitation this way:

> That which is gathered as data is modelled as the way things are, and then projected forward with the implicit assumption that things will not radically change or diverge from previous experiences. In this way computation does not merely govern our actions in the present, but constructs a future that best fits its parameters. (p. 44)

Within those parameters we are only able to construct a future that is a mechanical repetition of a given past, but not the new future that can come out of the spontaneous unpredictability of existence.

Psychoanalysis studies what we might call the existential grammar of our subjective life, the ways in which our affects are connected to the meanings we give to our experience. But this grammar is always incarnated in a singular vital being. Precisely because the emotions' draw from a non-representable pulsation, the living grammar of an embodied person is always open to the unexpected.[1] The very vitality behind our thinking and speaking, always unformed, always in movement, always in transformation, escapes the algorithm. AI's capture of experience can only replicate the form of the emergence, but not the emergence itself.

There is a difference between, for example, the memory that comes from the body and the conceptual memory of the intellect. This difference is poignantly illustrated in a scene from the Netflix series *Living with Yourself*, which tells the story of a man that finds himself forced to share his life with his clone. At some point the clone is trying to convince his counterpart's wife that he re-members everything "they" had done together, so it doesn't make any difference whether she is with him or her actual husband now, in the present. The man's wife tries to explain to the insistent clone that he might "remember" having been on their honeymoon with her, but that his (cloned) memory is only the mental blueprint of *that* occasion. Since he had not actually been there, his memories were lacking in precisely the shared experience that insufflates memory with sensibility and makes a concept. Representational memory falls short of bodily experience; it is composed of mere ideas and mental concepts, empty of emotions or sensible im-pressions. To confuse one with the other is to obviate precisely that which distinguishes spontaneous life from its mere mechanical repetition. As we have often observed, the fantasy of a future where we overcome the body misses the difference between cognitive knowledge and actual experience. We can digitally *inscribe* a thing but never *incorporate* it (Hayles, 1999); the thunder remains, but the lightning always eludes us.

In our digital re-creation of the real, the otherness that grounds the self vanishes in the sheer luminosity of the screen. Its density and singularity becomes no different than that of any other. When there is nothing there to ground the image, it becomes interchangeable, so that it can be substituted by anything else. The result is a free zone of random interactions, where everything acquires the same importance, which means everything loses all importance. Chatroulette gives us a poignant example. This online chat website, which allows one to interact with whomever person randomly appears on the other side, turns every body into a specter that is discarded just as easily as it was brought to being, by a mere click. The advertising for its offer is clear about this:

> Here you can meet a biker, a pop singer, a stamp collector, a beautiful dancer, someone very intelligent, funny, pleasant, simply the person of your type; or you can press the "next" button and continue the search. Random chat is somewhat like real life: you'll be provided with lots of different opportunities, but the final choice always totally depends on you (Internet advertisement for Chatroulette).

The irony, of course, is that if you can always and very easily discard what you have before you in search of another option, you will never choose: lured by the promise of infinite possibilities it becomes difficult, if not impossible, to exercise that "final choice," for there will always be lingering there beyond the next click, a new alternative that promises a better fate. We see this in the increasingly familiar experience people have when, on a meeting arranged by Tinder, they find their date surreptitiously scrolling through their phone, seeking the next set of available matches, as they are (supposedly) trying to get to know one another. This virtual parade may feed the boundless voyeuristic hunger triggered by its inexhaustible possibilities, but in the end, it is unable to engage even a fraction of our souls. The digital screen reduces everything to the same meaningless repetition, where each new image is nothing but the endless actualization of yet another option.

b *Virtual body*

We all sense, at some level, how the digital thins out the *existential density* of things. In "San Junipero," for example, there was a tacit acceptance of this thinning in foregoing death and entering the joy of immortal life. Despite its realism, experience there is always "merely" virtual, lacking in the darker dimensions of life, for which a certain nostalgia, even a melancholy sets in. In this story, this nostalgia hovers over the idyllic summer town, in those virtual cigarettes that, as we are told, have no taste and in the licentious pilgrimage of its inhabitants to The Quagmire, the sordid nightclub, site of boundless sex and violence, where people go to feel something who are desperate to *feel* anything.

How can we begin to characterize the difference between the sense of physical, lived embodiment and the sense of embodiment in virtual space? How is our virtual presence different from our everyday sense of bodily life? Merleau-Ponty (1999), as we know, speaks of a permanent dialogue that goes on between the body and the world, a speaking back and forth to one another. But once we enter the virtual, this dialogue stops. Even if we put on our Oculus Rift headset and have the experience of actually moving in space, there is always the feeling – as there is sometimes consciously, and always unconsciously when we dream (cf. our discussion of Nancy in Chapter 10) – that what we are doing is still a little removed from "real" experience. This becomes clearer when we take the headset off and our physical self takes charge again and remembers what was just experienced as being somehow hollow, as if we had been numbly watching from outside. When we are living a life of drudgery or mindless repetition, distant from our real desires, we can have that same sense of an absent world in our actual experience. Extreme sports, which involve a high degree of risk, have become such a common practice because it is one compensation for a life so detached from feeling, where one simply functions in repeated mechanical routines.

In our society today, mass shootings and mindless violence may be the price we are paying for our virtual lives. "We become machines at the price of our humanity," says Mazis (2002), commenting on the mindset of serial killers, who report "feeling a great distance from the experience around them, as if they were watching themselves and others from afar":

> In killing they get to experience the feelings of others: the horror and pain of the victims that becomes so palpable, so charged, it can jump the gap they've erected ... [T]here is [...] a sense something is missing, something that they are trying desperately to regain. (p. 15)

When we collapse the (human) virtual into its digital image, an immeasurable multidimensional organic whole is reduced to measurable zero-dimensional distances between points, where objects become binary coordinates in digital space. The entire horizon of subjectivity is impoverished, for, as Murphie (2002) points out, if we are to resonate with the world, we need that density and detail with which "we introduce elements of chance which molecularize the whole aesthetic process, throw[ing] it open to the full specificity of the entire world, at [each] moment" (p. 206).

This zero dimensionality is restructuring the relation between virtuality and the real, between our digital life and empirical reality; in other words, it is forcing us to revision our whole ontology. Murphie (2002) says it is "reconfiguring the relations between micro- and macro-perceptions",

> bringing to light the possibility that these relations are subject to change, and that different social machines, different conceptual apparatus may make it possible to have different bodies, different souls, or different zones of clear expression.... (p. 204)

Orality, writing and filming all have affected the way in which we imagine the soul and its relation to the body. With the modulation of modulations available in the digital, that relationship becomes even more perplexing.

Another episode from *Black Mirror*, "Striking Vipers," gives us a stirring example of this new complexity. In this story, two close male friends in their late 30s play a VR game, where they are able to inhabit a body of whichever sex they choose. Karl virtually assumes the body of a woman. In the game he/she finds himself/herself having erotic feelings for his/her (also heterosexual) friend, Danny, and eventually they engage in (virtual) sex together. The experience is traumatic, but at the same time transforming for both. Not only does Karl experience the particular physical sensations of a (virtual) female body without undergoing sexual reassignment surgery, but they both begin to have feelings of lust, jealousy, and desire for each other, which they would have never experienced and are disturbing and incompatible with their actual lives. Nevertheless, in this narrative, they end up incorporating their video-game life into their everyday. In other words, they discover in the virtual new dimensions of themselves, which initially disrupt their lives but eventually expand them, "without having to submit to a major reterritorialization" (Murphie, 2002, p. 204).

It would seem then that there is something superficial about these new bodies and souls since there is no real change that has happened. No sex operation was necessary, of course, but not even a significant redrawing of the boundaries in their social lives; no drastic changes necessary in their living arrangements, merely an almost perfect assimilation. William Carr (2010), for example, sees in this a clear sign of decadence and a gradual watering down of everything we have held dear. In *The Shallows* he makes this case:

> Our growing use of the Net and other screen-based technologies has led to the 'widespread and sophisticated development of visual-spatial skills.' We can, for example, rotate objects in our minds better than we used to be able to. But our 'new strengths in visual-spatial intelligence' go hand-in-hand with a weakening of our capacities for the kind of 'deep processing' that underpins 'mindful knowledge acquisition, inductive analysis, critical thinking, imagination, and reflection.' The Net is making us smarter [...] only if we define intelligence by the Net's own

standards. [But] if we think about the depth of our thoughts rather than just its speed [...] we have to come to a different and considerably darker conclusion. (p. 141)

We have already noted, when considering the phenomenon of post-truth in the last chapter, that we may be overestimating the value of concepts like "truth" or (in this case) "depth" that are so important to Carr's analysis; we might do well to try to see these new circumstances as opening realms of meaning that, rather than competing with the old values, instead broaden and enrich them.

   If the digital solution to this existential thinning is to make the virtual world "feel" even more real, then the non-digital solution would be to reconnect as well to the weight of the body and its in-evitable aging, rather than use the virtual to flee from it. But does virtual reality, in liberating us from space and time, not dissolve the microperceptions of our embodied selves? And in subjecting our perceptions to digital representations, does it not make us deaf and blind to the subtleties of physical experience? It's not that there is no body in the virtual world; the physical body itself gives rise there to an immaterial body. Whether we are sitting before a screen (immersed in a virtual world) or on a beach (immersed in the natural world), the body is always affecting and impacting how we are seeing, how we are experiencing the world. Body, affect and apperception are intimately interwoven, so that our thinking lives and our affective lives, even if virtual, seem to be inseparable from our physical bodies. But the di-gital dissociates us from the physical body, fostering a disembodied consciousness that seems to dispense with it. But does it, or can it, really?

2 The logic of transparency

a Newton's sleep

Representational thinking brings coherence and order to the play of differences that make up consciousness and psychic life. In its structuring capacities, the virtual makes good use of that ordering function. It may foreclose the unpredictability out of which life arises, but we nevertheless prefer the clean sharpness of a concept to the messy density of the experience it articulates. We turn to our screens so hungrily because of their power to virtualize the world, to move from virtuality to actuality, without effort. We have all become sentimentalists, wanting the luxury of an emotion without having to pay for it, as Oscar Wilde puts it. We flee indeterminate openness, seeking security in representational closure; we prefer its shallowness over complexity and depth; we disavow the negative. So we are prone to falling asleep to reality and then feeling falsely relieved by the clarity of the very concepts that have sent us to sleep. Nowadays, we demand not just *images* through which *to view* everything, but *perfect* representations – images sharper than anything we could ever perceive with our naked eyes. That's how compulsive we are now about guarding our sleep.

Our contemporary cultural condition is well illustrated by the mythical figure of Endymion, the beautiful young astronomer (or hunter), who chose eternal sleep over death so that he could lovingly gaze forever at Selene, the Moon Goddess. The name Endymion means "one who finds himself [closed] *within*, encompassed [by the beloved] as if in a common garment" (López-Pedraza, 1990, p. 19). This gives us an image of possession and mimetic stupefaction with one's love, that fairly pictures the way in which representations in our time have us, too, "encompassed […] as if in a common garment" enveloping us in a cocoon that keeps us closed "within" and separate from the world. It is entirely consistent then, that in the myth, Endymion is supposed to have received the power to sleep with his eyes open, which provides a wonderful image of a state of catatonia or catalepsy that also accurately depicts our contemporary 24-7 digital culture.

In our cultural evasion of everything a-subjective: silence, darkness, emptiness, indifference, death, we too constantly and collectively go to sleep. We prefer the mathematical perfection of our artificial inventions to the fateful opaqueness and complexity of the creations of reality. Screening the world now in perfectly sanitized HD images, for which we leave reality behind, our consumerist techno-scienticism is the most recent form of this Endymionic syndrome. Merleau-Ponty (2007) again:

> Science manipulates things and gives up living in them. It makes its own limited models of things. Operating upon these indices or variables to effect whatever transformations are permitted by their definition, it comes face to face with the real world only at rare intervals. Science is and always will be that admirably active, ingenious, and bold way of thinking whose fundamental bias is to treat everything as though it were an object-in-general – as though it meant nothing to us and yet was predestined for our own use. (p. 351)

We abandon the real and embrace its virtual copy. Concrete, temporal, existential change feels to us like a catastrophe; and the perfect impassivity of our statues, the eternal immutability of the Platonic forms – now in the razor-sharpness of the digital image turned into an idol of our faith in the Saving Power of technology – is meant as a denial of the unknown that shadows all experience.

The scanning, spying, sussing out behavior that proliferates in our voyeuristic era is endemic to the Pygmalionic impulse. Fastened by the safety of the image, we course through the digital, empowered to define the undefinable, see the unseeable, represent the unrepresentable. Our reduction of everything to its enframing generates our surveillance culture, its collective omniscience, and the emergence of a stunning kind of intelligence that can see and know everything there is to be seen and known.

As whatever we fantasize about can be virtualized, instantly, just as we imagine it, the immersive world of digitality becomes exclusively oriented around our whims, interests and desires, and subjected to their expectations. Apart from its making us oblivious of what stands beyond our intellectual grasp, this technological power diminishes the need for the creative and emotional struggle traditionally connected to the work of the imagination, and instead kindles the hybris inherent to technological power, the Promethean Titanism that triggers and is triggered by it. This capacity to have reality conform to our wishes awakens an insatiable craving that can lead to self-destruction.

It can be a fruitful and enlightening thing to have the virtual world at our disposal, yet it's a whole other matter when we start to expect or demand that the outside world also behave that way. This illusion does away with any higher instance than ourselves, divesting the world and existence of all mystery and transcendence. Having broken the connection to the unrepresentable, we can more easily think of the world as simply our property and guide all our decisions only in terms of ourselves. We become numb to our abysmal misuse of nature that's making the planet unsustainable; and we feed our narcissism, crippling any possibility of community and perverting all communication, social interaction, and the human ethos itself.

Western thinking for over 2000 years has indeed been tyrannized by the Platonic spirit of *sameness*; it is not surprising that philosophy and psychoanalysis are still equally committed to permanence over change, identity over difference, and immutability over temporal movement: Heidegger's (1996, §6, 26) "metaphysics of presence." In subordinating difference to sameness, however, we are allowing to escape from our attention what we might describe as the extra-propositional or the sub-representative origin beyond speech, prior to conceptual articulation; the void where everything originates. Turned into theories and arguments, thinking is encased in a bourgeois language and a mentality for which the unsayable has no use or even any sense. The result of this is a narrowing of experience and a rickety conception of the human subject; as long as we fail to find the "primordial silence" beneath the chatter of words "our view of man," Merleau-Ponty (1999) says, "will remain superficial" (p. 184).

Language is always partial, always fragmented, always dependent on something lived that it cannot represent. Merleau-Ponty (1999) speaks of a primordial silence that surrounds and precedes speech. Agamben (1995) talks of the mute and latent matter from which the word arises. Representation encircles everything in a single vestment, just as the moon encompassed Endymion and kept him closed within. Positivistic and totalitarian, the all-encompassing perspicuity of representation is no overview at all but a solipsistic cocooning, an abstraction to which Wittgenstein (2009) swiftly responds: "Back to the rough ground!" (§ 107).

However, if we consider an ontology of change, movement and difference, what is decisive is not so much what the concepts grasp but precisely what is beyond it. Shifting the discourse in the direction of difference, as we have been doing with Deleuze, makes the point of philosophical understanding no longer about structuring reality, but deconstructing it. Meaning breaks down, experience turns opaque, and we encounter indeterminacy. That sudden irruption of nonmeaning, of empty significations feels impenetrable and unavoidable. It is then that we need to move back from words to life, or rather bring words to life. As Merleau-Ponty (1999) observes:

> If every statement is incomplete and every expression is situated upon a silent tacit comprehension, then it must be that things are said and are thought by a Speech and by a Thought which we do not have but which has us. (p. 66)

In the face of the ineffable, we automatically reduce the world to a controllable and predictable object; in other words, we assume the scientific approach, the dream against which William Blake (Ackroyd, 1996) warned:

> Now I a fourfold vision see
> And a fourfold vision is given to me
> Tis fourfold in my supreme delight
> And three fold in soft Beulah's night
> And twofold Always. May God us keep
> From Single vision & Newton's sleep (p. 193)

b Pharmacology of the selfie

The Digital Age with its "black mirrors" makes us lose track of the complexity of our lives by its unlimited representational capabilities. But digitality, paradoxically, may also help to liberate us from that very fixation.

As we saw in the example in the Introduction of Frank's dream of his pre-Parkinson's father, the oneiric image derives its psychic power from the living source that the digital lacks. Although the digital image may also be unbidden -appearing unexpectedly as a "memory" on our screens by the magic of Facebook, for example-, and have a significant psychological impact, still our encounter with that random memory produced by the algorithm of the virtual platform clearly lacks the numinous force of the living image, its uncanniness and spontaneity. So, although the digital enhances and enriches our experience in various ways (it even allows us to replay the image as many times as we want), it lacks the dream image's autonomous singularity, which stands beyond representation and – *a fortiori* – is impossible to translate into digital code.

"Be Right Back," the episode of the *Black Mirror* series we examined already in Chapter 3, illustrates the difference we are alluding to. Not long after the protagonist, Martha, receives the artificial body of her boyfriend, Ash, programmed to act exactly like the original person, she discovers in the clone precisely the same shortcoming we have pointed out in the digitized image. What has been archived in Ash's digital footprint may register everything he did and said, so cloned Ash is constituted by everything that made up his actual life; yet being programmed from what the person already has been, it lacks the open virtuality that distinguished it from the living person.

What we are is not just that part of us that has already happened but, more intrinsically, the spontaneous vitality that remains behind the actual, in the depths of (living) matter. The enigma of each person is found in her own virtuality, that living potential constituted by all the forces that sustain her – from her historical and her genetic past – which have not yet acquired any actuality, yet undergird the life she lives as its unfathomable origin. The representation that has been digitized only repeats the same: it fails to capture the potentiality from which the new can emerge. It misses completely the play of difference that always stands behind the illusion of a stable identity in the living person. The person we are in the networks, the identity that we forge through the screen, insofar as it remains a sediment in the virtual world, a digitized actualization, is rivened from its living source; it reduces bodily experience to bare information.

The digital tempts us into the assumption that what it captures is the core of what we are, that indeed we are our representations. This is evident in that epidemic of self-expression and exhibitionism mani-fested in the Selfie phenomenon. The impulse to constantly take pictures of ourselves reflects a desperate demand for a permanent register, foisted on us, moreover, by a growing collective pressure in everyday public life to condense who we are in what we represent for others. This collective fever seems to be a revolt against impermanence, a desire to capture life and save it from the peril of extinction. It obeys a Pygmalionic instinct.

The phenomenon of the Selfie may work, as we have seen in the critique of stance two (Chapter 4), as a tired and repetitive image, an empty simulacrum that negatively inflates the self. Selfies give us the illusion of something unchanging. But doesn't the digital also offer a way to reverse that equation? What if it is exposing us, instead, in its static and sterile repetition, to the glaring void that is at the center of all representation: what if that underlying oneness turns out to be a figment of our imagination?

David Hume (1896) famously wrote, already in the 18th century:

> [W]hen I enter most intimately into what I call myself, I always stumble on some particular perception or other, of heat or cold, light or shade, love or hatred, pain or pleasure. I never can catch myself at any time without a perception, and never can observe any thing but the perception. [...] If any one upon serious and unprejudic'd reflexion, thinks he has a different notion of himself, I must confess I can reason no longer with him. [...] He may, perhaps, perceive something simple and continu'd, which he calls himself; tho' I am certain there is no such principle in me. (p. 134)

We are, indeed, nothing but a running stream, a flux, a flowing collection of different perceptions just passing through. In his words:

> [These perceptions] are nothing but a bundle or collection of different perceptions, which succeed each other with an inconceivable rapidity, and are in a perpetual flux and movement. [...] there [is no] single power of the soul, which remains unalterably the same [...] There is properly no simplicity in it at one time [...] whatever natural propension we may have to imagine that simplicity.... (p. 134)

As we saw in Chapter 8, Deleuze and Guattari (1994) claim that identity is nothing but "an optical 'effect' produced by the more profound game of difference and repetition" (p. 4). Identity is but the fleeting glimpse produced by the play of light and water on the surface of the river we couldn't enter twice.

So what if the narcissistic love manifested in the selfie phenomenon – this need to register one's every moment – is secretly seeking to return to that play, seeking to overcome representation precisely by the oversaturation of representations? In its obsessive need to capture the self, again and again in every new situation it encounters, it may become possible to intuit or see the play of differences that underlies the illusion of identity.

In her photography, Cindy Sherman is famous for playing with her own image. Her work is meant to undermine the conventional ways culture shapes our appearances. Although she has always insisted her images are not to be taken as personal statements, in her recent incursion into Instagram she has been posting photos of herself produced by a series of algorithms. As Andre Russeth (2017) writes, these faces that "have inflamed skin, warped noses, piercing eyes," create "a reality at once disorienting, disturbing." This array of images conjured by Sherman ultimately questions representational identity.

That obsessive repetition becomes a new means of exploration. Each selfie eventually shows that, no matter how many pictures I post of myself, I am never wholly *this* representation, and I am not *that* representation, or indeed any other. In the constant repetition of the same, we are confronted with the negative dimension of identity. An *enantiodromia* takes place again, that reveals the sedimented sameness of identity as ephemeral unrepresentable differences. "All identities are only simulated," proclaims Deleuze and Guattari (1994, p. 1) from their vantage point.

As we have pointed out several times already, nothing is more affirmative to the self, nothing more inflating, than the ceaseless stream of pictures produced by our phones. Yet the impulse contained in the Selfie seems to be, then, also about connecting to the dynamic, unnameable, plural forces – the differentials – from which consciousness arises. Where all representation is anchored, we are liberated from all representation.

We see that unmasking happening in the interactions we have in the Internet. The color-blind, gender-blind, age-blind web allows us to present ourselves in any one of many faces without being any one, and at the same being all of them. If we peel the onion of our digital identity, what we are left with is the abysmal yawning from which the self emerges. The digital may be helping us come face to face with groundlessness, with what the Eastern mind, in the Sacred Wisdom of *Sunyata*, identifies as the "emptiness" behind all representation (Varela, Thompson, and Rosch, 1993).

While the digital in its proliferation of images may invite us to encounter the groundlessness of identity, it also does the opposite, providing us the means to disavow it, defensively displacing and substituting our groundlessness with something fully representable in its digital rendering. This is the paradoxical power that we have been calling the pharmacology of the digital.

3 Digital centaurs

> and already the knowing animals are aware
> that we are not really at home in
> our interpreted world.
>
> R.M. Rilke (1989a)

a Towards the posthuman

Modern culture is rooted in Humanism, the belief that human being is the pinnacle of Nature, so that any other species or creature is subordinate to us; that reason is the infallible guide towards progress, so that anything that does not fit the demands of science's single vision is not important, and progress is defined in terms of our needs over all others. We are masters and possessors of Nature, as Descartes proclaimed. Everything is measured according to one single standard: human being. But even within the human it seeks to define by exclusion, according to parameters set by a biased ideal which rests upon a conception of humanity made to the image of Vitruvius' man: white, male, heterosexual, European, and enlightened. "Man" is seen as the measure of all things and at the summit of an ontological hierarchy that results in the exclusion of all diversity from equal importance: women, non-European, non-white, non-enlightened, non-heterosexual people.

Humanism has proved to be defective, partialized, distorting of (and blind to) the diversity of our nature. The proclamation of human rights, for example, ignores and so deprives all those that do not form part of the Western establishment. It discriminates and subordinates animals, plants, and nature as a whole, to human standards. It is tyrannical and exploitative, as it sees nature, merely as "standing reserve" for our needs, as Heidegger (1977b) puts it.

The growing new consciousness of our age rooted in feminism and evolving into the critique of hetero/gender normativity and other growing minority and civil rights movements, begins to undermine the very concept of man. The limitations of the model we have taken for granted for so long, make it suddenly a problem.

b Transhumanism and the Singularity

Freud claimed that there had been two blows to human narcissism before psychoanalysis. The first blow was that of Copernicus, when he demonstrated that human beings are not the center of the universe and left us thwarted in a new world. The second blow was Darwin's, when he proved that *Homo sapiens*, allegedly superior to animals, actually descended from the apes. The third blow would be given by psychoanalysis, which revealed a troubling truth (with which we have had to learn to live all of last century) that we are not masters, not even in our own house, because there's always a self behind the self that is doing things we do not know and that can unveil truths that we ignore about ourselves.

Artificial intelligence (AI), however, could be giving a fourth blow to our narcissism. With AI, it is also possible that a new kind of entity is being constituted, where human intelligence is not just enhanced but even surpassed to the point where the very notion of humanity comes into question. The neuroscientist Christof Koch (2012) even speculates that the web might have already become sentient, and asks:

> [B]y what signs shall we recognize its consciousness? Will it start acting on its own in the near future, surprising us in alarming ways by its autonomy? (p. 132)

Alarming, because in that case Artificial Intelligence would eventually reveal to us – again, and perhaps now indisputably – that human being, as we have understood it up to this point, may not be the peak of creation, but merely a step in a process where the products of human technology are extending and reconstituting Nature. They may be even displacing or just leaving behind our species, over-throwing it, divesting it of its alleged privilege; perhaps even proving it as dispensable as all other species that have preceded us. In other words, digital technology, and artificial intelligence in particular, may be subverting the very sense of who we are, showing that life, *zoe*, is unstoppable and chronically mutable, multifaceted and radically unpredictable; and that we are miniscule in comparison to that "raw cosmic energy that underscores the making of civilizations, societies and their subjects"(Rosi Braidotti, 2013, p. 55) that is now barging in on our species due to the emergence of the digital.

But perhaps the belief that our technological prowess – in this case, our creation of artificial superintelligence – is a practical danger that may obliterate us from the universe becomes a self-fulfilling prophecy. For insofar as mesmerizing us with the fantasy of an enhanced human future, it stops any reflection about the meaning of these develop-ments, the nature of human life itself, which then makes technology an actual threat. Taking our relationship with it as a matter of dom-ination and control delivers us directly into the hands of the beast it creates and persuades us of a looming disaster. "The superintelligence explosion," is what Bostrom (2014) calls it. But this is still a humanist fantasy. Both as the extinction of our race or as the utopian triumph of human reason, it is a product of the anthropocentic imagination that blinds us to the import of the present moment.

From the anthropocentric perspective, our technological mastery is idealized as our (final) victory over nature. This reaches its apotheosis in what's called the Singularity, a moment in the history of the species that, transhumanists claim, will mark a new and brighter beginning for human being (or, if we are pessimistic about the facts, it may be its utter demise). Experts[2] estimate that it is soon approaching: 2050, they predict, will be the year of its consummation. Enhanced by artificial intelligence, we will become Gods or else, overpowered by it, we will be extinguished. The Singularity[3] will be a moment

> ... in which our intelligence will become increasingly nonbiological and trillions of times more powerful than it is today – the dawning of a new civilization that will enable us to transcend our biological limitations and amplify our creativity. In this new world, there will be no clear distinction between human and machine, real reality and virtual reality. We will be able to assume different bodies and take on a range of personae at will. In practical terms, human aging and illness will be reversed; pollution will be stopped; world hunger and poverty will be solved. Nanotechnology will make it possible to create virtually any physical product using inexpensive information processes and will ultimately turn even death into a soluble problem (Kurzweil, 2005).

But this excessively exalted conception of our future becomes a myopic screen behind which we fail to ask ourselves the transcendental questions that a revolution like the one we are living demands of us, peremptorily and every day.

This transhumanist fantasy, whether utopian or dystopic, is merely an exacerbation of the humanist stance. Digital technology may very well be, not the beginning of a new era for humanity, as transhumanists think, but, quite to the contrary, precisely the "event" of which Foucault wrote in 1966, over 50 years ago, of the end of man or the beginning of a new conception of what it means to be human:

> man is an invention of recent date. And one perhaps nearing its end [...] If those arrangements [that had made it possible] were to disappear as they appeared, if some event of which we can at the moment do no more than sense the possibility – without knowing either what its form will be or what it promises – were to cause them to crumble, [...] then one can certainly wager that man would be erased, like a face drawn in sand at the edge of the sea. (Foucault (1989), pp. 421–422)

Transhumanism seems to rest, paradoxically, on those very "fundamental arrangements of knowledge" that are being shattered by the technological revolution.

The danger digital technology poses is much more fundamental than what, from the anthropocentric humanist perspective, is vainly and exclusively seen in terms of human survival and its victory over nature. Singularitarianism, in conceiving of technology as a mere instrument (that may, in fact, exceed us), fails to attend to the fact that it is intrinsic to our very nature, a power at the very heart of the enigma of being human. And it should be obvious that this Singularitarian vision completely misses the pharmacological nature of technology as Stiegler conceived it. Technology is not something that we make or possess but something we grow, or something that grows from us. By turning it into an object that we can manipulate at will, Singularitarianism explicitly relegates the task of reflection on the meaning of this "technological merge" to a secondary place, something we can attend to once we have solved the *real* problems. As Bostrom (2014) suggests,

> We could postpone work on some of the eternal questions for a little while, delegating the task [which philosophers dedicate their time] to our more competent [transhuman] successors, in order to focus our own attention on a more pressing challenge: increasing the chance that we will actually have competent successors [and not destructive to humans].... We thus want to focus on problems that are not only important but urgent [in the sense that their solutions are needed prior to the intelligence explosion...] to expedite the development of *control methods* that could render the machine intelligence revolution survivable and beneficial. (our italics, p. 256)

So we need "to expedite the development of control methods" to keep the danger in check, in order for us to survive the intelligence explosion, where machine intelligence surpasses human intelligence. Note the way Bostrom separates them from each other and so makes the machine an alien instead of a natural extension of our bodies and psyches. Bostrom says we need "the capacity of control able to mitigate the risk of an accidental lift-off of superintelligence" (p. 259), but what really matters about technology here is not itself technological, as Heidegger famously pointed out. It is existential.

We bring words back from their metaphysical to their ordinary use, says Wittgenstein, talking about how theorization needs to be brought down to the ground in order to give it life. We could say that we must bring back our technology from its melancholic entrancement and deliver it to the concreteness of our human condition. We must see technology, indeed, as an extension not of us, but of Nature that works through us, which we cannot overpass. Not technology as a tool, as a tool for production, but as a symptom or a screen against which we can see ourselves. We should see technology, in other words, not as something we own, but as something that owns us and is grounded, like us, in the unrepresentable.

c Digital ethics

> And in the dark crossing of the
> heart, there is no temple for Apollo
>
> R.M. Rilke (1989b)

i Technology

If we understand that technology is a means of engaging with the complex constellation of vital energies that constitute Nature, then we need to understand *how* we engage with its manifestations, both outside and within us. This concerns not only how we treat the earth, but also how we treat ourselves and each other. We cannot rush to the future filled with the excitement of transhumanism, leaving reflection on the nature of technology for later and hence, insofar as it extends us, reflection on its impact on ourselves.

We seem to think that we can solve the consequences of our technological excesses by means of more technology, without first addressing the question of how and why we are using it so self-destructively. Technology as a symptom can reflect us back to ourselves and reveal what it is we want, what we seek, desire what we desire. It can show us why we do the things we do, suffer and despair, abhor or revere. It may help us see what kind of creatures we are and where – as a species – we are headed. We need to see through our projections on technology, discern what fears and fantasies lie behind them. We need to discover under what aegis we have come to this, what conception of ourselves and our place in nature is responsible for our mindlessness. To continue along the same path, without understanding how and why we have arrived at our current crisis, is to risk blindly repeating what needs to be changed. This is what's most needed and not mechanical control methods to protect us from ourselves.

The technological modulation particular to the digital touches again the very core of the ontological centaur, radically unraveling its modern encasing, that is, the concept by which human being has been so far identified. The digital stretches the implicit duality of the ontological centaur to its utter limits adding to the already complex mix of human and animal, the cyborg, which gives further depth to the paradox.

If the monster we see menacingly approaching is something we have created in order to escape the confrontation with the complexity of life, then we will blindly walk into oblivion, inevitably continue along the path towards the catastrophe we imagine. But our technological fantasies are merely distractions to disavow our own mortal nature, merely houses of cards we are always constructing in the air to avoid coming to the rough ground of our hybridity, especially when further roughened by artificial intelligence and cyborg natures.

Like scientism, which believes that everything must pass through the scientific screen to guarantee truth and knowledge and the power of prediction and control, Dataism (now channeled and directed by capitalist consumerism) also believes that everything must be digitized, not, however, for the sake of anything as lofty as knowledge or truth, but for the sake of profit. It is oblivious to any Law that opposes its course along the craving for both money and power. Genetics, eugenics, cryogenics, and biotechnology are prey to becoming not only testaments of our misuse of technology, but also of greed and human stupidity.

ii The question of ethics

In the dawn of a new technological era endowed with the power of the digital, it is crucial to provide a new and broader conception of our species and of its place in nature. Donna Haraway (2016) and Rosi Braidotti (2013) bring *gravitas* to the issue, when they replace the detached, transcendental subject of humanism with what they describe as "subjects dying together," emphasizing, not man as the rational agent but humans that, like any other creature, suffer mortality, especially aggravated now by these apocalyptic times.

The emboldened virtual self vs. the immanent, here-and-now self of embodied life, constitutes a central ethical dilemma in our age. How much disavowal of the other's subjectivity are we entitled to in the name of digital self-expansion? Or, conversely, how much of the situation of our actual, everyday relatedness to other people and our environmental surround should we abstain from disavowing in order to curb the self-aggrandizing expansion inherent to digitality? In the present "crisis of humanism" there are various tasks required in view of a post-human future. One of them, as Braidotti (2013) writes, is that of reinventing and reimagining the connection with the nonhuman that humanism has torn. In general, we need to overcome our cultural fixation on sedimented sameness and embrace instead the fluid stream of difference that is becoming conscious in the world. But we also need to change our conception of and relation with technology.

Ruthless discriminating humanism and narrow-minded anthro-pocentrism, fueled and even further perverted by the greed of capit-alism, cannot any more underwrite digital technology.

Alejandro Jodorowski (2007), the oracular Chilean filmmaker, says a different kind of faith is needed to effect the necessary change at this new crossing. We must not only question everything – the meaning of philosophy, of politics, of economics, of morals – but we also need to be open to the transvaluation of the values that ground the current system – its culture and form of life – that is quickly crumbling before our very eyes. He claims we must convert from our staunch rationalism, our long-standing identification with reason, and begin to believe instead in the power of the emotions. We need, in other words, to think not (only) with reason, but more than anything *with feeling*: with the heart instead of from the head. This is, indeed, as we may remember, the shift Ortega y Gasset (1961) anticipated as the radical displacement of our age, which is already taking place as a response to humanism and in the midst of digital technology. It involves the dissembling or displacement of the paradigm that has sustained our whole culture until now. As Jodorowski cleverly puts it, it is not a revolution but a "re-evolution": a change in our way of seeing, a leap of consciousness, a second birth in language.

This complete reversal in culture will not occur if we are making sure we keep everything under control, busily fixing things "to miti-gate the risk of an accidental lift-off," as Bostrom (2014) (p. 259) puts it. We need to turn the technological phenomenon into a gateway, an entrance to a new consciousness, a different way of living. The change we need, we venture to say, is not only or not so much in the state of things, but in their meaning for us, because – in the words of Agamben (1993) we have already seen – it will not take place "in things but at their periphery, in the space of ease between every thing and itself" (p. 54). Perhaps Wittgenstein (1995) puts the point best, when he wrote in the *Tractatus*,

> If the will, good or bad, changes the world, it can only change the limits of the world, not the facts. [...] In short, in this way the world becomes, completely, another. It must, so to speak, grow or decrease as a whole. The world of the happy is different from the world of the unhappy. [*Die Welt des Glücklichen ist eine andere als die des Unglücklichen*] (6.43)

The change we need does not belong to our "interpreted world"; it takes place at its limits, at the point where things stand beyond representa-tion. The task ahead, then, is not only the solution of practical problems, but more than and before anything, the kind of inner transformation that changes the phenomena completely, yet (paradoxically) without actually changing them; just like the world of the happy man, which is the very same world but different than that of the unhappy.

Coda

As we have seen in our previous chapters, Deleuze, writing just before the advent of the digital age, allows us to see the virtual as a kind of immanent emergence in its own right, with its own play of difference built into it, thus pointing to an alterity or otherness that originates beyond the human subject. What may be happening in the digital age is the deliverance into a different topography of human nature, a refashioning of the ontological centaur that may be opening the path for the task of our age, namely, to cite Ortega y Gasset (1961) again, the exploration of the boundless vitality upon which reason stands.

Not only does this task begin to flutter in our new awareness of the reality of the virtual – which adds a further depth and complexity to existence – but also in the dark excesses of a blindly empowered technology. It involves a reconception of human nature – not only of the place of the virtual, but also of the place of the vital – that *extends* consciousness to the negative that yawns beyond our rational grasp and opens up a whole vast territory, where we may find an ampler place to live the paradox of human existence. It may be nothing other than the return to primordial emptiness, the very silence behind all language. Our immersion in virtual reality may be pushing us to confront the negative anew, the negative that lurks behind the virtual.

The deliverance of this age is to that vitality that stirs beyond our words and rationally constructed structures, to its ungraspable and unstoppable flux that has always nurtured reason. It is an awakening to the groundlessness of human existence, to the pulsating depth and darkness of life, that informs all our categories and ignites the spontaneity from which all things are given birth in matter.

Notes

1 This is why Bion (1994) advises that we start every psychoanalytic session without memory and desire, his short-hand for an attunement to the non-representable vitality of the present moment, an openness to the unexpected, that can be obscured by referencing what happened in the past (memory) or what we want to make happen in the future (desire).
2 Names of note here are Marvin Minsky, Hans Moravec, Raymond Kurzweil, Nick Bostrom, and Anders Sandberg.
3 The term "singularity" has a use in physics, in the General Theory of Relativity. However, there is no direct connection, but a mere analogy, between this use of the term and the sense in which it is used by transhumanism (Diéguez, 2017).

References

Ackroyd, P. (1996) *Blake: A Biography*. New York: Knopf.

Agamben, G. (1993) *The coming community*. Minneapolis: University of Minnesota Press.

Agamben, G. (1995) *Idea of Prose*. New York: State University of New York Press.

Bion, W.R. (1994) Notes on Memory and Desire. In F. Bion (Ed.), *Cogitations* (pp. 380–385). London: Karnap.

Blake, W. (1996) Blake records. Oxford: Oxford University Press. In Ackroyd, P. (1996) *Blake: A Biography*. New York: Knopf.

Bostrom, N. (2014) *Superintelligence. Paths, Dangers, Strategies*. Oxford: Oxford University Press.

Braidotti, R. (2013) *The Posthuman*. Cambridge: Polity Press.

Bridle, J. (2018) *New Dark Age. Technology and the End of the Future*. London: Verso.

Carr, N. (2010) *The Shallows. What the Internet is Doing to our Brains*. New York: W.W. Norton & Company

Deleuze, G., and Guattari, F. (1987) *A Thousand Plateaus*. Minneapolis: Minnesota University Press.

Deleuze, G., and Guattari, F. (1994) *What is Philosophy?* New York: Columbia University Press.

Diéguez, A. (2017) *Transhumanismo. La búsqueda del mejoramiento humanos*. Barcelona: Herder editorial.

Foucault, M. (1989) *The Order of Things. An Archaeology of the Human Sciences*. New York: Routledge.

Harari, Y. (2017) *Homo Deus. A Brief history of Tomorrow*. New York: Harper Perennial.

Haraway, D. (2016) *Staying with the trouble. Making kin in the Chthulucene*. Durham: Duke University Press.

Hayles, N.K. (1999) *How we Became Posthuman. Virtual Bodies in Cybernetics, Literature, and Informatics*. Chicago: University of Chicago Press.

Heidegger, M. (1960) *Sendas perdidas*. Buenos Aires: Losada.

Heidegger, M. (1977a) The Question Concerning Technology. In *The Question Concerning Technology and Other Essays* (pp. 3–35). New York: Harper Torch Books.

Heidegger, M. (1977b) The Age of the World Picture. In *The Question Concerning Technology and Other Essays* (pp. 115–154). New York: Harper Torch Books.

Heidegger, M. (1996) *Being and Time*. New York: SUNY Press.

Hume, D. (1896) *Treatise of Human Nature* (L.A. Selby-Bigge, Ed.). Oxford: Clarendon Press.

Jodorowski, A. (2007) *Alejandro Jodorowsky interview*. https://www.youtube.com/watch?v=WstYV_soyMw

Koch, C. (2012) *Consciousness: Confessions of a Romantic Reductionist*. Cambridge: MIT Press.

Kurzweil, R. (2005) *The Singularity is Near: When Humans transcend Biology*. New York: Viking Penguin.

López-Pedraza, R. (1990) *Cultural Anxiety*. Einsiedeln: Daimon Verlag.

Mazis, G.A. (2002) *Earthbodies: Rediscovering our Planetary Senses*. Albany: SUNY Press.

Merleau-Ponty, M. (2007) Eye and Mind. In T. Toadvine and L. Lawlor (Eds.), *The Merleau Ponty Reader* (pp. 351–378). Evanston: Northwestern University Press.

Merleau-Ponty, M. (1999) *Phenomenology of Perception*. New York: Routledge.

Murphie, A. (2002) Putting the Virtual Back into VR. In B. Massumi (Ed.), *A Shock to Thought: Expression after Deleuze and Guattari*. London: Routledge.

Ortega y Gasset J. (1961)*The Modern Theme*. New York: HarperTorchbooks.

Rilke, R.M. (1989a) The Duino Elegies. In S. Mitchell (Trans.), *The Selected Poetry of Rainer Maria Rilke* (pp. 151–214). New York: Vintage International.

Rilke, R.M. (1989b) The Sonnets to Orpheus. In S. Mitchell (Trans.), *The Selected Poetry of Rainer Maria Rilke* (pp. 225–255). New York: Vintage International.

Russeth, A. (2017) Facetime with Cindy Sherman: The Artist on Her "Selfie" Project for W, and What's Behind Her Celebrated Instagram. In *W Magazine*. Retrieved from https://www.wmagazine.com/story/cindy-sherman-instagram-selfie/

Varela, F., Thompson, E., & Rosch, E. (1993) *The Embodied Mind*. Cambridge, MA: MIT Press.

Wittgenstein, L. (1995) *Tractatus Logico-philosophicus*. London: Routledge.

Wittgenstein, L. (2009) *Philosophical Investigations*. Oxford: Wiley-Blackwell.

10 The tragedy of the virtual

> Methinks, by most, 'twill be confess'd
> That Death is never quite a welcome guest.
>
> Goethe, Faust

Prelude

All day and all night, the digital is continuously telling you to leave whatever you are doing (or not doing) and check in with it. It seduces with the promise of escape from the dull, slightly anxious moments that texture the everyday by transiting into a heightened reality that is undeniably more stimulating and satisfying.

Consider the familiar rote of digital life. At the end of the day, when we are finally ready to close the laptop for the night, we inevitably hesitate, and check again to see, just in case … one more thing; the sudden panic at the apparent loss of our phone, or the urge to check our social media in the middle of whatever we happen to be doing; the magnetic draw that beckons us voyeuristically to our neighbor's screen, and the allure of its unknown promise; the abrupt intrusion of someone's voice behind the digital stream, that forces us to pull out our AirPods and leave the virtual to respond, followed by the anxious return.[1]

For some, the passage into the virtual world involves a loss of reality. For others, it is because we can finally move into the virtual that we will no longer have to suffer the limitations endemic to the physical, the body, the flesh of our existence. We place loss, absence, and the passing away of things exclusively in one or the other of the two camps. Each, in their own way, tries to hold on to something that seems valuable and keeps out something that seems dangerous. Pushed to their extreme, they both lead to the same partition of virtual and real common to the pro and anti-technological stances.

But the tragedy is that such perfection is impossible, because when virtuality is actualized something is always lost, a potential must die for the actual to be born, for that potential to become real. Potentials are actualized by different technologies, and each involves a loss of its own. In the oral the virtual is rhizomatically actualized, whereas in the written, narrow paths, linear thinking, mathematics and logic are often imposed upon it. Each, the oral as well as the written, involves a loss. Yet each also fulfills its new role.

In our present day, we call the modulation enacted by the digital, "virtual reality." This term, however, carries within itself a hidden bias against the digital world. Since Plato, the virtual smells of fakeness to the scribal mind. But digital virtuality involves a complicated marriage of each of the previous media; it takes us back to the rhizomatic as well as makes use of rational logic and numbers; with the aesthetic power of images and sounds made available on screens by the digital media, it transforms language, both oral and written. The digital has its peril in its bewitching (hyper)realism, its rising above the transient with its beguiling power to simulate the empirical without having to include the body. That powerful mirage is the promised land for many, and a fake copy for others.

The anti-technologist, for example, wants to protect us from the invasive force of the digital which tries to replace what can only come from embodied life and its intrinsic relation to mortality with an inauthentic hyper-techno virtuality. So the digital needs to be placed under tight supervision and control, its influence diminished, to prevent it from impinging upon human virtuality. But with such a paranoid eye, the many ways in which the world today is being imbued with virtuality, in other words, how human virtuality itself is being expanded by the digital, is missed.

And then things take an even more complicated turn, as it becomes clear that part of the motive to see the digital as adversary is the feeling of threat imposed by its particular modulation of the virtual. The digital potentiates the radical rhizomatic edge that reveals life in movement, tapping into a virtuality that disrupts dichotomies and hierarchies. The digital opens and releases things, threatening ordering centers of power, against which the anti-technologists want to tighten their grip.

At first glance, we might think that the pro-technologists have found a way out of the rigid division that so clearly plagues the anti-technologist's position. In Floridi's concept of "on-life", or with the idea of the Internet of Everything, where external reality itself becomes a digital mirror, the intention to blend digital and actual life seems to succeed, so that virtual and real no longer oppose one another. But in truth it fails, because it relies upon the same stubborn opposition, and ends up replacing human virtuality with the digital virtual, without remainder.

Even though virtuality's inexhaustibility gives us the sense that there is always more, its very ephemerality is also a harbinger of loss. In any actualization of virtuality, in the digital no less than in the physical, there is privation. This intrinsic loss of being, touches everything, both real and virtual, empirical world and digital world, human virtuality and digital virtuality. The tragedy of the virtual is indeed that loss is inescapable, and anything that offers to transcend it is an illusion.

In what follows, we want to illustrate -from the perspective of the losses that follow in the wake of the digital-, what we have in mind when we speak of this tragedy. We tend to assume that overcoming impermanence, making the world feel more stable and coherent is one of the great benefits of the digital. However, the intuition behind our claim that a thinning or flattening occurs in the passage to digitality is also that it can be a detriment that threatens to erase the generative spontaneity of the human virtual.

Since we will be exploring the territory where human virtuality is nurtured by finitude – limitations, absences, endings – it will be hard for us not to allow what is sacrificed by the digital to overshadow and thus blind us to what is gained by it. Thus, the peril of this concluding chapter is to not sufficiently consider the alternative perspective, that the human virtual can be enhanced by the new mode for reckoning with loss that is opened up by the digital. Can our tragic vision be large enough, robust enough, to hold and endure the tension between diminishment and enhancement with the advent of digital virtuality? Is it possible to hold ourselves open to the tragic condition, without falling into the dichotomization of virtual and real that we have been working so hard to deconstruct?

Introduction

We can view the losses that are incurred in digital life from many vantage points: i) as a relational loss, since the constant preoccupation with our devices disconnects us from the people around us, especially those we are most intimate with, ii) as a communal loss, as the digital bursts into our shared, collective spaces, hampering our capacity to effectively read and empathize with one another, to feel our way into each other's experience and into what we have in common and iii) as an existential loss, where our unwitting embrace of digital virtuality paradoxically diminishes our capacity to access and bear the human virtual. These are three dimensions of what we are calling the tragedy of the virtual.

In the Virtual Within (Chapter 5), we examined how an inward orientation toward the mind – which mapped out the role psychic life plays in structuring how we take in and perceive the world – is steadily receding in the digital era. There is a remarkable outward turning of the very psychic stuff that used to comprise our subjectivity – fantasies, wishes, dreams – as we take up residence in the virtual world.

What once found a home in the innermost reaches of the self now winds its way through cyberspace.

Take tweets, for example. Thoughts, fantasies, and ideas that ran around in our mind are now showcased in a public forum, to whomever is willing to listen. The inside turned out, for anyone that wants to see. And what a rush! Bearing witness to the ephemera of our most private thoughts and feelings, the receptivity of the psychoanalyst now becomes dispensable, as she is multiplied in the gaze of so many others in the digital frenzy.

For Freud and Jung, the psyche has a life-force of its own that eclipses the conscious intentionality of the self. Within their own unique conceptual systems, each discovers a non-personal dimension out of which subjectivity arises. In Nancy's re-transcription of the Freudian drives, as we have seen, it manifests as a momentum that is inside us yet surpasses us. These depth-psychological accounts, with their emphases on psychic forces that are other to the intention of the subject, are one way of rendering this vitalizing non-personal (we might we even say non-human) source of subjectivity that we have come to call the immanent virtual. But what happens to this ultimately uncontrollable, non-sovereign source of vitality when it no longer emerges from the spontaneity of the psyche but in the algorithms of the digital?

In our digital lives, rather than traversing us, this surge is outwardly dispersed, impossible to contain, over-burdening the metabolizing function of the psyche. We are more susceptible today of being thrown off balance by the digitization of the self that encumbers its functions, as it tries to deal with the impinging demands of collective, networked experience. Exhausted by its relentless incursions, we begin to surrender the self's own autochthonous space/time structurings and allow the digital to become the new regulator and container of our psychic existence. What once derived from an energy that is both in us and surpasses us is now external and cybernetically produced, replacing our organic sense of the flow of existence with a demanding other, to whose mechanical pulse we must adapt, in order to continue to benefit from its riches. The virtuality inherent to the digital disperses our psychic energy into the nothingness of cyberspace, cutting us off from the very source that once sustained us. The only way to contain this dispersal, reel it back in, is to submit to the digital's precise ordering of the world. As I finally relent and snap a smartwatch to my wrist, I am stabilized by its predictable rhythms. There's a terrible irony here, for the digital fractures the self and then presents itself as that which can heal the fracture.

Of course, this is a partial description of what the intrusion of the digital into our normal lives feels like. We want to be careful not to get caught up in romanticizing the past, a worry we have had since the beginning of this project as non-digital natives facing our own personal and historical sense of loss, in having lived through a pre-digital era that is now vanishing. For us scribals, there is a sense of being overtaken by external rhythms foreign to what is natural to us. But not for a digital human. We need only think of those babies that before turning two are already conversant with a touch screen and are learning to interact as easily and smoothly attuned to the digital world, as we claim the mediation of the screen is fracturing. We recently heard of a 6-year-old child who had a terrifying nightmare and, after describing it to his parents the next morning, visibly disturbed, exclaimed: "Something is wrong with my computer. It must be broken!"

In acknowledging the hypnotic power of the digital to turn just about everything into an easily digestible representation of reality, is it possible to just stop for a moment and silently feel its weight, how it immunizes us from the unformed, non-representable aspects of experience? Can we let ourselves perceive, in that silence, how the digital presses against us, constricting and narrowing our range of being? That vague and dull feeling of being over-saturated by too much time on the screen alerts us to what is being displaced. When we replace human virtuality with digital virtuality something is erased. Encased in its limiting frames, where everything is predictable and controllable, we yearn for the whimsical spontaneity of non-digital life.

Yet, at the same time, the vitality of the psyche is not as displaced now as we may think. The digital virtual has its own form of spontaneity that offers a new kind of food for the psyche. The unexpected associations and connections that can happen in the virtual world animate and enrich our experience, opening us to its prolific rhizomatic expansion. Consider the ever-new combinations behind the undeniable explosion of creativity that we are witnessing in all of the arts and sciences. The digital becomes a vessel for the very energy that feeds our most dynamic affective and cognitive life.

It is easy for the non-natives among us to fall into the trap of blindly projecting onto that vitality our fears about what the digital may be opening up and releasing into the world, like a kind of modern-day Pandora's box, rather than seeing it as something inherent to who we are as humans and what we are potentially capable of. It might be its de-repressive aspects that we most fear, its freeing so much of the raw sexual and aggressive energy kept buried in the culture. This anxiety is not surprising, since things are so radically breaking apart today. The self is fracturing, as the political, legal, social, religious, and ethical institutions that held it together are unraveling. Is it a de-structuring energy that is breaking open the individual and cultural psyche in the name of new life and renewal? Or is it a destructive energy, unleashing chaos and mayhem into the social and political surrounds, as the Other becomes increasingly intolerable or threatening, and violence inevitable. Are we before the Apocalypse or is it a Renaissance?

1 Personal losses

a Digital mourning

As we have said from the very beginning, the way we deal with technology – how we conceive it, how we develop it – hangs on the attitude we hold towards loss and the ephemerality of experience. The role the digital plays in our virtual lives can be gauged by the ways in which we use it to manage the unpredictability and sheer unruliness of life. The energy unleashed by the digital takes things apart, making us ever more aware of the evanescent, while at the same time putting them back together, helping us face loss and absence.

But, just as it is immensely complicated to know what it really means to grieve a loss and come out on the other side, we don't know what it means, or if it is even possible, to mourn in the digital. The digital is a real trickster when it comes to loss, for what better means do we have today for disavowal than the virtual re-constitution of the object? We can live in the illusion that nothing has ever really passed because everything can always be recovered, virtually. We are seduced by this promise of pure, death-denying limitlessness, where there is no dispossession and thus nothing to mourn.

And then, with just a slight shift in perspective, the whole digital revolution seems at the same time to also be compelling us to wrestle with the reality of loss and contingency like never before. Virtual worlds appear and suddenly vanish, and new ones take their place, echoing and resonating with the coming-to-be-passing-away of our mortal condition. The digital reveals something about the cease-lessness of things ending. In its always indeterminate flux, it can teach us not how to deny loss, but how to bear it; how to creatively respond to those de-structuring forces that live inside ourselves and in the world. Though we have harshly criticized the constant flooding of the psychic by the digital, that deluge spawns the play beyond representation, and teaches us to let go; by its unceasing multiplication and generation of new life it leads us to a freer relationship with all that passes.

b Digital mirroring

The sweet melodious ring of the digital pulls us out of ourselves, impinging upon the immanence of our existence, what Winnicott (1960) calls our going-on-being. For him, the alternative to being is reacting, which takes us outside of ourselves. "[R]eacting interrupts being and annihilates" (p. 47). From the joyful self-forgetfulness of ordinary, everyday life, we become reactive to the digital's demand to take charge and return to the center of things. Yes, of course, we can lose ourselves in virtual worlds as well, but we have become so inured to the interruption, that we hardly notice its impingement anymore.

Over-exposure to the digital can cause what Robert Jay Lifton (1982) refers to as psychic numbing, that state of being where ordinary experience can no longer impress itself upon us. Unless it is pretty hyped-up, it has no chance of getting in. Increasingly benumbed, we are pulled to open up the most intimate spaces of the self to the digital (sleep, dreams, fantasy, sexuality, as well as the internal workings of our physiological life), as we crave its hyperreality to penetrate and break through the very psychic situation it has engendered. In unconsciously seeking to find and recover our loss of ordinary experience, we re-double our attachment and immersion.

What does it mean to fall asleep while holding your phone (an *ersatz* thumb), to prolong contact with it till the very moment at which you nod off, and then have it there, patiently waiting by your side, when you wake up, especially if you awaken in the middle of the night? The digital fills the gap between waking and sleeping; it protects against the darkness of night with light and presence; it shields us from silence and absence, making us less alone with our dark thoughts, less afraid. The smartphone in our bed is analogous to the child's teddy bear, helping to calm the distress of being alone while facing the terrors of the night. It fills in the nearly imperceptible fissures that occur in the transition from one state of being to the next.

But the smartphone, like the stuffed animal, is not only a transitional object that helps us bear absence and separation. It is also, as we have seen, a self-object, bestowing upon us an expansive mirroring of the self that well surpasses what any parent can humanly offer to a child. We have created an object that attends to you and only you, 24 non-stop hours every day, awake or asleep. It's hard to let go of it, and no wonder the panic when it is lost. Indeed, the average smartphone user (and god only knows the fetishistic perversity implied in measuring this), touches, swipes, or taps their phone 2617 times a day.

We find ourselves ill-equipped to move beyond this primary hunger for mirroring. We fail to develop the necessary internal, psychological faculties to bear and process what is other to the self. The digital, if we are not careful, can promote a self-object way-of-knowing the world, where virtuality becomes a prop for the omnipotence of the self. We buy into Facebook/Google/Amazon life because it offers a seemingly limitless world entirely structured to narcissistically magnify who we are and what we want. In our digital life, the world itself becomes an all-giving self-object that creates the illusion that the not-me is eradicated; but it does so at the cost of the plentifulness of the everyday.

As we have seen, a self-object constructively feeds our omnipotence and allows us to grow a self. But in order for development to proceed, at some point that self-object has to become a transitional one, so that we can begin to shape our narcissism in such a way that it does not have to deny the reality of the other, but indeed can learn to be fed from it. In our exploration of digital adolescence, we saw this as a piercing by the world (so necessary for growth) of the narcissistic cocoon from which the self emerges. A transitional object always has linkages beyond itself and its local realm; it's what brings the psyche into the world of externality. Today, it seems we know all too well how to make a child feel at home in our digital culture, but we don't know how to help them with the shift from narcissism to transitionality in life.

How do we bear witness to the spontaneity of our own being as opposed to the spontaneity that's generated by the virtual? In the unending buzz and dazzle that encircles us, we deafen to the quieter and more subtle inner voices, the ungovernable elements that are played out in dreams and fantasy. Given the brightness and clamor that emanates from the digital, it is nearly impossible to find the dark vessel of quiet necessary to nurture our interior lives. We no longer know how to protect it – or the interior lives of our children – from its intrusions. Because everything comes at us so quickly and clearly, so proximal to the central self, the non-egoic dimensions of our psychic life, that which is eccentric to it, slowly fades.

This infiltration into the psyche of highly concentrated digitized virtuality, as it is unleashed and played out in the virtual world, causes a collapse at the border between inner psychological truth and collective consciousness. We are no longer enriched by the meanings generated from their intimate and kindred association, nor can we make use of the vitality of their difference.

And to be as fair and pharmacological as possible, the question we keep returning to is whether digital virtuality is the cause of this collapse, or whether the digital is somehow, in some yet unforeseen way, helping us to deal with a collapse that has already happened. Winnicott's (1963) idea of the trauma that we anticipate, as a trauma that has already occurred, is helpful in seeing the digital as a placeholder for, a symptom of, perhaps a new form of virtuality. And yet, because the digital is such a trickster, we use it to evade the very thing it could be trying to teach us about the mortal nature of the virtual itself. Perhaps human virtuality is desperately trying to break through its digital vessel, enacting a return of the repressed to which we have not yet learned how to surrender or, much less even, begin to integrate.

c Digital melancholy

This paradox of technology that, on the one hand, extends the virtual while, at the same time, obstructing it, has shadowed every position and stance that we have explored with regard to the digital revolution. It might be profitable, then, to take another look to try to understand existentially how human virtuality is being affected by digital technology. We are indeed ontological centaurs, strange creatures with one foot in the finite world of material life and one foot in the infinite world of the virtual. Human being nowadays stands in a place where the fundamental tension between the infinite virtual, and the finite, concrete real is coming undone. It is the most paradoxical of circumstances, where what we dream up inside ourselves is threatened by the unlimited possibilities offered to us in the virtual world.

Adam Phillips (2012) explores this paradoxical dynamic as it arises in our mental lives. He calls it "the haunting myth of our own potential", characterizing it in these words:

> ... much of our so-called mental life is about the lives we are not living, the lives we are missing out on, the lives we could be leading but for some reason are not. (p. xi)

Phillips explores the dynamics or grammar of that spectral space, the haunted relation between our actual lives and their unrealized potential. Not only does imagination craft the life we lead (in the forms of society, language and culture); it also shadows that life with an unlimited number of unrealized possibilities that stalk it. Digital technology may be a response to (and indeed often a monstrous magnification of) that very stalking, for it introduces a radically new way of "actualizing" our unlived desire, where we can lead the lives we are missing out on, virtually. For instance, in Second Life, I can live as a man while I am a woman in my everyday experience. Or, as desire becomes potentiated in the virtual world, it can spill over into real life, with excessive and sometimes destructive effects, as we saw in *U.S.S. Callister* (cf., Chapter 7), where someone bullied in real life was able to get back at those that abused him, thus actualizing (virtually) his desire for revenge in ways that were unimaginable before our time.

Thanks to the digital, we can now reach back and re-encounter moments from our youth and past relationships – the lost objects of our college days, for example, that we have been able to locate from the archival wealth of the web – and re-live them in the present. In our virtual life, the object of our melancholic fantasy ("I missed my chance with this person and can never get it back") is restored and our desires fulfilled (or shattered) in unforeseen ways. One of the most extreme forms of haunting that result from the social media is the creeping anxiety we begin to feel, as – exposed to the lives of so many people – we find ourselves continuously and masochistically measuring our own lives against them, with all the things they do or have, which we don't. Watching the many stories in Instagram or Facebook can be a very erosive and indeed often corrosive experience, because we long to be there and enjoy the wealth of the lives we are voyeuristically watching, instead of reflecting on that feeling that we are missing out, alone as we are, on the other side.

The intercourse between the virtual and the actual is intrinsic to who we are today. Neither stands alone. The imagination of possibilities and their digital expression, and the paths we have taken in our concrete lives to actualize them, are fundamentally and inseparably united. This intermingling of the actual and the virtual involves not just, as Phillips (2012) points out, our having to live a "double life," "somewhere between the lives we have and the lives we would like" (p. xi), but a "triple life," for in the digital age we are all learning to live suspended in the tension between the virtual, the actual, and the digital virtual.

For us today, the unrealized potential dwelling in our minds can now be instantly actualized. Digital technology complicates the difficulty of our dual nature by materializing the virtual in the digital and interweaving it with the real. The ontological centaur acquires a further dimension, so how do we learn to think and live as *digital* centaurs? For Phillips, we need to "think ourselves as always living a double life, the one that we wish for and the one that we practise; the one that never happens and the one that keeps happening." (p. xviii). This new tripling of virtual/actual/digital literally casts us into an intensified version of this drama. There is "the one that never happens" (what always stays inside the mind); and now two adjoining tracks that always happen, in the real world and in the digital.

As desiring creatures, we are always, in some sense, missing out, for it is lack that constitutes desire. The digital collapses the paradoxical tension between the virtual and the actual, profoundly affecting the space between what never happened and what is always happening. Unable to bear missing out, to tolerate the unlived lives that we will never live, we turn the digital into an escape or a refuge. In the illusory belief that digital virtuality can overcome lack, we may be enacting the very form of disavowal that is at the core of perversion, according to Freud.

d Digital narcissism

Digital virtuality empowers a bold and expressive self, hungry for affiliation and partnership. It increases the speed by which we can contact the other, making him more accessible, our relationship more concentrated, more intimate, more focused. It does away with spatial limitations, brings people closer together, and frees us from being pigeonholed because of our appearance, race, cultural background, etc. It helps to open the self toward the world, creating fairer and more democratic spaces, where a fuller relationship to our common humanity can occur. Our relational lives are broadened, as more and more people can become important to us, and the events that happen around us take on ever greater significance. We feel more connected to our intimate circle of friends and family, our communities (digital and otherwise), and to the larger social and political movements afoot in the world. Linked to the same events simultaneously, we are more than just a global village, we sometimes seem to be a single mind. In the experience we had with the fire in the Cathedral of Notre Dame, for example, where the whole world shared their thoughts and feelings over the catastrophe happening online in real time, the virtual world dissolved the natural barriers that constitute our individualities, and amplified our experience of the world from our individual corners into a global space.

The digital takes away many of the obstacles that in the physical world prevent us from taking action. It expands the reach of our agency; it makes it easier to take charge of things and we feel a potent sense of efficacy in our lives. Because one of its main outputs is affectively charged, life-vitalizing meaning, it is no wonder that we are so eager to embrace its actualizations. If it is an addiction, it's an addiction to that which gives intensity and passion, and those are qualities we can never be in too short supply of.

However, this extraordinary sense of agency is shadowed by how the digital also unleashes the narcissistic strivings of our unconscious self. The very same appetite for intensive self expansion, can, in nearly imperceptible ways, devolve into a kind of self-aggrandizement which pushes us ever further into the all-too-human tendency to diminish, and even negate, the other. The strivings of the virtual self enact an expansiveness of the subject that has the potential to do violence to human intimacy since it depends upon the cues that come from close physical proximity. In that digital maneuver of being close in yet far away, we are unable to encounter the embodied presence of others; we become impervious of them and they of us, for as Gianpiero Petriglieri says of the Zoom encounter, there is a plausible deniability of everyone's absence:

Our minds are tricked into the idea of being together when our bodies feel we're not. Dissonance is exhausting... It's easier being in each other's presence, or in each other's absence, than in the constant presence of each other's absence. Our bodies process so much context, so much information, in encounters, that meeting on video is being a weird kind of blindfolded. *We sense too little and can't imagine enough.* That single deprivation requires a lot of effort. (Twitter Feed @Petriglieri, April 4, 2020)

Digitality grants us command over the virtual. It allows us to modulate our relationship to the other, to procure through the screen what I want and need from them to feed my own desires. As a by-product of the narcissism that is its life-blood, the digital becomes a weapon of subjugation.

Few people write as lucidly of our inalienable self-involvement as the Irish novelist John Banville (2000).

There is in me, deep down....a part that does not care for anything other than itself. I could lose everything and everyone and that pilot light would still be burning at my centre, that steady flame that nothing will quench, until the final quenching. (p. 30)

The digital reaches to the core of my being. It fuels that pilot light for us today in a way that is incomparable to anything that has come before. With my orgy of clicking (Gertz, 2018), I become omnipotent and immortal, the other be damned! If the narcissism within us can never be domesticated, what does it mean for us as a species to finally have at our disposal near total control of the virtual?

2 Collective losses

a Virtual privacy

Derrida (Derrida and Stiegler 2002) remarks on the erosion of our familiar distinction between public and private by the intrusion of the "telepowers." That intrusion has grown today, some 20 years later, as virtual reality has been liberated from its encasement in the private screen to emerge into the shared, public spaces of our lives. Since we feel freer and at the same time more compelled to expose our innermost self within the safe confines of the virtual world, and, since our devices are with us wherever we go, we find ourselves engaging with the intimate dimensions of our private digital lives in public, regardless of where we are or who might be around. Since there are very few, if any, places left where our technological extensions are prohibited, public life and digital life have become nearly synonymous.

This ever greater tolerance for the digital presence in collective life is the counterpart to its seeping into our most intimate spaces and private acts. Fantasies that used to be contained within ourselves are acted out, first in virtual reality, and now outside in the world.

An unconscious resistance overtakes us when someone tries to pull us out of our digital immersion, calling us to the demands of life that are happening right now, there before us. Once in the grip of that resistance, we feel empowered to refuse the demand for tolerance that has always helped to contain communal life and keep our discourse and relational exchanges civil and relatively peaceful. In that refusal, we liberate ourselves from the frustrating and "annoying" (as the digital youth call it) impositions that others make upon us. When the others are virtualized, as we have learned, they do not impinge in the same way. The digital screen becomes a protective layer, a sleeve that precisely allows us to determine how much of the other we let in and how much we decide to keep out.

In the same way that inner, psychological space has become so unbearable that we flee to our phones (e.g., in moments of transition) when we cannot tolerate the impending feeling of absence or emptiness, we are equally compelled to retreat into our private, virtual world whenever we enter public space. This may be an attempt to deal with the overexposure that we are subjected to, with the omnipresent camera, always there, just at the edge of our awareness. Enter nearly any store today, look up, and there you are on the video monitor. Whatever city street we happen to be walking on, whatever building we might wander into, the feeling of being surveilled is with us all the time. Paranoid and suspicious of each other, we retreat further into our virtual worlds, as a response to the dysphoria generated by the ever-present watching eye. The smartphone becomes a line of flight, a means of escape, in pursuit of the very privacy and internal space that has been sacrificed.

And paradoxically, that public space seems to have emptied out. The earbud/screen nature of digital life makes it feel as if there is no communal space that we are sharing together, each of us is so singularly locked into a world that is always somewhere else. We are not really there, and there is the growing sense that no one else is either. Deaf and blind to the aesthetics of shared space, our social surrounds begin to feel antiseptic and deadened, like the waiting room of a doctor's office.

When we are at the airport, for example, we buy our packaged drinks and snacks, locate the nearest charging station, and take a seat, crowded in with everyone else. Needing to disconnect from an increasingly cold, unoccupiable, non-human environment, we dive into our virtual cocoon. So as to escape from where we are and who we are with, we psychically anesthetize ourselves in an obsessive engagement with our devices. Overexposed in our private life due to the digital, we flee further inside it in a vicious circle that starts to seep into collective life as well, leaving the space inside the screen as the only inhabitable place left.

Look around in a subway car, or a crowded bus stop, and notice the small crises of dissociation happening. Everyone swept into their own mini-world of self-interest and concerns that causes our awareness of the primacy of communal engagement to recede. The polis is erased. The all-important encounter with the other, at the root of inter-subjective life, shifts from outside in public space to inside the private-digital, making the already deadening and claustrophobic outside spaces to feel even more closed-in and lifeless. Compare, for example, Starbucks, the prime instance of the sanitized coffeehouse and Caffè Florian, which, on the contrary, is famous for its bohemian ambiance, glamour and social effervescence. The exchange between people in a Starbucks no longer happens in the context of lively shared social engagement as it does in the famous Venetian cafe, but in the private space of earbuds and screens. In both, talking and gesturing abound, but in the franchise, nearly all of it is turned inward, toward a ghostly other, an absent presence.

Although the turn to our screens shields us from the demands and realities of public life, it should also be noted that the digital has added an entirely unique aspect to private life. Through the security of our phones we are taken into this new space of connection and digital interaction. We may be alone and alienated from those that are in our immediate physical proximity, but inside our shared virtual worlds we feel closely connected to whomever we might be chatting with. We experience two moods simultaneously: the intimacy of a living room and the estrangement of a public square.

Consider the virtual connections that have become an indis-pensable means to live a social and professional life. The virtual other is both here in our lives and at the same time not. This new form of contact engenders a truly distinctive source of intersubjective spon-taneity. Whenever I crave the immediacy of the distant other, I can call her forth and, presto!, there she is, right in front of me. Without the encumbrance of having to traverse physical space and time, we videochat, in any public space, as, for example, when I am riding the train, shopping in the market, walking across the mall, surrounded by actual others who are then compelled to bear witness to this very peculiar display of private/public behavior.

But with a slight change of perspective, nothing that important seems to be really lost. Instead, we perhaps notice something positive previously occluded by our bias. New venues for communication with the other open up, where there is less hiding and more transparency (even if, at times, involuntary). Nowadays it is common for people to

260 Philosophical issues of the virtual

showcase their private interactions with others in a platform where others can enter freely, make comments and interact in various ways through the open chat room. Little by little, it seems, we are starting to loose our reservations about letting people witness whatever is taking place in our personal spaces, so that it seems everyone now can have their own show, as many people do now, for example, in Instagram Live. And as our portable devices become more sophisticated, allowing us ever more frequent immediacy with the other, the public becomes private, the private public until, eventually, there is no difference between them. Indeed, the very boundary that held them in some kind of livable tension rapidly dissipates.

b Virtual containment

In its investigations of the unconscious dynamics of our interior lives, psychoanalysis repeatedly stumbles over the question as to the difference between satisfying an impulse in actual life (reality) in contrast to the mode of satisfaction that is intrinsic to the mind (fantasy). The actualization of a desire within the realm of fantasy, dream and memory – all dimensions of the virtual within – uncannily echoes its counterpart in the real. When we dream of doing something we really want to do, it's as if we have actually done it. But what criteria do we have for the comparison between actual and imagined gratification? Virtual satisfaction can match, and even exceed, at times, the satisfactions that happen in the real. But isn't any satisfaction always rooted in some kind of unfathomable mix of virtual and actual?

Fantasies seldom stay inside as pure fantasies. They are most often accompanied by a drive for action, for some form of actualization outside the mind. We find ourselves caught up in the ubiquitous struggle to contend with the impulses embedded in our fantasies, that urge for action. We want something, and become frustrated or angry when our desire is thwarted. We feel envy when someone else has what we want and we do not. Desire's lack draws us out toward people and objects, in a never-ending quest for satisfaction or permanence.

Acting out describes a psychic breakdown in which a person is compelled to live something out in actual life that cannot, but most likely should, be held within the space of their own mind. It represents a failure of containment, where what cannot be psychically metabolized is unconsciously thrust against the world, often in destructive and harmful ways. For example, consider the common experience of discharging one's anger against another person because of an inability to process within oneself the underlying affects that gave rise to that aggressive outburst, whether it be sadness, jealousy, rejection, etc. We can't hold something inside, so we force it to the outside, on to the other.

This characterization of acting out assumes its opposite, that there is a way of containing (or expressing, satisfying, fulfilling) our instinctually driven lives that converts what we are compelled to express literally, in an impulsively driven act, into a non-action action. Here, the impulse is held and experienced as a psychological rather than literal reality. The psychic processes of the mind –reflection, mentalization, metabolization, etc. – help us de-literalize, and thus contain our impulses, holding them as metaphoric or symbolic or virtual realities. The experiential fulfilment may take place in one's dream or fantasy life, or, in how it changes and affects one's psychological comportment and attunement to the world. Holding the tension of an impulse and experiencing it as a psychic rather than a literal reality, opens us to different dimensions of the world, aspects of existence often difficult to bear, yet important to face; these are erased when the impulse is acted out.

The digital virtual provides us a new means of obtaining the experiential fulfilment of our desires that -like the virtual within – does not require an actual other or object or specific place or time. But-unlike the virtual within – it can happen on-demand, exactly when we want it to. What does it mean to satisfy our desires in virtual reality, and how do such fulfilments mark the real?

With the advent of virtual reality, the difference between psychic expression and literal action gets terribly obscured. Given how accurate our simulations are becoming, it is now evermore difficult to distinguish whether an experience happened virtually or actually, online or offline. All sorts of tensions are collapsing and new ones arising. We are forced to re-think what acting out can even mean in our time, given how the digital is able to provide such a rich and accessible platform for the enactment of our innermost fantasies and desires. And as we struggle to understand the consequences of this new mode of instantaneous, on-demand wish fulfilment, we have to come to terms with the meaning of this difference for our virtual lives.

Virtual reality may very well be the preeminent space for the exploration of psychic fantasy and active imagination, which Jung calls dreaming the dream onward. By granting experiential fulfillment to our most primordial drives, it lets us live out our impulses as virtual realities, thus providing a crucial safeguard against their being (consciously or unconsciously) acted out in the world. Virtual reality and psychic reality are close and intimate cousins, each mutually extending and drawing each other out. The virtual can replicate the inner workings of dream and fantasy only now in a realm outside of ourselves that is much easier to access and control.

Once again, in the spirit of the pharmakon, we are brought face-to-face with a central paradox: on the one hand, the virtual world provides expression and containment for our impulse-driven lives, furthering, as it were, our own psychic virtuality, and thus, diminishing our tendency to act out, while, on the other, it can become the perfect platform for evacuating those impulses within ourselves that we are no longer able to contain or bear.

In the course of these chapters, we have made many positive links between virtual reality and Winnicottian potential space, that balancing point between fantasy and reality that allows for the actualization of our inner virtuality. From this vantage point, it seems reasonable to consider the digital virtual as an outstanding form of potential space, which fusing together our most vital desires to this dreamspace of experiential gratification, liberates the imagination, giving life purpose, direction, and intensity.

Virtual space enlivens and animates the play that is always taking place between self and other. Since the risk of action in the virtual world is relatively small compared to what we live out in the real, it offers a powerful mode of containment, for we can be a lot less careful about our use of the other as a screen upon which to enact our projections. This protected, sheltering quality engenders a nurturing space for the free expression of desire to chart its own path, sexual and otherwise, as we can live out any identification we want, become any new kind of self or inhabit any new kind of other. We are emancipated from the religious, economic, gender, and political strictures that have so restrained us. Libido, desire, the force of our sexuality and the play of our narcissism, can be given freer reign.

However, the capacity of the digital for containing and expressing our impulses and desires can precipitously flip into its opposite, and empower a highly intensified form of acting out. As we know from everyday life, states of psychic equilibrium, – where we feel certain that we have a good handle on a particular yearning, and are doing well at containing it – can suddenly and unexpectedly devolve into a moment of impulsive action. The same can occur, in a more magnified and dramatic way, in the virtual world. Desire finds itself narcissistically encased inside a hallucinatory reality that is blindly driven toward its own fulfillment.

The unending possibilities of the digital virtual can suddenly turn into a dystopian space for psychic disavowal, a crass home for trolling and ghosting, where the worst tendencies in ourselves are acted-out upon a virtual stage, now shared by all. The virtual world enables us to blow by the reality of the other in the name of our narcissistically driven satisfactions. We see this emblematically in the erotically driven, aggressive everydayness of our social media lives. Or, in an even more sinister way, by the use of Twitter and Facebook for political gains. There is a persistent temptation (or even a habit now) to use it as an evacuatory chamber for what is most disavowed in ourselves.

c *Virtual leaking*

As our fantasy lives take up residence in the actualizations offered by the virtual, something about the precarious balance between containing an impulse and acting it out is profoundly and dangerously destabilized. Masud Khan (1993) describes how certain individuals who suffer from an incapacity to dream -by which he means that they cannot actualize within their own psyche the experiential space in which a dream occurs – find themselves exploiting social space to act out their fantasies. In the newly proliferating forms of mass violence, as our innermost fantasies of mayhem, death and destruction are acted out in the public square, what, for Khan, was exploitation, takes on a more malignant turn today. The very impulses, aggressive and destructive in their nature, that the virtual has given us so much opportunity to explore safely within its secure borders, seems now to be escaping from its digital container and entering our shared empirical world.

New forms of mass violence are taking place all over the world: mass shootings in nightclubs, movie theaters, concert halls, schools, houses of worship, the proliferation of vehicle-ramming attacks, bombs being set off at city events, etc. as well as the rising anger and aggressiveness aimed at whoever is different than us (i.e., the denigration of the immigrant, the foreigner, the stranger, the other). The ugliness and destructiveness inherent to everyday social life that has always been with us is sorely aggravated by the digital.

These new modes of violent acting out and denigration of the other uncannily resonate with the particular structure of the self-other relationship that flourishes in the virtual world. Rather than unconsciously turning toward social space to act out my dreams and fantasies, I can now freely exploit the virtual. In VR I can let loose and do whatever I want. I immerse myself in a space in which being able to play-out my aggression toward others stirs up great excitement and passion. I can maltreat and abuse them, and ultimately destroy them at my will; and, if I am so moved, I can do it over and over again, with total impunity. But, as we have seen with the protagonist of *Black Mirror's U.S.S. Calister*, or with what happens on the dark web, or even Twitter, this can take its own spontaneously destructive turn.

The violence that is opened up by digital virtuality is no longer contained by the screen, it seems to be leaking out everywhere. Consider this recent story from the *New York Times*:

> Duped by a man she met on the Internet who lived nearly 4,000 miles away, an 18-year-old Alaskan woman lured her best friend to a popular trailhead and carried out a murder-for-hire plot on the promise of millions [....] Six people [were] ... arrested in the case,

which the authorities described as a catfishing scheme. Catfishing is when a person uses a false identity online to lure someone into a relationship. Mr. Schilmiller [the anonymous figure behind the scene][...] directed Ms. Brehmer [the 18 year old] to sexually assault two minors and send him videos of those crimes [...] Mr. Schilmiller told investigators that Ms. Brehmer communicated with him throughout the killing, and sent him Snapchat photos and videos of Ms. Hoffman [the murder victim] when she was tied up and after she was killed. (Vigdor, 2019, p. 23)

For the protagonists of this story, it is clear that the distinction between virtual and real destructiveness is no longer operative.

In addition to these overt acts of violence that mimic the ethos of the virtual world, there are also more subtle ways in which the digital has become the new carrier of human aggression. Cyberbullying and trolling are obvious examples. It seems no longer necessary or perhaps not even possible anymore (as is poignantly evident in the aggression and verbal violence enacted in the digital networks) to process within oneself the underlying affects that give rise to our negative feelings, which we so easily now force on to the other in the virtual space of the social media.

Moreover, in a kind of everyday posture when in public, we strap our devices to our belts (like a kind of digital open carry) so that they are there, ready at hand, to defend or aggress. Whether it's whipping out our phones to look something up to prove someone wrong when we are in an argument or precipitously snapping a picture or filming the action in a tense situation, especially where there is a conflict of interest. We dissuade or threaten, implying, "I am now capturing your words (or your actions, or that little piece of reality that is in contention between us), so you better watch yourself." Digital surveillance is not only done by governments and corporations now; individuals also use their own private tracking devices to spy, ensnare, and entrap.

When these new virtual rules set the standard for our social behaviors, the other in real life becomes as dispensable as the virtual object on our screen. There is an imperiousness to digital behavior, a lack of empathy for the other, that threatens civility and abrogates our sense of what it means to live as a local citizen with neighbors, rather than as a digital citizen linked to virtual others. Disconnected from our common humanity, we do not know what to do with the odd feelings that are aroused by the robotic voice that replaces the human, when sharing personal information on the phone, or when we are having trouble keying-in our food order on a touchscreen (with the cashier standing right across from us, sneering, instead of helping). We become victims of digital objectification and as a consequence find ourselves, unwittingly, objectifying the world around us. Deep down inside the omnipotent self, we feel entitled, for example, to walk down the street looking at our screens, carelessly bumping into people as if they were mere objects in our way; or to text and drive, recklessly endangering not only our own lives, but the lives of everyone else.

What is problematic for the individual, and even worse for the culture, is when we start treating real others in our lives as mere extensions of our own selves. We expect the world to behave like the digital, where there are no limits to what we can have, as everything is repeatable and replaceable so we can casually dismiss the fact that others are separate centers of subjectivity.

Digital virtuality offers a powerful way of enframing experience so that there is less friction and obstacle between the self and what it desires, as well as what it disdains and wants to assail against. That self-aggrandizing mode of relating to the world has such a powerful grip on us that though the laptop might be closed, the phone on a shelf charging, somehow the digital is still pulsing through us as we make our way through the interpersonal spaces of the world. It is not so simple as just switching-off, or taking a digital-free holiday away from it.

3 Ontological losses

> However lonely in appearance, a color is in the company of its kin -all its potential variations. The spectrum is the invisible grip background against which «a» color stands out. It is the ever present virtual whole of each color apart.
>
> Brian Massumi (2011)

a Digital transparency

Jung (1971) is famous for saying: "The psyche creates reality everyday. The only expression I can use for this activity is fantasy" (p. 52.) As the digital infinitely expands the horizons of our thinking and feeling life, it serves as a great awakener of psychic fantasy. We scroll through our social media and news feeds hungry for images and narratives that will set the imagination in play. Whether participating in multiplayer video games, assuming the role of an avatar in a Second Life–like setting, or tapping into the vast array of erotic possibilities available in the virtual world, the symbolic and metaphorical dimensions of the mind are emboldened. Like sulphur, the digital ignites fantasy and inflames desire. Psyche comes alive, becomes real, in the virtual world.

The digital opens up shared, collective spaces for dreaming that approximate the imaginative occurrences within ourselves, as we fantasize and have reveries about each other and our experiences.

Indeed, what would Jung – who urges us to dream the dream onward and actively engage with the denizens of our imaginal lives – think of the dreamscapes opened up by virtual reality? Would he not affirm their potential for making contact with the creative psyche? And wouldn't the Freud who wants to free us from sexual repression, extol the erotic possibilities opened up in cyberspace, as they give expression to every form of polymorphous perversion, lifting out of repression an unending variety of sexual combinatory practices? The virtual world provides an immediately engageable, free-associative platform for fantasy that enables us to become conscious and interactive participants in the dreaming experience. And just like the inner world of psychic reality, where we engage our fantasies without having to act them out in the world of "real" others, the virtual offers a parallel mode of containment, where what we most ardently desire can be lived out "virtually" rather than "actually."

We have been staging the ongoing dialogue between the virtuality that lives inside us in the form of the virtual within and digital virtuality, where the very fantasies that lie latent in the mind come to life on the screen, with ever greater immediacy, precision and clarity, as our technological sophistication advances. We have understood the irresistible draw of the digital in terms of its capacity to transform the dullness of the everyday into moments where a passing thought, a whisp of an idea, can suddenly spring to life, appearing before our eyes, as virtually real. This possibility for instantaneous revitalization becomes a powerful seduction, an ongoing temptation to turn to the digital in order to enliven the mind, stir the imagination. What we pursue in the virtual world is not so different, in this sense, from what we seek with certain mind-altering drugs. With digitality, however, we are able to deliberately modulate our virtual dreams in a way we are unable to with anything else.

We have insisted upon keeping an eye on the transit between the ordinary occurrence of mind in "real" life and this elevated and somewhat transcendent state of experience, where meaning and intensity are always ready-to-hand. We have spoken about the losses that occur in the leave-taking to the digital, which we steadfastly refuse to acknowledge, as we strive to keep those departures veiled from ourselves and those around us. Indeed as we become more virtually connected to each other, surrounded by interactive intelligent gadgets that begin to make our digital life seamlessly feed into our "real" life, a hope arises that they will become so well blended together, that we will lose all awareness of when we leave one to enter the other and thus ultimately arrive at Floridi's (2014) utopian "on-life".

It's as if the ultimate aim of this infusion of digital virtuality into the everyday real is to reproduce within the experience of our digital lives the complex awareness that takes place when we sleep. As Nancy (2009) describes it:

> The quite singular awareness of the dream [is such] that this awareness thinks itself, and does not think itself as awareness of a world contrasted with it as a waking world is. At every instant the dreamer thinks he is in the waking world and knows he is in the dream world, whose simultaneities, compossibilities, confusions do not escape him, but also do not surprise him enough to make him emerge from the dream. (p. 8)

We read Nancy's distinction between the dreamer thinking he is in the waking world and yet knowing he is in the dream world, as involving the difference between experiencing the dream (as if you are awake, and in your actual life), and a kind of pre-knowledge that forms a backdrop to dreaming awareness in which in some sense you "know" you are in the dream world.

This "quite singular awareness" which does not differentiate between a dreaming and a waking world, but somehow manages to hold both together is parallel to what happens for the infant in transitional space. As Winnicott explains:

> the essential feature in the concept of transitional objects and phenomena is *the paradox, and the acceptance of the paradox:* the baby creates the object but the object was there waiting to be created and to become a cathected object ... [I]n the rules of the game we all know that we will never challenge the baby to elicit an answer to the question: did you create that or did you find it? (Winnicott, 1971, p. 89)

This background "knowing" can suddenly emerge when something in the dream becomes too disturbing and we signal to ourselves that this is only a dream and wake ourselves up. In that moment, the dream's simultaneities, confusions, etc. break through the illusion that what is happening in the dream is actually occurring in waking life. This dexterous singularity of awareness falters, potential space breaks down and the dream and waking world clash. But then the paradox is refused, for we do indeed elicit an answer to the question: are you actually awake or is this just a dream?

The aspiration for us today as virtual reality pioneers seems to be to create this same kind of singular awareness, where real life and virtual life are held together in some form of potential space where it no longer occurs to ask, "Did you create that or did you find it?" We seek to effect a transitional space for our digital lives, where we can learn to hold and accept, without challenge, its many paradoxes.

One example of such a paradox is that while in virtual space we can partake of the dreaming experience without being asleep. Virtuality is akin to a waking dream, where we move around in a fantasied world, not of our own making, yet we are awake and aware. Any type of imaginative engagement, whether it be art, film, drama, literature, or music, offers us some version of this waking dream experience. But virtual reality, in its creation of an immersive, three-dimensional world, which fully captures and engages our whole being, is second only to our actual dreaming life. And here too, we are free to act without consequences, in accordance with our own inclinations and in total anonymity.

Because of its unparalleled immersive quality, it is easier to lose or escape from ourselves in virtual reality than it is in our ordinary engagement with the arts or in the occurrence of our everyday fantasy lives. Whether watching a show, painting a picture, writing a poem, reading a book, or gossiping with friends, we are inside these activities at the same time as we are in the world. The ongoing impingements of life, as our attention wavers or we are brought back to something we had tried to forget, keeps the two, virtual and real, in some kind of inescapable, dynamic tension. When we engage our virtuality through the arts, we learn creative and generative ways to cultivate this tension, what Gordon Bearn (2013) calls "life drawing." Even though we have not yet made dinner, or figured out what to do about the children's homework, we struggle to bring our attention back to what we were reading or listening to, the poem that we were writing, the conversations that we were having, etc., re-finding the potential space that is always vulnerable to break-down and loss. Unlike the total envelopment of the dream, they remain distinct, and we always find ourselves with one foot in each world. Other than a nightmare waking us up, there's no real worry about the breakdown of potential space when we dream. Ordinarily we take it for granted that we stay enveloped inside the dream, even though there can be a back-and-forth shift of perspectives between being inside the events that are happening to us and being outside them, as an observer, at some distance. These alterations of awareness seem to have a life of their own, as different dreamscapes evoke different moments on the spectrum between identification and dis-identification with the dreaming "I."

In contrast, in our engagement with virtual reality, our everyday consciousness is highly involved in setting the stage, choosing which characters to identify with and deciding from which perspective to view the action. In virtual reality, the ego has near total jurisdiction over how things happen, how a particular scene will ultimately unfold, whereas the events of a dream seem to just happen on their own accord. They arise "from a situation that I am in and, as I, do not define or create" (Scott, 2007, p. 147). As it gives itself over to the shifting identifications with the events and people on the dream stage, there is more porousness to the dreaming self than its waking counterpart.

In virtual reality there is, however, as we have seen in many instances, a similar kind of free and open plasticity at play, a shape-shifting and fluid occurence of our own multiplicity, with many new possibilities for cross-and-counter identifications that are very nourishing to experience in the world. When we dream, however, we do not stop and question that this fluidity of encounter, where one person or event or affective reality can so spontaneously morph into another, is anything other than an experience of waking life in a dreaming world. The existential force of the dream is an outgrowth of this highly condensed medium where affect and existence coalesce, where the dreamer is fully engaged with the expressive singularity of what he or she is living in the moment.

But in the virtual world, where we leave our body behind, and give ourselves over entirely to the artificial fluidity of the algorithmic guide, a dissociation occurs. Our engagement is held by a wounded thread that results from the excision of our body from the proceedings and a full dependence on the structures predetermined by the net. When we watch our dreams being played out on a screen, especially one that is programmed for us, the free arising, naturally spontaneous psychic image is subdued. In order for the virtual to manifest as virtual reality, an existential thinning of experience occurs, as we have already seen.

Dreams are not simply a projection, whose every character wears a mask that hides the self, as we saw with Freud (and which is even more central in Jung). Quite the contrary, the worldliness of the dream and its characters have an autonomy all their own that is not of our making and certainly cannot be reduced to only a projection of the self. When we dream, we are profoundly engaged with the otherness of our existence. Digitally induced virtual worlds try to overcome the unbridgeable gap that separates dream life from waking life by creating a virtual other that is now under our control. However, simulated otherness and actual otherness are fundamentally different and we must come to terms with the existential impoverishment of the former. Or are they so different? Awake or asleep, we are always dreaming. It's just that now there is another way.

Dreams are remarkably elusive, fundamentally outside our control. When we go to sleep at night, we never know where they will take us, and when we awaken, we struggle to recapture the affective quality of the events that were lived with such immediacy during the night. Our efforts at retrieval go only so far, for no matter how hard we try, the recollected dream is permeated with gaps and absences, the losses of unrecoverable experience. The impossibility of bringing the dream back into full presence, its withdrawing, evanescent quality, evokes the non-representational dimensions of the psyche that we have repeatedly been calling forth. Perhaps the digital is so gripping because it persuades us to believe that nothing escapes its representation, that everything is susceptible to being digitized without remainder; and thus we can finally vanquish, as perhaps no other technology has so effectively done ever before, the ineffable aspects of human experience.

As whatever we fantasize about can be represented to us, instantly, just as we imagine it, this mode of virtuality diminishes the need for the creative and emotional struggle required by the work of the imagination. But it also activates our insatiable cravings to have reality conform to our wishes, seducing us into the hybris inherent to technological power. The Promethean Titanism that triggers and is triggered by it is essentially oblivious of what stands beyond representation.

We see an example of the bewildering places this new-found control over the virtual may be taking us in Wim Wender's 1991 film *Until the End of the World*. In this story, a new technology is developed that allows people to watch their own dreams. As the main characters experiment with it, we witness them being overtaken by a rapacious hunger to re-play, again and again, their dream videos. In the end, we find them glued to their screens, totally bewitched, voyeurs to the inner workings of their psychic lives, an apt image, if ever there was one, of a modern-day Platonic cave. Early Hikikimories of the 20th century.

Wender's film can be read as a prognosis for the increasing fervor we find in the digital era to procure some kind of objective analysis of what goes on inside ourselves, some way of reading the surface to unlock its hidden depths. Of course, Foucault (1973), in the *Birth of the Clinic*, already identifies this trend to probe beneath empirical perception, as he explores the epistemic changes that occurred in the 18th century when physicians first dissected the human body. They cut it open in order to make visible what was always hidden to the human eye beneath the surface, what could only, up to that moment, be inferred. In our era, technology not only makes the body ever more transparent, allowing us to send exploratory micro-cameras along the most recondite corners of the organism, but now also seems to promise overcoming the problem of the inscrutability of the human psyche, of desire, of who we "really" are emotionally inside ourselves as opposed to what we present to the world.

The psyche, however, in contrast to the digital self, is fundamentally indeterminate. It can never be entirely known, or made fully transparent. As we have seen, there is an un-representable core to the self that is active and alive within us, even if ungraspable. We can never truly know ourselves, and in turn, for the same reason, the people we are most deeply attached to will also always remain, at some core level, a mystery.

No matter which way you slice it, the self-other continuum is encompassed by not-knowing, unpredictability and ex-centricity which stirs up a terrible anxiety that is baseline for us as humans. In its remarkable ability to bring out of concealment that which resists appearing, digital technology is a balm. We might be seeking a technological solution to what is not only a psychic condition, but an ontological one. The obdurate unknowability of the self and the other, the indeterminacy of human existence, and the unbearable uncertainty about all things is endemic to being alive. Indeed, as Žižek (2012) puts it,

> one cannot look "objectively" at oneself and locate oneself in reality; and the task is to think this impossibility itself as an ontological fact, not only as an epistemological limitation. In other words, the task is not to think this impossibility as a limit, but as a positive fact. (p. 239)

b Digital aura

We seek not just technological mastery of the world outside but also inside, of the self. As we do with nature, we compel the psyche to give up its secrets. We monitor our sleep to know at what exact points in the night we are dreaming or whether and how much we snore. We use brain imaging technology to have represented to us on a screen what is happening in the dreaming mind. If we do our research right, we can strip away the many masks of other selves, knowing in advance of meeting them, any troubling or dark life-events that may be lurking in their background. Our innermost affective states, and these self-same states in the other, can now be eerily detected and revealed.

In an op-ed for the *New York Times*, David Brooks (2019) writes, for example, about the use of A.I. technology to diagnose and predict depression. "[A]fter listening to millions of conversations, machines can pick out depressed people based on their speaking and visual patterns." (p. A23). Not only can depression be detected, but suicidal thoughts as well:

> In his book "Deep Medicine," which is about how A.I. is changing medicine across all fields, Eric Topol describes a study in which a learning algorithm was given medical records to predict who was likely to attempt suicide. It accurately predicted attempts nearly 80 percent of the time. By incorporating data of real-world interaction such as laughter and anger, an algorithm in a similar study was able to reach 93 percent accuracy. (p. A23)

The machine picks up clues about a depressed person that we, as family or friends or clinicians, with our ordinary powers of empathy and perception, are unable to detect. It reads us better than we can read ourselves. It sees through our masks. No Winnicottian false self, no Jungian persona, no Freudian ego, is safe. Now we can even be told, similar to how a swab of the tongue can reveal our ancestral DNA, what set of feelings are lodged deep in the core of ourselves. Better than a lie detector, the digital is becoming an affect and desire detector, offering ever-new readings to the self. Furthermore, as we make our way into the public domain, we are constantly being scanned; with the vast and rapid improvements of facial recognition technology, there is no hiding, cameras everywhere and in everything.

We need only reflect upon the fact that before a child is 2 years old, typically, it will have been already photographed and videotaped by ultrasound equipment even before birth, and its every move and experience will continue to be registered for many purposes. As Marcel O'Gorman (2015) writes:

> [M]y children live in a culture where their recorded images circulated in the world before they did, will be disseminated in multiple locations and contexts while they are alive, and will remain in databases and media archives long after they die. They might store their digital assets on a commercially run server to be opened by their survivors after their death, and as morbid as the thought may be, their own children may create eternal video monuments to play at their funerals and store them for replay on whatever social media outlet is most popular at the time. (p. 10)

All of this behavior that empowers us to define the undefinable, see the unseeable is endemic to the representational impulse that courses through the digital and generates a collective omniscience (Lévy, 1997), a stunning kind of intelligence that can see and know everything there is to be seen and known. But the artificiality of such an intelligence – the fact that all it can see, discern, detect is of a representational character – does away with a dimension of human experience that should not be forgotten. Since the agenda is precisely to maintain things under control, tightly scaffolded within this representational enframing, human creative engagement with the world is covered over, disavowed and ultimately obliterated. Thus this omniscience, for the sake of a false comfort, does away with any opaqueness, shrouding existence's natural (as opposed to artificial) virtuality, making us less and less able to recognize its aura, and to perceive the existential density of reality.

This shines a new light on a core difference between human virtuality and virtual reality. If indeed, the unknowable and the non-representable are the very source of the human virtual, and such a force is foreclosed in virtual reality, then it follows that virtual reality can only offer a simulation of human virtuality, a knock-off, as it were. Digital life is enframed, held inside the limits of its own representation, or as Scott (1996) put it in his distinctive reading of Heidegger's *The Question Concerning Technology*, it takes place inside a "definitive, ordering center… [that] hold[s] things in place according to silent demands for a certain manner of presentation" (p. 69):

> In a time of technology [especially given digitality] things are given to appear and to have significance by their usefulness. They are fitted to purposes based on our needs, plans, and interests […] Technology […] names a manner of appearing in which things are for the sake of something else. (p. 70)

We see this clearly now as every past media is funneled into the uniformity of digitization, the enframing of which homogenizes experience and makes us gradually incapable of discerning anything outside that enframing. It numbs us to human expressiveness and vulnerability. For example, we become deaf to the warmth and timbre of the human voice that is displaced by the ubiquity of loudspeakers in public spaces as much as in the private reception of our smartphones, or in the AI devices that talk to us throughout the day. In growing accustomed to the voice of our interlocutors' Zoom images fragmenting, spacing out, speeding up, and de-synchronizing from their gestures, we are gradually being desensitized to the uniqueness and physical integrity of the personal. By the constantly running present moment of the digital, we are distracted from the historical depth that the non-digital brings to us. Even though the digital expands the representational powers that were limited by the materiality of the previous media, it does away with something of the opaqueness that gives actual experience its profundity.

If we hearken back for a moment to Heidegger's description of the technological world as a wish world, Jared Russell (2020) tells us that for the philosopher wishing "is about a kind of anticipation that refuses possibility: wishing wishes for something to be objectively present-at-hand. […] The wish-world is driven to actualize the real, fleeing the reality of the possible" (p. 108). He continues:

> This world endlessly celebrates its ability to extract from itself an actuality that it is driven to prioritize over its being as possibility. This describes how the scientific spirit is betrayed in being reduced

> to the production of quantifiable, calculable results, and in such a
> way that not only encourages but that insists on statistical
> thinking as the measure of understanding and knowledge.
> (pp. 108–109)

In extracting from itself an actuality, we want to say, this mode of
being loses the virtual as possibility. Just as in Benjamin, the art object
loses its aura (the object's density) to mechanical reproduction, in the
age of digital imaging, the image, then, also seems to lose it.

But while it may be true that the digital image has lost the aura of
the material image, it is also true that it generates other modes or
types of auras. By magnifying, accelerating, photoshopping, or subjecting it to any of the functions by which we are able to examine it,
we discover new depths that change and extend our horizons beyond
what we might have perceived without digitization. Why not think,
in the spirit of McLuhan that with its amputations, digital life also
brings along its novel extensions? Perhaps it is by attending to the
new emergences that we may gradually begin to carve out the space
within which to reconfigure our vision of what is to come.

Coda

We have attempted to articulate a psychology and philosophy that
acknowledge modes of virtuality that transcend digital life, such as
those found in the inner reaches of the psyche, in the mind, in the
aura of the object and in the immanence of the world. Perhaps it is
inevitable that this new extension of our virtual life cast a shadow that
paradoxically narrows our access to modulations of the real that stand
outside the digital. After all, this would not be something new for, as
we know, with each new technological addition there is always a
corresponding subtraction.

But in prizing the human virtual against the artificiality of the digital, we fall into the authentic/inauthentic trap we have tried so assiduously to deconstruct. The digital gives us unparalleled access to a
mode of emergence unseen with any preceding technology. But, the
seduction of unending potentials offered by it makes us forget the
acute sense of loss we feel with its encroachment upon the magical
incantation of that existential interface of mind, imagination and
embodiment that is the human virtual, and takes us to the other side,
where it is digital virtuality that now becomes the "real" magic.

If indeed our technologies help us overcome the passing away of
things by giving us access to an infinite realm of emergence, then it is
impossible not to be haunted by what it must at the same time always
foreclose. The effort to not polarize is thus continuously thwarted, for
each new modulation makes us recoil from what seems to threaten

reality. In its foreclosures, changes and movement, something is always left behind to mourn. Ghosts are with us from the moment we modulate the virtual; every technology builds upon the hallowed grounds of the immanent virtual.

Nowadays, perhaps because of our unprecedented experiences with virtual space, it becomes easier to assume there is no loss either when leaving the empirical to enter the digital, or when forced to exit digital life and come back to non-hyper realized ordinary reality. Because they seem to have become interchangeable and we can inhabit both places at once without any tension, we see only differences when moving from the digital to the empirical. Paradoxically, however, the virtual – the very thing we want to hold on to – can be degraded in both worlds. Too much time spent in our virtual screens can numb us to the vitality of the physical world making it feel empty, spent, tedious, not exciting enough, not playful or inventive enough. But, conversely too, the vitality of the digital can also be stolen because of its own over-exposure.

One would think TikTok knows this, when it warns its users to "go outside" for a while before coming back, when they have spent too much time on it, insuring that way that they indeed will return! Play video-games all day, stay glued to the screen wherever you move – mindlessly walking through crowds in the streets, oblivious to your surroundings, compulsively checking and updating your feeds, absent to the world of physical things – and the digital itself, that area of inventive freedom and spontaneity, dries up.

And then there's the digital at night. Experiments have shown that the blue light from digital surfaces suppresses the hormone melatonin, which promotes sleep, so blocking our access to the bounties of bodily rest, replacing them instead with the pixel-flickering infinite light offering. Physical exposure to virtual screens has an Endymionic effect. Just as Endymion, the mythological ephebe, as we know, swapped mortal vigil for immortal sleep so that he could permanently satisfy his desire for the Moon goddess, we also end up in a sort of trance where, stripped of the refuge of sleep, we are rendered numb and creatively impotent. A knot is tied that stunts the natural course of the vital flow and hence of human virtuality itself. Instead of enlivening, that intensity and continuous use deflates or buries us under the plaque of habit, luring us – in its eternal promise for something always better – to the particular unending quest for the impossible object that constitutes the dynamics of digital-addiction.

Transcending the constraints both of the body and its temporality, the human virtual constitutes the experience of a dimension of life beyond empirical existence, where we "rise above," as it were, our material nature. A hybrid "of the natural and the supernatural" is how Ortega y Gasset (1968) characterized this duality in our human condition. We want to say instead, a hybrid of the actual and the virtual. The virtual is the human mind churning bits of empirical reality and experience through the mill of the imagination, engendering the unending fantasies that crowd and illuminate our perception always, whether in vigil or sleep. Memory rides tandem with these images to conjure virtual life and – like Dyonisus' wine is said to have been invented to make humans forget their suffering mortality – it brings us peace in the midst of the ephemeral world and impending death.

What would human life be if memory didn't hold what has already passed and imagination what is to come? How could we bear human existence if not? Cut off from the virtual, human experience would be deadened, and the vibrancy, spark and vitality of the world gone. We saw this with trauma, where, premature exposure to the virtual overwhelms the psyche and renders it fragile and impotent to build the inner structures that would contain it. The power of the virtual is thus reduced, and as memory and fantasy lose their vivifying influence, imagination itself becomes dangerous, and the passing away of things unbearable.

Maintaining a connection to that which enlivens experience, as we have seen with Winnicott, is a life-long task that is tied to learning to bear our mortality. What animates the virtual, as it moves through mind and world, is its openness to contingency, the fact that things can spontaneously move in any direction, at any time. Cut yourself off from a relationship to the non-governable dimensions of experience that seeks to unravel what is fixed and stable in our thinking and living, and the virtual petrifies. A life that is not attuned to them, and so does not, in at least some of its dimensions, avow the reality of loss and death, is a life inert and emptied of meaning.

The very life-blood of the virtual, what makes it flow, is this ultimately uncontainable, yet generative force at work in the psyche, in the world. Jung (quoted in Edinger, 1974), in his own idiosyncratic use of the term, calls this vital energy, God. He writes:

> To this day God is the name by which I designate all things which cross my willful path violently and recklessly, all things which upset my subjective views, plans and intentions and change the course of my life for better or worse. (p. 101)

The pygmalionic, in its chronic propensity to freeze reality, to stop time, is nothing other than a response to the terror of this reckless and violent, untameable flow that potentiates life through its destabilization. Insofar as it partakes or even originates as a response to that terror, the digital can seem as if it were predicated on an unconscious desire to rid the world of all its uncertainties. But the irony is that the very impulse to codify the world, make it into a picture, enframe it, as we saw with Heidegger, confronts us again with the fact that the very source of the human virtual is the unrepresentable, in its radical flux; that it has always been there, haunting our certainties with its ghostlike insistence upon absence, lack and contingency. The virtual, therefore, is underwritten by a torrent of vital energy that we must sediment but which itself is always de-sedimenting our reality. The danger is to fall into the stultifying expectation of a static, permanent world and become enchained to it.

Deleuze gives voice to a mad, proliferating energy at work behind experience, anticipating the utter intensity in which the virtual is actualized in the digital era. As our perception of things changes be-cause of the prosthetics and other extensions of our bodies and minds through which we now perceive them, the digital (re)introduces the rhizomatic vantage point from which we can better understand the paradoxical nature of the pharmakon.

Note

1 We impulsively sent a friend an email right after we had finished writing these opening paragraphs, asking him to read it. He instantly wrote back: "Beautiful. I love it, and ironically was sitting on the toilet playing digital chess against a computer using the new app my son downloaded on to my phone. It was a crucial play when you e-mailed so I thought: "Ooh I'll just finish this game before I see what you wrote,' how perfect was that?... P.S. I won the game."

References

Banville, J. (2000) *Eclipse*. London: Picador.

Bearn, G. (2013) *Life Drawing: A Deleuzian Aesthetics of Existence*. New York: Fordham University Press.

Brooks, D. (2019, 28 June) Op ed. A.I. can save you life. *New York Times*, p. A23.

Edinger, E. (1974) *Ego and Archetype: Individuation and the Religious Function of the Psyche*. Baltimore: Penguin Books.

Floridi, L. (2014) *The 4th Revolution: How the Infosphere is Reshaping Human Reality*. Oxford: Oxford University Press.

Foucault, M. (1973) *The Birth of the Clinic: An Archaeology of Medical Perception*. London: Tavistock Publications, Ltd.

Petriglieri, G. @gpetriglieri Twitter feed, April 4, 2020.

Phillips, A. (2012) *Missing Out: In Praise of the Unlived Life*. New York: Farrar, Straus and Giroux.

Gertz, N. (2018) *Nihilism and Technology*. London and New York: Rowman & Littlefield International.

Jung, C.G. (1971) Psychological Types. In R.F.C. Hull (trans.), *Collected Works of C.G. Jung* (Vol. 6). Bollingen Series XX. Princeton: Princeton University Press.

Khan, M.M. (1993) The Use and Abuse of Dream in Psychic Experience. In Flanders, S. editor. *The Dream Discourse Today*. London: Routledge.

Lévy, P. (1997) *Collective Intelligence: Mankind's Emerging World in Cyberspace*. Cambridge, MA: Perseus Books.

Lifton, R.J. (1982) Beyond Psychic Numbing: A Call to Awareness. *American Journal of Orthopsychiatry*, 52(4), 619–629.

Massumi, B. (2011) *Semblance and Event: Activist Philosophy and the Occurrent Arts*. Cambridge: MIT Press.

Nancy, J.L. (2009) *Fall of Sleep*. New York: Fordham University Press.

O'Gorman, M. (2015) *Necromedia*. Minnesota: University of Minnesota Press.

Ortega y Gasset, J. (1968) *Meditación de la Técnica*. Madrid: Revista de Occidente.

Russell, J. (2020) *Psychoanalysis and Deconstruction: Freud's Psychic Apparatus*. London: Routledge.

Scott, C.E. (1996) *On the Advantages and Disadvantages of Ethics and Politics*. Bloomington and Indianapolis: Indiana University Press.

Scott, C.E. (2007) *Living with Indifference*. Bloomington and Indianapolis: Indiana University Press.

Vigdor, N. (2019) Online Friend Baited Woman to Plan a Murder, Police Say. *New York Times*, June 19, p. 23.

Winnicott, D.W. (1960) Parent-Infant Relationship. In *The Maturational Processes and the Facilitating Environment* (pp. 37–55). Madison: International Universities Press.

Winnicott, D.W. (1963) Fear of BreakdownWinnicot, C., Shepherd, R., and Davis, M. In *Psycho-Analytic Explorations* (pp. 87–95). Cambridge: Harvard University Press.

Winnicott, D.W. (1971) The Use of an Object and Relating Through Identifications. In *Playing and Reality* (pp. 86–94). London and New York: Tavistock Publications.

Žižek, S. (2012) *Less then Nothing: Hegel and the Shadow of Dialectical Materialism*. London: Verso.

Postscript: Digital life in the time of the pandemic

Who would have thought that as we were on the brink of sending our text to the publisher, the COVID-19 pandemic would strike, stunning the world and awakening a new kind of collective consciousness. How could we possibly ignore it, when, making human contact perilous, it has abruptly thrust us further into the virtual world and intensified the transformation that was already underway in human life and was the very object of our investigations?

Just before it began, physical space was still sharply distinguishable from the virtual, or, rather, our physical life was separate from what was at most a supplementary digital existence. But now, forced as we are by the circumstances to be more fully submerged, a fusion of actual life and virtual life is taking place. Floridi's' "on-life" seems to have finally arrived. The pharmacological dimensions of this plunge, however, could not go unmentioned on our watch.

What could be more disruptive to the comfort and diversions achieved in our technological era than a pandemic? What could be more threatening to the sweep of capitalism that has already infected the planet, subjecting its well-being to the fluctuations of a volatile stock market and human greed, than the dramatic advent of this plague? It has pushed us all into one single space, where we now hear the same stories, are obsessed with the same issues, and afraid of the same dangers. This pandemic has done the unimaginable, halting our habitual civilized lives, suspending everything we took for granted, and infusing the everyday with a hallucinatory experience of global proportions. In the numbing pre-COVID anticipations of a comfortable, predictable, and controllable digitized world, we had anesthetized ourselves from the unpredictability and uncertainty of actual life. But this sudden jolt, this irruption of the virulent force of nature has fractured the normality of civilized culture, awakening us to the fact that we have been living in a bubble, tightly secured by the technological enframing of the world.

As we finish writing this book, the pandemic rages on; new hotspots keep emerging in different parts of the planet, second and even third waves threaten, making the virtual world our inescapable refuge. We are spending more time now communicating and interacting on screen than in the physical presence of others. And as we seek shelter from the virus, our digital devices thrust us into the open space of the digital virtual, and its infinite possibilities. Sociability, intimacy, and close contact are made even more possible now without the need of bodily co-presence, or geographical proximity. In this new, unforeseen circumstance, we find ourselves suddenly and frantically betrothed to the virtual world as our bodies become dispensable.

Paradoxically, as our social worlds are rapidly and profusely expanding, we are increasingly isolated from one another. Those fortunate enough to suddenly have time on their hands (and the safe haven of their homes) initially responded to the confinement by virtually reaching out, manically, to everyone they knew (and many they did not), breathlessly trying to recapture the life, past, present (and even future) that seemed to be rapidly slipping away. Virtual interaction became a safeguard from cultural mayhem and crisis.

Our central concern of the book, the virtual world, suddenly acquires unprecedented urgency: what happens to us when simulated reality becomes the order of the day and our social and emotional lives shift to the virtual? And what does it mean, or what will it occasion, that our primary contact with our closest friends, colleagues, family, and everyday human interaction is mediated through a two-dimensional flat screen and digital algorithms? After hours and hours on chat and Zoom and the Internet, this pandemic plunge into the virtual makes us feel an increasing sense of disconnection from the outside world, other bodies, animals, plants, natural and even artificial objects.

Synchronistically, we had already included in our last ruminations E.M. Forster's (2009) story, *The Machine Stops*, written just over a century ago, with a prophetic imagination that conjured up a dystopian society eerily similar to ours today. Set in subterranean Earth, its citizens are already spending their life shut inside a small cell, never seeing one another in person, only telecommunicating through what Forster describes as Zoom-like devices. They were all connected through a powerful machine that – by means of a console complete with all the necessary controls – supported daily life and made physical contact not only unnecessary but, in most cases, even inconvenient or undesirable.

Forced by the coronavirus to spend most of our waking hours inhabiting virtual space, one need not be too pessimistic or have too much imagination to realize that Forster's future may be very close already to our present. What's truly uncanny about this story is how clearly it depicts the most negative aspects of the technological pharmakon. A century before the birth of the World Wide Web ("the Machine" of contemporary digital life), Forster anticipated some of the most immediate and obvious perils of our present world. His prophecy is the end of man, the end of nature, and our ultimate submission to the machine. *The Machine Stops* is as striking and tragic as a Cassandrian mirror, and it should give pause to any fantasy of technological liberation.

In this story, humanity has been overtaken by "the Machine," which provides all comforts and meets all needs, except the need for human contact which it seems to have made increasingly unnecessary. It tells the tale of Vashti and her son, Kuno, who live on opposite sides of the world. It begins with Kuno beseeching his mother to visit him in person, and her adamantly resisting the idea, feeling that seeing each other every day on the screen is quite plenty. She shuns any disruption of her comfortable life inside the Machine, which provides for her every need and fulfills any desire she may have at any time. She sees no need to leave her room, whereas Kuno, by contrast, yearns for real contact and real experience. "I want to see you not through the Machine...," he pleads with his mother, "I want to speak to you not through the wearisome Machine" (p. 3).

Kuno's mournful words reverberate for us today, as it becomes ever more clear that even if the virus subsides we can anticipate a future of sustained social distancing and virtual contact. We are steadily becoming habituated to interacting with small thumbnails, which may be rarefying our perception and ripping away the aura of things transformed now into data and information. While good enough for general communication, in these connections, the non-verbal aspects of bodily interaction are attenuated in the reduced visages that we become to each other. Forster highlights the way in which the discernment of the other's state of mind through the subtle gestures intrinsic to physical encounters are blunted in the virtual image. Vashti can only guess about her son's emotional state, as she tries to read him through the mediation of the screen.

> She fancied that he looked sad. She could not be sure, for the Machine did not transmit nuances of expression. It only gave a general idea of people – an idea that was good enough for all practical purposes.... (p. 5).

But despite this sudden reduction of social interaction to virtual contact, Vashti describes it as an enormous advance in human intercourse, for, as she says proudly, one can be connected to "several thousand people" (p. 2). But in our situation, with so many people to snapchat, tweet, or text, this supposed "advance" seems to be a loss rather than a gain. So much time spent on virtual platforms is having deleterious effects on our bodies and psyches. Being able to connect virtually with friends, colleagues and family far away was once a great luxury and privilege, but now it is fast becoming an oppressive necessity. Every time we are called back to the screen for yet another Zoom session, the space we enter begins to feel like solitary confinement. We experience an expansion of social connection, yet, behind the screen, we remain (and ever more glaringly in this pandemic) isolated and alone. It's better than nothing, we keep telling ourselves, trying to keep our mounting distress under control and feeling indeed overburdened and exhausted. What is there to do with such a glaring and unbearable paradox?

It is truly amazing how Forster's description of life inside the Machine foretells our digital life today, even its ability to soften the rough edges of loneliness and melancholy, flooding us with its electric blue light.

> For a moment Vashti felt lonely. Then she generated the light, and the sight of her room, flooded with radiance and studded with electric buttons, revived her. There were buttons and switches everywhere – buttons to call for food, for music, for clothing. There was the hot-bath button, by pressure of which a basin of (imitation) marble rose out of the floor, filled to the brim with a warm deodorized liquid. There was the cold-bath button. There was the button that produced literature. And there were of course the buttons by which she communicated with her friends. (p. 6)

In the virtual world, every desire is within immediate reach; instantaneous wish fulfillment becomes the primary mode of digital action and control. But in this way, we are facing the quickly approaching dystopic future of an "Amazoned" world, filled with smart speakers awaiting our every command, and made possible by a workforce of robots, drones, and low-wage workers monitored by digital surveillance. What the pandemic is making painfully clear is how Machiavellian our economic infrastructure has become, unceasingly stimulating us by offering to deliver to our front porches with warp speed all our wishes and fancies. "Though it contained nothing," writes Forster of Vashti's room, "it was in touch with all that she cared for in the world" (p. 6). The digital offers us a world that although virtually plenty, is materially depleted. This is what Flusser is alluding to when he says, as we remember, that the digital renders the one-dimensional world of writing to the digital's own zero dimensionality; though capable of fulfilling all our desires, the virtual world is wholly devoid of dimension.

Charlie Brooker imagines that zero dimensionality of the digital in another Black Mirror episode, "White Christmas." He describes a future world where it becomes possible to digitally clone an individual's consciousness, reducing it to "a cookie" which is simply placed in a virtual limbo. When time bottoms out and space is voided, the zero dimensionality of the digital becomes a petri dish of sadistic manipulation. The virtual clone becomes a slave living in a kind of eternal hellscape where nothing ever happens, and where her sole function is to attend to the menial tasks of life demanded by her original.

Yet at the same time that the digital seems to be literally emptying reality of all dimension, something else seems to be taking shape. Universal connectedness becomes a new reality that is not only empowering the individual but also forging a collective mind. This has become poignantly clear in the events surrounding the brutal death of George Floyd in 2020 at the hands of a police officer, which, captured by the smartphone of a 17-year-old high school junior, went viral and set off a firestorm of protest and rage. Digital virtuality has powerfully contributed to a sudden and universal response – unheard of in human history – uncovering the pervasive problem of police brutality in America and racial injustice all over the world.

The digital has also made the experience and the struggle against the pandemic a global matter, where we have reacted together, as one single, albeit fractured, world community. Everyone around the planet is made privy to the same information (and misinformation); we simultaneously learn the daily count of infections and deaths in every country; we witness together the virus's ravaging of everyday communal life and its spread across the surface of the globe, and we suffer as well the various attempts to contain it.

The interconnected globe has become, after all, already an extension of our minds, "a virtual world," as Pierre Lévy (1997) wrote just before the turn of the century, "which is at the same time a society of animated signs, a shared organ of perception, cooperative memory, and space for communication and navigation" (p. 112). He pointed this out when the digital world was still in diapers, and he added that we may "have the opportunity to collectively think through our future and alter its course" (p. xxiv):

> Faced with the choice of turning back or moving forward [...] humanity has a chance to reclaim its future, not by placing its destiny in the hands of some so-called intelligent mechanism, but by systematically producing the tools that will enable it to shape itself into intelligent communities capable of negotiating the stormy seas of change.... even if we manage to achieve a condition of personal immobility, the landscape will continue to flow and tumble around us, infiltrate us, transform us from within. We are no longer in historical time, with its references to writing, the city, the past, but within a moving and paradoxical space that comes to

> us from the future. ... Time is not now anymore a succession of events ... Time now is errant, oblique, plural, indeterminate, like that which precedes all origins. (p. xxv)

Lévy's description astoundingly corresponds to the transformation of time during the pandemic. Days run into nights, as weeks and months seem to pass without the rhythm and structure of familiar experience that once anchored life to predictable routines. The temporality marked by the virtual world has nearly overtaken the internal human sense of time, transmuting it into something errant, plural, and indeterminate, impossible to keep track of. Something is coming at us fiercely, propelling us into the future, and we are struggling to hold on.

Forster's story offers a more dystopic vision of this future. In the last remaining book in Vashti's world, she has the means to eradicate unpredictability:

> By her side, on the little reading-desk, was a survival from the ages of litter – one book. This was the Book of the Machine. In it were instructions against every possible contingency. If she was hot or cold or dyspeptic or at a loss for a word, she went to the book, and it told her which button to press. The Central Committee published it. In accordance with a growing habit, it was richly bound. (p. 8)

In our pandemic times, where we have only limited access to experts to help us deal with the small material breakdowns of everyday life, we increasingly depend on the infinity of the Youtube archive for instruction. Analogous to rule 34: "if you can imagine it, there's porn of it," we might add a rule 35: "if you run into a problem with any of the many objects that surround you, there is a video for it."

If Lévy is correct, and there truly is a collective mind emerging, a shared organ of perception, we can almost sense its haunting manifestations as Youtube mesmerizes us into thinking and feeling, over and over again, that perhaps there is really nothing unique about us or any particularity in our life, that individuality may in fact be an illusion. Someone else, somewhere else, has run into the very same problem, and goes to the same source that prescribes the very same actions to all. Just as Vashti's book, Youtube tells us precisely what button to press.

"The Machine" makes up for the losses of our confinement and the imposition of social distancing, actualizing our desire with every possible material satisfaction and the luxury and comfort possible in our technological age. We no longer need a singular book, a set of books, or even a whole library, for today the Internet is our shield against contingency. And if, as we have been claiming, contingency underwrites the human virtual, then the attempt to digitize the physical world, and thus make everything controllable, is tantamount to its repression.

For Stiegler, moreover, because of our increasing dependence on the Machine, there is nowadays, in advanced contemporary capitalism, a growing numbing or "proletarization" of the individual. The digital network has become a black box that hides from all but the specialists what goes on inside it, or how its algorithms work. The common man is clueless about how things that happen happen. He slowly sinks into stupidity.

We have witnessed in the advent of the digital a sort of Copernican Revolution, like the one Kant claimed he had effected with his philosophy. Kant had said that we could not possibly hope to have certain knowledge of the world if the subject had to conform to the object, for there was always uncertainty in our encounter with things when it was on their own terms, with the many opacities inherent to matter that makes certain knowledge impossible. But if we conceived of knowledge not as the result of our minds conforming to the world, but rather of the world, of things, conforming to our minds, then just an introspective look would suffice for us to discover the mental structures that render knowledge certain.[1]

Forster seems to be echoing Kant when Vashti claims that the civilization before her had "mistaken the functions of the system, and had used it for bringing people to things, instead of for bringing things to people" (p. 9). We can now see that the Internet of Things indeed brings the whole world to us so that we don't need anymore to reach out to it. This is of course something invaluable for us now, as we can find refuge from the viral infection in the safe areas of a virtualized world. But in so effortlessly replacing reality with its nearly perfect simulation – the experience of cycling through the French countryside, for instance, with the Peloton bike that brings that experience into our living room – we may be seduced by the comfort and clarity of the VR screen so that we begin to value better the constructed world rather than the natural, and eventually not even notice the difference. So satisfied are we with its virtual replacement that we could, as Vashti did, start to wonder about "those funny old days, when men went for change of air instead of changing the air in their rooms!" (p. 9):

> Few travelled in these days, for, thanks to the advance of science, the earth was exactly alike all over. Rapid intercourse, from which the previous civilization had hoped so much, had ended by defeating itself. What was the good of going to Peking when it was just like Shrewsbury? Why return to Shrewsbury when it would all be like Peking? Men seldom moved their bodies; all unrest was concentrated in the soul. (p. 11)

The Tragedy of the Virtual in a Pandemic Age is summed up very well at the end of the story by Kuno's admonitory words:

> Cannot you see [...] that it is we that are dying, and that down here the only thing that really lives is the Machine? We created the Machine to do our will, but we cannot make it do our will now. It has robbed us of the sense of space and of the sense of touch, it has blurred every human relation and narrowed down love to a carnal act, it has paralysed our bodies and our wills, and now it compels us to worship it. The Machine develops – but not on our lines. The Machine proceeds – but not to our goal. We only exist as the blood corpuscles that course through its arteries, and if it could work without us, it would let us die. (p. 26)

Oliver Sacks (2019), at the end of his life, also saw this story as a prophetic fable for our own world, in which our digital devices have made us lose an important part of who we are and how we behave with one another. As he lamented, "This is how I feel increasingly often about our bewitched, besotted society, too."

The great loss in Kant's Copernican turn was that the world as it is in itself becomes unreachable outside the structures imposed on it by the mind. The Romantics argued that what had been sacrificed for the sake of certainty was what was most important to human being, which happens to always lie beyond the confines of intellectual or re-presentational understanding. Are we too, in bringing the world closer to us by digitization, not also losing what is most valuable in human life? In so rapidly replacing a world that required a body to enter it with the disembodied world of the screen, aren't we in danger of disregarding the imponderable aspects of physical existence that are irreducible to any representation? Or are we not also gaining something that we may be yet unable to discern in the rarified experience of the virtual screen?

Note

1 Of course we are over-simplifying here. That introspective look is a complex rational task of what Kant calls "a transcendental deduction", where we un-cover the necessary conditions for the possibility of our knowledge of things.

References

Forster, E.M. (2009) Kindle Edition, Copyright © 2009 by IAP. Las Vegas, Nevada, USA.

Lévy, P. (1997) *Collective Intelligence. Mankind's Emerging World in Cyberspace.* Cambridge, USA: Perseus Books.

Sacks, O. (2019) The Machine Stops. *The New Yorker*, Feb 11, 2019.

Index

265–6, 270, 274, 276, 280; active (Jung) 261; bodily 31, 44; collective 31, 195; erotic 132, 133, 135; human 26; sexual 136, 176, 181

immediacy 2, 22–3, 25, 44, 72, 76–8, 80, 82, 113, 128, 144, 163, 178, 184, 187, 219, 259, 260, 266, 269; absolute 78; emerging 82

impoverishment 25, 33, 65, 179, 204, 207–8, 210, 269

incorporation (Hayles) 224

indexicality, indexical 28, 97; character 36, connection 36–7

individualistic subjectivity 113–14

infant 64, 120, 130, 142–3, 145–51, 153–5, 158–9, 172, 182–3, 185–7, 190, 267

information 1, 15–16, 22, 24–6, 32–6, 45–7, 65, 73–4, 76, 85, 99, 116, 130–1, 183, 208–9, 217–9, 224, 233, 238, 257, 264

inscription (Hayles) 224

Instagram 2, 53, 80, 86, 103, 117–18, 135, 157, 159, 185, 189, 235, 255

interaction 1, 2, 24–5, 38, 45, 54, 66–7, 77, 80, 93, 99, 102–4, 111, 133, 170, 174–5, 182, 192, 195, 219, 225, 231, 235, 259–60, 271; social 77, 104, 231; verbal 25, 102; virtual 133, 175, 192

Internet 6–7, 14, 24, 38, 55, 73, 75, 81, 84–5, 100, 116, 130–4, 173, 176, 182, 188, 190, 223, 226, 235, 247, 263, 280, 284–5

intersubjective life 123, 182, 259

intuition 31, 55, 112, 204, 248

Jaar, N. 96–8
James, W. 76
Jodorowski, A. 242
Jonze, S. 180
Joyce, J. 206
Jung, C.G./Jungian 116, 168, 173, 178, 249, 261, 265, 266, 269, 272, 276

Kalsched, D. 124
Kant, I. 63, 285
Khan, M. 263
Klein, M. 140
Knafo, D. 134
knowledge 3, 8–9, 22, 62, 73, 75–6, 82, 94, 97–8, 205, 208, 211, 225,

228, 239, 241, 267, 274; arboreous 98; coherentist 76; Descartes' tree of 98; intellectual 94; positive 62; preknowledge 267; scientific 9; self–knowledge 55

Koch, C. 237
Kohut, H. 119, 188–9
Krebs, V.J 15
Kriegman, D. 120
Kurzweil, R. 238
Kūki Ningyō (Koreeda's film) 135

Lacan, J. 64, 76, 132, 140, 150
Lachmann, F. 182
language 2, 4, 9, 12–13, 16, 19, 23–6, 29, 38, 42, 44, 47, 74, 97, 119, 132, 195, 206, 208–9, 220, 231–2, 242–3, 247, 254; bourgeois 25, 231; cinematographic 29; as first technology 23; mediation of 42; as mode of expression 25, 42; non–representational dimension of 270; oral 23, 25, 44; ordinary 206, 208; representational 209; as tool 25; written 25

Laplanche, J. 62
Lars and the Real Girl (Guillespie's film) 135
Lemma, A. 182
Lévy, P. 73, 135, 272, 283–4
Li, O. 113
Lifton, R. 252
libido 85, 131, 133, 178, 262
life drawing (Bearn) 268
liking 170, 190
linear/linearity 8, 24, 26–7, 30–1, 44, 47, 79, 98, 105, 206, 211, 215, 217, 247; logic 24; one–dimensionality 44; text 26; writing 30, 47
living matter 34, 233
Living with Yourself (Netflix Series) 225
Livingstone, A. 121
Locke, J. 76
logic 13–14, 24, 27, 31, 37, 48, 50, 77, 82, 97–8, 160, 174, 204–8, 211, 214–16, 218, 229, 247; structures of writing 31; transparency (Baudrillard) 229; of the visual 27
López–Pedraza, R. 129, 230
loss 26, 15–16, 22, 24, 28, 33–5, 46, 64–8, 78, 81–3, 87, 106, 112, 114, 116, 122, 128, 130–1, 137, 144–5,

For Product Safety Concerns and Information please contact our EU
representative GPSR@taylorandfrancis.com
Taylor & Francis Verlag GmbH, Kaufingerstraße 24, 80331 München, Germany

www.ingramcontent.com/pod-product-compliance
Lightning Source LLC
Chambersburg PA
CBHW050336270326
41926CB00016B/3475